PLANT INTELLIGENCE

AND THE

IMAGINAL REALM

BEYOND THE DOORS OF PERCEPTION
INTO THE DREAMING OF EARTH

STEPHEN HARROD BUHNER

Bear & Company
Rochester, Vermont • Toronto, Canada

Bear & Company
One Park Street
Rochester, Vermont 05767
www.BearandCompanyBooks.com

Bear & Company is a division of Inner Traditions International

Library of Congress Cataloging-in-Publication Data
Buhner, Stephen Harrod.
  Plant intelligence and the imaginal realm : beyond the doors of perception into the dreaming earth / Stephen Harrod Buhner.
      pages cm
  Includes bibliographical references and index.
  ISBN 978-1-59143-135-0 (pbk.) — ISBN 978-1-59143-836-6 (e-book)
  1. Plants—Psychic aspects. 2. Dreams—Miscellanea. I. Title.
  BF1045.P55B84 2014
  133'.258—dc23
                                                                    2013044901

Printed and bound in the United States by McNaughton & Gunn

10 9 8 7 6 5 4

Text design and layout by Priscilla Baker
This book was typeset in Garamond Premier Pro with Bauer Text Initials, Avenir, and Find Hand used as display typefaces

Illustrations on pages 105, 156, 157, 161, 162, 165, and 408 copyright © 2014 by Kim Lindemyer and used by permission of the illustrator
Graphic representations of minke whale and white-beaked dolphin songs copyright © by Aguasonic Acoustics and used with their permission

To send correspondence to the author of this book, mail a first-class letter to the author c/o Inner Traditions • Bear & Company, One Park Street, Rochester, VT 05767, and we will forward the communication, or contact the author directly at **www.gaianstudies.org**.

For Flick

The night comes too soon for those we love

CONTENTS

ACKNOWLEDGMENTS

For those who have written about the journey, taking it themselves, refusing to settle for secondhand gods. My students who for the past thirty-five years have also been my teachers. And: Benjamin Bailey-Buhner, Mary Brown (on bass), Phil Brown (on lead guitar and vocals), Tom Clemens, Kevin Compton (on blues guitar), Don Conoscenti (the greatest unknown musician in the United States), Eric Hansen (on vocals), Julie McIntyre, Harry Pickens (on piano), Calixte Raifsnider, Erika May Randolph (on flute), Trishuwa, and, of course, Melanie and Jeff at the Buckhorn (who make playing out like playing at home), Linda and Shelly at the Mine Shaft in Madrid (ditto), and Rodney Henderson (who makes us smile when he drums).

A Note to
the Reader

*Watch with glittering eyes the whole world around you, because the
greatest secrets are always hidden in the most unlikely places. Those
who don't believe in magic will never find it.*

ROALD DAHL

This book is a user's manual about the techniques and states of perception necessary for directly interacting with the Gaian system, perceiving the deeper patterns in Gaian movements, and understanding the meanings within those patterns. In many respects it is a manual for becoming a nondomesticated explorer of the natural world, something that used to be called, long ago, a natural philosopher, what might now be called a *wild scientist* as opposed to a domesticated one.

Unlike the majority of books being written about the state of Earth/ human relationship and the problems that face us, this book does not list all the troubles and then, at the end, call for more regulation, urge you to write your congressional representative, insist you recycle or buy an (absurdly expensive) environmentally friendly car, or plead for you to give money to nonprofits. As Einstein so eloquently put it, *We can't solve problems by using the same kind of thinking we used when we created them.* So, this book is about how to actually think differently, the processes involved, and how they will alter your perceptual frame if you use them. It then urges you to do one thing: whatever the hell it is that *you* think you should do in response. It is in your own individual genius that the answers lie, not in the pronouncements of experts who have no conception of the local environment in which you live every day of your life. Letting the experts run things is how we got into this mess to begin with.

Thus this book is specifically meant for those who understand what it means to look with glittering (i.e., luminous) eyes. For that is the understanding that binds us together, that lies at the heart of thinking differently. If you are a mechanicalist or die-hard reductionist (or even someone who thinks humans are somehow innately different, i.e., more special, than all other life-forms on this planet) this book will only irritate you, upset your stomach, and cause you to mutter over and over again, "Wrong! Wrong!" Please read Richard Dawkins instead.

Plant Intelligence and the Imaginal Realm is the fourth in a series of five (or perhaps six, or seven, or eight) books that began, long ago, with *Sacred Plant Medicine* (Inner Traditions, 1996), and which also includes *The Lost Language of Plants* (Chelsea Green, 2002) and *The Secret Teachings of Plants* (Inner Traditions, 2004). (Note: *Lost Language* contains a depth look at chemical communication among plants and their ecosystems; *Secret Teachings* a depth look at heart perception, synchronization of heart fields, and EM field dynamics.) As with those latter two works, some of the material in this book, especially in the first half, is somewhat technical. That density exists as part of a long-term project to create a map of human interaction with the natural world that actually has something to do with the real world, an area in which our current maps, inherited from the late nineteenth century, are tremendously deficient. You don't have to read those parts—you can just skip around if you wish. In fact, I urge you to have fun and from now on take in what has relevance to you and to ignore the rest. After all, it's your life, you should spend it how *you* want.

THE GILA WILDERNESS, 2013

FIRST MOVEMENT

Touching
the Foundations
of the World

~

Any intelligent fool can make things bigger, more complex, and more violent. It takes a touch of genius—and a lot of courage—to move in the opposite direction.

ALBERT EINSTEIN

In the pronoun we, I of course included the starfish and the redwood forest, the segmenting egg, and the Senate of the United States. And in the everything which these creatures variously know, I included "how to grow into five-way symmetry," "how to survive a forest fire," "how to grow and still stay the same shape," "how to learn," "how to write a constitution," "how to invent and drive a car," "how to count to seven," and so on. . . . Above all I included "how to evolve," because it seemed to me that both evolution and learning must fit the same formal regularities or so-called laws.

GREGORY BATESON

We have learnt that nothing is simple and rational except what we ourselves have invented; that God thinks in terms neither of Euclid nor of Riemann; that science has "explained" nothing; that the more we know the more fantastic the world becomes and the profounder the surrounding darkness.

ALDOUS HUXLEY

For we now recognize the nature of our disease. What is wrong with us is precisely the detachment of these forms of experience—art, religion, and the rest—from one another; and our cure can only be their reunion in a complete and undivided life. Our task is to seek that life, to build up the conception of an activity which is at once art, and religion, and science, and the rest.

R. G. COLLINGWOOD

On earth there is no escape, no exit, from global ecology.

DORION SAGAN

THE SOFT FLUTTER OF BUTTERFLIES

I never was a good student in school—though first grade was fun. We made hand prints in wet plaster and walked in the woods looking for butterflies and learned the Spanish words for chocolate and hello.

That first summer after school was wonderful. I got bright new shoes and ran and played with my friends and we flew kites whose tails fluttered in the wind and the days were as long as forever. But next year, school was different.

Our teacher stood ramrod stiff at the head of the class and she was tall and thin and the mole on her chin quivered with indignation. Her face disapproved of itself and she wrinkled her nose when she talked as if she were smelling something polite people didn't mention.

She marched to school wearing a backpack filled with rocks (to make her posture better) and she hit our hands with a ruler if we were naughty and gave us demerits if we talked out of turn and taught us that every word could only be pronounced one way and that the dinosaurs were giant cold-blooded reptiles who died because their brains were too small and it took a week for the nerve impulses to get from their tails to their heads.

I didn't like her very much and I began to think that school was something I would rather not do.

But when I told my mother I was informed that I didn't have a choice in the matter and that school was good for little children and that go I would. So, the years went by, as years do, and some teachers were better and some were not and I became as unconscious as unconscious could be.

I remember the day I began to wake up.

Our sixth-grade class was being unruly and the teacher was suffering from it and we were informed that the only thing she wanted to hear out of our mouths was nothing. A girl in the next seat asked if she could borrow a pencil. I turned to her and said, "Sure. Here." And so I was sent into the hall for talking out of turn. It was winter and I wore short sleeves and thin brown pants and the hall of the new school was as cold and dim and empty as damaged hearts.

The hall lights were turned off during class to save electricity and the pale winter sunlight trickled in from the windows at each end of the long hall and the floor was linoleum and the walls lined with metal lockers and the ceiling lights were little square recessed boxes and every little tiny sound echoed as if I were in a metal tube and the alienation and loneliness of the place went through me like a sigh from the mouth of god and left me trembling in its wake.

And then, for some reason that day, I got mad.

It occurred to me there was something wrong with this place and though I did not know it at the time I was beginning to realize there is a difference between schooling and education. And I just decided that I wouldn't put up with it any longer and so I walked.

I left that place and walked the three miles home, down the endless winter sidewalks with their stark leafless trees and the long, snow-plowed streets, and took the key from under the milk box and let myself into the silent and empty house. And later still, I carefully watched from behind the pale window curtains as the blue car, with the teacher and the vice-principal inside, pulled slowly up in front of the house. I watched as they opened the car doors and got stiffly out. I watched as they walked up the frozen flagstones and then the icy steps to the front door. And I remained silent all through the ringing of the bell.

And I remember later the 105-degree fever and the bed-and-myself floating in space and the visions and the voices and my wonder at what

I was experiencing. And then I went back to school and I was once again quiet and good but some sleeping thing inside me was stirring and not god nor parents nor school systems could keep it much longer in its box.

Then my parents moved to Dallas, Texas, and it was 1966 and I began to listen to the Beatles and the Stones and Bob Dylan and the sleeping thing inside me began to rattle the lid of its box and sometimes the sounds it made were really, really loud.

It was a bad time and a bad place for that sleeping thing to make noise.

The suburbs of Dallas were filled then (as they are now) with the Avon-decorated faces of our mothers and the absence of our fathers and a generation of children were growing up displaced persons and some kind of wildness was beginning to creep out of the emptiness inside us. Our hair grew longer and a strange light began to gleam in our eyes and we discovered words like "fuck" and "shit" and "No." And our elders began to fear us and I found it was possible to be arrested for walking with long hair.

Handcuffed and taken to the local lockup, my mention of the Bill of Rights was greeted with laughter. I was denied a phone call and held without knowing if anyone knew where I was. I was told I had no right to counsel and my jailers amused themselves by telling me I would never get out, that they had called my mother and she said for them to keep me, and that I would soon be put in general lockup with "the others."

But, perhaps, if I told them who I bought my drugs from (assumed from my long hair), they would "go easy on me." Perhaps, if I were cooperative, they could intervene, tell the judge I had been helpful, and arrange my release (I still wasn't sure what the charge was—I didn't know, then, about walking with long hair). But I didn't cooperate and even so, twenty-four hours later, my mother did show up to take her wayward, fifteen-year-old, very terrified son home. They had collectively felt some experience with Texas justice would teach me something. It did. I have hated the abuse of power ever since.

And the lid of the box came off and that sleeping thing inside me came out and I have never put it back again and I never will.

How hard it is to honor these most important of our teachers.

My school, of course, was not amused and informed me I no longer need attend (I was a bad influence on the other children) and I finally knew too deep for words that they were not interested in me as a human being but only in my compliance and I filed emancipation papers and worked that summer emptying garbage cans (learning a lot about my neighbors' lives) and saved my money and then, just after Christmas, I left that town, hitchhiking West. I was sixteen and on January 1, 1969, I arrived in Berkeley, California, with $50 in my pocket and a tattered Boyscout backpack with two changes of clothes.

The Berkeley protests had been going on all that summer and fall and the students at the university still carried gas masks to class every day. I met some people who lived in a flat on Telegraph Avenue and they said I could live in their walk-in closet for $25 a month. They kept green cans of military rations under their beds and hung gas masks on a coat-rack near the door and after a while one of the guys said he thought I should take a high school equivalency test and go to college and so I did.

That first day of class, sitting right in front of me, there was a trans-vestite and s/he had long purple fingernails and a lot of makeup and I never had seen anything like that in my life.

There was a man with a wild red beard and wild red hair and he told me stories about living for a year in a cabin he'd built in the mountains after he'd left high school and about building a ship and sailing around the world and about the typhoon that hit him off the coast of Mada-gascar and wrecked the ship and cast him, wretched and gasping, on the shore. Then he was found by a beautiful woman who offered him fruit and nursed him until he was well. And then they had great sex for the longest time. Then, much later, he decided to leave and he worked his way back to America on a tramp steamer with a load of green hides and he never could get rid of the smell. And I am sure that he (as I do) smells it yet.

A boy in my class knew Cesar Chavez and he'd helped him organize the first migrant worker protests in California and he was Hispanic and played the guitar and was handsome and could sing so beautifully that it almost broke my heart and he told us not to eat grapes because of the boycott.

One of my roommates was called Stone and she was from Georgia and was a stripper in the Tenderloin in San Francisco. She made more money than the rest of us together and was putting herself through school to become a psychologist. Another was a psychopharmacologist who used to get pure liquid LSD from Sandoz in Switzerland for his master's degree program at the University of Iowa but they all injected it instead of giving it to the chimpanzees and now they couldn't publish their research. And he knew Owsley and sometimes I would see Jerry Garcia walking along the street and James Taylor played at a little venue and only eighty people were there and I had never had such fun in my life.

The university didn't care if I came to class, nor how I looked, and my professors weren't interested in their students complying or conforming, only in their learning. And I loved it. But then the People's Park Massacre happened and the war went on and the riots grew bigger and the years got longer and I didn't know what I wanted to do—or be—so I left and moved to the high mountains of Colorado and rebuilt a nineteenth-century cabin in woods.

I learned to work a wood-burning stove and to cut firewood and to survive 32 feet of snow over a winter and to put snow chains on my car and how to build an outhouse that didn't smell and to identify wild plants in the mountains and sometimes to use them for my food and medicine.

But I didn't know what I wanted to do with my life so I went to university again and the teacher in my first class looked like Santa Claus. He had a big stomach and a huge white beard and he laughed a lot. He told us his name was Ben Sweet (Sweet by birth, sweet by disposition) and the name of his class was "On the challenge of being human." My other teachers did not seem to care about the challenge of being human and instead they taught us to think about mathematics and analyze different chemicals and as the months went by I felt further from myself. And the only thing that seemed to make sense was Ben Sweet and the way he talked to us and urged something in the deeps of us to come out—the way he looked, and listened, as if he had no other place on this Earth to be except with us, as if there were nothing more important in his life than what we had to say at just that moment in time.

And one day I found myself thinking that I wanted all my teachers to be like that and realized I didn't care if I never did learn to "make a living" and I thought, "Why not?"

So, I made a list of every person I had heard of that had moved me the way Ben Sweet did and I decided I wanted to meet and learn from every one of them. And I kept thinking, "This is crazy," but some other part of me kept saying, "Why not?" And for some reason I listened to what it said.

That paper is old now, as wrinkled as this face I see every morning in the mirror. We both have the marks of years upon us; the houses we've lived in and the moving vans and the storage boxes and the mountains of Colorado and the high plains desert of New Mexico and the long nights when the deeps rose up and demanded answers and all the friends who took a different path and that I've never seen again.

I take it out and spread it on the table. The childish scrawl of my younger self looks up at me from that ragged, lined notebook paper. The names, filled with their simple hope, straggle over the page . . .

Buckminster Fuller, Robert Bly, Jacques Cousteau, Robert Heinlein, Joan Halifax, Stephanie Simonton, Elisabeth Kübler-Ross, William Stafford, Jane Goodall, Gregory Bateson, Eric Fromm, Frank Herbert, Ashley Montagu, Margaret Mead.

I was so young then and the world was so new and my whole life was before me.

Elisabeth Kübler-Ross dressed with no sense of fashion; she was plain and tall and thin. Her body was always moving, so full of energy that it quivered, constantly seeking an outlet in some comment, gesture of hands, or facial expression. Elisabeth's face was strong and masculine and she chain-smoked and didn't care if people didn't like it. Her eyes penetrated everything they touched and they were the deepest blue and looking into them was like peering into some deep mountain pool that's so clear you can't tell how deep it is. Down in those deeps were things I couldn't quite make out, things I didn't understand, experiences maybe or some aware part of her that looked back, waiting for me to notice it. I could feel whatever it was deep inside, touching parts of me that I did not know I possessed. And those parts of me . . . I could feel them begin to stir under its touch.

When she talked to me—or to anyone the week we spent with

her—she was fully present; she looked back, she *really* looked.

"How did you come to your work?" someone asked. And she told us, her intonations filled with the thick shapes of her German-Swiss language.

"I was a young doctor and it was just after the war. I had heard stories of the terrible things that had happened in the concentration camps and I wanted to see for myself. So, I went to Majdanek in Poland. It is just outside the town of Lublin.

"The gates of the camp stood open, raggedly smashed back as if a tank or truck had burst through them. Rusting barbed wire straggled away, as far as I could see, in either direction from the gate posts. There was a feeling about the place, or maybe it was just a feeling in me, as if I were standing at the opening of a huge, dark room—a room that contained some immense presence.

"By the gates there was a table and a young woman with dark, raven hair. She had to ask me several times for my name. She carefully wrote it down in the book where they kept a list of all the visitors. Then she looked up and smiled a sad, quiet smile, and waved me in. And so, I began to walk, to see the camp, to see the truth of that place for myself.

"There were rusting railroad tracks and weeds growing up between them, and abandoned railroad cars sitting on the tracks, the doors thrown open. Inside the first one were thousands of shoes, tiny children's shoes, quiet now from their running and laughing, no longer a part of children's lives. I could not take it in, thousands of children's shoes, all moldering together. Then I looked into the next car and for the longest time I could not make out what I was seeing. Suddenly I realized . . . it was filled with tangled mats of human hair, hair that the Nazis had shaved from the heads of the people in this camp, hair to be used for mattresses.

"There is a shock that comes when you see something that the world you have grown up in has no place for; the mind cannot conceive it and it feels as if the fabric of the world has torn and you have stumbled and are falling through into some in-between place that you never knew existed.

"So, in shock I stumbled back from the railroad cars filled with hair and children's shoes and turned and began walking. I don't know where I was going.

"Soon, I found myself in front of a wooden barracks. The interior was shadowed and empty and my footsteps echoed on the rough floorboards. I stood a minute to let my eyes adjust to the pale light filtering in from the doorway in which I stood and the small windows up under the eaves of the roof. In the shadowed gloom I could see the tiers of wooden bunks where the people had slept, one above the other, three in all, the last one close against the ceiling. There was still a faint odor of unwashed bodies—of fear, and of ancient grief.

"I walked down the long passageways that ran between the tiers of bunks on either side, looking around me. Then I saw—on the walls, roughly scratched, sometimes carved, into the wooden planks—hundreds of initials, and names—the last desperate messages to the living. And among those messages—I couldn't believe it—were hundreds and hundreds of butterflies. Butterflies, everywhere. In the midst of that horror, the children had scratched butterflies into the walls!

"I still remember the pale sunlight and its touch on that room. The light seemed worn and tired, as if defeated over the course of days and years by what had been held in that shadowed building. I remember the feel of the wooden floors beneath my feet, and the smell—of wood, and people, and lost hope—and the silence touched only by the slight echoing of my footsteps—as if the whole world had stopped breathing. And the feeling, the feeling that was consuming me as I stood there under the impact of those butterflies.

"Then I felt someone behind me and I turned and found the young woman from the gate standing there, watching me. There was a sweetness about her and her eyes were calm but there was something else, too, in the lines of her face, as if a great wave filled with grief had swept across it and left traces of its touch for all the world to see.

"I, still caught under the spell of the place, did not know what to say, what to do. I had never conceived of such things happening. She saw that in my face and gestured and we walked outside.

"'My name is Golda,' she said, and then told me her story.

"She was born in Germany and was half Jewish. Her father was taken by the Gestapo in 1939 during the early arrests. She and her mother, brother, and sister lasted longer; they were taken in 1944 and, eventually, sent to Majdanek.

"'After we arrived,' she said, 'they herded us into a line at the door of the gas chamber. My mother, my brother, and my sister were in front of me but the room was filled after my sister was pushed in, crying. They tried to force me in as well but the door would not close no matter how hard they pressed it against my back, so they pulled me out and slammed the door closed. And so, for some reason that I will never know, I survived.' She looked toward the crematorium, pointed to the chimney. 'The ashes of my mother, brother, and sister floated up from there that day.'"

Elisabeth looked at all of us in the room. None of us were moving. We were still, hardly breathing, caught spellbound. "I had never experienced such cruelty," Elisabeth said, "and my heart was being crushed. But the young woman seemed oddly unaffected by it, so I said to her, 'But you look so peaceful. How can you be peaceful when your whole family was killed here?'

"Golda looked back at me—those peaceful eyes!—and said in the most penetrating voice I had ever heard, 'Because the Nazis taught me this: There is a Hitler inside each of us and if we do not heal the Hitler inside of ourselves, then the violence, it will never stop.'"

Elisabeth stopped then and waited, letting what she had said reverberate in the room, penetrate into the depths of us. Then, softly . . . "So I asked her, 'What are you doing now?'

"She told me she was working in Germany, at a hospital for German children injured during the war, the children of the Nazis who had sent her family to Majdanek. I was shocked. I asked her why. 'How else,' she asked, 'can I heal the Hitler inside me but to give to them what they took from us?'"

When Elisabeth was done many of us were crying, some were weeping deeply. She looked at us in that way she had and said, "Now you are *feeling* like human beings not acting like dispassionate scientists." Then she paused and said again, so softly . . . "There is a Hitler inside each of us, and if we do not heal it within ourselves, these things will never stop."

There was something in her voice that day, some invisible thing that my younger self did not consciously understand but could only feel. And it went into the depths of me and there it remains still. And sometimes when I feel the cruelty in callous and indifferent men, when I hear the velvet violence hidden in the innocuous-seeming words of a mother speaking to her child, when I see the people among us from whom the powerful have stolen the future—and the present, when I feel some rage inside me wanting to do harm because I feel so helpless that I can find no other thing to do, that teaching, in the depths of me, rises up again into awareness and I see that young woman in Majdanek and I feel her eyes looking into me and I hear Elisabeth's voice once more and I begin to think outside the box again.

There is a difference I learned, long ago, between schooling and education. Do you feel it now, in the room with you?

I was never able to find it in the analysis of chemicals or in degree programs or in any of my schools. But sometimes I find it in the soft flutter of butterflies, in the wildness of plants growing undomesticated in a forest clearing, in the laughter and running of young children, their hair flowing in the wind, and sometimes, sometimes I find it in the words of teachers who come among us from time to time—out there, far outside these walls, in the wildness of the world.

1
RECLAIMING
THE INVISIBLE

The most beautiful thing we can experience is the mysterious. It is the source of all true art and all science. He to whom this emotion is a stranger, who can no longer pause to wonder and stand rapt in awe, is as good as dead.

ALBERT EINSTEIN

I am made to love the pond and the meadow, as the wind is made to ripple the water.

HENRY DAVID THOREAU

I hold to the presupposition that our loss of the sense of aesthetic unity was, quite simply, an epistemological mistake. I believe that that mistake may be more serious than all the minor insanities that characterized those older epistemologies which agreed upon fundamental unity.

GREGORY BATESON

There are experiences we have as children, each and every one of us, that find a place deep inside us where neither time nor wounds can reach or damage them. And those experiences? They light our way through the world for the rest of our lives. Many of us forget them as we grow older, yet still they remain, shaping who we are at a level too deep for words. They shape, yet they also wait. They wait to be remembered, wait for the time when we *need* to remember them, when we need a particular kind of light to find our way in darkness.

Some of those experiences are memories of moments when, for some reason, never to be completely understood with our rational mind, the day-to-day world changes. In those deeply charged moments, the very quality of reality shifts and the alteration is so striking, the feeling impact so strong, the effect on psyche so deep, that it is not possible for the depths of us to truly forget.

As if it were happening now, I remember the first time . . .

My grandfather was sitting at his desk . . .

the very one where I now write these words

and I was walking along the hallway, going outside to play, when I caught a glimpse of him and stopped at the door of his room, hesitating tentatively on the threshold. Then, for some reason that day, my internal world quieted in a way I had never before experienced. I became aware of a special quality to the sounds in the room. Silence itself took on a penetrating quiet-sound of its own, like a word filled with deep meaning which has reached out and touched the very foundations of the self. Every tiny noise emerging in that magical silence took on, itself, a special kind of sound, a special kind of meaning. It seemed to me that I could hear, truly hear, for the first time: the creak of the chair, the slight rustling of drapes, the movement of my grandfather's hands among his papers, his breathing—and the simple, quiet susurrus of my own inhale and exhale. Each sound seemed almost to shimmer and each and every one of them resonated deeply inside me. I felt some kind of *communication* coming out of those sounds into me.

The light, filtering in from the windows, was charged with a quality I had never seen before; it seemed to glow with a special light of its own. A shimmering luminescence came from inside it, as if I were seeing a deeper form of light, quietly existing, normally invisible, inside the day-to-day sunlight I was used to. Sensuous, liquid, alive, luminous. And everything in the room was immersed, literally bathed, in it.

I remember seeing the dust motes as they slowly moved in the quiet air currents, each catching a piece of that golden light, then vanishing again as they turned in the slowly drifting air—a light rain of golden sparks of light, appearing and disappearing to my wondering eye. And like the light itself, every object in the room seemed to gently shimmer, a soft luminescence emerging from inside them, bringing out colors in their surfaces I had never noticed before. They seemed almost like living stained glass, lit from within.

Time itself had changed, as if it were suspended—like the dust motes in the air. There was so much *time* and it was so slow I could take as long as I needed to sense each and every thing. And what is more, I felt companioned. Companioned by *everything* in that room: the sunlight, the sounds, the smells, the desk, the lamp, the papers and pens, the curtains, the chairs, every physical object. *Everything* had taken on a kind of intelligent awareness and caring and each and every thing in that room was gently companioning me in that single, suspended moment in time. I felt part of a living, breathing, aware, intelligent universe, and what is more . . . I felt wanted by that universe, as if I had come into the arms of my deepest and truest family. I felt at home in a way I never had before.

I had entered some, heretofore unknown, magical world, a world that lies underneath and behind the one that most of us see every day. And oddly enough, I could tell, even at that young age, that my grandfather was caught up in that world with me. Somehow, we were caught spellbound in a special time and place, where the usual rules of this world were, for a brief moment, suspended. Our breathing slowed, our very being paused a moment and calmed, and in some way that I did not understand, we were connected. I could feel a current of energy moving between us, and both of us were joined similarly to the room and the light and the sounds all around us and to every physical object in that room.

Everything seemed to have somehow become more itself. Everything seemed charged with meaning, some deep meaning that I could feel but not understand, at the time, with my mind. There was a look of understanding that passed between my grandfather and myself that day and a closeness that I have never forgotten. And for a brief moment in time, something from inside me flowed into him and something from inside him flowed into me. And our bodies and our eyes acknowledged the reality of it in that simple glance even though our minds had no words to describe it.

Then, in an instant, it passed, and we were left as we had been, but . . . changed. A powerful wind of deep meaning from the heart of the world had passed through that room, and we, standing in its path, had felt it move through us, and, in that moment of touch, it opened our eyes and our ears and our hearts to something deeper in the world around us and in ourselves. Then it was gone, leaving us changed, different, in its wake.

It was much later in life that I came across these sentences by the poet William Stafford, a man I deeply admire . . .

> *I was as if in a shell that glowed. All the big, dim reading room became more itself and had more meaning because of what I was writing. The alcove at the east end where the literature-browsing books were (a favorite of mine) was darker and more velvety. My steps, walking back to the boarding house to work, were ritual steps, feet placed carefully on the storybook world.*[1]

and began to understand that such moments happen for all of us. My stumbling upon that magical world was not an isolated event, not something unique to myself. And as I began to look for them, I found the tracks of others who had passed this way before me. Manuel Cordova Rios spoke of it this way . . .

> *As my glance wandered in the treetops I became aware of undreamed beauty in the details of the textures of leaves, stems, and branches. Every leaf, as my attention settled on it, seemed to glow with a greenish golden light. Unimaginable detail of structure showed. A nearby bird song—the irregular arpeggios of the siete cantos (seven songs)—floated down. Exquisite and shimmering, the song was almost visible. Time seemed suspended; there was only now and now was infinite. I could separate the individual notes of the bird song and savor each in its turn. As the notes of the song were repeated, I floated in a sensation that seemed somewhere*

between smelling an elusive intoxicating fragrance and tasting a delicate ambrosia.[2]

And Thoreau like this . . .

In the midst of a gentle rain . . . I was suddenly sensible of such a sweet and beneficent society in Nature, in the very patterning of the drops, and in every sound and sight around my house, an infinite and unaccountable friendliness all at once like an atmosphere sustaining me. . . . Every little pine needle expanded and swelled with sympathy and befriended me. I was so distinctly made aware of the presence of something kindred to me, even in scenes which we are accustomed to call wild and dreary, and also that the nearest of blood to me and humanest was not a person or villager, that I thought no place could ever be strange to me again.[3]

And Albert Hofmann like this . . .

There are experiences most of us are hesitant to speak about, because they do not conform to everyday reality and defy rational explanation. These are not particular external occurrences, but rather events of our inner lives, which are generally dismissed as figments of the imagination and barred from our memory. Suddenly, the familiar view of our surroundings is transformed in a strange, delightful, or alarming way: it appears to us in a new light, takes on special meaning. Such an experience can be as light and fleeting as a breath of air, or it can imprint itself deeply upon our minds.

One enchantment of that kind, which I experienced in childhood, has remained remarkably vivid in my memory ever since. It happened on a May morning—I have forgotten the year—but I can still point to the exact spot where it occurred, on a forest path on Martinsberg, above Baden, Switzerland. As I strolled through the freshly greened woods filled with bird song and lit up by the morning sun, all at once everything appeared in an uncommonly clear light. Was this something I had simply failed to notice before? Was I suddenly discovering the spring forest as it actually looked? It

shone with the most beautiful radiance, speaking to the heart, as
though it wanted to encompass me in its majesty. I was filled with
an indescribable sensation of joy, oneness, and blissful security.[4]

These experiences are not strangers to human beings. They have
accompanied our species through millennia. As children all of us experienced them in one form or another—even if we no longer consciously
remember that we did. Such moments are an integral part of what it
means to be human and someplace in all of us such memories are tucked
away. But as we are schooled, as life has its way with us—and with our
hearts—those memories come less and less to the conscious mind. We
learn . . . not to follow our hearts, not to grow *outward* into the world . . .
but to grow up, away from those kinds of memories and experiences, and
away from the world. In so doing, we grow away from something essential to our humanness, to our habitation of this world. We can no longer
see or *feel* what is within the surface sensory inputs that we receive; we
can no longer experience the luminous with which we are surrounded.
We have lost, as James Hillman once put it, the response of the heart
to what is presented to the senses. The early-twentieth-century German
writer and poet Gottfried Benn captured this state of being, our almost
fanatical orientation toward surfaces, in his observation that, "[for those
in the West,] reality is simply raw material, but its metaphysical background remains forever obscured."[5]

"Its metaphysical background." What a beautiful phrase, what beautiful implications in that line.

Albert Hofmann describes the impact that the loss of the metaphysical background, our loss of the sense of aesthetic unity, has on us as
human beings.

The experience of such a comprehensive reality is impeded in an
environment rendered dead by human's hands, such as is present in
our great cities and industrial districts. Here the contrast between
self and outer world becomes especially evident. Sensations of alien-
ation, of loneliness, and of menace arise. It is these sensations that
impress themselves on everyday consciousness in Western industrial
society; they also take the upper hand everywhere that technological

*civilization extends itself, and they largely determine the produc-
tion of modern art and literature.*[6]

And that is why, you know, that literature, that art of any sort, is so
tightly controlled now, that it is so *schooled*. For

> *You must not extend awareness further
> than your culture wants it to go.*

Do you understand what I mean here?

Art—real art—connects artists, and their art, *and* those who experience their art, to the metaphysical background of the world, to the
imaginal world that lies deep within the physical. That is, in part, its
ecological function. And that is why the continuing assaults on the imaginal (and its explorers) are so pervasive, why the schooling of artists—
of writers, musicians, painters, sculptors—has become so mechanical,
so oriented toward surfaces, toward form. For if we should recapture
the response of the heart to what is presented to the senses, go below
the surface of sensory inputs to what is held *inside* them, touch again
the "metaphysical background" that expresses them, we would begin to
experience, once more, the world as it really is: alive, aware, interactive,
communicative, filled with soul, and very, very intelligent—and we,
only one tiny part of that vast scenario. And that would endanger the
foundations upon which Western culture, our technology—and all
reductionist science—is based; for as James Hillman so eloquently put
it, "It was only when science convinced us that nature was dead that
it could begin its autopsy in earnest." A living, aware, and soul-filled
world does not respond well to autopsy.

Nevertheless, despite our cultural immersion in surfaces, our "growing up," and our schooling, somewhere inside each of us, those memories
reside. Someplace deep inside, we remain children, those younger parts of
ourselves woven into our being just as the rings of trees—and their earlier stages of growth—are still within them. These parts remain accessible
within us, natural expressions of our aliveness. All of us have the capacity
to free those parts—and their unique perceptual experiences of the world.
All of us still have the capacity for a deeper kind of perception.

and from time to time
it still breaks through our habituated notperceiving
. . . despite what our culture wants

Sometimes, merely reading about it can again bring the experience alive once more. Robert Bly, speaking of Thoreau, talks about that this way . . .

> *As we read Thoreau's work, especially his prose, we slowly become aware of a light in and around the squirrel, the ant, the woodchuck, the hawk, that belongs to them and not to the eyes observing or the brain producing words.*[7]

Throughout the years, I have met many people who have had moments of perceiving the light in and around the squirrel.

for that is what all my years of teaching have been about

Without exception, all of them have reported how difficult it has been to keep that perceptual experience alive. From every corner of life it seems, has come the demand to abandon it: from school, religion, culture, and family. The pressure to abandon the metaphysical background of the physical world is immense. There is not a one of us who *feels* the movement of the invisible inside us who does not experience that pressure, nor struggle with the demand to conform to surfaces as our orienting position. To discuss openly this deeper kind of experience, to conversationally mention that

> *yesterday as I sat among the rock formations and trees of the Gila I felt a change come upon me. I could feel the soul of that place as a delicate feather touch upon all my senses and, in that moment, a light began to emanate from every stone, every plant and tree, even the soil itself. I dropped then, into a silence as deep and still as any I have known. And as I listened I began to hear, as Aldo Leopold said I would, the music that lies deep within these hills.*
> *It seemed as if I had come home to a place I had always known,*

the place in which my true family resides. I felt companioned, and loved, and as I began to look deeper, I could sense, even see, the living connections between everything around me; there were golden threads moving through the world, weaving all the apparently separate organisms and objects together. I reached out and touched the nearest and a certain feeling came over me. And I suddenly realized I could follow that feeling through my enhanced sensing, home to where it originated, deep in the foundations of the world.

I let myself go. And as I moved deeper, following the thread home, I began to discover unexpected truths about each and every thing that that particular thread passed through. I saw that flowers menstruate and that pine pollen is filled with testosterone and that our sexuality is only a specific instance of a general condition. And as I continued on, I began to understand that the innovation we call sex is woven deeply into every aspect of what we call Earth.

Then, as I grew tired, my gaze began to relax. I realized, irrevocably, there is no part of this world, including myself, that is not connected to every other part; the surface that we have taken to be the world is but the beginning.

is to break incredibly strong conventions of what is allowable to speak of in our culture. If, instead of talking about the weather, one were to say, as the poet Theodore Roethke once did, that

Suddenly, in the early evening, the poem "The Dance" started, and finished itself in a very short time—say thirty minutes it was all done. I felt, I knew, I had hit it. I walked around and I wept; and I knelt down—I always do after I've written what I know is a good piece. But at the same time I had, as God is my witness, the actual sense of a Presence—as if Yeats himself were in that room. The house was charged with a psychic presence: the very walls seemed to shimmer. I wept for joy.[8]

one would suddenly find that conversation has ceased, that conversational companions are looking uncomfortable, that an awkward silence has fallen, that, if the companions are scientists, they have become twitchy and soon will begin to argue with what has been said—with the *reality* of what has been said, that if they are fundamentalist religionists of any sort (even of science or humanism), they have become afraid. How difficult it is to speak of these things, of this kind of experience. And how much have we lost in consequence.

Those of us who have experienced *a light in and around the squirrel,* those of us who have kept those memories, and experiences, alive inside us, find ourselves, in the West, in a strange country, strangers in a strange land.

The remarkable writer Terry Castle wrote of what this experience is like, not for us who experience the livingness of the world, but for women who one day discover they love women. The discovery that one is fundamentally different from the others with whom culture is shared is a difficult, sometimes insurmountable, experience. But for some, as Castle comments, there is the "potential for a certain radical mental freedom."

It makes sense: to embrace one's sapphic feelings—to come out to oneself—is necessarily to rethink the world. For not only is one made at once to confront one's apparently permanent alienation from the "normal" or mainstream, one finds one has to adjudicate, in the most piercing and personal way, on a raft of ethical, religious, and scientific questions. Are one's desires felonious or unnatural, as most traditional belief systems (distressingly) continue to insist? Or are they something rather more benign—simply a "variant" expression of human sexuality? If the latter is the case, couldn't one view same-sex passion, in turn, as perhaps a useful evolutionary adaptation? As an age-old demographic reality, possibly hardwired into the souls of some, that actually enriches and diversifies human civilization? Such questions are unavoidable and pressing; for no matter how timid and law abiding one is by nature, at the moment of self-recognition one suddenly finds oneself conspicuously in the wrong in the eyes of the world—caught out in a posture of stark and shocking defiance. By merely existing, one does fairly spectacular damage to entrenched presumptions about sexuality and society.

For some women the challenge is too much. . . . Yet in others,
the experience prompts an intellectual liberation. . . . An entire edi-
fice of socially imposed sexual myths, assumptions and taboos sud-
denly begins to look termite-ridden, carious, morally indefensible.
The world itself is seen to be wanting; everything must be adjusted
accordingly.[9]

Castle refers to this adjustment as adapting "to the cognitive challenges of self-acceptance." That is, once we can deny our nature no
longer, no longer force ourself into the paradigm of "normal" that the
cultural and social world around us insists upon, we begin to accept that
we are different, fundamentally so, from those around us. We encounter the cognitive challenges of self-acceptance and, in so doing, begin to
come to terms with what and who we really are.

Although Castle's linguistic tour-de-force is about women loving
women (in particular three women of note born in the 1890s) it is appli-
cable to any person who finds their personal orientation to be outside
social norms. And here, when talking about a light that is in and around
the squirrel's body, we are talking about perceptual sensing outside the
norm. To rephrase:

Are we engaging in a "variant" expression of human perceptual
sensitivity? If so, couldn't this be viewed, in turn, as perhaps a use-
ful evolutionary adaptation? As an age-old demographic reality,
possibly hardwired into the souls of some, that actually enriches and
diversifies human civilization?

And is it not true that we, *by merely existing, do fairly spectacular damage to*
entrenched presumptions about the nature of reality and society? Those of
us who carry the seed of this perception within us, as something we cannot and do not particularly want to repress, by our mere presence upset
the "normal" orientation of our Western society and culture. And once we
begin to truly accept ourselves and our perceptual experience as normal . . .

An entire edifice of socially imposed reality myths, assumptions and
taboos suddenly begins to look termite-ridden, carious, morally

*indefensible. The world itself is seen to be wanting; everything must
be adjusted accordingly.*

We, in accepting what we do and are, in accepting the reality of *what* we
perceive, have come out to ourselves.

We extend our awareness further than society wants it to go, specifically through our capacity for shifting consciousness in a particular
way. And when we do this, when we open those perceptual doors to
see deeper into the world, we begin to enter another world entirely; we
begin to leave the merely human world behind; we begin to see from the
world's point of view. And the view from there is much, much different
than the view from our cultural orientation, irrespective of our particular
subculture. Taking on that view, being able to see *deeper* into the meanings within material forms, does disturb the existing paradigm. Simply by
existing, by reflecting back to the culture something outside its frame of
reference, those of us who perceive in such ways really do *fairly spectacular damage to entrenched presumptions about* the nature of reality. But
there is every reason to view this capacity as a crucial evolutionary adaptation, a capacity hardwired into all living organisms and which serves a
specific purpose. Given the situation we find ourselves in, as individuals,
as a culture, as a species, it is a capacity that is essential, for as Albert
Einstein once said . . .

> *We can't solve problems
> by using the same kind of thinking we used
> when we created them.*

Which seems obvious but what is actually believed by most people
(including most scientists) is that if we only do what we have been
doing, just more vigorously, things will turn out differently.

> *You do know that is the definition of crazy, don't you?*

What is really true is that we must abandon the normal channels of
thought we, as a species, have used the past century or more, step outside of our habituation of perspective, and enter new territory. Not

just put our toe in the water, but immerse our whole being, our whole mind and spirit in a very different paradigm and perceptual experience. This means that

You must abandon your preconceptions

and travel into the world itself, as it really is, and find out for yourself what is true, and find, as well, just what you, yourself, are meant to do in this lifetime. And to do that, to really see deeply into the world, means using perceptual capacities that our culture habitually denies.

Despite our culture's willful ignorance, deeper perceptual experiences and paradigmatic shifts in cognition are spontaneously emerging with more frequency, and much more strongly, into the human species. For using this different kind of perception and thinking *is* the way out of our predicament, the way to solve the problems that those older kinds of thinking have caused. It is an evolutionary necessity.

This book is about developing the skill of intentionally altering perception in order to perceive the light in and around the squirrel. It is about learning how to consciously use it as a tool of perception and cognition. But it is also about what happens after that initial step. Once you see again with the eyes of a child, feel with the undefended heart, once you can enter that state at will, then what? That first step, essential as it is, is merely opening the doors of perception. What happens then if you walk through those doors, into the heart of the world? What happens to you as a person? What do you find out there, far out there, in the wildness of the world, far away from all human habitation and thought?

Come, journey with me, and I will show you.

2

"THE DOORS OF PERCEPTION"

First you must learn to see.

BARBARA MCCLINTOCK

Listening means learning to hear.

ROBERT WISE

Music is feeling, then, not sound.

WALLACE STEVENS

There are things known and things unknown, and in between are the doors of perception.

ALDOUS HUXLEY

*A*ll organisms encounter a specific kind of environment from the moment they are born. And every one of them has to be able to perceive that environment, take in information about it, and process that information in order to survive. There are no organisms that can or do exist in complete isolation from their environment and there never can be.

not even scientists

There is no way to stand here and look at the world over there, as if there were no connection between the two except an observing brain.

such dissociation is in fact pathological

Every organism is deeply interwoven into the ecological matrix from which it is expressed. And every organism possesses an interface, a place where the outside world and it touch.

and that touching is continual

At that interface are located specific organs for the perception of the exterior world—for the perception of *not me*. This is true even of the tiniest of life-forms, such as viruses.

and of bulkier ones, such as neuroscientists

Viruses have, just as we do in the skin that covers our bodies, an outer protein envelope. The surface of the viral protein envelope is studded with receptors (just as the surface of *our* envelope is). These are the unique sensory organs that the viruses use to gather information about their surroundings. They are the interface portals, the doors of perception, that allow the viruses to survive, that allow them, as well, to find the cells they are most suited to live within.

As physician and viral researcher Frank Ryan comments . . .

Viruses have a kind of sensation that could be classed as intermediate between a rudimentary smell or touch . . . they have a way of detecting the chemical composition of cell surfaces. . . . This gives a virus the most exquisite ability to sense the right cell surfaces. It recognizes them through a perception in three-dimensional surface chemistry.[1]

Every living organisms *has* to have a means to perceive informational inflows in order to survive; *every* living organism possesses mechanisms to do so.

Once environmental inputs are perceived, all organisms possess specific capacities for processing those informational inputs. Every one of them can determine the nature of the incoming information, its potential impact on the individual organism's health, and can decide what to do in response. They *have* to be able to do this in order to survive.

These truths are fundamental yet their implications are nearly always overlooked; it is hard to avoid the conclusion that this "overlooking" has been intentional. For the implications directly counteract nearly everything we have been taught about ourselves and the world around us.

Because all life-forms, irrespective of their nature, must, to survive, have a sense of *not me*, they all have a sense of self, they are in fact *self-aware*. Because all life-forms, irrespective of their nature, must, to survive, be able to analyze the nature of the *not me* that approaches them and, further, must be able to determine its intent, and further, be able to craft a response to that intent, all life-forms are, by definition, *intelligent*. Because all life-forms have to be able to determine the intent of the *not me* that approaches them, they also have to be able to determine *meaning*. In other words, all living organisms can not only process data, they also engage in a search for meaning, an analysis that runs much deeper than linear cause and effect. Thus, three capacities—self-awareness, intelligence, and the search for meaning—that have (erroneously) been ascribed as belonging *only* to human beings, are in fact general conditions of every living organism.

thus, the essential nature of the conflict between reductionists and those of us who actively feel the living intelligence of the world around us

These three attributes of living organisms have an important place in this book but to get to them I need to play with something else first, something obvious, but something that is commonly overlooked. And that something is specific to experiencing the metaphysical background of the world, and that is the doors of perception.

The Doors of Perception

The doors of perception are in fact the sensory portals through which we experience the world. In human beings, as in most animals, informational environmental inputs are processed through the sensory modalities all of us are familiar with: sight, sound, taste, touch, smell, and feeling—which is similar to touch but different from emotion, i.e., how a place *feels* to you when you encounter it. (This is, in fact, a primary, and sixth, sense that all human beings possess—we could not survive without it.) We possess the capacity to perceive the world around us through the use of sensory capacities that have been developed over long evolutionary time. And these sensory capacities are deeply interwoven with the complexity that we know of as the world. They are a primary point of interface between *me* and *not me*. For the ecological sophistication that we call Earth to exist, those interfaces must, of necessity, be extremely sophisticated as well.

The world is filled with sensory events that have to be processed; all living organisms are immersed in those events—continually. And every single one of those sensory events are filled with meanings, some relevant, some not. We (and every other self-organized life-form that exists) not only possess specific receptors on our body surfaces that allow us to process those inputs but our central nervous system possesses specific neural networks whose job it is to work with, or process, those sensory inflows as they move deeper inside us.

All sensory inflows in *every* organism that exists are analyzed below the level of conscious awareness as to their nature *and* the meanings embedded within them. The function of the sensory-specific neural networks within us is to make sense of, and regulate the inflow of, the extremely large sensory data stream that touches us. And the amount of data within such sensory inflows is massive, though commonly we don't notice that it is.

If you

look around the room, now,

that you are in, and allow yourself to take in everything in your visual field, you can see just how much visual data there is.

There is an incredibly rich range of shapes, and functions, and relationships of objects to each other, and shadows, and light reflections off surfaces, and subtleties of colors and textures, in fact millions of bits of visual sensory inputs in just this one place alone.

But until you began to *intentionally* look around you, you probably had little conscious awareness of the *amount* of data in your visual field. Specific parts of your neural network were acting to reduce the amount of incoming data reaching your conscious awareness. Most of your (conscious) attention was on reading this book, *not* on the visual field in which you sat immersed as you were reading it.

And even though these words are moving into you through a visual medium—the printed words on this page—as you became immersed in this book, you no longer saw the words as a visual input. You'd left that surface orientation behind. You began, then, to work with, and experience, the meanings that these words are only the containers for. Once you did, you saw, not words on a page, but pictures of the things I am speaking of and, too, into your experience came the sound of my voice and the feelings that accompany the meanings that these words have inside them. You were, until I woke you from it, engaged in a form of dreaming.

A special kind of dreaming,
central to everything this book is about,
and one that no one had to teach you how to do either

A rich sensory experience occurs during such dreaming but what you were not doing to any great extent was paying attention to the complex visual field that surrounded you as you dreamed. You were, at an unconscious level, *restricting* the amount of visual sensory information that flowed into your conscious mind.

All organisms learn to do this after they are born, to restrict the background sensory inputs that are not relevant to immediate tasks. And the more familiar your surroundings are, as are those in your house or on your regular route to work, the less such visual inputs tend to intrude on your awareness. It is possible, as you probably know, to drive to work or back home from a familiar place and not remember any details of the trip. During such drives, a part of you filters out the sensory inputs of the drive from your conscious awareness—but the unconscious parts of you *do* pay attention to all the visual data coming in. *They* drive the car for you; they just don't bother your conscious mind with the details. And they would not unless something actually needed your conscious attention, like a

Garbage truck!

suddenly emerging from a side street.

This phenomenon is common to all living organisms. They all have mechanisms for taking in and processing sensory data—and they all have mechanisms for reducing the amount of sensory inflows. They possess what are called sensory gating channels—or as William Blake and Aldous Huxley more comprehensively described the phenomenon, we all have within us the doors of perception.

Sensory gating channels can be thought of as tiny apertures or gates or doors in specific sections of the nervous system's neural network. They are similar to the lens in our eyes

you see

that can expand or contract as needed to increase or decrease the amount of data allowed in. They act to prevent sensory overload. In other words, if we consciously perceived everything that was coming in simultaneously as it was happening we would be overwhelmed with sensory experience.

> *This is, in fact, what many schizophrenics and those on hallucinogens experience—and it happens for a specific reason that is most definitely not pathological. It is crucial to our habitation of this planet and this book is about, in part, learning to open sensory gating channels at will to whatever degree is desired—to open the doors of perception.*

If there were no sensory gating, every sound, every smell, every feeling, every visual input would emerge into awareness without any ability to shut it off. This is what William Blake, someone who could intentionally alter the degree of aperture of his sensory gating channels, was referring to when he said . . .

> If the doors of perception were cleansed everything would appear to man as it is, Infinite.

And as he quite rightly went on to say . . .

> For man has closed himself up, till he sees thro' narrow chinks of his cavern.[2]

"Narrow chinks of his cavern." What a beautiful way to put it, that habitual narrowing of sensory gating channels that most of us experience. In essence, when sensory gating channels are narrow, as they commonly are, we only perceive a very small part of the world around us. Only a tiny bit of the radiance of the world can shine in through the narrow aperture that is left; the rest of it is gated out.

> Gated communities do then
> have some relation to the real world

There is a reason for this, as brain researcher Arash Javanbakht notes . . .

> In a world where we are simultaneously bombarded with a great deal of stimulation, we learn to focus our attention on important stimuli, while filtering out (gating) less relevant stimuli. Sensory gating (SG) is a way of habituation to repetitious and unimportant stimuli for the brain to reserve its limited resources to focus on important stimuli that need processing.[3]

It helps us focus on what we have determined, through experience, schooling, and cultural habituation, to be important. It also protects us from sensory overload. For it is true that, if gating did not exist, if the nearly infinite amount of sensory expressions that exist in the world flowed in without restraint every minute of every day of our lives, we simply could not function—we would experience what many researchers refer to as cognitive fragmentation. We would drown in a sea of sensory inputs. As neuropharmacologist Franz Vollenweider observes . . .

A fundamental feature of information processing dysfunction in psychosis is the inability of these patients to screen out, inhibit, filter, or gate extraneous stimuli and to attend selectively to salient features of the environment. Gating deficits may cause these subjects to become overloaded with excessive exteroceptive and interoceptive stimuli, which in turn could lead to a break-down in cognitive integrity and difficulty in distinguishing self from nonself.[4]

We need some sort of gating, and some control over gating, in order to function within the sea of sensory communications in which we are embedded. Hence, neural mechanisms for filtering sensory data inflows exist in the neural networks for every type of sensory input that we experience, including our nonkinesthetic *feeling* sense (what I have called *heart perception* in *The Secret Teachings of Plants,* Inner Traditions, 2004). Researchers in a number of disciplines have been working for over three decades to map (and label) the neural gating channels that control sensory input flows.

They are doing this to learn how to pharmaceutically normalize schizophrenic conditions and to make a case for the continued illegality of drugs— very bad ideas, for reasons I will get to . . . eventually.

Sensory Flow Through the Brain

Researchers talk of P50 or N100, P200, N40, N50, M50, M100, N400, and so on gating channels. There are, in fact, a series of gating channels that exist in every sensory neural network, not just a single one. It can be visualized

even more accurately than the lens of an eye

as being similar to a series of locks on the river of incoming sensory flows.

For example, during auditory processing, sound inputs flow through the ear, then the brain stem reticular formation, then the medial septum (these two being called the lemniscal pathway), then the hippocampal region (which also includes the amygdala), then the thalamus, then the auditory cortex, then finally the cerebral cortex.

> *These latter three being called the nonsensical,*
> *I mean the nonlemniscal, pathway*

The central clearing center, as it were, for all sensory inputs is the hippocampus. It is here that all pathways converge.

> *It is this organ that is concerned with*
> *orienting us—in both physical space*
> *and the rich field of meanings through which we move*
> *every day of our lives*
> *It is the part of us that works most deeply with meanings,*
> *with the meanings that are embedded within every*
> *sensory input we receive*

As researchers comment, the hippocampus (of which there are two, one on each side of the brain) is specifically "concerned with interpreting the significance of sensory stimuli, to orient the organism in its environment."[5] And this most definitely includes the meaning fields in which we are embedded. From here all the sensory inputs, except that of smell, are funneled to the thalamus (or thalami, there are two, one on each side of the brain), for routing to specific areas of the cerebral cortex.

Sensory gating processes occur every step along these neural pathways, located in the limbic, striatal, pallidal, and thalamic structures of the brain. Only what the pre-attentional parts of the self determine is important is allowed to reach conscious awareness.

> *The gating in the deeper sections of the brain occurs nearly instan-*
> *taneously, within 50 milliseconds—that is 50 thousandths of a*

second—much more quickly than in the hippocampus which takes 250 milliseconds to process the incoming data stream.

The unconscious or pre-attentional parts of the self that analyze sensory inputs and then determine what or what not to let through may vary in their function: they may be a part of us that are focuses on protection of the self or a part that engages sensory phenomena with a sense of wonder or even a part that is measuring sexuality levels in people at a party. If the area of interest (or concern) of any particular deeper part is activated, then the sensory gating will open more widely—allowing more inputs to reach conscious awareness. If the unconscious parts determine that the sensory inputs have no importance, sensory gating narrows—and the sensory inputs remain outside our awareness. These deeper parts of us allow sensory inputs to touch our consciousness *only* if *they* determine those inputs are important enough.

though you, your conscious self, can override that decision
. . . if you want to, that is

The pre-attentional parts of the self use a complicated analytic process to determine relevance. They weigh a large variety of factors to gauge relevance; this includes such things as the intensity of the sensory inflow, its novelty, the degree of contrast between a sensory stimulus and its sensory background, and its rarity.

When it comes to novelty, the pre-attentional parts of the self look for patterns of similarity, that is . . . how similar is this new sensory input to ones that have gone before? They, in essence, engage in a comparative analysis in order to determine whether something is novel or not. But the new sensory input must be novel in a specific way. Specifically, because every new inflow of sensory data is *not* in fact identical to those that went before,

no event is ever identical to any previous event

each new sensory input does present the self with novelty. To override the continual novelty of the world there is a certain novelty *threshold* that must be reached before a new sensory stimulus is considered to actually be *novel*. So, while all the white daisies in the garden are slightly different from one another you won't generally perceive any of them as novel.

unless you decide to

But should you come upon a pink one in that sea of white, it will automatically capture your conscious attention.

Then there is intensity: Sensory inflows of any sort that occur past a certain threshold or *degree* of intensity *always* reach conscious attention. A sudden, loud sound in the kitchen, as opposed to the continual and familiar sounds of the refrigerator jogging in that room, will always capture conscious attention. This allows us, at the simplest, to determine safety levels in our environment.

Hey! Did you hear that? . . . Shush . . . Listen . . .
Is someone at the door?

Then there is degree of contrast: When determining contrast, the pre-attentional parts analyze incoming sensory data against the background inputs. As an example, if you are at a party where many people are talking, not only is the sound gated but the semantic meanings in the hum of conversation are also gated. Essentially, both sound and the meanings-in-the-sounds are reduced in intensity so you don't get overwhelmed by the incoming sensory inputs. However, should you hear your name from across the crowded room,

Did you hear what happened between Michael and Jenny?

the gating channel that is contrasting sound meanings in the room will open more widely and allow the sensory input through. It signals the cerebral cortex to pay attention. Once signaled, the cortex, in association with other parts of the brain, uses stochastic processes to enhance the signal so that what is being said can be heard in detail.

Well, he put the moves on her during a workshop.

What happens, in experience, is that out of the sea of sound, your name just jumps out and is clearly heard—even if you were not consciously listening to that particular conversation. At that moment you consciously begin to listen and as you do, and as the pre-attentional parts of the brain open channels more widely, more and more of the conversation can be heard.

What I heard is that she actually told him to fuck off,
right in the middle of the lecture.
Geesus! The guy's an idiot!
Yeah, and then he . . .

One of the ways that your neural system facilitates this process is through the near-immediate creation and release of specific neurotransmitters. These affect gating levels and processes in the central nervous system and brain.

Glutamate and GABA (gamma aminobutyric acid), acetylcholine, dopamine, serotonin, melatonin, testosterone (and other androgens), estradiol (and other estrogens), noradrenaline, nicotine, and a host of less common but still powerful neuroactive compounds such as DMT are all generated and released into the system in a unique combination each time, depending on the incoming sensory inputs and their meanings.

Hearing your name in such a circumstance will always signal the unconscious self to open gating more widely, for any attention intentionally directed toward *you* by outside organisms will *always* (potentially) have something to do with your safety.

I heard he's going to get fired.

That always overrides gating.

In general, every sensory message, irrespective of its nature, flows through the same pre-attentional parts of the brain during the initial gating. Once this early gating occurs, the remaining sensory bits are routed to the thalamus which then sends them to the specific portion of the brain that specializes in that particular sensory modality: the primary visual cortex for vision, the primary auditory cortex for sound, the primary somatosensory cortex for touch, and so on. After processing in those centers, they are sent to the cerebral cortex—which itself performs a final gating—and then they reach conscious awareness. During sleep, the thalamus, if we are blessed, acts to cut off nearly all sensory inputs so as to not alert the cerebral cortex and cause waking.

Each of these specialized areas is capable of extremely detailed discrimination in very tiny modulations of the sensory inflows. The auditory cortex, as an example, processes the sound inputs that have not already been gated earlier in the stream. It specifically works with tone, pitch, harmony, loudness, and beat patterning or timing. In people that use auditory inputs as a primary or major area of sensory processing

musicians for instance

there is much less gating of sound in the deeper levels of the brain than in nonmusicians. In consequence, much more sound input reaches the auditory cortex. Because the auditory cortex is continually used to work with larger amounts of sound inflows (with more subtlety), it becomes highly developed and shows tremendous plasticity, that is, continuous new neuronal development. Frances Densmore, for example, the ethnomusicologist who recorded thousands of Native plant songs in the early twentieth century, could perceive pitch differentiations as tiny as $1/32$ in deviation. (She had as well total recall and prefect pitch.) The more a sensory modality is consciously used to analyze incoming sensory inflows, the more sensitive it becomes, and the larger the neural network within it becomes.

this applies to the feeling sense,
that is, heart field perception, as well

In the primary auditory cortex, different neurons respond to different tones. Each neuron or neuron group in that region of the brain is, in fact, specific for particular tones. The neurons adjoining those sensitive to one tone are themselves sensitive and respond to tones that are similar but slightly different and so on across the whole range of sounds humans can perceive. From long-term and extensive use, in musicians, the neurons become highly sensitized to tiny modulations in every incoming sound. As well, the neurons in the cortex synchronize with each other creating much larger fields of perception for variations in the sound inputs. This increases sensitivity to sound perception. And, from the stimulus of continued and highly focused use, more neurons form in the organ, creating, again, more sophisticated sound perception. Over time, the organ itself becomes much more *aware*. It begins to actively look for and respond to fields of sound communication and, in combination with the hippocampus, actively works to pull the inherent meanings out of the sound field.

Thus, when musicians play, that part of the self is highly involved in the *expression* of sound. It is partnered with the conscious mind; they become allies in the process of sound-making. An exquisitely developed *feeling sense* also comes into being which blends together with the parts concerned with sound generation creating a unique synaesthesia of sensory perception and expression. This blended sensory capacity is concerned with the *exact* expression of meaning through sound. Fingers, lips, breath, the auditory neural network, and *the feeling sense*—that is, *how* the music feels—all act as one unified coherent organism of expression. Tiny shifts in any of these systems cause tiny modulations in the meaning-filled sound field that, ultimately, produce a musical outcome far beyond any combination of the parts.

When musicians listen to incoming musical or sound inflows, they listen for those exact kinds of tiny, invisible, modulations that no one else can hear. And if they are playing together in a group, they then modulate their sound expression in response to what they are hearing. What occurs then is a living communication between a group of people who are working intensively with something invisible—something that is more than the sum of the parts, the thing that comes into being at the moment of self-organization. You can't point to it, but you can always feel it when it's there . . .

and when it's not.

This dynamic is what the poet William Stafford was describing (though he was talking about writing) when he wrote . . .

> *Just as the swimmer does not have a succession of handholds hidden in the water, but instead simply sweeps that yielding medium and finds it hurrying him along, so the writer passes his attention through what is at hand, and is propelled by a medium too thin and all-pervasive for the perceptions of nonbelievers who try to stay on the bank and fathom his accomplishment.*[6]

In musicians, or those who, over a long time, attend closely to sound modulation (as good actors and writers also do), the entire auditory neural network becomes an active, intelligent sensing organ. Over time, unique invisibles, perceivable only because of the sensitivity and openness of the sensory gating in that neural network, are able to be heard and, as well, expressed *through* the activity of that part of the self. This is what Goethe was talking about when he said that

> *Every new object, clearly seen, opens up a new organ*
> *of perception in us.*

Using that part of the brain as a primary sensing organ, actively extending its gating parameters, literally remakes it. More neurons form, the brain region becomes more plastic; it becomes highly sensitive to the lightest touch of sensory inflows. A new organ of perception emerges that can be used to consciously perceive tiny modulations of the meanings held within a much larger spectrum of the sensory modality being used.

Children who begin working at an early age with music have, as habit, much less pre-attentional or unconscious gating in the neural network that attends to sound. Gating, in general, develops over time and with exposure, the pre-attentional self learning to gate whatever is not important to the conscious mind. Children, by nature, have much less gating than adults—gating tends to narrow over time. If children begin working with sound early on, auditory gating remains much more open—it never narrows as it does in others. Since the importance of sound perception remains high in those who begin young, the systems in the auditory neural stream allow more sound through to the conscious mind, simply as habit throughout their lifetime.

In those who begin working with music at a later age, the simple decision to pay attention to sound, and tiny modulations of sound, will override established gating parameters and start the sensitization of auditory neurons.

though it takes awhile

As it is developed *as a habit of daily behavior* over a long enough time period (several years minimum) the neuronal fields become increasingly sensitive, neuronal synchronization begins to occur, the neuronal fields extend, and more neurons form. The sensory zone, as it does in all musicians, increases in size. The pre-attentional parts of the self take the top-down decision by the conscious mind to attend to sound as an *override*. This resets unconscious gating parameters; and if you work at it long enough, the resets will be permanent.

Gating "Deficits"

Gating activity outside of the normal bell-shaped curve for the population of the United States is, generally, considered to be pathological. The more widely open gating channels are, the more likely someone is to be defined as clinically abnormal and to be labeled, one way or another, as having "stimulus filtering difficulties" or "gating deficits."

P50 (a.k.a. P1) gating systems have to do with the gating or modulation of auditory perceptions. Nonmusicians (and some musicians) that have "less robust" P50 gating are often considered (by psychologists) to have higher rates of "perceptual modulation" difficulty. For nearly all people, a new sound that occurs in the field of background sounds within which we are immersed daily signals our conscious minds to pay attention. This causes us to focus on the new sound. Once identified, its nature determined, and safety level appraised, conscious focus shifts away from it (if safe), to whatever we were doing before. Those with "less robust" gating have, as habit, a more open P50 system, and many more incoming sounds make it into conscious perception.

Wait! What is that!
What?
Don't you hear it? Something's moving in the house.

In other words people who have this gating channel more open can in fact hear things that most of the rest of us cannot. And the more open the channel is, the more they hear. People with very open P50 channels commonly report being "flooded with sound" or hearing "everything at once." In other words, the unconscious mechanism that filters sound lets more through, so much so that, in some cases, the people exist in a sea of sounds that tend to overwhelm consciousness. This is often complicated by the fact that, commonly, they also have more open N100 channels.

N100 (a.k.a. N1) gating channels are those that trigger increased *attention* and activation of memory. When this channel is also open not only are there more sounds being consciously perceived but conscious attention is directed to each and every one of those sounds. Further, a rapid cross-correlation of new sensory inputs with previous experiences is generated in order to determine subtle meanings and differentiation within them. Those with "less robust" N100 gating tend to overinclude "irrelevant" sensory inputs and meanings into the focus of attention. For such people, to the unconscious part that analyzes background sounds, all sounds remain relevant and so it signals that conscious attention must be paid to the incoming sounds. The more open this gating channel the more difficult it becomes to shift attention away from the incoming sounds. Not only can the person be overloaded with incoming sounds, they have great difficulty in removing their attention from the individual sounds themselves.

Soldiers with PTSD often have trouble with these two gating channels; they take in more sounds, are highly alert to any tiny new sound in their auditory surroundings, and rapidly cross-correlate new sounds with old ones, seeking out their potential danger. (This will also keep adrenal stimulation high, putting them into a high alert status most of the time.)

Although studies on gating "problems" have occurred with various "abnormal" states (such as PTSD, migraines, bipolar disorder, Asperger's, Parkinson's, Alzheimer's, ADHD, and autism) most of the work has occurred with those labeled schizophrenic. A common complaint among this group is of "sensory inundation and inappropriate orienting to irrelevant stimuli," and this includes a great deal more than just sound. It is often spread across the sensory spectrum. Essentially, they perceive a lot of things other people don't and they don't know how to sort it out. In them, the doors of perception are more widely open than in the rest of the population, sometimes much more widely so.

"Inappropriate orienting to irrelevant stimuli," by the way, is a cultural definition, not a functional one. In other words, those with significantly open sensory gating channels are orienting themselves to sensory inputs that most other people do not notice and attributing importance to the meanings in those sensory inputs that other people do not.

> *Further, they don't know how to interpret the sea of meanings they are experiencing. They tend to use the cultural metaphors (and standards of normalcy) they have internalized to explain what is happening, the majority of which are inaccurate maps of the metaphysical background of the world. Those metaphors just don't work at helping orient the person in time, space, or meaning. Often they make things worse. It's a software problem that extends itself as well to clinicians. Few of those that treat the condition actually have access to the metaphysical background of the world themselves or even understand what access to that world means. In consequence, not only are the interpretations by "schizophrenics" of their meaning inflows "crazy," so are the informational interventions by their caretakers.*

This behaviorally orients those with this kind of widely open sensory gating far outside the cultural norm. In cultures that recognize the importance of this capacity, this group of people are trained to use their enhanced perceptual capacities for the benefit of the group.

> *there would then be many more holy people among us*

Schizophrenic states, in fact, share a large number of common features with the experiential states generated by hallucinogens indicating that schizophrenia is not in fact an abnormal state but is itself an altered state of consciousness. Part of the major problem attending schizophrenia is what it is *defined* to be, that is, abnormal, rather than an altered state of consciousness that has a specific ecological function for the species. In the West such states are labeled as an illness and are almost always medicated.

Most psychoactive drug use is proscribed for exactly
the same reason . . .
You must not extend perception further than the
society wants it to go

There are very few people in the West (and virtually none who are clinically schooled) who understand how to train someone in the use of that enhanced perception. Once such gating dynamics are labeled abnormal, accepted to be neuropathological, there is generally no alternative (in that system) except pharmaceutical suppression.

But when it comes to the whole concept of "abnormal," a deeper look begins to reveal inherent problems. Studies have found that one-fourth of "healthy" individuals in every Western population commonly report sensory inundation, difficulty in stimulus filtering (stimulus overinclusion), and problems with orienting to inappropriate stimuli. It is much more common among artists (writers, musicians, painters, and so on), those who use psychoactive drugs, and the gifted. It is also common among people who have been exposed to severe environmental stressors such as war. Rather than abnormal, it is, rather, a common experience of the human species. Despite this, there are strong cultural reasons why more widely open gating channels are suppressed.

You are not going out of this house with your hair
like that young man!
(Hey wait! Come back here!)

Nevertheless, the capacity for opening the doors of perception is built into us and every species of life on this planet for a reason.

and that reason is central to the purpose of this book

As well, it's *natural* to us, for when we are born our gating channels are very, very open.

3

"AND THE DOORKEEPER OBEYS WHEN SPOKEN TO"

Mind at Large has to be funneled through the reducing valve of the brain and nervous system. What comes out at the other end is a measly trickle of the kind of consciousness that will help us to stay alive. . . . Certain persons, however, seem to be born with a kind of bypass that circumvents the reducing valve. In others, temporary bypasses may be acquired either spontaneously, or as the result of deliberate "spiritual exercises," or through hypnosis, or by means of drugs. Through these permanent or temporary bypasses there flows . . . something more than, and above all something different from, the carefully selected utilitarian material which our narrowed, individual minds regard as a complete, or at least sufficient, picture of reality.

ALDOUS HUXLEY

What one commonly takes as "the reality," including the reality of my own individual person, by no means signifies something fixed, but rather something that is ambiguous—that there is not only one, but that there are many realities, each comprising also a different consciousness of the ego.

ALBERT HOFMANN

To know how cherries and strawberries taste, ask children and birds.

GOETHE

The door to the soul is unlocked; you do not need to please the door-keeper, the door in front of you is yours, intended for you, and the doorkeeper obeys when spoken to.

ROBERT BLY

During early life, the sensory gating channels in every individual in every species find their own "default" setting. That is, as the organism ages, through experience with informational inputs and feedback from family and culture about what is relevant and what is not, the sensory gating channels themselves develop their own particular range of action. The amount of incoming sensory data that reaches conscious awareness is then held to some constant that does not have to be monitored. It becomes automatic. And within any animal species there is considerable variation among the default settings that occur. Some individuals will have very narrow sensory gating channels

Get off my lawn!

others will be widely open.

Oh, I like the blue streaks in your hair!

This directly affects the perceptual field that is experienced in day-to-day life *and* the amount of information they take in through sensory data. Widely open channels can be restricted to a single sense, such as smell, or they can cover several sensory mediums: feeling, seeing, and hearing for example.

Unfortunately, most researchers studying gating dynamics in children are, as with "schizophrenia," focused on "normal" versus "abnormal" gating. And all children are expected to fit into the defined "normal" range of behavior. Sensory gating dynamics outside that culturally determined "norm" are defined as abnormal and researchers note that

> *Individuals with these characteristics have been classified as having sensory processing deficits (SPD). Such behaviors disrupt an individual's ability to achieve and maintain an optimal range of performance necessary to adapt to challenges in life. The manifestations of SPD may include distraction, impulsiveness, abnormal activity level, disorganization, anxiety, and emotional lability that produce deficient social participation, insufficient self-regulation and inadequate perceived competence.*[1]

Those terms, if you look at them more closely, are exterior, "authority" generated terms; they relate directly to the paradigm in place in those authorities. They really don't have much to say about the interior experience of the children so labeled. So, let's reorient from exterior to interior.

"Distraction" then becomes boredom; "impulsiveness" becomes self-generated explorative behavior based on what captures interest; "abnormal activity level" is thus high-energy levels generating multiple task interests; "disorganization" is failure to follow rigid organizational regimens set by others; "anxiety"—well, we all know that one: what the hell kind of world did I get born into?; "emotional lability" is, in fact, a wide range of emotions that are accessed when adults or the exterior culture don't want them to be. In other words, should you have ever read Mark Twain, what is being described is "Tom Sawyer syndrome," a once common state of being in many if not most children. The more widely open the sensory gating channels are, the more the child's behavior alters from what is currently held to be the cultural norm in the West.

On average, some 5 to 10 percent of all children in the West fall into this category. They are defined as having sensory processing disorders and the focus is on using medication to get them to maintain "an optimal range of performance." Among gifted children the incidence of more widely open sensory gating channels is much higher, as high as 35 percent according to some. They possess, as a result, "a global heightened awareness to sensory stimulation."[2]

In spite of the movement to label "a global heightened awareness to sensory stimulation" abnormal, it is, in fact, a condition natural to all of us. In infancy, gating is very widely open. At that time *all of us* experience a global heightened awareness to sensory stimulation. As we age gating tends to narrow, but not uniformly. While *all* gating narrows as we age, in each of us some gating channels remain more open than others. And this is true across the species as well, for some people the gating average across the whole sensory spectrum becomes very narrow . . .

> *i.e., people that used to be called "narrow minded"*
> *(Pop quiz: in what year did the narrow minded take control?)*

for others gating remains very open, especially among young children, artists, schizophrenics, specialists of the sacred such as shamans and Buddhist masters, and those ingesting psychotropics.

Researchers Michel Kisley et al. comment . . .

> *Before ten years of age, and as young as 18 months old, sensory gating measures are extremely variable from child to child. . . . A correlation between increasing age and stronger response suppression was uncovered, even within this restricted age range.*[3]

The neural networks responsible for sensory gating begin to process data as soon as the child is born . . . and to some extent prior to birth (since both sound and light perception occur in the womb). The networks, in essence, begin responding to environmental cues (including those of the parents, culture, and exterior environment) and modulating sensory gating function based on those cues. And the hippocampus is perhaps the central organ in the brain responsible for processing sensory data and acting as a gateway for inflows. As Kisley et al. note: "The cholinergic innervation of the hippocampus, which is crucial for intact sensory gating, exhibits extensive remodeling during pre- and early postnatal development."[4] It displays a great deal of plasticity in response to incoming sensory flows; the more it works with meaning and the more sensory input it is sensitive to, the more it shifts its neural structure as it sensorally interacts with the world.

Because newborns have minimal gating, they tend to experience everything *simultaneously* as it happens. They take in nearly all the field of sensory inflows in which they exist, and from every sensory modality. They are literally immersed in a sea of meaning-filled sensory inputs. Because they don't yet have language nor any presets determining what things "mean," they work with meaning directly and learn, through experience, to determine the nature of the meanings they encounter. In other words, they are working with the metaphysical background of things directly, without prejudice. Or, as Eric Berne once described it . . .

> *A little boy sees and hears birds with delight. Then the "good father" comes along and feels he should "share" the experience and help his son "develop." He says: "That's a jay, and this is a sparrow." The moment the little boy is concerned with which is a jay and which is a sparrow, he can no longer see the birds or hear them sing. He has to see and hear them the way the father wants him to. Father has good reasons on his side, since few people can go through life listening to the birds sing, and the sooner the boy starts his "education" the better. Maybe he will be an ornithologist when he grows up. A few people, however, can still see and hear in the old way. But most of the members of the human race have lost the capacity to be painters, poets, or musicians, and are not left the option of seeing and hearing directly even if they can afford to; they must get it secondhand.[5]*

Very young children don't have the intermediary of language—they don't have a *sign* in place of the *thing*. They "see and hear in the old way."

> *And that is what this book is about. It is recovering this ability, and using it intentionally, to interact with the metaphysical background of the world. It is about becoming aware. It is about giving up getting things "secondhand."*

As infants age, sensory gating processes develop, uniquely for each one of them. The older the child, the more sensory gating clicks into place. As Kisley et al. comment about their research: "The correlation between sensory gating and conceptual age was significant."[6] By age eight the gating channels begin to take on what will be the default state in adulthood. This further solidifies, narrowing more, at the onset of puberty and generally is in place by the end of adolescence.

Younger children, because gating is still much more widely open, are by nature more attentive to the sensory flows coming in to them, respond with greater attentiveness to stimuli considered irrelevant by adults, and generally have a greater sense of wonder about the world since most stimuli are novel to them. They have not yet learned to relegate the sensory inflows from the world to background noise.

> *The world is still filled with wonder and magic; they still see with glittering eyes. It is, in part, their openness to the touch of the world upon them, their sense of the livingness of everything they encounter, that so strongly affects all of us who encounter them.*

Crucially, every developmental stage that we go through as we grow (including middle and old age) has a different gating dynamic. Thus, in each stage of growth we perceive different aspects of the sensory field in which we are embedded. They are, in essence, a series of lenses through which we can perceive different layers of the reality field through which we move.

Every developmental stage has a different *function* and thus *what* it is going to perceive from the field around it is directly related to that function. Each particular stage acts as a focusing mechanism that shifts gating in particular ways, thus altering the sensory data that is perceived. This acts at the unconscious level to affect what type of sensory inflows are considered important at that time in life and thus what makes it to the conscious mind. The functions of the different developmental stages are each interpreted as a distinct *task set* by the parts of the CNS that gate sensory inflows at the unconscious level.

> *I will get to task sets in a minute*

So the sensory inflows are gated differently as ego states change, both during the developmental stages of life *or* when previous developmental stages are intentionally regenerated later in life.

One of the reasons that Luther Burbank could directly work with plants to co-create most of the food plants we now take for granted is that he routinely accessed earlier developmental stages, in essence, taking them on as a lens through which to experience the world. This shifted his sensory gating dynamics, opening the doors of perception much wider, allowing a much richer sensory perception to occur. It allowed him to work with the metaphysical background directly. As Helen Keller once remarked of him . . .

> *He has the rarest of gifts, the receptive spirit of a child. Only a wise child can understand the language of flowers and trees.*

This capacity to moderate the doors of perception through the activation of younger developmental stages also points to one of the great lies of our time: human beings are not single egos but are instead composed of multiple ego states.

> *multiple personality disorder*
> *is only a pathological expression*
> *of a general condition*

Different parts of the self—irrespective of calendar age—come to the fore at different times, depending on environmental demands. All of us know this, we just don't *know* it. There is not a one of us that has not had an argument with ourselves about something we wanted to do but that another part of us felt we should not do.

> *Go ahead, eat the cake!*
> *(No, I shouldn't, I gained too much weight last week.)*
> *C'mon, eat it. Look at it, can't you just taste it right now?*
> *(Stop it! Don't make me.)*

This kind of complexity in the psychological structure of the personality is a long-standing evolutionary innovation. It allows for extremely sophisticated responses to environmental challenges. One element of this is the deeper perception of meanings in the world that can occur through the alteration of sensory gating by a simple reorientation of internal consciousness from one developmental stage to another. As brain researcher Mark Kiefer comments: Consciousness is not the "simple result of processing in a single 'consciousness' module."[7] There are multiple "modules" or ego states that together make up the "us" that we know as our unique selves. Together these "consciousness modules" form something greater than the sum of the parts, though there is not a one of us who has not and does not tend to take on, from time to time, one of those modules or ego states to the exclusion of the others.

> *Policeman: Why did you run if you hadn't done anything?*
> *Suspect: Well, when I saw you a part of me said run.*
> *Policeman: That part of you is an idiot.*

Nevertheless, it is possible to form an alliance between all the various ego states or modules in which something much more than the sum of the parts comes into being as *a synchronized whole.*

this is what inner council work is

Then, when desired, *any* of the various ego states or modules can be taken on as the primary lens being used through which to see the world. This gives us sophisticated *perceptual* options through which to analyze the meanings in which we are embedded, which gives rise to a much greater range of behavioral choices.

The *way* we saw the world at infancy or at four or at eight is still an accessible capacity. Those developmental stages exist in one form or another in all life-forms;

> *there is a reason that puppies, and kittens, and young children, and newly emerging plants all have such a similar feeling to them. These developmental stages occur across genus and species lines— they exist for a purpose*

they are evolutionary innovations. They allow for unique perceptions of the world, and unique types of interactions with environment. Each developmental stage or consciousness module allows different aspects of the layered complexity of the world within which we are immersed to be perceived. That is a primary part of their function.

It is an aspect of the emergent behaviors
that occur in all self-organized biological systems

Like cells into organs into organisms on the physical level, psychological and social organization shows the same sort of innovative development. In perceiving different layers of the complexity of the world, we are able to work with different meanings, meanings that themselves are shaping aspects of the world around us below the level of linear perception. This then allows for tremendous behavioral innovation in response, for we can then affect patterns of movement below the level of their gross behavior. As Tsuno and Mori note . . .

> *Mammalian brains have a remarkable ability to use sensory infor-*
> *mation about the external world and the interoceptive state to*
> *choose an appropriate behavior from among a wide range of reper-*
> *toire of behavioral responses. Changes in behavioral state are accom-*
> *panied by internally coordinated changes in the information*
> *processing mode of local neuronal circuits, including those in the*
> *cerebral neocortex and the hippocampus.*[8]

We can intentionally alter how we process sensory data simply by an alteration in state: *"Changes in behavioral state are accompanied by inter-nally coordinated changes in the information processing mode of local neu-ronal circuits."*

It is very difficult to understand the language of plants if you cannot open sensory gating channels more widely. Many people who have learned to do so, as Helen Keller noted about Luther Burbank, begin to take on a unique kind of childlikeness, for that younger part of the self, to whom such behavior is natural, begins emerging into the world as habit.

Intentionally Shifting Gating

While gating channels normally operate at an unconscious level to process out irrelevant data, all gating channels can be intentionally opened further, and there are a number of ways to accomplish this. Simply having intent, the decision to consciously focus on some particular incoming sensory flow, is one of them.

For example, when you focus conscious attention on reading these sentences, the unconscious parts that are gating visual inflows allow your conscious intent to override their narrowing of the sensory gates. They no longer act to gate inputs as they normally do. In consequence the words on this page begin to stand out as individual identities. If, on the other hand, you happen to casually see a newspaper lying on a table as you pass by, you might see that it is covered with words, but you won't necessarily notice the words themselves. At an unconscious level you have gated them out. Similarly, if you casually opened this book and glanced at a page, though you might "see" the words, you would not necessarily be actively attentive to them as individuals or to the meanings inside them. The incoming visual messages—in this instance, the meanings in the words and sentences—are "gated" because the unconscious parts of you have determined they are not, at that moment in time, important enough to pay attention to. This keeps you oriented to the surface of the visual world.

> *this same kind of gating, trained into us from childhood, is why it is often so hard to see the meanings in the sensory communications that come to us from the natural world around us, the reason why we can't experience the metaphysical background of the material world—it's why we remain oriented to surfaces, as a culture, as a people. It is why reading the text of the world is now so uncommon in the West.*

All that it takes to change this is your *decision* to read, your intentionally focusing on the words as individuals. This creates a shift in gating parameters. The unconscious parts of you that gate both visual inputs and meaning open more widely in deference to the conscious mind's intent.

Interestingly, attentional override can also occur without actually *focusing* the eyes on a single object; you can do it just as well with what some people call luminous eyes, or soft-focused (peripheral-like) vision. It is not necessary to look directly at something to see more deeply into it. As gating researcher Martin Eimer notes . . .

> *Attention can be voluntarily directed to specific objects and locations within the spatial field independent of overt eye movements. Stimuli at attended-to locations are detected with higher speed and accuracy as compared to stimuli presented outside the attentional focus.*[9]

In other words, you can let yourself take in the visual field as a soft-focused field of visual experience and simply focus your attention, not your eyes, on something in that visual field and that will override gating. You will begin to take in more sensory data about that particular thing and it will then be processed at deeper levels of meaning by the hippocampal region. This particular kind of seeing in fact tends to gate much less of the visual field than focused vision. If you look at one thing closely, say the coffee cup on the table, the rest of the visual field tends to be gated out. But if you look at the whole visual field and simply let your attention focus on the cup a much greater range of visual input will be retained.

Irrespective of how you do it, it is always possible to override the automatic gating of sensory inflows by intentionally focusing awareness on incoming sensory data.

> *This is sometimes referred to as a "task set." In essence, you have set yourself a "task"—e.g., learning music or reading—and that decision, and interest level, override the unconscious gating defaults that have previously been in place.*

By consciously making the decision that certain sensory inflows are more important than others, your conscious mind increases their novelty against the background sensory inputs. This, nearly immediately, overrides previous gating settings.

The classical view of unconscious sensory processing

in other words, the previous definitive statements about the nature of reality that the majority of scientists proclaimed as true

is that gating is an unalterable automatic process once sensory gating defaults are set in childhood. It had been assumed that there could be little conscious control—or possible control—over the process. This perspective is, regrettably, still deeply ingrained within the work of nearly all neuroscientists and psychologists/psychiatrists. One of its problems, which becomes apparent when it is examined more deeply, is that an "autonomous" process should, by definition, be invariant within each individual. But studies of sensory gating show that it is *never* invariant . . . in anyone. Gating parameters tend to move across a spectrum in all people (and to be variant across populations as well). In other words, there are moments in our lives that all of us open our gating channels much more widely. The belief that gating is fixed flies in the face of the need for a species to be adaptable to altered circumstances; such inflexibility would place a tremendously powerful limit on cognitive responses to environmental perturbations.

What is more accurate is that unconscious gating defaults act in concert with environmental and cognitive demands and the needs of the cerebral cortex and thus are continually in flux depending on circumstances and environmental inputs. As researchers Kiefer et al. observe . . .

Unlike classical theories, refined theories assume that automatic processes are critically dependent on higher-level, top-down factors such as attention, intentions, and task sets that orchestrate the processing streams toward greater optimization of task performance. Given this dependency on the precise configuration of the cognitive system one might as well speak of conditioned automaticity.[10]

As they continue . . .

Attentional influences originating from task sets enhance task-relevant unconscious processes while attenuating task-irrelevant unconscious processes. Much as conscious perception is influenced by attentional mechanisms, unconscious cognition is assumed to be controlled by top-down signals from the prefrontal cortex that increase or decrease the sensitivity of processing pathways for incoming sensory input. Processing in task-relevant pathways is enhanced by increasing the gain of neurons in the corresponding areas, whereas processing in task-irrelevant pathways is attenuated by a decrease of the gain. Gain is a parameter in neural network modeling, which influences the probability that a neuron fires at a given activation level. Single cell recordings in non-human primates have shown that the likelihood of a neuron firing, given a constant sensory input, is enhanced when the stimulus dimension that is preferentially processed by the neuron is attended to.[11]

In other words, it is possible, simply by deciding to do so, to increase the "gain" of your perception, to alter the automatic gating presets that we have habituated. We can learn to increase our sensory sensitivity at will, to open our sensory gating channels more widely when we wish to do so, to engage directly with the meanings held *within* those sensory inflows. We can alter our programming, even at the unconscious level. In fact, *every* door in the neural network that gates sensory inputs can be altered if desired. We can, in fact, open the doors of perception if we wish to do so, as widely as we wish to do. The ability to alter unconscious sensory gating at will, as Kiefer et al. comment, "ensures the adaptability of cognition even in the unconscious domain."[12] And, the more we practice intentionally opening the doors of perception, the more easily and more fully we can do so. As Kiefer et al. comment . . .

Attentional amplification of sensory awareness in any sensory medium is achieved by top-down signals from prefrontal cortex that modulate activity of single neurons in sensory brain areas in the absence of any sensory stimulation and significantly increase baseline activity in the corresponding target region.[13]

Increased sensitization in a sensory neural network, once initiated, is sustained by the synchronization of the rhythmic activity of the enhanced neural group within and between other neural groups in the central nervous system (CNS). In other words, the new functional state creates, in essence, a small biologic oscillator in the CNS to which other neural groups in the CNS synchronize, thus enhancing and stabilizing the new state that has been initiated in that particular neural pathway. Neuroimaging in the brain shows that once the areas of the brain that process incoming sensory data are sensitized to incoming data, that is, once the gating channels are opened more widely, the sections of the brain that gate that particular type of sensory data stay open. The baseline gating level increases even if the degree of sensory stimulus is not increased. The metaphysical background of the world begins to emerge into sensing on a regular basis.

We can't solve problems
by using the same kind of thinking we used
when we created them.

Or as Albert Hofmann once put it . . .

All attempts today to make amends for the damage through envi-
ronmentally protective measures must remain only hopeless, superfi-
cial patchwork, if no curing of the "Western entelechy neurosis"
ensues. . . . Healing would mean existential experience of a deeper,
self-encompassing reality.[14]

The opening of sensory gating channels beyond the current setting parameters dictated by our culture is a necessity. To think differently, we must *actually* think differently. And in this, intent is important.

What you intend when you approach something in the world determines, to varying extents, the degree of sensory gating that occurs as you perceive that phenomenon. Intent, task demands, cognitive template, and gating defaults all affect what you sensorally perceive when a part of the exterior world and you meet. More colloquially, all of us see what we expect to see.

and this is true even of scientists . . .
just because they know how to use a hammer

does not mean they can use it well
it is not the tool that is crucial to the art
but the ability of the craftsman

Nevertheless, the perceptual frame can be changed. The amount of sensory input that is being gated can be altered simply by the desire to do so—though specific *actions* are necessary to carry out that desire.

Altering sensory gating parameters are most easily accomplished in one of three ways, and we've already talked in some depth about the first one: 1) having a task that demands a greater focus on incoming sensory data flows. The others are: 2) regenerating a state similar to that which occurred during the first few years of life, or 3) by altering the nature of the gating channels themselves by shifting consciousness (which is somewhat different from re-generating developmental stages).

In somewhat more depth then: 1) Focusing on a specific task that demands greater sensory sensitivity, say for instance if you go out into the backyard and sit next to a plant, and then focusing on the color of its leaves in the minutest of detail, to the exclusion of all else and, in the midst of that experience, asking yourself

How does it feel?

will significantly increase both the visual and feeling inputs that are normally gated for you by your unconscious. This will immediately begin allowing you to access the deeper metaphysical background of the world as it pertains to that particular plant growing in that particular eco-range. In essence, focusing on tasks that demand greater sensory inflows enhances the sensitivity of the neural pathways that are involved in that particular sensory flow, reduces gating, and activates more relevant neurons in that pathway. The deeper meanings in the sensory flows are then more accessible to your awareness.

Alternatively, 2) if you should take a minute to sit quietly, breathing deeply the while, until you are very calm, and then if you were to

see the little child you were standing in front of you

and notice how that child that you were looks to you, how they feel to you, and if you were to then begin to talk with that part of you, your sensory gating of visual, auditory, and feeling stimuli will begin to change. The gating channels will begin to open more widely. If you should take it further, should you then imagine your grown-up body as being similar to those chocolate bunnies, the ones that are hollow inside, the ones whose hollowness follows the shapes and patterns of the exterior body, should you see your grown-up body from the back of itself as hollow and

> *should you then ask that little child to step around behind you and to, very carefully, place their face just behind your face, until it is snugly in place, their eyes right behind your eyelids. Should you then slowly open your eyes and let them see the world through your eyes, the entire perceptual field will shift. The amount of incoming sensory data will increase—immediately—in all six sensory mediums. Most especially will the feeling, seeing, and hearing senses become more sensitive. This is the experience of fully reinhabiting your interbeing with the world.*

And of course, the more closely you get to reactivating a newborn, infant state in this way, the less sensory data that is gated and the more inflows you have access to, inflows that can become nearly infinite in their richness and complexity. From this place, with this habituated skill, you can begin to directly access the metaphysical background of the world. You can fully reinhabit your interbeing with the world.

Or, finally, 3) if you wish, you can shift consciousness itself more directly by directly increasing the apertures of your sensory gates, by opening the doors of perception themselves more widely. You can do this a number of ways,

> *hallucinogens are one of them*
> *meditation is another*
> *habituation to constantly feeling*
> *the touch of the world upon you is another*

for there are multiple ways to open those doors of perception, both directly and indirectly. The doors exist for a reason . . . and our ability to narrow or expand them at will exists for a reason. It is a natural capacity that all organisms have, intended by structure and ecological function, to open the doors of perception.

Repression-Driven Gating

The sensory stimuli we encounter do not, in and of themselves,

except under unusual circumstances

determine whether or not we pay attention to them; *we,* ourselves, do. In fact novel stimuli of great intensity (which usually are not gated) *will* be gated if they do not conform to the nature of expected sensory inputs. In other words, we notice, in the visual field around us, those things that fit into our paradigm, our template. Those things in the fields around us that are not deemed relevant to the "template" we are using are not noticed.

For instance, if the paradigm in which you are immersed has as a primary assumption the belief that there is no feeling sense (in the way I am using it in this book) then, to a greater or lesser extent, that feeling sense will be gated. Those who have lost, as James Hillman put it, the response of the heart to what is presented to the senses, are sometimes so trained to believe that the objects outside them have no "feeling reality" to them that all feeling inflows of that sort are gated entirely.

Specifically: Studies of the individuals who attribute living or non-living status to exterior objects have found that how those things are perceived is completely dependent on the search template that is in place at the time. In other words, the template itself determined whether one could "see" living and nonliving attributes in exterior objects. The researchers noted, in the usual convoluted wording, that

These findings suggest that action intentions sensitize congruent and desensitize incongruent unconscious processing pathways. We propose that an attentional top-down signal enhances unconscious processing of the stimulus dimension that matches the current

intention. This attentional sensitization mechanism results in sub-liminal priming effects on responses to visible targets only for stimu-lus dimensions that are congruent with the current action intention.[15]

In other words, what you believe—that is, the descriptions of the world around you that you received in childhood—act much like software; they program what is perceivable by your conscious mind.

What you can perceive is also affected if you are trained to concentrate on a single sensory modality over all the others. If this occurs, all the other modalities decrease in importance and are subsequently more strongly gated. This often makes it difficult to access other sensory modalities. For instance, if you are sensorially trained to concentrate on didactic sound, that is, words

William F. Buckley

then an environmental pressure or external demand for you to move into visual processing or feeling processing presents difficulties since you, while in verbal didactic, are strongly gating those modalities at an unconscious level. Being confined to a single modality, habituated to it by schooling or culture or environment, is tremendously debilitating.

It is a form of ecological reclamation of the self
this learning how to perceive through all the body's senses

For example, during studies focused on interpreting meaning it was found that continued focus on the meaning in words (which uses visual, auditory, and feeling senses) enhances the future ability to determine meaning irrespective of the medium conveying it. However if the focus is shifted to classifying letters by shape (which restricts the sensory modality to the visual only), the ability to determine meaning decreases. In other words, focus on form inhibits the ability to determine the meanings that underlie form. The effect takes place at the unconscious level, at the level of gating. Long-term focus on the exterior of things, as a habit, reduces the capacity to find meaning—at all. It inhibits the ability to work with the meanings that are held inside the visual sensory inflows. Meaning becomes strongly gated while form perception is not. Or as Gregory Bateson once put it . . .

> *The human being, depersonified in his own talk and thought, may indeed learn more thingish habits of action.*[16]

This finding is consistent irrespective of the type of study. As another example, researchers have found that if people are asked whether a word refers to a living or nonliving thing (tree, rock, ball, girl, plant), they become subliminally primed to attend to the meaning of things, in this instance *livingness*. But if they are asked to determine whether a series of words end in a vowel or a consonant (garden, bottle, ocean, leaf) they become subliminally primed to focus on *forms* of things, not their inherent meanings. In the first case, they become subliminally primed to look for livingness in subsequent interactions; in the second they are primed to look at the exterior shape or surface of things. Long-term training in one perspective or the other actually creates a long-term template that automatically gates incoming sensory data. It becomes increasingly more difficult, with age, to alter the settings.

> *This is what Charles Dickens was writing about*
> *when he wrote his book* A Christmas Carol

Another study, in which participants were asked to determine whether or not a capital letter in a word was a vowel or consonant (jewEl, fAble, oRacle, breaTh) found that it strongly disrupted subsequent semantic processing of unconsciously encountered words. In other words, the ability to determine the meaning in words, at an unconscious level, was inhibited. In a similar way, the focus on the form of an object: which leg is larger on that chair, on that table, on that bed—which leaf shape is more oval among those three different plant species—disrupts subsequent *meaning* processing.

> *This is why taxonomists know so very little about plants*
> *and why physicians are so often terrible healers*

People trained in such an exterior focus get stuck on surfaces and can no longer find depths, can no longer experience the metaphysical background of matter. Their unconscious simply gates it out. As Kiefer et al. note, again in an insult to clear languaging, "The capture of visuo-spatial attention by unconscious stimuli likewise was shown to depend on the match between the stimulus feathers and a fitting top-down search template."[17] In other words, some things have to be believed to be seen or, another way of putting it: if you assume something is not there, then, to you, it won't be.

In substantial ways, the reductionistic science that has been practiced since the mid-twentieth century has programmed all of us, to varying extents, to gate the *meanings* that flow into us from the world. For some of us, so strongly, that life indeed feels meaningless. This is what Vaclav Havel was talking about when he said . . .

> *The relationship to the world that modern science fostered and shaped now appears to have exhausted its potential. It is increasingly clear that, strangely, the relationship is missing something. It fails to connect with the most intrinsic nature of reality, and with natural human experience. It is now more of a source of disintegration and doubt than a source of integration and meaning. It produces what amounts to a state of schizophrenia, completely alienating man as an observer from himself as a being. Classical modern science described only the surface of things, a single dimension of reality. And the more dogmatically science treated it as the only dimension, as the very essence of reality, the more misleading it became. Today, for instance, we may know immeasurably more about the universe than our ancestors did, yet it increasingly seems that they knew something more essential about it than we do, something that escapes us. The same is true of nature and of ourselves. The more thoroughly all our organs and their functions, their internal structures, and the biochemical reactions that take place within them are described, the more we seem to fail to grasp the spirit, purpose, and meaning of the system that they create together and that we experience as our unique "self."[18]*

We can change this if we wish, but it does involve intent, the decision to actually do something different, the decision to in actuality change the self. It takes work to begin developing, then using, another type of thinking entirely. Or as Luther Burbank put it, "It is repetition, repetition, repetition that habituates the skill."

Unconscious Overrides

Interestingly, studies have found that there is often a very deep conflict between the gating imposed by schooling, culture, and parenting and the gating that the evolutionarily innovated living system you know as yourself would actually prefer. The parts of the brain that determine gating settings respond to imposed parameters as the child develops *however* . . . deeper than all those are the evolutionary dynamics that underlie our species emergence. One of the simplest is the drive for survival, in other words, your very deep sense of self-protection. If, in the field of sensory inflows in which you are immersed, the parts of the self that gate inflows pick up sensory-encoded meanings that can affect your self-organizational integrity, they will have a very deep evolutionary drive to signal your conscious attention. However, if the paradigm or lens through which you view the world around you does not allow you to receive those signals consciously,

this can be thought of as repression-driven gating

then the unconscious parts of the self may begin to override the conscious programming. In response your emotional state or behavior may change, sometimes significantly. You just won't know why.

> *Let's not go to the movies tonight.*
> *Why not?*
> *I don't know, it just doesn't feel right.*

In essence the pre-attentional parts that gate sensory flows, in assessing the meanings in incoming sensory data, have determined that what your conscious mind has decided to do is a threat to system integrity. This tends to activate responses from both the hippocampal regions, which includes the amygdala. The amygdala functions, as researchers comment, to detect the emotional "salience" of incoming sensory data and to relate the proper emotional value to each input. In other words, the meanings in sensory inflows *always* create an emotional response in that part of the brain. For most people in the West, these kinds of emotional responses are usually gated because the conscious mind has accepted a paradigm that discounts their importance. However, if the pre-attentional parts of the self determine that it is important enough, they will let the emotional response through to the conscious mind. You will feel funny, you just won't know why.

The emotional response to each tiny incoming sensory bit can tell the conscious mind

if you pay attention to how you feel
in the same way that musicians pay attention to sound

a considerable amount about the meaning inside every particular sensory input that you experience. We may not have yet identified the nature of the meaning inside a sensory inflow, for instance

the dog we see lying on the path we are about to step onto.

But our (*fear*) or our (*joy*) tells us a great deal about the intent of the dog, even if we don't know why we are having that particular, nearly instantaneous, response in the moment of visual input.

It is possible, just as it is with the auditory training of musicians, to begin using the feeling sense actively. This will increase neuronal development in the hippocampal and the cardiovascular (heart) system and with practice, over time, increase sensitivity to tiny modulations in that sensory flow. Sensitivity to the tiniest shifts in feeling will develop, just as they do in musicians with sound complexes. And, with experience, the ability to determine the meanings inside those feelings will become a reliable skill. In other words, it becomes possible to immediately know the intent of the dog as soon as it is seen/nonkinesthetically felt.

Communicatory inputs from the world can occur through any of the six primary sensory modalities at any time. The important thing is to first develop the capacity to *feel* the deeper meanings inside any of the sensory modalities, second to seek their meanings, and third to craft congruent responses.

We move through a sea filled with currents of sensory stimuli every waking moment of our lives. What we normally perceive of that rich sensorial input is incredibly tiny. More to the point, the meanings within those sensory flows are as numberless as the sensory inputs themselves. And we perceive only a tiny amount of them. Nevertheless, we can increase the gating channels that reduce those flows and thus take in increasingly large amounts of meaning-filled sensory stimuli.

we can become sensitive to the touch of the world upon

We can begin to directly interact with the meanings that flow into us from the world every minute of every day of our lives. Those meanings are directly related to what is *happening* in the world around us, in the communication between plants, the intelligence of animals, the functioning of Gaia.

and every organism on this planet has sensory gating, and the ability to increase it when needed, we are not alone in this

Once sensory gating channels are expanded, the organism can take in more meanings, and the increased knowledge opens up significant new avenues of behavior, response, and innovation. That is the reason that mechanisms exist in every organism (and throughout the ecosystems of the Earth) for the expansion of sensory gating channels; the reason why there is no "normal" setting for gating channels in a population; the reason why some people have gating channels so tremendously open. The very functioning of the world depends on it.

4
"EVERYTHING IS INTELLIGENT"

Every component of the organism is as much of an organism as every other part.

BARBARA MCCLINTOCK

Materialism contains a prodigious depth that materialists are a long way from fully grasping.

ERNST JUNGER

Intelligence: 1) the ability to learn or understand or to deal with new or trying situations. 2) the ability to apply knowledge to manipulate one's environment.

MERRIAM-WEBSTER'S DICTIONARY

Astonishing! Everything is Intelligent!

PYTHAGORUS

Insofar as we are a mental process, to that same extent we must expect the natural world to show similar characteristics of mentality.

GREGORY BATESON

*I*n spite of considerable evidence to the contrary few of us are taught that all life-forms on Earth are highly intelligent. Nearly all children in the West are still taught by both school and culture that intelligence is a primary attribute of the human species and that all other life-forms on Earth are less intelligent, usually in some sort of descending pyramidal hierarchy with people at the apex and so on down. Thus, it would be humans, dolphins, chimpanzees, dogs, and so forth, through birds and lizards to insects then plants and microbes and then, I guess, maybe air molecules or something—they are pretty stupid. This is a rather grim holdover from nineteenth- and early-twentieth-century thinking and it is terribly incorrect. The foundational problem with that view is that all living organisms, it turns out, are self-organized and all of them show emergent behaviors. As Michael Crichton once commented . . .

> *It did not take long before the scientists began to notice that complex systems showed certain common behaviors. They started to think of these behaviors as characteristic of all complex systems. They realized that these behaviors could not be explained by analyzing the components of the systems. The time-honored scientific approach of reductionism—taking the watch apart to see how it worked—didn't get you anywhere with complex systems, because the interesting behavior seemed to arise from the spontaneous interaction of the components.*[1]

Unfortunately for reductionists, one of the "interesting" behaviors that arise in complex systems, once biological self-organization occurs is—always—intelligence in the system.

Self-Organization

Nothing has undermined the older, more mechanical view of the world than spontaneous self-organization and the resultant nonlinearity of living systems—and their implications. As mathematician Steven Strogatz puts it . . .

> *In every case, these feats of synchrony occur spontaneously, almost as*

if nature has an eerie yearning for order. And that raises a profound mystery: Scientists have long been baffled by the existence of sponta- neous order in the universe. The laws of thermodynamics seem to dictate the opposite, that nature should inexorably degenerate toward a state of greater disorder, greater entropy. Yet all around us we see magnificent structures that have somehow managed to assemble themselves. This enigma bedevils all of science today.[2]

"Eerie?" Strogatz's word choice is deeply revealing. *Eerie* means "strange and frightening" and its synonyms are: *uncanny, sinister, ghostly, unnatural, unearthly* (nice one), *supernatural* (and so on). The majority of reductive scientists, when they experience this fundamental aspect of reality, experience one overriding emotion: fear. Self-organization leads to an inescapable conclusion: there is more going on than mechanical reductionism perceives or can explain. (*Bedevil* is interesting as well: "to torment mercilessly, plague, worry, annoy, frustrate, be possessed by dev- ils, bewitch," and finally . . . "to spoil or ruin." "It ruined our good time and our lives are now plagued by merciless Earth devils.")

Such self-organization always begins the same way, or as research- ers Scott Camazine et al. put it, "At a critical density a pattern arises within the system."[3] Thus, when a container is packed with increasing numbers of molecules, at a certain point, which can never be predicted, the random motions of the billions and billions of molecules will sud- denly show a sudden alteration in behavior, all of them will spontane- ously synchronize. The molecules begin to move and vibrate together. They begin acting in concert, actively cooperating, and become tightly coupled together into one, interacting whole exhibiting a collective, mac- roscopically ordered state of being. They become a unique living system of which the smaller subunits (the molecules) are now only a part. At such a moment, the molecules have combined into a system that is *self- organized*. A phase change occurs. Something more than the sum of the parts has come into being. And . . . it just happens.

Like water turning into ice.

And you can't predict what the system will look like after the phase change. For instance, at one degree above freezing water is still liquid, but a simple decrease of one degree in temperature causes a sudden shift in the water's state, a *phase transition*. A very tiny change, as small as $1/100$th of a degree once the temperature is approaching freezing, will cause the water to change its physical form. Suddenly.

Synchronization occurs abruptly and, unless it is something you have already experienced, it's impossible to know that it's going to happen. One moment there is one state, the next something entirely new comes into being.

> *This why the potential for a phase change in Earth environment is so dangerous. Such a shift will not be a simple alteration in what we have always known. It will be like water to ice, something completely different, so different in fact that none of the current cultural and scientific assumptions/pictures will be of use to our survival.*

And that new thing? Neither its physical nor its behavioral nature can be predicted from a study of its parts—from an analysis of the prior state. As Camazine et al. comment . . .

> *Complexity and complex systems generally refer to a system of interacting units that displays global properties not present at the lower level. These systems may show diverse responses that are often sensitively dependent on both the initial state of the system and nonlinear interactions among its components. Since these nonlinear interactions involve amplification or cooperativity, complex behaviors may emerge.*[4]

There is no linear additive process that, if all the parts are taken together, can be understood to create the total system that occurs at the moment of self-organization; it is not a *quantity* that comes into being. It is not predictable in its shape or subsequent behavior or its subsequent qualities. There is a nonlinear *quality* that comes into being at the moment of synchronicity.

There is also not just a shift in form in that moment of self-organization but also the emergence of new behaviors. That is, the system begins to act. As physicist Paul Davies comments, nonlinear systems "possess the remarkable ability to leap spontaneously from relatively feature-less states to those involving complex cooperative behavior."[5] And those behaviors? They can be as different as water to ice. It can be something like, oh, I don't know, like . . . pathogenic bacteria all over the Earth suddenly becoming completely resistant to antibiotics, all at the same time. Or Earth temperature suddenly jumping 20 degrees Fahrenheit and staying there . . . forever.

The system begins to display something other than synchronicity, it begins to *act* as a unit, to have behaviors. And just as a study of the parts of a self-organized whole cannot give an idea of the larger whole's nature, so too the study of the smaller parts' behaviors cannot give an idea of the larger system's behavior. As Camazine et al. note, "an emergent property cannot be understood simply by examining in isolation the properties of the system's components. . . . Emergence refers to a process by which a system of interacting subunits acquires qualitatively new properties that cannot be understood as a simple addition of their individual contributions."[6] Or as systems researcher Yaneer Bar-Yam puts it, "A complex system is formed out of many components whose behavior is emergent, that is, the behavior of the system cannot be simply inferred from the behavior of its components. . . . Emergent properties cannot be studied by physically taking a system apart and looking at the parts (reductionism)."[7]

Or as Goethe put it over two centuries ago . . .

> *Life as a whole expresses itself as a force that is not to be contained within any one part. . . . The things we call the parts in every living being are so inseparable from the whole that they may be understood only in and with the whole.*

The whole, tightly coupled system, at the moment of self-organization, begins to act upon its microscopic parts to stimulate further, often much more complex, synchronizations. A continuous stream of information begins flowing back and forth, extremely rapidly, between the macroscopic, ordered whole to the smaller microscopic subunits and back again (interoceptive) so that the self-organizing structure is stabilized, its newly acquired dynamic equilibrium actively maintained. This information stream also immediately includes the external environment, where a similar, rapid flow of information occurs (exteroceptive), in order to more fully enhance stability. In other words, the system becomes deeply engaged in processing *interoceptive* and *exteroceptive* data, analyzing it, and altering its self-organized state based on that analysis. The system is now displaying what is called *emergent* behaviors.

At some point the increasing number of molecules that self-organized crossed a *threshold* beyond which occurred that moment of self-organization. On one side there was nothing but randomized molecular movements, on the other there was sudden self-organization and emergent behavior. All self-organized systems remain very close to this threshold, just barely on the self-organized side of it. It is this dynamic balance point, near the edge of chaos, that makes the system so responsive to the interoceptive and exteroceptive inputs, that leads to an incredible capacity for innovation in self-organized systems. Michael Crichton described it impeccably . . .

> *Even more important is the way complex systems seem to strike a balance between the need for order and the imperative for change. Complex systems tend to locate themselves at a place we call "the edge of chaos." We imagine the edge of chaos as a place where there is enough innovation to keep a living system vibrant, and enough stability to keep it from collapsing into anarchy. It is a zone of conflict and upheaval, where the old and new are constantly at war. Finding the balance point must be a delicate matter—if a living system drifts too close, it risks falling over into incoherence and dissolution; but if the system moves too far away from the edge, it becomes rigid, frozen, totalitarian. Both conditions lead to extinction. . . . Only at the edge of chaos can complex systems flourish.*[8]

This threshold line, that edge between anarchy and frozen rigidity, is not a like a fence line, it is a *fractal* line; it possesses nonlinearity. It is, in fact, much like a coastline, and like a coastline its exact orientation in space and time ebbs and flows. At the moment the threshold is crossed, at the moment when self-organization occurs, the new living system enters a state of dynamic equilibrium. From that point on, the self-organized system retains an elegant sensitivity to that threshold point; it exists just on the balanced side of that threshold and so constantly monitors any incoming energy flows that touch it, for each incoming energy flow causes the system to move slightly too close to the line again—a process that can cause it to lose organization entirely if allowed to go too far. As that occurs, the system analyzes the nature of the flow it has encountered and crafts a response to it which will restore the balance point. A very simple example of this is

Juggling

If you have ever learned to do simple juggling (or even seen someone do it) there is a point, when all the balls are up in the air, where an almost magical balance point suddenly comes into being. (This happens with unicycles and their riders, too.) Before juggling you have balls here, juggler there. A dynamic system separated into its parts, not, at the moment, in dynamic equilibrium. When the juggler picks up the balls and throws them into the air, for a moment, they are still isolated parts. But then there is that magic moment when the juggler finds the balance point. At that instant he and balls become one unified whole, existing in a state of dynamic equilibrium; they have crossed a threshold of self-organization. Juggling occurs.

But once it does, immediately, the juggler begins to slightly move his hands and feet—this way and that way—to maintain the balance point.

this is emergent behavior

Tiny perturbations, exceptionally tiny disturbances of the balance point, a slight movement of a ball this way or that, indicate to the juggler just how that perturbation can affect the dynamic equilibrium. So, he moves his body, his feet, his hands to keep the balance point intact. But there is no way for any juggler to think those perturbations through with the linear mind—it takes too long—by the time he does, the balls will have fallen. The conscious mind is too gross a tool, too slow, too focused on parts rather than wholes. So, at a very deep, unconscious level some part of the juggler takes in that perturbation, extracts the meaning within it, and then alters his movements to maintain the balance point. Those perturbations are *communications,* but they have to be analyzed extremely quickly and a response initiated just as fast in order to not drop the balls. It must be done by *feel,* intuitively; that is, by some other part of the self than the part that thinks linearly.

> *Once the balance point is found, the sensory gating channels open more widely in order to respond to minute alterations in that balance point. The body, sensory channels, and conscious mind achieve a synaesthesia, a unity of perceptual analysis and response. The more accomplished the juggler, the more open the sensory gating channels become in response to the task set, and the more complete the synaesthesia. The entire process takes place in a state very similar to dreaming. It's done by feel, below the level of conscious awareness. In response to the intent to juggle, the conscious mind steps back and allows the rest of the self to take over, for only in that way can juggling occur, the balance point kept. As soon as the linear mind becomes dominant, the balls will fall, the balance point lost. (This says a lot about the ultimate success of the West using the linear mind to solve problems.)*

Juggling is a simple example of a complex, nonlinear system existing in a state of dynamic equilibrium close to the threshold of self-organization. It captures the kind of behavior of whole systems that chaos theory or nonlinearity attempts to explain. There is an inherent indeterminancy in these kinds of systems. There is no way to predict what perturbations will occur at any moment in time nor is there a way to predict a living system's responses to them. You can start off with two identical-as-possible jugglers at the same spot on a performance floor and you will never be able to predict where they will end up in the room or the movements they will use to juggle the balls. The best you can say is that they will most likely be in the same room and, if they are good, they will probably manage to keep the balance point intact.

Every living (system, phenomenon, organism) is like this. *Every* one of them exists close to that threshold and every one works, at much greater degrees of complexity than a juggler manipulating his balls

Editor: Shouldn't you change that sentence?
Writer: No, I don't think so, what's wrong with it?

to maintain the balance point that came into being at the moment of self-organization. This is done through a tight coupling to both the internal and external worlds.

In self-organized systems the information from the smaller subunit (in this example, the juggler's balls)

Editor: Wait a minute!
Writer: What?

travels to the larger whole as chemical cues, or electromagnetic fluxes, or pressure waves, and so on. The larger system, the juggler, takes in the information, analyzes it, and alters his behavior. In other words the system alters its nature to incorporate the changes (interoceptive inputs) so that it can keep its self-organizational state intact. The information generates a response to it by the system.

Information from the external world (exteroceptive inputs) is taken in similarly. For the juggler, floor perturbations which alter how the feet are balanced, the flow of air in the room, comments from the audience, and so on, all affect his stance, orientation, and balance, which affect his capacity to keep his balls in the air. So that exterior-to-the-system information is taken in and, again, below the level of conscious awareness, behavior is altered to keep self-organization—the homeodynamic balance—intact. And this type of process works very well in living systems. As James Lovelock notes . . .

No one doubts that humans are in thermostasis, yet our core temperatures range from 35 to 40°C and our extremities from 5 to 45°C. This may appear imprecise, but it serves us well.[9]

Informational pulses travel back and forth from the system to both its parts and the exterior world, extremely rapidly, and last as long as the system itself remains self-organized. Based on the information gathered, the system then alters its functioning—from millisecond to millisecond.

In living systems, unlike jugglers and balls, the amount of analyzed information is considerably larger, many millions of times larger.

Everything Is Intelligent

In order to maintain the self-organized state, the living entity that comes into being in that moment—the thing that is more than the sum of the parts, of necessity—must immediately develop mechanisms for analyzing two things: inflows from the exterior world toward the *me* that now exists (exteroceptive inputs) *and* the functional state of the parts that have self-organized to make up the whole (interoceptive inputs). Failure to analyze the inflows can result in death, i.e., the loss of self-organization. As well, dysfunction of any of the parts can also lead to loss of self-organization.

> *This is why every part matters to the whole. Remove the lungs, liver, and pancreas and whether or not you have a brain becomes irrelevant. Remove the plants, the forests, the waters and whether or not you have scientists or opposable thumbs becomes irrelevant.*

Inflows from the exterior world, from *not me* toward *me,* have of necessity to be understood. Their nature—but more importantly their *intent*—has to be determined, and once that occurs a response to the inflow has to be crafted. By all useful definitions of the term this *is* intelligent behavior; it is also the way dictionaries such as Merriam-Webster's define it . . .

> *The ability to learn or understand or to deal with new or trying situations [or] the ability to apply knowledge to manipulate one's environment.*

Interestingly, the word, intelligence, comes from the Latin phrase *inter legere*—it means, simply, "to choose." And, in fact, a crucial additional, and almost-always-overlooked, aspect of intelligence in living systems is that they possess the capacity to innovate behavior, that is, to generate unique solutions to the environmental challenges that face them. They have the ability, as the Latin root of the word indicates, to *choose*. The comparative zoologist Richard Lewontin describes it like this . . .

> *Much of the uncertainty of evolution arises from the existence of multiple possible pathways even when external conditions are fixed. It is a prejudice of evolutionists who give adaptive explanations of the features of organisms that every difference between species must be a consequence of different selective forces that operated on them. . . . Populations subject to identical selective conditions may arrive at quite different evolutionary endpoints, so that the observation that two species differ is not* prima facie *evidence that they were adaptively differentiated.*[10]

Thus, if you take two plants, same genus and species, and plant them in identical environments, just as is true with jugglers, they will end up at slightly, or sometimes very, different places. Their leaf patterns, chemical structure, and dynamic interactive interface with their surrounding environment will not be the same. Faced with the same environmental pressures, each will choose slightly, or very, different responses—from a large number of possible choices—to those environmental pressures. And what they choose, and in consequence what happens afterward, can't be predicted. As Lewontin goes on to say, "The characteristic of a living object is that it reacts to external stimuli rather than being passively propelled by them. An organism's life consists of constant mid-course corrections."[11]

"Mid-course corrections." That is the capacity of a living organism—and that includes everything from viruses to human beings—to choose among multiple effective options in response to incoming environmental pressures. It is in fact indicative not only of the capacity to choose but also, most distressingly for reductionists, of free will. In other words, every living organism on this planet (including such self-organized systems as the white blood cells in our bodies) has the capacity to analyze the nature of outside forces that touch them, determine their intent, and then to exercise judgment in determining from among a number of potential responses which one to implement. That this is true, and has been known to be true for a very long time, does nothing to stop the extreme discomfort engendered by saying it out loud. Most people, including the majority of scientists, have been taught that human beings are somehow innately different from the other organisms on this planet.

nevertheless we are not

We are different only in the specific ecological functions we serve—just as every living organism is—but we are not different in our underlying capacities from the other life-forms on this planet. And that most definitely includes intelligence. Our intelligence is only a special instance of a general condition.

When researchers in the late nineteenth and much of the twentieth century began examining the world for intelligent life-forms, they, regrettably but understandably, used themselves as a template for finding it.

Perhaps that is why they have had such trouble finding it
Just sayin'

They began judging all life-forms by human norms. In other words, they looked for language that seemed like our own, tool making that seemed like our own, social organization that seemed like our own. They rather insistently projected a human-centric orientation onto the exterior world. Any organism that had some of the human attributes they deemed indicative of (human) intelligence was accorded more value than those organisms that appeared to have less. Or, from another frame of reference, they were using as a measuring stick the concept of the evolutionary pyramid or escalator. Specifically: "We emerged from the primordial ooze

Martha!

and slowly we turned, step by step, and in a world red in tooth and claw, we crawled up out of the clinging slime. By dint of our superior intelligence, we rose to the top of the evolutionary pyramid, the supreme life-form on this planet. Finally, from a heaving sea of blind, striving life-forms, each struggling for continued existence, awareness emerged. (The

Earth, nay, even the Universe itself, did thus become conscious of itself.) And we stood on the pinnacle of our greatness, alone, looking out at the great void of the universe wondering, 'Is there anybody else out there?'" Or as Robert Heinlein once put it . . .

Man is a rationalizing animal not a rational one.

And, as it happened, scientists, looking out at the void, did notice some sophisticated (human-like) attributes in some other life-forms. Dolphins seem pretty smart and chimpanzees, too. Then dogs maybe, or parrots. Not sure about janitors, though.

Still, those early researchers, standing on the pinnacle of their greatness, were, in their own fashion, finding that intelligence in one form or another was an attribute of the living organisms they were studying. Whether it was the discovery that prairie dogs have a complex language; that in fact they describe the movement of other animals through their territory in great detail, including, if those animals are humans, distinctions in the color of their clothes; or the finding that chimpanzees can sign up to 3,000 words (and even invent their own words for objects they haven't been taught words for) and then teach the ability to use sign language to their offspring; or that their memory is better; or

Pop quiz: How many words of chimpanzee can the most intelligent primatologist speak? (Hint: a lot less than 3,000 . . . Hmmm, let's see what number starts with a "z"?)

the discovery that dogs can add and subtract, or that ravens make tools, or that dung beetles navigate by the stars, or that amoeba farm bacteria for food, or that crocodiles and alligators design and use tools to more easily capture water birds, or that elephants can learn to speak human language, or that dolphins use nonlinear mathematics in seeking and finding their food, examination of the living organisms around us continually reaffirms that intelligence is an attribute of living systems—even when using humans as the yardstick for measurement. Nevertheless, despite this, there remains, among most researchers and nearly all nonresearchers, the belief that humans are the only organisms with *real* intelligence; dolphins may be as smart as us from that frame of reference (probably not) but chimpanzees are more properly thought of as much lower on the scale of evolution—in another million years they might think as well as us . . . maybe. But the other animals? They are much further back, much lower on the scale.

Just because prairie dogs have made up specific prairie dog words for "fat guy with red shirt" doesn't mean they are intelligent.

And besides, animals, even birds, are like us;

sort of

they are very close behind us on the evolutionary escalator—compared with things like bacteria—and so have developed some rudimentary capacity to think—just not very well. If they were as advanced as us on the escalator they would think just like we do, but they *are* behind us, back there, on a lower step, a reminder of where we came from not so very long ago.

Bless their hearts!

Or as Lynn Margulis (and Dorion Sagan) once put it, "Our intolerant slogans continually denigrate the nonhuman life with which we share this planet."[12] But while the evolutionary escalator is an incredibly common expression of a belief in human exceptionalism, it doesn't have any real basis in ecological reality. The view is one Darwin specifically rejected, which makes it all the more ironic that it is the neo-Darwinians that have spread it about so much. Darwin's own perspective, as the English philosopher Mary Midgley comments, is much different, he did . . .

not see evolution as an escalator, but as a sinuous, branching radiating pattern—not a staircase, but perhaps a bush or seaweed. Life-forms diverge from each other to meet particular needs in their various environments. Our own species figures then only as one among the many, with no special status or guarantee of supremacy. This notion has, however, always been found far less exciting than the escalator model, which has been enormously popular ever since it was promoted by Herbert Spencer, in spite of Darwin's own rejection of it and its evident complete irrelevance to this theory.[13]

The cerebral hypertrophy that so many reductionists celebrate as evidence of human superiority, that they insist puts us on the top of the evolutionary ladder, is in fact only a projection coming from their particular psychological orientation. In fact, as Midgley comments, the old picture of man's rise to dominance . . .

showed brain evolution dramatically as a series of successive conquests, in which at each level of life a new brain area and its faculties came in to rule the rest, culminating in man and final victory of the cerebral cortex, or some specially splendid part of it. . . . Detailed neurological work has, however, worn away almost every aspect of this seductive picture. As Stephen Walker, a neurological psychologist says, "One still has a sense of regret that this charming and convincing tale must be discarded. The weight of evidence is now if anything more in favour of the unhelpful suggestion . . . that all the fundamental parts of the vertebrate brain were present very early on, and can be observed in lampreys.[14]

Our brain is not especially unique, nor does it confer on us any special faculty not already present in the system from which it emerged. Nevertheless, brain chauvinism has continually led to ridiculous "utopian" projections like this one by molecular biologist William Day . . .

[Man] will splinter into types of humans with differing mental faculties that will lead to diversification and separate species. From among these types a new species, Omega Man, will emerge either alone, in union with others, or with mechanical amplifications to transcend to new dimensions of time and space beyond our comprehension.[15]

Or as the science-fiction writer Greg Bear once put it, "we are now in charge of our own evolution." As Midgley comments . . .

world pictures like this are not primarily science. The science that is supposed to justify them is really a small part of their content. They are actually metaphysical sketches, ambitious maps of how all reality is supposed to work, guiding visions, systems of direction for the rest of our ideas.[16]

Everything in that frame is judged in terms of the human, as if we are outside the ecological matrix in which we are embedded, as if evolution ended once and for all with our emergence, with the development of our brains. And this kind of thinking has invaded nearly every aspect of human life. As Rupert Sheldrake puts it, "The evangelists of science and technology have succeeded beyond the wildest dreams of the missionaries of Christianity."[17]

The trouble is that this worldview is not accurate to the world itself or to the findings of researchers in scores of fields. Unfortunately nearly everyone in the West believes significant aspects of it to be true. Our thinking has been corrupted by bad software, an inaccurate description of reality. In consequence, our experiences of ourselves, of the world, and many of our behaviors have been corrupted as well.

The widely disseminated picture of our human exceptionalism is grounded in the assertion that we possess a unique form of intelligence due to our unique, hypertrophic brain. But this belief is not true; it has become a kind of intellectual imperialism. It has been, and still is, used to denigrate the orientation that many people still experience, that the world, and the other organisms with which we share this Earth, are alive, intelligent, and aware. It has been used to stifle the response of the heart to what has been presented to the senses. This has resulted in the creation of a conceptual monoculture that can't see outside its limitations. Such imperialists have set out to conquer the superstitious natives inhabiting the dark continent, the place where the general populace lives. Midgley makes the point that arguments such as Day's rest in a belief in human beings as "an isolated will, guided by an intelligence, arbitrarily connected to a rather unsatisfactory array of feelings, and lodged, by chance, in an equally unsatisfactory human body."[18] Or as Susan Sontag once described it: "consciousness harnessed to flesh,"[19] as if there could be consciousness without the emergence of the self-organized system we call the body. This type of dissociation is a common side effect of the materialist and very reductionist view of the world most of us are trained in. But as Midgely notes, this system of thought is not reason, not science, but behavioral examples of, as she puts it, an unexamined, "exuberant power fantasy." It is bad software, generated out of unexamined psychological frameworks.

The evolutionary escalator metaphor and the assumptions of what constitutes intelligence (and value) that are embedded within it create, automatically, behavior that is very dangerous to every other life-form on this planet—in fact to the health of every ecosystem this planet possesses.

We can't solve problems
by using the same kind of thinking we used
when we created them.

The belief in our unique intelligence is, and always has been, a lie. And while this "power fantasy" is slowly eroding in the light of unavoidable animal intelligence—as Giorgio Samorini notes . . .

Studies on animal behavior are providing ever more data in direct contradiction to behaviorism's rejection of animal mentality, and more and more scholars and researchers are distancing themselves from the behavioristic paradigm and beginning to admit the possibility of perceptive consciousness in animals.[20]

—it is certainly not eroding when it comes to simple, non-brain-possessing life-forms such as viruses.

Nevertheless, *intelligence* emerges as an aspect of self-organization in living systems. *Always.* What is actually true is that once self-organization occurs the capacity for analysis, innovation, and response all occur contemporaneously. And the degree of intelligence in living organisms, irrespective of whether they have a "brain" or not (or are an animal or not), is exceptional. This finding is beginning to pervade nearly every field of science, laying waste to the older paradigm. But most scientists are still very reluctant to accept what is becoming obvious. As Paul Davies comments . . .

> *To date biology is rooted in the old physics, the physics of the nineteenth century. Newtonian mechanics and theromodynamics play the central role. More recent developments, such as field theory and quantum mechanics, are largely ignored. In spite of the fact that the molecular basis for life is so crucial, and that molecular processes are quantum mechanical, atoms are treated like classical building blocks to be fitted together. Distinctively quantum effects, such as nonlocal correlations, coherence, and phase information, let alone possible exotic departures from quantum mechanics as suggested above, are not considered relevant.*[21]

Again: the degree of intelligence in living organisms, irrespective of whether they have a "brain" or not (or are an animal or not), is exceptional, and examples abound. For instance, the capacity to engage in mathematical computation and differentiation is common. As Richard Lewontin observes . . .

> *In* Cladocera, *small fresh-water arthropods, reproduction remains asexual as long as conditions of temperature, oxygen dissolved in the water, food availability, and degree of crowding remain constant. Then, if a sudden change in these conditions occurs . . . the* Cladocera *switch to sexual reproduction. . . . The organisms are detecting a rate of change of an input, not its absolute value. They are performing mathematical differentiation.*[22]

The capacity for mathematical analysis and differentiation is supposed to be limited to human beings. But it is not. You can also find it, sadly for reductionists, in slime mold. Jeremy Narby, in his book *Intelligence in Nature* (Tarcher, 2005), reveals that the "slime mold, *Physarum polycephalum,* can consistently solve a maze. . . . [W]hen food is placed at the start and end points of the maze, the slime mold withdraws from the dead-end corridors and shrinks its body to a tube spanning the shortest path between food sources. The single-celled slime solves the maze in this way each time it is tested."[23] Toshiyuki Nakagaki, the researcher conducting the study, commented that

> *Even for humans it is not easy to solve a maze. But the plasmo-dium of true slime mold, an amoeba-like organism, has shown an amazing ability to do so. This implies that an algorithm and a high computing capacity are included in the unicellular organism.*[24]

This capacity for mathematical differentiation and computation is wide spread. *All* self-organized biological systems possess it. One of the more amazing examples is the Clark's Nutcracker.

An Elegant Symbiosis

The Clark's Nutcracker is a bird, a member of the Corvidae family of birds which includes crows, ravens, jays, and magpies. It's a large bird, as most members of the family are, and it has a long coevolutionary history with certain pine trees, the white pines in particular.

White pines are a member of what are called the stone pines. These pines are similar in that once their seed-filled cones mature, the cones themselves do not open for the seeds to disperse. Unlike other pines, the cones of stone pines do not possess the tough fibers needed to pull back the scales and release the seeds. The only way for the seeds to exit the cones is if an animal breaks them open. The pine seeds (or nuts) of the white pines are exceptionally high in lipids, amino acids, and other nutri-ents, so it is not surprising that they are a preferred food source for a number of animals, including humans. But the Clark's Nutcracker's rela-tionship with the white pine is special.

Like most coevolutionary ecosystem relationships, the one between the white pine and the Nutcracker remained unrecognized (by Western scientists) until very recently. The person most responsible for bringing to light its complexity is Ronald Lanner in his remarkable book *Made for Each Other* (Oxford University Press, 1996).

Again, the cones of these pines never open enough to release the seeds. Massive shaking of the trees during powerful wind storms won't do it. Even if the scales themselves break off (which they can do since they don't possess the fibers of other types of cones) the seeds will remain in place, for the seeds are clasped just slightly behind the part that most often tends to break away. Since the cones don't open by themselves, and since the seeds are how the tree reproduces, an outside actor is necessary. For the white pine, it is birds, most commonly the Clark's Nutcracker, with whom the plant has developed a highly sophisticated mutualism.

The Clark's Nutcracker possesses a sublingual pouch in its throat in which it can store up to 100 white pine seeds at a time. When the bird finds a cone, it opens the scales as delicately as a (competent) surgeon with a scalpel performs an operation. The scale is picked away, the seed taken up, and it's then stored in the sublingual pouch. When the pouch is full, the bird begins depositing the seeds in caches spread over an area of up to ten square miles around the stand of trees it is feeding on. Some 30,000 seeds in 10,000 locations—two to five seeds each—are stored every year. The bird then feeds on the seed store during winter and the months afterward, until the trees produce seed again.

The remarkable thing, however, is the bird's capacity for both memory and mathematical calculation. Researchers have found that the birds can remember the location of every seed cache for up to two years. As well, they remember which locations seeds have been harvested from and which have not. Even more remarkable is *how* the birds find the caches they have created when they need to harvest more of the nuts. They unerringly return to the *exact* site of their cache in order to retrieve them. To get an idea of the enormity of this task, really *think* of what they are doing when they dig up a cache.

Pine nuts are relatively small, perhaps a quarter of an inch wide and half an inch long—at most. There are three seeds per cache on average. When caching the seeds, the bird makes a depression in the ground with its bill, two to five of the very tiny nuts are inserted into it, and then it is covered over. Remember: there are up to 10,000 of those locations spread out over a ten square mile area. Yet when the bird needs more food it unerringly flies to the *exact* location of a cache and digs it up, even when the landscape is covered with winter snow.

Naturalists have, for centuries, pondered just how the birds could do this. They first thought that smell was involved, but extensive work found that *only* the bird who hid the seeds could find them; no other Clark's Nutcracker could. So, it couldn't be smell. Other hypotheses were explored and likewise found to be inaccurate. Finally one researcher, Stephen Vander Wall, thought that the birds must be using their memory of landscape features to find the seeds. So, he went to an area where a Clark's Nutcracker had caches and *moved* landscape features (e.g., large rocks). Once he had, the birds could no longer find the seeds.

It turns out that Clark's Nutcrackers use a highly sophisticated form of triangulation to determine cache locations. When they make a cache they visually locate two landscape features in order to triangulate their cache.

say a rock and a tree

The landscape features are large enough so that during heavy snow they can still find their caches. The birds take an exact measurement—by eye—to the rock and the tree in order to fix the cache location in their mind. They can then locate the cache—a cache that is rarely larger than half an inch wide—within the ten square mile section in which they hide their seeds. But really, *think* about what this entails.

First, the birds must remember the location of at least 10,000 caches. Second, they can remember the same number of caches from the previous year. Third, they can remember every cache from which they take seeds and those from which they haven't. Fourth, they also have visual *overflight* cues in memory for each and every cache that they make. This allows them to locate the general area, from the air, as they are flying toward one of the seed stores. And these memories are foundational—it is only on the ground that their capacity for triangulation has relevance.

And finally, *think* about what they are doing when they are actually finding (or originally triangulating) a cache. They can measure *exactly* by eye the distance from where they are standing to both a stone and a tree. Exactly. This means to within tiny fractions of an inch. If they were to be only two inches off the triangulation would fix a different location; they would not find the cache. They literally have to dig right on top of the seed store to find it.

But *think,* too, about how stones and trees really are in the real world. They are not perfectly symmetrical posts that are standing completely vertical. The bird has to look at an exact spot on the rock *and* on the tree in order for the measurements to be accurate. Most rocks, and trees, are rather ragged in their shape. Each section of the rock will be slightly closer or farther away from the place the bird is standing; each section of the rock, if used as the triangulation point, will give a slightly different measurement. So the bird not only has to remember the landscape features themselves but the exact spot on that feature that they previously used.

And . . . there is even more to it than this. *Think* about what they are doing. They are measuring distance *by eye* as accurately as a measuring tape, to within millimeters. Further, they are doing this by using *no known* mathematical system. When we use a measuring tape, we are using a system of numbers that is human invented. What are the birds using? And further, how are they storing it in memory? To be stored in memory the measurements have to be encoded in some form and that form has to have an internal consistency to it. In other words it has to possess the same kind of structural integrity as our system of mathematical measurement.

The birds have some way of measuring distance and as well some way of encoding that measurement in memory. In other words, they have a system for measuring units of distance—but of course not the same one that our species developed—that is also, as ours is, infinitely flexible. Since no cache is going to be the exact same distance as a previous one they have to have a system which includes a large variety of "numbers." Each triangulation is different, each a different measurement (or number) of distance. There are numerous implications in this. Here are three of them: 1) mathematical relationships that are inherent in Universe can be perceived, and utilized, by more organisms than the human; 2) numbering systems are arbitrary and are only metaphors for those mathematical relationships—they are not foundational; 3) organisms other than the human not only have the capacity to perceive distance but also differentials— they can add and subtract; 4) they possess a sense of congruency—they know when they have the right answer—and the wrong one.

To get an idea of this latter capacity, *remember* how such a thing occurs in your own experience. You can re-create it now, if you wish, simply by taking something on your desk or table and moving it to a new location.

Begin by looking at what you are going to move, say a fork on the dining room table. *Look* at its location. Memorize it as exactly as you can. Once you have the location in mind, take it and move it, however far you wish, to another location on the table. Then when you are ready, move it back, but . . . do it this way.

Move it half way back and ask yourself, is this the right location? You will get some sort of an internal response to that question, a negation. It will feel a particular way, a way that tells you, "No, that is not it." So . . . move it again, again just a portion of the distance. And once more ask, "Is this it?" And again you will get a negation, a particular feeling that tells you it is not in the right place.

> *You are using here a holistic gestalt of mathematical differentials rather than a linear, reductionist numbering approach. But it gives you an exact sense of distance and relationship.*

Now, as closely as you can, move it back to the exact spot it was initially in. And ask again. Even though there might be subtle differences in its location the spoon will be close enough that some part of you will give, instead of negation, an affirmation, "yes, that's it." You engaged in an analysis of distance differentials by eye, just as the Clark's Nutcracker does. And you did it by the fork's relationship to landscape features just as the bird does, by getting a gestalt of distance relationships between the fork and the landscape features that surrounded it. But remember here: the distance line that the bird measures from the cache to the tree, from the cache to the rock, is a great deal farther than the distance from the fork to the table edge, the distance from the fork to the cup. And understand as well that the landscape features the bird uses are nonlinear, that is, they are not straight-edged like the edge of the table or the coffee cup you might have used.

> *Try the exercise again, outside, in a natural landscape, using a nut lying on top of the ground in the midst of a sea of plants. It is very different from doing it on the simple linearities we know of as*

tables, much harder in fact. Yet, interestingly, some other, unusual factors come into play in natural systems. There is a quality of living-ness in a natural system that adds something to the process, making it harder in one way, easier in another. Harder for the linear VSP (Very Serious Person) mind, easier for the childlike self.

Still . . . you knew when the location was correct by how it *felt*. Like you, the bird possesses an internal sense of congruency, a feeling sense that tells him when his measurements are accurate. But also, remember, the bird is *remembering* up to 20,000 locations over long time spans.

Could you, next week, or next year, remember the exact location of the fork?
And then move it back to that spot as closely as you just did?

Clark's Nutcrackers have some mechanism for encoding each location in memory so that they rarely forget it. They are, as well, due to the dis-tances involved, using a form of distance *triangulation* much larger in scope than that with the fork. The birds are working with their orienta-tion in space in relation to multiple landscape features that exist at some distance from the cache.

So . . . they land, look at landscape feature one, get a measurement that is *exact*. Then they look at feature two and get another exact mea-surement, then combine the two measurements into a gestalt of their location. Then they check it against their memory. If they get a "no," they adjust their position and check again, until they get a "yes," then they dig. If you think even more deeply into this process you begin to see that they are in fact measuring both length and differentials. Just as with Richard Lewontin's description of *Cladocera,* the birds are engaging in mathematical differentiation.

Clark's Nutcrackers use prodigious memory. Really *think* of what they can remember, that is, cache locations from two years, that is *20,000* loca-tions. However, each of these locations has a number of aspects that have to be remembered as well: 1) every cache that still has seeds and which ones do not; 2) overflight visual recognition of the general location of all 20,000; 3) the landscape features they are using for triangulation for all

20,000—that is 40,000 landscape features; 4) the exact spot on the landscape feature from which to measure—40,000 of them; 5) the distance from feature one—20,000 distances; 6) the distance from feature two—another 20,000 distances.

And they also use mathematical differentiation by measuring and adjusting their position in order to find the cache location. I can't think of a human being that could do the same thing

What about Rainman?

except for maybe some people who are autistic; they show the same capacities for memory and measurement.

But weren't we also talking about the white pines?
What do they get out of it?

This is how the white pines propagate. It is a form of pollination, or rather an innovation on pollination as we usually define it. The white pines, like all pines, are wind pollinated. But unlike most pines, whose seeds are carried from the cones to the Earth by the wind (which limits their spread), the white pines seeds are carried to new locations, up to ten miles away, by birds and there they are planted in the ground *at exactly the right depth for optimum sprouting*. The seeds that the birds do not eat, and they very rarely eat all of them, germinate, and grow new pines. This is how the pine forest spreads to new locations.

Many scientists commonly recognize now that birds, especially members of the Corvidae, are exceptionally smart. (Not as smart as us, but not bad really.) But when it comes to discussing bacterial or viral intelligence, organisms that most definitely do not have brains,

We want braaaaains

things begin to get much more difficult.

5
WE WANT BRAAAAAINS

A mind is an aggregate of interacting parts or components.

GREGORY BATESON

It is unlikely that intelligence as a biological property originated only with Homo sapiens.

ANTHONY TREWAVAS

It was difficult to believe that extremely stupid creatures with brains smaller than pinheads were capable of construction projects more complicated than any human project. But in fact, they were.

MICHAEL CRICHTON

Rightly did Darwin pin up a paper warning himself to be careful about using the words "higher" and "lower."

MARY MIDGLEY

Two things are infinite: the universe and human stupidity; and I'm not sure about the universe.

ALBERT EINSTEIN

*I*n spite of continual reports on intelligence in all self-organized biological systems, "brain chauvinism" is still rampant. One of the things most troubling to human centrists, mechanicalists, and reductionists—fundamentalists of any sort really—when it comes to general intelligence in living organisms, is, again, the lack of a brain.

Wait a minute, are you saying that reductionists lack a brain?

Actually, the thing that troubles most of these sorts of people when it comes to seeing the reality of the living organisms around them is their deeply entrenched belief that consciousness and intelligence reside in the brain. And the more consciousness and intelligence there is, the more "special" the brain must be. Thus, for a very long time, such people insisted that it was brain *size* that mattered. Unfortunately, when confronted with the brain of a blue whale (really, really big) they began to look stupid, so they shifted their orientation to brain size in relation to body size,

which led to problems in a number of their marriages,

thus putting humans back where they belonged. On top of the evolutionary pyramid. But it turns out that brains don't actually have to look like brains in the human sense of the term. *Braaaaains* are not necessary in order to have a brain. The brain that we think of as a necessity for intelligence is only one possible form a neural network can take and that is determined by ecological function and species shape; it is not essential to intelligence. As neurologist Antonio Damasio puts it, "the mind is embodied, not just embrained."[1] The desire for braaaaains, unsurprisingly, just turns out to be too anthropocentric. It says a great deal about the psychological orientation of reductionists and very little about the world *out there.* And the world out there has been making this plain, with increasing insistence, for some time, nowhere, perhaps, more so than in the rise of antibiotic resistant bacteria. As science writer Valerie Brown comments, "It is clear that bacteria are not what the general run of humans thought they were, and neither are humans. Bacteria are the *sine qua non* for life. . . . The idea that humans are separate from and superior to everything else in the biosphere has taken a terminal blow from the new knowledge about bacteria. . . . There's no going back."[2]

(Our) Resistance Is Futile

Antibiotic resistant bacteria are now one of the (human) world's most serious emerging problems. Although most people have seen a news report about it one time or another, few realize that *all* the world's bacterial researchers now admit that within our lifetimes antibiotics will become increasingly useless. Or, as researcher Mark Lappe once put it . . .

*The period
once euphemistically called
the Age of Miracle Drugs
is dead.*

Very few people are aware that infections from resistant bacteria, often picked up in hospitals during routine procedures, are the third leading cause of death in the U.S. (In 1999 they were fourth.) Very few people know, as well, that the world's leading pharmaceutical companies have stopped research and development on new antibiotics—there are virtually no new ones in the pipeline. Within the next few decades, we face, as many bacterial researchers have pointed out, the emergence of untreatable epidemic diseases more deadly than any known in history. Or as David Livermore, one of Britain's primary bacterial resistance researchers, puts it . . .

It is naive to think we can win.

It wasn't supposed to be this way; when antibiotics were commercially introduced in 1946 they were considered to be miracle drugs and many prominent researchers and physicians loudly proclaimed the end of infectious disease—for all time—was at hand. The trouble is that the lens through which most scientists viewed the world then (as regrettably, many still do) pictured the world as an essentially static background against which human beings acted. In other words, it was seen as a passive set, much like a stage set used for a play, and human beings were seen as the only actors on that stage.

we stand here, *the world is over* there

Or as Mary Midgley puts it, "The really strange and disturbing thing about [it] is the alienation of the human operator from the system he works on. He appears outside the system. He is an autonomous critic, independent of the forces that shape everything around him."[3] He has no relation to the world from which he has been expressed, no feeling connection to the other life-forms on the planet.

Out of this came the belief that we could make substances to kill the germs that sometimes killed us and the only thing that would happen is that less of us would die. The assumption was that the bacteria

who as anyone can see possess no brain

would just blindly die off leaving us a disease-free life. In consequence, human beings have been flooding the Earth with millions of pounds of antibiotics each and every year for a very, very long time. And these antibiotics? They are not biodegradable except under very special circumstances. Once we excrete them out of our bodies, or throw them away, or when industries dump them or their industrial byproducts in landfills, they go into waste treatment streams or the soil or underground aquifers relatively unchanged where they then impact the bacterial underpinnings of the planet . . . forever. They never go away.

In an extremely short period of geologic time the Earth has been saturated with several *billion* pounds of nonbiodegradable, often biologically unique pharmaceuticals designed to kill bacteria. Many antibiotics (literally meaning "against life") do not discriminate in their activity, but kill broad groups of diverse bacteria whenever they are used. The worldwide environmental dumping, over the past 65 years, of such huge quantities of synthetic antibiotics has initiated the most pervasive impacts on the Earth's bacterial underpinnings since oxygen-generating bacteria supplanted methanogens 2.5 billion years ago. As bacterial researcher Stuart Levy comments . . .

It has stimulated evolutionary changes
that are unparalleled in recorded biologic history.[4]

What are these evolutionary changes? At the simplest level, the development of exceptionally sophisticated resistance mechanisms in *all* the bacterial populations of the world. In response to the impact of *not me* on the bacterial *me,* bacteria have begun generating tremendously sophisticated behavioral and physical responses. Bacteria have literally begun rearranging their genomes. As those genomes shift, their physical structures alter, sometimes considerably. It has been two and a half *billion* years since anything approaching this degree of change has occurred in the bacterial populations of Earth. But this kind of response is inevitable in any self-organized system; as Francisco Varela et al. observe, a biological network

> *will reconfigure itself to an unspecified environment in such a way that it both maintains its ongoing dynamics and displays a behaviour that reveals a degree of inductive learning about environmental regularities.*[5]

Bacteria are, literally, remaking themselves in response to antibiotics. As soon as they encounter an antibiotic that can affect them, however minutely, they begin generating possible solutions to it. The variety and number of solutions they can generate are immense, from inactivating the part of the bacterial cell that the antibiotic is designed to destroy, to pumping the antibiotic out of their cells just as fast as it comes in, to altering the nature of their cellular wall to make them more impervious, to even using the antibiotic for food.

The old-style, neo-Darwinian, explanation for bacterial resistance, which regrettably still can be found in many newspapers and technical books, is that when a person takes an antibiotic all the *susceptible* bacteria are killed off but . . . there are always a few that are naturally resistant to the antibiotic. These survive to spread and thus resistance emerges. Occasionally you will also see statements that spontaneous mutations (the neo in neo-Darwinism—and, no, these Neos know nothing about white rabbits) are arising that are naturally resistant to antibiotics;

these mutated bacteria survive, have offspring, and thus spread.

The truth is much different. Bacteria literally analyze the antibiotics that they encounter and generate responses to them. They actually *remake* their genome in order to alter their physical form. And this solution? It is passed on to their descendants. In essence, this is the passing on of acquired characteristics, something Lamarck insisted was possible and that neo-Darwinians have ridiculed ever since.

Ironically enough, it was Alexander Fleming, the discoverer of penicillin, who first warned of bacterial resistance. He noted as early as 1929 in the *British Journal of Experimental Pathology* that numerous bacteria were already resistant to the drug he had discovered and by 1945 he warned in a *New York Times* interview that improper use of penicillin would inevitably lead to the development of resistant bacteria.

At the time of his interview just 14 percent of *Staphylococcus aureus* bacteria were resistant to penicillin—by 1953, as the use of penicillin became widespread, 64 percent–80 percent of the bacteria had become resistant and resistance to tetracycline and erythromycin were also being reported. (In 1995 an incredible 95 percent of staph was resistant to penicillin.) By 1960, resistant staph had become the most common source of hospital-acquired infections worldwide.

this is an exponential growth curve . . .
things don't usually work out well
in these kinds of situations

So, physicians began to use methicillin, a *B*-lactam antibiotic that they found to be effective against penicillin-resistant strains. Methicillin resistant staph (MRSA) emerged within a year. The first severe outbreak in hospitals occurred in the U.S. in 1968—only eight years later. Eventually MRSA strains resistant to all clinically available antibiotics except the glycopeptides (vancomycin and teicoplanin) emerged. But by 1999, fifty-four years after the commercial production of antibiotics, the first staph strain resistant to all clinical antibiotics had infected its first three people.

This rate of resistance development was supposed to be impossible. Evolutionary biologists had insisted that evolution in bacteria (as in all species) could only come from spontaneous, usable mutations that occur with an extremely low frequency (one out of every 10 million to one out of every 10 billion mutations) each generation. That bacteria could generate significant resistance to antibiotics in only thirty-five years was considered impossible. That the human species could be facing the end of antibiotics only sixty years after their introduction was ludicrous.

Bacteria are the oldest forms of life on this planet and they have learned very, very well how to respond to threats to their well-being. Among those are the thousands if not millions of antibacterial substances that have existed as long as life itself has existed. The world is, in fact, filled with antibacterial substances, most of them produced by other bacteria, fungi, and plants. Bacteria, to survive, learned how to respond to such substances a very long time ago. Or as Steven Projan of Wyeth Research puts it, bacteria "are the oldest of living organisms and thus have been subject to three billion years of evolution in harsh environments and therefore have been selected to withstand chemical assault."[6] And our antibiotics? Most of them are actually just slight alterations of bacterial substances that are already common in the world, primarily in fungi—substances that bacteria have long been aware of and are highly responsive to.

Once a bacterium develops a method for countering an antibiotic, it systematically begins to pass the knowledge on to other bacteria—not just its offspring—at an extremely rapid rate. Under the pressure of antibiotics, bacteria are interacting with as many other forms and numbers of bacteria as they can. In fact, bacteria are communicating across bacterial species, genus, and family lines, something they were never known to do before the advent of commercial antibiotics. And the first thing they share? Well, it's resistance information.

Bacteria can share resistance information directly, or simply extrude it from their cells, allowing it to be picked up later by roving bacteria. They often experiment, combining resistance information from multiple sources in unique ways that increase resistance, generate new resistance pathways, or even stimulate resistance forms that are not yet necessary. Even bacteria in hibernating or moribund states will share whatever information on resistance they have with any bacteria that encounter them. When bacteria take up any encoded information on resistance, they weave it into their own DNA and this acquired resistance becomes a genetic trait that can be passed on to their descendants forever. As Gaian researchers Williams and Lenton comment . . .

> *Microbe transfer between local populations carries genetic information that changes species composition and thus alters the nature of each community's interaction with its local environment.*[7]

"The nature of each community's interaction with its local environment" changes. One aspect of that: as bacteria gain resistance, they pass that knowledge on to *all* forms of bacteria they meet. They are not competing with each other for resources, as standard evolutionary theory predicted, but rather promiscuously cooperating in the sharing of survival information. "More surprising," one research group commented, "is the apparent movement of genes, such as *tetQ* and *ermB* between members of the normal microflora of humans and animals, populations of bacteria that differ in species composition."[8] Anaerobic and aerobic, Gram-positive and Gram-negative, spirochetes and plasmodial parasites, all are exchanging resistance information. Something that, prior to antibiotic usage, was never known to occur.

And, irritatingly, bacteria are generating resistance to antibiotics we haven't even thought of yet. For example, after placing a single bacterial species in a nutrient solution containing sublethal doses of a newly developed and rare antibiotic, researchers found that within a short period of time the bacteria developed resistance to that antibiotic *and* to twelve other antibiotics that they had never before encountered—some of which were structurally dissimilar to the first. Stuart Levy observes that "it's almost as if bacteria strategically anticipate the confrontation of other drugs when they resist one."[9]

They are also teaching each other how to become more virulent, in other words, how to make their disease impacts stronger, by sharing virulence factors among themselves through the same mechanisms they use to share resistance information. In fact, they are acting in concert so well in response to the human "war on disease" that it has led Levy to remark that "One begins to see bacteria, not as individual species, but as a vast array of interacting constituents of an integrated microbial world."[10] Former FDA commissioner Donald Kennedy echoes this when he states that "The evidence indicates that enteric microorganisms in animals and man, their R plasmids, and human pathogens form a linked ecosystem of their own in which action at any one point can affect every other."[11] Bacteria, as a group, are, in actuality, an extremely large self-organized system that covers the entire world.

The largest ecosystem known is the bacterial world that exists in the basalt layers two miles deep in the ocean, underneath and inside the basalt layers that exist another 100 to 500 feet beneath the water. This "seam" of bacterial life extends completely around the globe, a single unified ecosystem that is foundational to everything above it.

And, despite constant press to the contrary, bacteria are *not,* at root, disease organisms. As Lynn Margulis comments, "Most bacteria have far more important things to do on this Earth than to devour our tissues while we are still alive, drink our blood when we are old and weak, or fight with us over who will eat our food first. . . . Those who hate and want to kill bacteria indulge in self-hatred. Our ultimate ancestors, yours and mine, descended from this group of beings. Not only are bacteria our ancestors, but also . . . as the evolutionary antecedent of the nervous system, they invented consciousness."[12] What we have been taught about bacteria—in our schools, in a million television advertisements, by our medical system—is, in fact, not true. They are not disease organisms bent on our destruction. They are something else entirely, the foundation of all life on this planet. As Margulis makes plain, "Bacteria are not really individuals so much as part of a single global superorganism."[13] And that superorganism is in actuality an incredibly large community of highly intelligent interactive subparts, just as our white blood cells are of us (or as we, as individuals, are of the human communities in which we live). The different species of bacteria that exist are members of a much larger community than it once appeared to twentieth-century thinking. And they are not taking the presence of pharmaceutical pollution lightly; they are responding to the environmental disruptions caused by antibiotics socially, as a group. And they are using capacities that, until now, human scientists insisted they did not have. As Valerie Brown notes: "In a series of recent findings, researchers describe bacteria that communicate in sophisticated ways, take concerted action, influence human physiology, alter human thinking and work together to bioengineer the environment."[14]

They aren't stupid at all; in fact bacteria are very, very intelligent.

Bacterial Intelligence

Bacteria are considered, by those who have deeply studied them, not only to be intelligent but also to posses a sophisticated language and a highly developed social capacity. They are, in reality, not all that different from us. As bacterial researchers Eshel Ben-Jacob et al. put it . . .

> *Bacteria use their intracellular flexibility, involving signal transduction networks and genomic plasticity, to collectively maintain linguistic communication; self and shared interpretations of chemical cues, exchange of chemical message (semantic) and dialogues (pragmatic). Meaning-based communication permits colonial identity, intentional behavior (e.g., pheromone-based courtship for mating), purposeful alteration of colony structure (e.g., formation of fruiting bodies), detection-making (e.g., to sporulate) and the recognition and identification of other colonies—features we might begin to associate with a bacterial social intelligence.*[15]

Those qualities are ones formerly limited, in reductionist minds, to humans and other fur-bearing mammals. But there is more disquieting news, the researchers note that there exists an "inheritable colonial memory" among bacterial colonies; in other words, what they learn, they pass on to their descendants.[16] They care for and teach their offspring. And it gets worse: they build cities.

Colonies of bacteria, Ben-Jacob notes, "have developed intricate communication capabilities, including a broad repertoire of chemical signaling mechanisms, collective activation and deactivation of genes, and even exchange of genetic materials. With these tools they can communicate and self-organize their colonies into multicellular hierarchal aggregates, out of which new abilities emerge."[17] Within these colonies (cities), as he goes on to say, "Each [bacterium] has internal degrees of freedom, informatic capabilities, and freedom to respond by altering itself and others via emission of signals in a self-regulated manner."[18] The cities are an aggregate of individuals who work together and, very specifically, those individuals have the ability to make choices; they possess free will.

James Shapiro, at the University of Chicago, is particularly plain-spoken on this; bacteria are indeed sentient beings and they work together to solve the problems facing them.

> *Forty years experience as a bacterial geneticist have taught me that bacteria possess many cognitive, computational and evolutionary capabilities unimaginable in the first six decades of the twentieth century. Analysis of cellular processes such as metabolism, regulation of protein synthesis, and DNA repair established that bacteria continually monitor their external and internal environments and compute functional outputs based on information provided by their sensory apparatus. . . . My own work on transposable elements revealed multiple widespread bacterial systems for mobilizing and engineering DNA molecules. Examination of colony development and organization led me to appreciate how extensive multicellular collaboration is among the majority of bacterial species. [Studies] show that bacteria utilize sophisticated mechanisms for intercellular communication and even have the ability to commandeer the basic cell biology of "higher" plants and animals to meet their own basic needs. This remarkable series of observations requires us to revise basic ideas about biological information processing and recognize that even the smallest cells are sentient beings.[19]*

"Sentient beings." A revolutionary recognition that contradicts *everything* that most people, and most scientists, currently believe about bacteria. He expands this considerably by noting that "each bacterium is, by itself, a biotic autonomous system with its own cellular informatics capabilities (storage, processing and assessment of information). These afford the cell plasticity to *select* its response to biochemical messages it receives, including self-alteration and the broadcasting of messages to initiate alterations in other bacteria."[20] Shapiro concludes his twenty-three-page paper with this remarkable statement . . .

> *The take-home lesson of more than half a century of molecular microbiology is to recognize that bacterial information processing is far more powerful than human technology. . . . These small cells are incredibly sophisticated at coordinating processes involving millions of individual events and at making them precise and reliable. In addition, the astonishing versatility and mastery bacteria display in managing the biosphere's geochemical and thermodynamic transformations indicates that we have a great deal to learn about chemistry, physics, and evolution from our small, but very intelligent, prokaryotic relatives.*[21]

Shapiro calls the extensive cooperation among bacteria "sociobacteriology." Other researchers, such as Susanne von Bodman et al., note that because of what is now being understood, bacteria must be viewed from a "social evolution perspective." They comment that it is clear that bacteria are highly social. Bacteria recognize kin, that is, they perceive related offspring just as other life-forms do, and they help protect them in order to support their reproduction, just as other life-forms do. Von Broadman et al. observe that "by helping a close relative reproduce, an individual transfers genes to the next generation, albeit indirectly; this class of cooperation is altruistic." Further, they note that bacteria have mechanisms for limiting bacterium activity that is too selfish because of its antisurvival impacts on the bacterial colony. They comment that "cheater cells are suppressed or inhibited so that they cannot take over a population."[22]

> *So, you're saying*
> *that bacteria actually prosecuted the bankers . . .*
> *But that we didn't?*

Bacteria, in fact, show just the same sorts of complex and sophisticated behaviors that humans do, from language, to sentience, to intelligence, to the creation of cities, to cooperation in groups, to complex adaptation to their environment, to protection of offspring, to species memory that is handed down through the generations. And, if the definition of tool is extended, as it should be, to the creation of chemicals

or even sophisticated, insulated, electrical circuitry

And yes, distressingly for reductionists, bacteria do make such things. Bacteria at the bottom of the ocean create insulated electrical cables to heat their cities. Scientists, who first found them, generated some pictures; here's an artist's rendering of what those cables look like.

So bacteria's capacities include intelligent tool making. Our belief that *braaaaains,* that is, an organ that looks somewhat like the one in our heads, is necessary for intelligence is just plain wrong. As the molecular biologist Anthony Trewavas comments . . .

> *Very early on, analogies were drawn between the connections that [bacterial] phosphorylation enables between bacterial proteins and the connections between neurone dendrites in higher animal brains. This led to their description as a phosphoneural network. The properties of these networks include signal amplification, associative responses (cross talk) and memory effects. Subsequent investigation indicated learning and the realization that these simple networks provide individual bacteria with informed decisions.*[23]

And as neuroscientist Peggy La Cerra observes . . .

> *The hallmark of animalian intelligence systems is the capacity to predict likely costs and benefits of alternative paths of behavior. This logic is evident in our most ancient ancestors, bacteria. [As an example] E. Coli is a single-cell organism with a single molecule of DNA. This simplest of animals exhibits a prototypical centralized intelligence system that has the same essential design characteristics and problem solving logic as is evident in all animal intelligence systems including humans.*[24]

Neural networks are generated any time a biological self-organization event occurs. And "the computational capabilities" that we recognize as integral to intelligence, as Chakrabarti and Dutta comment, naturally "emerge out of the collective dynamics of the network, which is nonlinear."[25] From that comes, as Trewavas observes, "Information processing, learning, memory, decision making, choice, predictive modeling, associating memory, sensory integration and control of behavior." These are, as he notes, "all aspects of biological intelligence."[26] These capacities are present in *every* biological organism—yes, that includes viruses.

Viruses creates communities, just as bacteria do. But what is even more interesting about viruses is that they act, in a number of circumstances, much like a group of cooperating carnivores such as a pride of lions or wolfpack—or, perhaps more accurately, humans. In fact, they seem to "shepherd" their flocks.

Researchers studying emerging viruses have noticed an interesting phenomenon. As more human beings are born, there is a consistent spread of human habitation into once undeveloped ecoranges. The previously existing environment is removed, houses are built, people move in. The former populations of plants and animals are displaced. However, one of the major things that has been overlooked is that viruses have also lived in those regions for a very long time—in a healthy symbiotic balance with their hosts, both plant and animal. It is possible to think of them as an invisible herd or pack species, spread with the same kind of density throughout those ecoranges just as deer or birds are. As Frank Ryan describes it . . .

The swarm analogy has implications that go beyond the mutational evolution within a single infected [individual]. The "species" swarm is nothing less than the genomic diversity of the entire virus proliferation across the genomic landscape of the entire infected species.[27]

In other words, in some senses, viruses should be thought of, not as individuals, but as a self-organized whole—a swarm—composed of many, many individual viruses, each with a slightly different genomic structure, that acts as an extensive intelligent organism. And that organism? It really, really doesn't like its habitat being destroyed.

Human beings, moving into a previously undisturbed ecorange, represent, in essence, the introduction of a new predator species. The existing animal groups are displaced, displacing in turn their viral symbionts. Mathematical modeling has found that the relationships of emerging viruses most closely resemble predator-prey relationships. That, in fact, viruses in an ecorange feed on their hosts identically to the way large mammal predators feed on *their* prey. But in this instance, they don't usually kill their hosts, they just scavenge nutrients from them, i.e., feed on them. As researchers Villarreal et al. comment, such mathematical models "resemble predator-prey dynamics in which the viruses act as predators on their host prey."[28] Only in certain circumstances do they kill their prey and when they do, the process follows the same predator-prey dynamics that exist in larger carnivores. Frank Ryan comments that

The microbes that kill people, particularly those that kill huge numbers in sweeping epidemics, follow, in many ways, the same universal law of predator and prey. It is part of this complex gestalt that the balance is shaped by the behavior of the prey. If the prey moves—if it changes, if its numbers increase or decrease, if its ecology alters—the predator must move with it.[29]

And like most predators, viruses are very, very intelligent. As Ryan observes . . .

In a sense every sufferer evolves his or her own strain of virus, and within each sufferer the strain is not a single viral genome but a

swarm of thousands of related genomes, all furiously mutating, meta-morphosing, driven by a genomic intelligence the like of which had never been imagined before. Self-regulating, it could speed its own production up or slow it down at will, overwhelming the failing immune system with novelty from week to week, even from day to day. . . . [Studies found that] there were genes that switched production of virus off or on, others that hugely accelerated the viral assembly line, jacking up production a thousandfold when the infected cells encountered a stimulatory antigen. There were still others that had the opposite effect, that switched off this positive feedback burst of replication. The more people studied the virus, the more strategically calculating is behavior appeared. . . . In other words, the virus coded itself for long-term survival, during which it could reproduce itself endlessly without necessarily killing huge numbers of host cells.[30]

Again, they don't normally kill their host species. In well-established virus-host relationships, in exchange for a hospitable living environment the viruses offer certain benefits to the host species, among which is the protection of that host species from external threats. For example, in the case of the simian herpes-B virus, *Herpesvirus saimiri.*

If a rival species of monkey begins encroaching on its host's territory, the virus will immediately jump species. In the new monkey species, the virus is deadly. It generates an incredibly fast acting cancer, the encroaching species dying from fulminating cancer of the lymphatic system. Within its host species, however, the virus is benign and never causes disease. The viral swarm responds to an encroaching species much as humans do when a competing carnivore begins taking their livestock. Many of the emerging viruses that human beings are encountering as disease organisms are acting similarly for similar reasons.

Portions of the viral swarm, the herd/pack of closely related viruses that live in a particular host species in a specific ecorange, will, in fact, immediately jump species if the integrity of their hosts and ecorange is threatened. Neo-Darwinianists have said that viruses enter new hosts "by accident," that such jumping is counter to the organism's survival and thus counter to "survival of the fittest" ideology. However, it appears that this is a well-honed and long-standing survival strategy, as Frank Ryan comments . . .

The attacking virus is programmed to injure and kill, even if in doing so this portion of the swarm sacrifices itself in an evolutionary cul-de-sac. The symbiotic relationship is well served by this sacrifice. This is as important as it is a radically different perception.[31]

Viruses, in fact, show altruistic behavior, just as bacteria do. Swarms are, in actuality, distributed intelligences, a form of neural net spread throughout multiple organisms. And they, like all self-organized systems, act to stabilize and retain their self-organized state. Thus they protect their ecological territory . . . and their hosts from intrusions of other species.

The world is not a static backdrop across which humans can move, building their suburbs where they will, the only intelligent actors on the planet. They call it the American dream, as George Carlin once put it, because you have to be asleep to believe it.

Attempting to kill off microbial groups because they cause human disease is fraught with peril. And while it is true that the introduction of antimicrobial substances in the millions of tons does stimulate rapid alteration in microbe genomes, that is not the only cause of the genetic innovations. As Yoshida et al. comment, "Mathematical modeling shows that this kind of cryptic dynamics occurs when there is rapid prey or host evolution for traits conferring defense against attack."[32] In other words, simply enhancing the defense of the prey against its predator—by, for instance, the creation and use of millions of tons of antibiotics—results in immediate alterations in the predators. With bacteria it stimulates rapid evolutionary innovation—*whether they encounter the antibiotics or not*—in order to reestablish predator-prey homeodynamis. Or as Hilker and Schmitz put it, "Parasite removal from food webs can have catastrophic effects."[33]

Though the rise of bacterial (and viral and fungal) resistance has begun to stimulate a moderately wide recognition among scientists that microbial intelligence exists—a recognition very much lacking among most physicians and the general populace—it is for plants that the majority of scientists retain the most derision. I mean there is just nothing *stupider* than a carrot.

and besides they don't have a brain either

Plant Intelligence

The deep intelligence possessed by plants has been explored, and discussed, by many people of note over the past several centuries, including Goethe, Luther Burbank, George Washington Carver, Masanobu Fukuoka, Jagadis Bose, and the Nobel Prize–winner Barbara McClintock. Nevertheless, their research and findings have usually been dismissed, irrespective of its competence. As Brenner et al. comment about Bose (and the concept of plant intelligence in general) . . .

> *Bose's overall conclusion that plants have an electromechanical pulse, a nervous system, a form of intelligence, and are capable of remembering and learning was not well received in its time. A hundred years later, concepts of plant intelligence, learning, and long-distance electrical signaling in plants have entered the mainstream literature. . . . Nevertheless, the concept of plant intelligence [still] generates a considerable amount of controversy.*[34]

The discomfort among reductionists has been so extreme that, as Baluska et al. (2005) note, for a very long time, the reports of a sophisticated plant nervous system "was labeled as pseudoscience and 'doomed' for oblivion."[35] Research indicating intelligence in plants, whenever it appeared, irrespective of the source, was consistently attacked by "mainstream" researchers as mystical, a romanticization of the natural world, or as anthropocentrism.

> *But really, when you think of it,*
> *we have a lot more in common with a plant than a car.*
> *Mechanomorphism—the projection onto Nature of a mechanical*
> *nature—is a lot more ridiculous than the idea of*
> *plant intelligence ever could be*

As Anthony Trewavas once put it, "The use of the term 'vegetable' to describe unthinking or brain-dead human beings perhaps indicates the general attitude [toward plants]."[36] In consequence, most of the work by Goethe and the others has been ignored, and in many cases forgotten.

Even Barbara McClintock, whose work on corn transposons eventually earned her the Nobel Prize, was ostracized for over a decade, because of the discomfort her work caused. And while her work was eventually recognized, her methodology, like that of Goethe et al., has been dismissed. As one of her colleagues once put it . . .

I respect McClintock's work; I just don't like her mysticism

Despite this, plants, it turns out, really are highly intelligent and yes, they do have a brain. It's just that no one ever looked in the right place. Oh, wait! There was someone, a long time ago, who did look in the right place.

His name was Charles Darwin.
(Oops!)

Darwin commented in one of his last works, *The Power of Movement in Plants,* that

> *It is hardly an exaggeration to say that the tip of the radicle thus endowed [with sensitivity] and having the power of directing the movements of the adjoining parts, acts like the brain of one of the lower animals; the brain being seated within the anterior end of the body, receiving impressions from the sense-organs and directing the several movements.*[37]

This book of Darwin's, his second to last, has been long ignored. It contains some of the most powerful insights about plants since Goethe's work nearly a century before. (Jagadis Bose, during the latter nineteenth and early twentieth centuries would take it considerably further.) Darwin had two genuinely deep insights that are paradigm altering: 1) that the root of the plant is in fact its brain; and 2) that the plant is using sensitive, and intelligent, analysis of it surroundings to navigate through the soil.

But Darwin's insight was just the beginning; depth analysis of plants since the turn of the (new) millennium is finding that their brain capacity is much larger than Darwin supposed, that their neural systems are highly developed—in many instances as much as that of humans, and that they make and utilize neurotransmitters identical to our own. It is beginning to seem that they are highly intelligent—perhaps as much or even more so than humans in some instances. (They can even perform sophisticated mathematical computations and make future plans based on extrapolations of current conditions. The mayapple, for instance, plans its growth two years in advance based on weather patterns.)

> *But, that can't be true. They just sit there when we kill them*
> *(yeah? and no matter how fast a human runs, the lion*
> *still finds him tasty.)*

Increasing numbers of researchers, in a multiplicity of fields, are beginning to acknowledge that intelligence is an inevitable aspect of all self-organized systems—that sophisticated neural networks are a hallmark of life. Some researchers are becoming quite vocal in attacking what they call the "brain chauvinism" of the old-school (male) scientists who are still clasping firmly to their bosom (26A) the shreds of twentieth-century scientific certitudes. Kevin Warwick, a cyberneticist, observes succinctly that, "Comparisons (in intelligence) are usually made between characteristics that humans consider important; such a stance is of course biased and subjective in terms of the groups for whom it is being used."[38] In other words, rationalists, who have long attacked the concept of intelligence and awareness in Nature as antirational Romantic projection, have been themselves been merely looking at and for their own reflection in the world around them—and, of course, finding the world wanting. But what especially activates their antirational subjectivity is whenever the organism in question appears to not have a brain, such as with bacteria, viruses, and most especially plants.

Plants and Perception

The old paradigm about plants, which is very common and (unfortunately) still believed by most people, is that plants are "passive entities subject to environmental forces and organisms that are designed solely for accumulation of photosynthetic products." But as Baluska et al. continue . . .

The new view, by contrast, is that plants are dynamic and highly sensitive organisms, actively and competitively foraging for limited resources both above and below ground, and that they are also organisms which accurately compute their circumstances, use sophisticated cost-benefit analysis, and that take defined actions to mitigate and control diffuse environmental insults. Moreover, plants are also capable of a refined recognition of self and non-self and this leads to territorial behavior. This new view considers plants as information-processing organisms with complex communication throughout the individual plant. Plants are as sophisticated in behavior as animals but their potential has been masked because it operates on time scales many orders of magnitude longer than that operation in animals. . . . Owing to this lifestyle, the only long-term response to rapidly changing environments is an equally rapid adaptation; therefore, plants have developed a very robust signaling and information-processing apparatus. . . . Besides abundant interactions with the environment, plants interact with other communicative systems such as other plants, fungi, nematodes, bacteria, viruses, insects, and predatory animals.[39]

As with all self-organized systems, plants continually monitor their internal and external worlds for informational/functional shifts in the relevant fields. If they are focusing externally, once they note a shift, they work to identify its nature and meaning, and its likely impact on their functioning. Then they craft a response.

Plants continually monitor every aspect of their environment: spatial orientation; presence, absence, and identity of neighbors; disturbance; competition; predation, whether microbial, insect, or animal; composition of atmosphere; composition of soil; water presence, location, and amount; degree of incoming light; propagation, protection, and support of offspring (yes, they recognize kin); communications from other plants in their ecorange; biological oscillations, including circadian; and not only their own health but the health of the ecorange in which they live. As Anthony Trewavas comments, this "continually and specifically changes the information spectrum" to which the plants are attending.

That's a brilliant phrase, "information spectrum," and its deeper meanings deserve to be teased out a bit. It reflects the truth that every living organism is immersed in a bath of sensory inflows every moment of their lives. Every part of those sensory inflows contains depth information about what is going on around that organism; the sensory inflows are in fact encodings of meanings, communications from the complexity of the scenario in which the organism is embedded. And the use of the word "spectrum" is, well, brilliant. Just as light can be separated into a spectrum of colors, each with different impacts, so too the bath of sensory inflows is a spectrum of simultaneously occurring informational inputs, each of which can be teased apart and focused upon should the part of the organism that gates sensory data indicate it is important enough to do so. In one of his most insightful statements Trewavas comments that, in general, "There is no unique separate response to each signal in this complex [of informational inflows] but merely a response issued from an integration of all environmental and internal information."[40] In other words, unless there is an informational inflow that the plant's sensory gating mechanisms identify as crucial to respond to,

> *such as extensive leaf damage from spider mites which will stimulate the plant to focus more specifically*

the plant normally does not use any form of linear cause and effect processing of data. It integrates the entire informational inflow that surrounds it into one holistic gestalt at each and every moment in time and generates a response that comes out of a unique, and very important, state of being.

> *It is actually a kind of dreaming*
> *And not the kind of dreaming you are thinking about either*
> *But a different kind of dreaming entirely*
> *(It's like the dreaming you do when you are reading this book)*
> *That dreaming is the central core of what this book is about*
> *It is the kind of dreaming that Goethe was engaged in*
> *When he learned about plant metamorphosis*

And Luther Burbank when he looked deep into the plant
And saw every environment its ancestors had ever lived in
And the same kind that Barbara McClintock did
When she watched individual chromosomes in corn shift their structure
It is the same state of mind that writers enter when they create worlds
It is also how Gaia dreams the world into being
And it is the kind of dreaming you can do, too, if you wish,
If you decide to walk through the doors of perception
And find out what is on the other side

As Trewavas continues, these plant responses are highly intelligent. "Given the plethora of signals that plants integrate into a response, autonomic responses do not occur. Signal perception is instead ranked according to assessments of strength and exposure." In other words, typical sensory gating as it exists in all organisms. But then he notes, as researchers in so many other fields are now doing, that the living organism, in this instance a plant, actually *chooses* the optimum response from a plethora of alternatives. As he says, potential "responses can be rejected; the numbers of different environments that any wild plant experiences must be almost infinite in number. Only complex computation can fashion the optimal fitness response."[41]

Some plants, such as sundew, are so sensitive to touch, for example, that they can detect a strand of hair weighing less than one microgram (one millionth of a gram) to which they then respond. But what is more revealing is that they can determine with great specificity *what* is touching them. Raindrops, a common experience in the wild, produce no response. This kind of mechanosensitivity, which is, in plants, similar to what we call our sense of touch, is used much as we use our own: The plants analyze what is touching them, determine its meaning, and craft a response. And that response many times involves rapid changes in their genetics, phenotype, and subsequent physical form. As McCormack et al. comment, "Plants perceive much more of their environment than is often apparent to the casual observer. Touch can induce profound rapid responses . . . in *Arabidopsis,* changes in gene expression can be seen within minutes after touch, and over 700 genes have altered transcript levels within 30 min."[42]

Many of the research papers that found a lack of intelligent response in plants, and that have been cited endlessly in the past by reductionists, were conducted in laboratories. Trewavas remarks succinctly that such results should have been expected. Laboratory studies will always misleading in this way, for wild plants live in *wild* not tame environments.

> *No such simplicity of circumstance is available to an individual wild plant, which in meeting an almost infinite variety of environmental states must construct individual responses to improve its own fitness. No genome could contain the information that would provide an autonomic response to every environmental state. And even cloned individuals do not exhibit identical responses.*[43]

The only place that *un*intelligence, that systems of simple linear cause and effect, can reliably be found is in systems created by human beings—or in their laboratories. As Ilya Prigogine and Isabelle Stengers comment . . .

> *The artificial may be deterministic and reversible. The natural contains elements of randomness and irreversibility. This leads to a new view of matter in which matter is no longer the passive substance described in the mechanistic world-view but is associated with spontaneous activity.*[44]

In wild systems intelligence, free will, choice, innovation, sophisticated adaptation are inherent. These capacities in plants, as in us, are due to extremely sophisticated neural networks and are as Baluska et al., observe, "specialized for neuronal-like activities based on plant synapses."[45] A "brain," as we think of it, is just not necessary. Trewavas comments that

> *It is now known (1) that various steps in metabolism act like many Boolean compute logic gates such as AND, OR, and NOR and are termed chemical neurons, (2) that these chemical neurons can act as pattern-recognition systems, (3) that proteins can act as compu-*

tational elements, and (4) that protein phosphorylation using about 1,000 protein kinases in both animals and plants provides for enormous numbers of complex elements of control, switching mechanisms and including both positive and negative feedback interactions. . . . Even in simple networks collective computational properties arose with parallel processing and extensive numbers of associative memories emerged as attractors occupying part of the network. . . . The cell in which zillions of molecular events occur at a time computes in parallel fashion, just like a brain. . . . The cellular network perceives continual environmental variation through a multiplicity of receptors. . . . Such networks learn either by increasing the synthesis of particular constituents or by changing the affinity between particular network steps by post-translational modification. Memory is simply the retention with time of the enhanced pathway of information flow and can be accessed by other pathways through cross talk. Cellular networks capable of these properties are entitled to be called intelligent.[46]

Plants, in fact, possess a highly sophisticated neural system and while it does not look like our "brain," it really is, in actuality, a brain. In fact, once you get over brain chauvinism, it's not all that different from our own.

The Plant Brain

It is common for people to view plants, for example a tree, as having a "head" and "feet," the head being the tree or its canopy, the feet being the root system. But it turns out that our orientation is incorrect.

This kind of human misorientation is not uncommon. A well known environmental activist once told me, "Old growth forests are monocultures; there is very little diversity of life in them." And many people have used that thinking to support the cutting of old-growth forests. But it turns out that he was (as are so many others) guilty of two-dimensional thinking. If you go upward, into the canopy of the forest, you will find one of the most complex and diverse ecosystems on Earth. There are plants and insects and animals there that make the diversity found in younger forests seem simplistic in comparison. And if you go into the soil surrounding those trees roots, you will find the same kind of complex community of life. Plants, in fact, construct within themselves a three-dimensional gestalt of their local space that includes not only the three-dimensional space of the rhizome world in which the root/brain exists but also of the canopy world that comes into being as the plant matures. Plants, in fact, negotiate both their form and behavior through a three-dimensional maze space—a topological surface that is continually changing in shape—that is constrained by the energy/movement of multitudes of other actors. And within those zones a diversity of life emerges that could not exist otherwise. Neither the Earth nor plants are limited to two-dimensional thinking it seems, just people.

In complex organisms the head, or anterior pole of the body, is the part that processes information, the posterior pole the part that engages in sexual reproduction and excretion of waste. From that orientation plants live with their heads in the Earth, their asses in the air. We love the smell, usually, of their reproductive organs and pick them to give to our beloveds (a highly suggestive though unconscious act). We don't, most of us, really know plants at all.

If you can get your head around that picture, the root system of a tree being its brain, its head, and the part we normally see being its lower body, you will probably experience a sense of disorientation accompanied by nausea.

what we think of as "up," isn't

That, again, is the experience that accompanies the restructuring of software. It is a direct experience of how *off* our accepted pictures of the world generally are and just how different the world really is from what we have been taught. The plant brain does exist and it is just as elegant as our own, in many respects more so. As Frantisek Baluska et al. comment . . .

Although plants are generally immobile and lack the most obvious brain activities of animals and humans, they are not only able to show all the attributes of intelligent behavior but they are also equipped with neuronal molecules, especially synaptotagmins and glutamate/glycine-gated glutamate receptors. Recent advances in plant cell biology allowed identification of plant synapses transporting the plant-specific neurotransmitter-like molecule auxin. This suggests that synaptic communication is not limited to animals and humans but seems widespread throughout plant tissues.[47]

And as Trewavas amplifies . . .

Learning and memory are the two emergent (holistic) properties of neural networks that involve large numbers of neural cells acting in communication with one another. But, both properties originate from signal transduction processes in individual cells. Quite remarkably, the suite of molecules used in signal transduction are entirely similar between nerve cells and plant cells. . . . Learning results from the formation of new dendrites, and memory lasts as long as the newly formed dendrites themselves. The neural network is phenotypically plastic and intelligent behavior requires that plastic potential. Plant development is plastic too and is not reversible; many mature plants can be reduced to a single bud and root and regenerate to a new plant with a different structure determined by the environmental circumstances.[48]

In other words, if you take the cutting of a plant from one location and plant it in another, as the neural system of the plant develops in the soil, analyzing its surroundings all the while, it alters, as it learns, the shape and formation of emerging neural net *and* the plant body it develops. This, more effectively, fits it into the environment in which it is now growing. In short, plants possess a highly developed root brain which works much as ours does to analyze incoming data and generate sophisticated responses. But what is more, the plant brain that emerges *always* fits its functional shape to the environment in which it appears. The plant neural net, or brain, is highly plastic when compared to ours.

A unique part of the plant root, the root apex (or apices, which are the pointed ends of the root system) is a combination sensitive finger, perceiving sensory organ, and brain neuron. Each root hair, rootlet, and root section contains an apex; every root mass millions, even billions, of them. For example, a single rye plant has more than 13 million rootlets with a combined length of 680 miles. Each of the rootlets are covered with root hairs, over 14 *billion* of them, with a combined length of 6,600 miles. Every rootlet, every root hair, has at its end a root apex. Every root apex acts as a neuronal organ in the root system. In contrast, the human brain has approximately 86 billion neurons, about 16 billion of which are in the cerebral cortex. Plants with larger root systems, and more root hairs, can have considerably more brain neurons than the 14 billion contained in rye plants; they can even rival the human brain in the number of neurons. And when you look at the interconnected network of plant roots and micorrhizal mycelia in any discrete ecosystem, you are looking at a neural network much larger than any individual human has ever possessed.

I still remember seeing a great, ancient maple send shudder after shudder through its trunk one year—for days on end. The entire tree was undulating; I'd never seen or felt anything like it before. Some dimension of the world that I had never encountered before was intruding itself into my experience. It literally felt like the underpinnings of my world view were crumbling. It seemed as if the tree were having an epileptic seizure, something far outside my experience of trees. Then, with a great crash one day, a single giant, diseased limb came hurtling down from the canopy, at which point the shudders ceased. In a flash of insight then, I understood that trees self-prune, that they self-caretake, that I had only the barest understanding of the plant world and finally grasped Einstein's observation that "we still do not know one thousandth of one percent of what nature has revealed to us."

While humans and many other animals, for example, have a specific organ, the brain, which houses its neuronal tree, plants use the soil as the stratum for the neural net; they have no need for a specific organ to house their neuronal system. The numerous root apices act as one whole, synchronized, self-organized system, much as the neurons in our brains do. Our brain matter is, in fact, merely the soil that contains the neural net we use to process and store information. Plants use the soil itself to house their neuronal nets. This allows the root system to continue to expand outward, adding new neural extensions for as long as the plant grows.

> *Old growth plants then begin to take on a much different character than their younger offspring. There are states of being that only come into play with age, and with the extensive development of expanded neural fields; the neuronal structure in an ancient redwood or old growth* Artemisia absinthium *is different from that in younger plants . . . so are the memories and life experiences held within that neuronal structure. Plants become wise, too, as they age. We are not the only ones capable of it. You can literally* feel *the difference such maturity brings in encountering old growth trees—the young just don't have it.*

In addition, the leaf canopy also acts as a synchronized, self-organized perceptual organ which is highly attuned to electromagnetic fields. It can be viewed, in fact, as a crucial subcortical portion of the plant brain.

As Baluska et al. comment, the root apices

> *harbor brain-like units of the nervous system of plants. The number of root apices in the plant body is high, and all 'brain units' are interconnected via vascular strands (plant neurons) with their polarly-transported auxin (plant neurotransmitter), to form a serial (parallel) neuronal system of plants. From observation of the plant body of maize, it is obvious that the number of root apices is extremely high. . . . This feature makes the 'serial plant brain' extremely robust and the amount of processed information must be immense.*[49]

Plant biologist Peter Barlow adds that the tips of the roots "form a multiheaded advancing front. The complete set of tips endows the plant with a collective brain, diffused over a large area, gathering, as the root system grows and develops, information" crucial to the plant's survival.[50] And, as he continues: "One attribute of a brain, as the term is commonly understood, is that it is an organ with a definite structure and location which gathers or collects information, which was originally in the form of vibrations (heat, light, sound, chemical, mechanical, . . .) in the ambient environment and somehow transforms them into an output or response."[51] By this definition, plants do have brains just as we do, but given their capacity to live for millennia (in the case of some aspen root systems, over 100,000 years) their neural networks can, in many instances, far exceed our own. Old growth aspen root systems can spread through as much as a hundred acres of soil creating a neural network substantially larger than Einstein's or any other human that has ever lived. They are, sometimes, far, far more intelligent than human beings. Plants, it must be realized, possess a spectrum of neural networks, just as mammals do. Some plants possess extremely large networks, others possess smaller networks. In other words, "brain" size occurs across a considerable range, just as it does with mammals. Nevertheless, all plants are intelligent (just as are all mammals). They are all self-aware. They all engage in highly interactive social transactions with their communities.

So, that carrot?
It was murdered, yes.

For their neural networks to function, plants use virtually the same neurotransmitters we do, including the two most important: glutamate and GABA (gamma aminobutyric acid). They also utilize, as do we, acetylcholine, dopamine, serotonin, melatonin, epinephrine, norepinephrine, levodopa, indole-3-acetic acid, 5-hydroxyindole acetic acid, testosterone (and other androgens), estradiol (and other estrogens), nicotine, and a number of other neuroactive compounds. They also make use of their plant-specific neurotransmitter, auxin, which, like serotonin, for example, is synthesized from tryptophan. These transmitters are used, as they are in us, for communication within the organism and to enhance brain function.

The similarity of human and plant neural systems and the presence of identical chemical messengers within them illustrate just why the same molecular structures (e.g., morphine, cocaine, alcohol) that affect our neural nets also affect plants. Jagadis Bose, who developed some of the earliest work on plant neurobiology in the early 1900s, treated plants with a wide variety of chemicals to see what would happen. In one instance, he covered large, mature trees with a tent then chloroformed them. (The plants breathed in the chloroform through their stomata, just as they would normally breathe in air.) Once anesthetized, the trees could be uprooted and moved without going into shock. He found that morphine had the same effects on plants as that of humans, reducing the plant pulse proportionally to the dose given. Too much took the plant to the point of death, but the administration of atropine, as it would in humans, revived it. Alcohol, he found, did indeed get a plant drunk. It, as in us, induced a state of high excitation early on but as intake progressed the plant began to get depressed, and with too much it passed out.

and it had a hangover the next day

Irrespective of the chemical he used, Bose found that the plant responded identically to the human; the chemicals had the same effect on the plants nervous systems as it did the human.

This really should not be surprising. The neurochemicals in our bodies were used in every life-form on the planet long before we showed up. They predate the emergence of the human species by hundreds of millions of years. They must have been doing something all that time, you know, besides waiting for us to appear.

The vascular strands that support the plant body, giving it its rigid structure, also act as the peripheral nerve system for the plant. The plant's neurotransmitters travel along the nerve system carrying information to the periphery, just as they do in our bodies. The plant roots engage in finely detailed analysis of their environment and communicate with the rest of the plant via neurotransmitters. The leaf canopy, as well, is taking in considerable data about the exterior world above ground. That data is sent to the root brain system, again via neurotransmitters for analysis.

GABA is present in high levels in the mammalian brain where it plays a major part in neurotransmission. It is also involved in the development of the nervous system through the promotion of neuron migration, proliferation, and differentiation. GABA strongly affects neuronal growth during cortical development, promoting DNA synthesis and cell proliferation, stimulating neurons to assemble into functional networks of axons and dendrites. It, along with auxin, plays similar roles in the formation of plant root neurons.

The plant root neurons work through the use of synapses, very similar to our own. "Moreover," as Baluska et al. comment, "not only have neuronal molecules been found in plants but plant synapses are also present which use the same vesicular recycling processes for cell-cell communication as neuronal synapses."[52]

The neuronal plant cells in the root exist in what is called the transition zone of the root apex. Baluska et al. note that "as cells of the transition zone are not engaged in any demanding activities, such as mitotic divisions or rapid cell elongation, they are free to focus all their resources on the acquisition, processing, and storing of information."[53] *Storing of information,* that means memory. As they continue: "Smart plants can memorize stressful environmental experiences and can call upon this information to take decisions about their future activities."[54] That is, they plan ahead.

The root apex is covered with a root cap which is designed to protect the apex *and* which also possesses sophisticated sensing capabilities. It screens the environment it encounters for large numbers of factors, processes the information, and alters its, and the plant's, behavior accordingly. "As a result," as Baluska et al. note, "roots behave almost like more active animals, performing very efficient exploratory movements in their search for oxygen, water, and ions."[55]

Plant Social Communication

Roots of plants are exquisitely aware of *self* and *not-self* and engage in sophisticated interactions with a wide range of living organisms. They, as Baluska et al. comment, are "capable of forming facultative cell-to-cell junctions with cells of other organisms (plants, fungi, bacteria). These correspond to 'immunological synapses'—specialized cell-to-cell adhesion domains that involve the plasma membranes of the two organisms that are opposing each other. Such adhesive domains are also sites of active cell-to-cell transport of molecules and metabolites."[56]

The plant roots enter into symbiotic relationships with bacteria, fungi, and other plants that are highly sophisticated. Bacteria form colonies on roots systems and produce nitrogen nodules, which the plant can then use as a nitrogen source, something the plants cannot do on their own. And in exchange the bacteria gain nutrients they need to survive. Roots also form close attachments with fungal mycelia. In fact, most plant roots are part of a sophisticated root/fungus communal network that can extend over miles. The mycelia provide immune enhancing compounds and various neurochemicals for the plants again in exchange for nutrients that supports the development and immune function of the plant body and root brain, just exactly as they do in us when we take them as herbal medicines.

This highly developed mycelial/plant root system connects all the plants in a particular ecorange into one self-organized whole that, itself, possesses capacities not perceivable in any of the parts. In essence, a large, self-organized neural network develops. This leads to the emergence of a unique *identity* in every identifiable ecorange on Earth.

It is possible then, if you reclaim your capacity to feel,
to make intelligent contact with the intelligence of any ecorange
in which you are embedded
to establish rapport and deep friendship
and to learn from that relationship,
to, in fact, learn to "think like a mountain"
from the mountain itself

The emergence of self-organized ecoranges generates the potential for highly adaptable responses to environmental perturbations that might affect that ecorange. Within that system, all the plants are continually communicating with each other, sending chemical communications along the mycelial network to other plants in the community. (Plants also speak using auditory signals through a complex sound-based language that is far more ancient than the human though it exists in a much subtler sound spectrum than our own.)

a biological internet that existed long before our pale imitation

If plants in the system detect that another plant in the mycelial network is ill, unique compounds are generated by the plants most able to do so and sent through the mycelial network to where they are needed. The medicinal compounds in plants have been used for millennia to heal the individual plant, other plants in the ecorange network, and the insects and other animals that make that ecorange home. This kind of cooperation, while irritating to kill-or-be-killed reductionists, produces an ecorange much more adaptable to environmental perturbations than would occur if each organism were constantly fighting each other (as neo-Darwinists would have us believe). The old lie that Nature is Red in Tooth and Claw, that life is a constant struggle for survival in an implacably hostile environment, just doesn't bear up under close examination, Life-forms die, yes, but they also help other members of their family, and other members of their species, and the members of other species off and on throughout their lifetimes. Just as we do. As Richard Lewontin comments . . .

> *To be convinced that all behavior on the part of others, without distinction, is hostile, is a form of mental illness.*[57]

The surprising thing is that we have allowed the mental illness of the neo-Darwinians to affect all of us, and our cultures, for so long.

Within ecoranges, there is a continual exchange of information that flows as volatile chemicals through the air. These chemical exchanges are in fact a highly complex form of communication, a language, that is taken in through plant stomata, analyzed, and responded to. There is also a highly complex communication that moves through the soil community, also quite often through the release of volatiles into the immediate rhizosphere surrounding the plant roots. And many chemicals are released into the mycelial network for travel throughout the ecorange. These interactions are highly intelligent and individually generated out of each self-organized plant entity. "The underground roots are," as Baluska et al. comment, "engaged in social activities that require self-awareness."[58] Like bacteria, plants form social communities that are tightly coupled together. And similarly to bacteria, plants

> *show just the same sorts of complex and sophisticated behaviors that*

humans do, from language, to sentience, to intelligence, to the cre-
ation of cities, to cooperation in groups, to complex adaptation to
their environment, to protection of offspring, to species memory that
is handed down through the generations. And, if the definition of
tool is extended, as it should be, to the creation of chemicals that
are designed to produce specific impacts on environment, their
capacities include intelligent tool making.

Older plants send out volatiles to younger plants that contain within them information about chemical responses to predation. A bean plant, being fed upon by a spider mite, can analyze from its saliva just what type of spider mite is feeding on it. It then will craft a specific phero-mone, releasing it from its leaf stomata as a volatile chemical into the air. That pheromone will call to the plant the *exact* predator that feeds on that particular spider mite. Older plants store this information as a kind of cultural learning that is then passed on to younger generations. Old growth plants are repositories of the acquired learning of the species. Cultural learning and transmission is, in reality, common throughout the Gaian system. Chimpanzees teach their young to collect termites with a stick, and how to make the stick.

Which is harder than it sounds; the stick must be shaped exactly.
Scientists who tried to do so, failed . . .
continuously

Cultural memory among all nonhuman species is a crucial element of ecosystem functioning and health. As Michael Crichton comments, "Animals raised in isolation, without parents, without guidance, were not fully functional. Zoo animals frequently could not care for their offspring, because they had never seen it done. They would ignore their infants, or roll over and crush them, or simply become annoyed with them and kill them. . . . Adapative behavior was a kind of morality; it was behavior that had evolved over many generations because it was found to succeed—behavior that allowed members of the species to cooperate, to live together, to hunt, to raise young."[59]

The recognition that the accumulated learning of generations is passed on by the current members of *every* self-organized biological system to offspring is deeply uncomfortable to those who believe that cultural memory is nonexistent in organisms other than the human. It confronts a common and deeply held belief in human exceptionalism. Nevertheless, moths in South American jungle habitats have been found to pass on cultural learning to their offspring. So have bacteria. So have plants. That we do so is only a specific instance of a general condition.

The killing of mature members of any species leads to a reduction not only in biomass and species density and diversity but also in that species' accumulated knowledge of how to most efficiently fill its ecological niche and interact with the rest of the ecosystem around it. The accumulated wisdom of the species is severely reduced or, sometimes, even lost in the process.

Thus the tremendous loss of human languages around the globe that were generated out of thousands of generations of human interaction with specific habitats by unique groups and which encode unique understandings of ecosystem functioning is a tragedy greater than we yet know.

And this accumulated wisdom of individual species (and ecosystems) is essential for the maintenance of Earth homeodynamis. For example, plants, as do bacteria, will teach other species of plants—that do not yet know how—how to resist specific herbivores that are feeding on them. *Artemisia tridenta* plants have been found to teach neighboring tomato plants how to resist foraging herbivores by showing them how to increase the accumulation of proteinase inhibitors in their leaves. They, as well, have been found to teach wild tobacco, *Nicotiana attenuata,* how to increase production of various plant chemicals such as methyl jasmonate to slow herbivore predation.

These extensive social communities of plants, these self-organized ecoranges, do not exist in isolation. The vast interlocking series of ecoranges across the Earth themselves communicate with one another, just as plants within a single ecorange communicate with each other. They *coevolve.* As Michael Crichton once put it . . .

By the twenty-first century, it was clear that coevolution wasn't limited to paired creatures in some isolated spinning dance. There were coevolutionary patterns with three, ten, or n life-forms, where n could be any number at all. . . . The outcome of this complex interaction was always changing, always evolving. And it was inherently unpredictable.[60]

The boundaries of these ecoranges, by the way, like the boundaries of all self-organized systems, are very porous. There is a constant flow of energy, and information, into and out of them. They are all tightly interwoven into the larger ecosystem of the Earth itself. Each acts locally, each acts globally. They are part of a highly complex and redundant system for maintaining the homeodynamis of the Earth. They develop more complexity over time, for the greater the complexity, the greater the ability to maintain homeodynamis.

Killing off mature ecosystems results in the loss of cultural learning among the world's ecosystem communities. Or as Albert Einstein once observed, "Technological progress is like an axe in the hands of a pathological criminal."

And they reproduce . . . just as the smaller self-organized systems we know of as life-forms do. As Lenton and Williams note, "Although reproduction of an ecosystem is clearly less faithful in its replication than reproduction of an organism, there is still enough short-term heritability of collective environment-improving properties for communities with them to spread across the global system."[61]

The world is made up of a series of nested self-organized systems within other nested self-organized systems within other self-organized systems. They, together, make up the much larger system we know as Earth, the living, self-organized biological organism that James Lovelock named Gaia. And all of them are intelligent.

6

GAIA AND "THE PATTERN THAT CONNECTS"

In the human spirit, as in the universe, nothing is higher or lower; everything has equal rights to a common center which manifests its hidden existence precisely through this harmonic relationship between every part and itself.

GOETHE

Bacteria are Gaia theory's fundamental actants, and through symbiosis and symbiogenesis, connect life and matter in biophysical and biosocial entanglements. Emphasizing symbiosis might invoke the expectation of a re-inscription of the human insofar as the ubiquitous interconnectivity of life ultimately connects everything to the human. I want to argue toward the opposite conclusion: that bacterial liveliness suggests a profound indifference to human life. As such, symbiosis does not efface difference, nor its vigorous refusal to be absorbed within human formulations of world-remaking, including environmental change. Bacterial indifference's radical asymmetry suggests the need for non-human centered theories of globality.

MYRA HIRD

A proper understanding of the Earth requires the abolition of disciplinary boundaries.

JAMES LOVELOCK

All reality is political, but not all politics is human.

GRAHAM HARMON

The Gaia theory has found such powerful purchase in the human world because it reminds us of something many of us intuitively know to be true (and which every four-year-old child understands): that the world is alive, intelligent, aware, communicative, and filled with soul; that we are not alone; that we are part of something much larger than ourselves; that we are companioned by millions upon millions of related life-forms; and that the dead, mechanical world we have been taught about in school does not exist . . . and never has. It restores a crucial dimension to human life, and human habitation of this planet.

As well, it alters human relationship to the whole. We become, in that moment of understanding, no longer exceptional, no longer special, no longer the most important species on the planet. We become just the same as everything else on Earth, no different from a plant or a bacterium, possessed of certain attributes and skills, with a unique ecological function—just as every life-form has—but not the crown of creation, never destined to rule the universe, never again to hold the hubristic position as the height of evolutionary development—the first moment the Universe (or the Earth) became conscious of itself. Or as Lynn Margulis once put it . . .

> *Perhaps the greatest stumbling block in the way of widespread acceptance of Gaia is the implicit shadow of doubt it throws over the concept of the uniqueness of humanity in nature. Gaia denies the sanctity of human attributes. If intricate planning, for instance, can be mimicked by cunning arrays of subvisible entities, what is so special about* Homo sapiens *and our most prized congenital possession, the human intellect? The Gaian answer to this is probably that nothing is so very special about the human species or mind. Indeed recent research points suggestively to the possibility that the*

physical capacities of the brain may be a special case of symbiosis among modified bacteria.[1]

And this is perhaps why it has been so bitterly resisted and attacked by so many scientists, why so many have tried so hard to shove Gaia into the room, lock the door behind her back, and turn on the gas. As one scientist once said to the founder of Gaia theory, James Lovelock . . .

> *Gentlemen! We are here to discuss serious science,*
> *not fairy stories about a Greek Goddess.*[2]

But as Lovelock comments in response . . .

> *We [as scientists] had become so used to thinking in terms of cause and effect that we no longer seemed to realize that the whole could be more than the sum of its parts. . . . The Earth self regulates its climate and chemistry so as to keep itself habitable and it is this that is the sticking point for many, if not most, scientists. Such a conclusion could never have come from reductionist thinking, and that is why arguments with biologists and others over Gaia have been so acrimonious for so long. The fact that reductionist science cannot offer a rational explanation for quantum phenomena like entanglement, nor of whole systems phenomena such as emergence, does not mean that these phenomena do not exist. Their existence confirms the limits of the Cartesian view of the universe. . . . Eminent representatives of the Earth and Life sciences secure in their disciplines ignored the fact that organisms massively alter their environment as well as adapting to it, and they did not see the evolution of the organisms and the evolution of their environment as a single coupled process. . . . I know it is unrealistic to expect them to welcome a theory like Gaia, which not only asks them to join together as if married but also to take a vow to believe in the phenomena of emergence.*[3]

Or as Richard Lewontin once put it, "Biologists suffer from a bad case of physics envy." It is hard to give up being special, to realize the extent of personal ignorance—and to realize that such ignorance can never be altered. Irrespective of how much we work at it, we will never understand all there is to know about the universe or this planet. We are children counting grains of sand at the seashore—and we will never be anything else. The impact of that realization forces a deep humility. There is nothing the arrogant hate more. As Michael Crichton, in his book *The Lost World*, once put it . . .

> *They maintained that arrogance, he knew, by resolutely ignoring the history of science as a way of thought. Scientists pretended that history didn't matter, because the errors of the past were now corrected by modern discoveries. But of course their forebears had believed exactly the same thing in the past, too. They had been wrong then. And modern scientists were wrong now. No episode of science history had proved it better than the way dinosaurs had been portrayed over the decades. . . . Because the Victorians believed in the inevitability of progress, they insisted that the dinosaurs must necessarily be inferior—why else would they be extinct? So the Victorians made them fat, lethargic, and dumb—big dopes from the past. This perception was elaborated, so that by the early twentieth century, dinosaurs had become so weak they could not support their own weight. Apatosaurs had to stand belly-deep in water or they would crush their own legs. The whole conception of the ancient world was suffused with these ideas of weak, stupid, slow animals.*[4]

That kind of thinking is still being applied to bacteria . . . and to plants . . . and, well, to nearly every life-form except Ph.D.s. (And at that, Ph.D.s in the Western world; the ones from Nigeria—bless their hearts!—just aren't very good.) It is a common projection applied to nearly every part of the natural world. *They* are stupid; *we* are not. *They* are lower on the evolutionary pyramid; *we* are more evolved. *They* are at the effect of mechanical processes they do not understand; *we* stand outside those processes and, unlike them, can manipulate the laws of matter and universe as we choose, creating our environment as we see fit.

they're called specialists
'cause they're so darn special

Despite this, the future belongs to those who understand the implications of Gaia theory, and who are willing to embrace it. For those who are willing to be humbled, who don't mind, such humbling opens the doors of perception onto a world that is much different from most scientists will admit. For as Frank Herbert once put it, "The mystery of life is not a problem to solve but a reality to experience."[5] And the experience of that reality is not limited to those with advanced degrees, as their possessors so often maintain; quite the contrary, it is the birthright of every human being on this planet.

and that, most definitely, includes you

LUCA

For nearly the entire history of life on this planet, 85 percent of that history in fact, life consisted solely of microorganisms. The last universal common ancestor (LUCA) for every life-form on this planet was bacterial. Again: The last universal *common* ancestor for *every* life-form on this planet was bacterial.

monkeys are the least part of the conceptual problem

In fact, every life-form we see—again, *every* life-form, including you and me—is simply a modification of bacteria in a more complex form. We are complex innovations of the bacterial communities of the Earth extended over very long time lines. And we really aren't that important, in spite of how numerous we appear to be. We are only a *tiny* part of the biomass of the planet. While plants make up over 90 percent of that biomass by weight, bacteria are still the dominant, and most numerous, life-forms. There are some 5×10^{30} bacteria on this Earth. That is 50 followed by 30 zeros (nine zeros is a billion, to put it in perspective). Another 5×10^{18} continually circulate in the atmosphere. And that bacterial biomass? It is *fundamental* to Earth. Gaia would not exist without it. As microbiologist Carl Woese puts it, "If you wiped out all multi-cellular life-forms off the face of the earth, microbial life might shift a tiny bit. . . . If microbial life were to disappear, that would be it—instant death for the planet."[6]

The Gaian ecosystem, the self-organized system that we know as Earth, came into being with the emergence of the global bacterial community. That bacterial community still is the foundation of this world. It *is* Gaia. It is the interconnected network of millions of bacterial biofilms, individual bacteria, and symbiogenic, bacterially generated, complex life-forms that lies deep within the crust of the Earth (perhaps by as much as 5 kilometers), covers the entire surface of the planet, and extends at least 50 kilometers above the Earth's surface.

The Earth itself is around 4.5 billion years old but sometime in its first half to one billion years of existence bacterial life emerged.

> *The numbers these guys sling around? They sound impressive,*
> *but they're only gross generalizations,*
> *they don't exactly know—and narrowing it down?*
> *it's like trying to get a taxonomist to definitely state*
> *the number of species in a genus . . .*
> *there's 30 or maybe 60 or for sure 89*
> *(taxonomy is a science?)*
> *so let's just say . . . it's been a right smart piece of time*

The oldest human-discovered fossilized bacteria (and oldest biofilms) are nearly 3.5 billion years old. And at their emergence, those self-organized bacterial groups began to modulate their environment in order to facilitate their continued existence—just as all life does. Eventually those bacterial colonies

> *the earliest ecoranges on the planet*

spread throughout the entire world, eventually coming together as one tremendous superorganism. As researchers Sonnea and Mathieu put it, bacteria came to "form one global, exceedingly diversified, yet functionally unified peculiar being."[7]

Once that self-organized system emerged, it began to modulate the environment at a global scale in order to keep its self-organized state intact. It began to function at a level of complexity impossible for the linear mind to grasp. As Michael Crichton (yes, I do quote him a lot—he's fun) once put it . . .

> *Do you realize the limits of our understanding? Mathematically, we can describe two things interacting, like two planets in space. Three things interacting—three planets in space—well, that becomes a problem. Four or five things interacting, we can't really do it. And inside the cell, there's* one hundred thousand *things interacting.*[8]

That's just one cell; there are more cells interacting on this planet than can be counted. The complexity that occurs during self-organization of a biological system—on any scale, from cell to planet—can never be understood with linear thinking *or* reductive approaches. The great Japanese farmer Masanobu Fukuoka captured this understanding when he said that

> *The causal relationship between factors in nature are just too entangled for man to unravel through research and analysis. Perhaps science succeeds in advancing one slow step at a time, but because it does so while groping in total darkness along a road without end, it is unable to know the real truth of things. This is why scientists are pleased with partial explications and see nothing wrong with pointing a finger and proclaiming this to be the cause and that the effect.*
>
> *The more research progresses, the larger the body of scholarly data grows. The antecedent causes of causes increase in number and depth, becoming incredibly complex, such that, far from unraveling the tangled web of cause and effect, science succeeds only in explaining in ever greater detail each of the bends and kinks in the individual threads. There being infinite causes for an event or action, there are infinite solutions as well, and these together deepen and broaden to infinite complexity.*[9]

He deeply understood that Nature was nonlinear, a self-organized complexity that could not be grasped or understood through reductionism. Such a Newtonian framework works best, and perhaps only, with billiard balls.

which we aren't . . . and neither is that plant

There are webs of complexity that tie everything together, and they are more numerous than the stars in the night sky. At the moment of self-organization of the bacterial membrane, complex feedback loops, both interoceptive and exteroceptive, immediately formed. Information from both locations began traveling in a huge, never-ending river composed of trillions upon trillions of bytes of data to the self-organized, more-than-the-sum-of-the-parts living system that had come into being. The system began, in that instant of self-organization, to modulate both its interior and exterior worlds in order to maintain its state. It began to modulate its environment.

Some of the earliest self-organized systems that formed after bacteria were the bacterial biofilms.

essentially small clusters of bacteria who live together

These occurred throughout the world, and later, as the colonies grew larger, they merged together to create the biosphere. Biofilms, when closely examined, are, in essence, three-dimensional physical structures—a type of bacterial city. They are created by single or multiple bacterial species, and allow the bacteria to more easily regulate their environment, moving it toward what is optimum for their survival, much the same as our cities do for us. From one perspective, the biosphere can be understood as a complex three-dimensional biofilm that extends from deep in the Earth to the edges of space. That Gaian biofilm continually regulates the environment of the Earth; it is, for instance, what keeps the oxygen content of the atmosphere at 21 percent. Oxygen, a highly reactive gas, will, when left to its own devices, combine with other elements to achieve a stable state, but on this planet, it does not. It was that insight that began James Lovelock's understanding that the Earth is a self-organized system regulating its own environment. In spite of reductionists' discomfort, such regulation has been found to occur anytime a living, self-organized system emerges. As Williams and Lenton comment about such systems, "the environment is consistently regulated to habitable conditions, even in the face of severe external perturbations."[10]

Once such a tightly coupled, three dimensional self-organized system forms,

beginning let's say at the bacterial level

it, *always,* begins to regulate its environment. Over time it begins to innovate; it acts to create more complex forms

such as biofilms

to better stabilize its self-organized state, to better regulate its environment. And there is a good reason for this: With increasing complexity of the system, as Timothy Lenton and Hywel Williams note, comes "a marked increase in robustness against extinction."[11]

The self-organized bacterial membrane that is Gaia has constantly, over very long time lines, increased the complexity of its structure in order to stabilize itself and to more effectively deal with perturbations to the system. This increase in complexity includes the generation of millions upon millions of complex forms of life, all with complex behaviors, all tied together through webs of connection and relationship. All an irremovable part of the web of life. All of them a part of Gaia, all of them Gaia in one form or another.

And what the Gaian system develops during one period of time to enhance stability, it then utilizes later, in other innovated complexities. As Gregory Bateson put it . . .

Every evolutionary step is an addition of information to an already existing system.[12]

All life-forms are a kind of living information, transforms, as Bateson put it, of messages. Not, by any means, actors against a static background. But rather, information added to an already extant and very complex information system. There is, in consequence, a pattern that connects each part to each other and to the whole. A pattern that runs through everything that Gaia has done. As Frank Herbert noted . . .

> *There is in all things a pattern that is part of our universe. It has symmetry, elegance, and grace—those qualities you find always in that which the true artist captures. You can find it in the turning of the seasons, in the way sand trails along a ridge, in the branch clusters of the creosote bush or the patterns of its leaves.*[13]

The original neural networks that are present in all bacteria and their communities have been expanded in both shape and extent over long time lines. All the living self-organized systems that we know of as life-forms contain neural networks based on the original bacterial network that emerged. And the neurochemicals that bacteria originally developed have been refined over long time lines and are now used by virtually every life-form that exists.

> *Our neural network is only a modification*
> *of an already extant neural reality*
> *that pervades the entire Earth ecosystem;*
> *it is only a specific instance of a general condition*

This expansion of the neural net, in multiple forms, all interconnected, facilitates the intake and processing of environmental information at ever more sophisticated levels for the Gaian network as a whole. Each self-organized system, that is, each subset of the larger whole, possesses a drive to fulfill its ecological function within the whole, and each possesses a sophisticated neural network with which it gathers data about the local environment in which it exists. Each also possesses free will as to how it accomplishes its function and how it responds to environmental perturbations. Gaia does not use top-down control over the parts that make up the whole.

> *that approach is the least adaptable and least functional of all*

The parts are relied upon to use their own analyses and choices as to how to respond, in essence, giving Gaia a network of trillions upon trillions of neural networks all working in their own sphere to help maintain Gaian homeodynamis.

and all utilizing their own inherent genius to do so

In the face of this, our science, our mentation, our civilization are, none of them, particularly brilliant or unique or in any way special. We haven't really done that much.

Just think of the *time* and innovation involved so far . . . think, as only one example, of the tremendous innovation in bacterial *shape* that has occurred in the billions of years since the Gaian system formed.

It took a half *billion* or more years for life to emerge; a *billion* years later the earliest forms of blue-green algae (which are actually bacteria) and simple fungi were generated. The first sponge-like animals emerged 650 million years ago, land plants about 500 million years ago, the first land animals 400 million years ago. The earliest human ancestors only three million years ago,

human beings as we know them now emerged only 35,000 years ago,
human "civilization" only four thousand years ago.
(Or maybe it's seven thousand, scientists aren't sure—
they found some old cheese pots recently . . .)
We are babies; we've just arrived.
It would be amusing really, when scientists,
with a life span of 80 years,
look at the Earth and pronounce it not alive
because it does not fit into their preconceptions
if it weren't so dangerous

Symbiogenesis

All the complex life-forms that we see were formed through symbiogenesis, a term coined by the person who first recognized its existence, Lynn Margulis.

Symbiogenesis is the formation of more complex life-forms from the union of two dissimilar, simpler ones. The mitochondria in our cells, that power our metabolism, were formerly free living bacteria, as are the chloroplasts that power those of plants. All complex life-forms are generated through just this kind of cooperative joining, over long evolutionary time, with information built upon information, complexity always increasing in order to more fully stabilize the system. And all such symbiogenic joinings produce life-forms that are not only more complex but whose capacities cannot be predicted from a study of the parts that joined together. As Myra Hird puts it . . .

Symbiosis entails the unfathomably messy entanglements that constitute temporal assemblages that sometimes emerge as symbiogenetic singularities.[14]

That is a particularly brilliant, if complex, phrase, no word unnecessary, yet a perfect description of the phenomena we know as life-forms. "Unfathomably messy entanglements." "Temporal assemblages." "Symbiogenetic singularities." "Hard to read at one go."

But symbiogenesis? It has upset a lot of people. Most especially those who believe that

Martha!

slowly we turned, and step by step we dragged ourselves up out of the primordial ooze, until we arrived at the pinnacle of our greatness. Nevertheless, we are just complex forms of bacteria, part of a complex self-organized bacterial biosphere. Thus philosopher Keith Pearson, most rightly, describes symbiogenesis as the "filthy lesson" of our true connection with the natural world. He observes, in his understated way, that it "continues to play a subversive role in biology since it challenges the boundaries of the organism."[15] And such challenges just don't stop; our boundaries are extremely porous. Viruses, for instance, perform a really irritating function of intermingling the DNA from every species on Earth with every other. As Richard Lewontin puts it . . .

> *It used to be thought that new functions had to arise by mutations of the genes already possessed by a species and that the only way such mutations could spread was by the normal processes of repro-duction. It is now clear that genetic material has moved during evolution from species to species by means of retroviruses and other transposable particles. . . . What is so extraordinary in its implica-tions for evolution is that transposition can occur between forms of life that are quite different, between distantly related vertebrates, for example, or even between plants and bacteria. . . . Thus, the assumption that species are on independent evolutionary pathways, once they have diverged from each other and can no longer inter-breed, is incorrect. All life-forms are in potential genetic contact and genetic exchanges between them are going on. . . . The evolu-tionary "tree of life" seems the wrong metaphor. Perhaps we should think of it as an elaborate bit of macramé.*[16]

Horizontal gene transfer between all life-forms on this planet, often through mosquito bites which transmit viruses in and out of organisms, is, along with symbiogenesis, one of the main driving forces in genetic innovation. We contain within ourselves the DNA of plants, insects, and bacteria, and viruses. We are, in fact, the "other" that we have been try-ing to kill. There isn't, ultimately, any truly separate species; there isn't, ultimately, any pure bloodline of any sort any place on this planet.

For most people, the recognition that we are at root simply bacte-ria, morphed through symbiogenesis into a more complex form in order to fulfill stabilizing functions within the self-organized Earth ecosystem, truly is a filthy lesson.

> *This is the redwood forest?*
> *But it's so dirty.*

It undermines any claim to specialness on our part; it simply makes us one of the many, held to the same constraints as any life-form on the planet. It undermines not only the human specialness articulated in many religions but also the belief in our specialness that permeates all Western science. As Lovelock puts it, "The entire range of living matter on Earth, from whales to viruses, and from oaks to algae, could be regarded as constituting a single living entity, capable of maintaining the Earth's atmosphere to suit its overall needs and endowed with faculties and powers far beyond those of its constituent parts."[17]

"A single living entity?" (That would include us as a subpart.) "Faculties and powers far beyond those of its constituent parts?" (That would indicate, of course, that we, as subpart, have capacities far less than that of Gaia. In other words that our capacity for thinking is exceeded by something nonhuman.) It is no wonder it has upset so many. In essence, a superorganism has emerged as a self-organized whole and that really is what the biosphere is. Lynn Margulis, as Myra Hird notes, has commented that "the biosphere as superorganism arises as an emergent property of complex symbiotic durations."[18] And it just sort of happened—all at once when critical mass was reached—water into ice, a phase change.

Margulis adopted the term "autopoiesis" to describe that phase change. It means: "self-making." As Margulis puts it, autopoiesis is the "autonomous organization of dynamic processes occurring within a closed operational whole."[19] In other words, it is the spontaneous appearance of a self-organized entity possessing emergent behaviors. And *everything* within that self-organized system, every "part" (yes, including us), is *allopoietic,* that is subordinated to the homeodynamis-maintaining goals of the autopoietic whole that came into being at the moment of self-organization. And, as with all self-organized systems, intelligence, awareness, the search for meaning, and the capacity for innovation in behavior is inherent in the system and every part of it. Or as biologists Humberto Maturana and Francisco Varela put it, autopoietic organisms "have individuality: that is, by keeping their organization as an invariant through its continuous production they actively maintain an identity that is independent of their interactions with an observer."[20]

"An identity that is independent of their interactions with an observer." Hmmm, there are implications in that line . . .

What has been important over the long evolutionary time lines, and still is, is not any particular organism or any particular period of life expression or any particular form life on this planet takes or has ever taken, but simply the continuance of the self-organized system itself. The *form* it takes is irrelevant to the system, the only crucial foundational aspect is continued self-organization. The various forms that have emerged over the lifetime of Gaia are innovations designed to maintain homeodynamis and to carry out the ecological functions that help it to do so. There has been, in fact, a great unfolding and movement of forms across long time lines. They appear and disappear and then still others emerge as message-material expressions of new complexities of information. All of them have been, and are, integral to the continued self-organization of the whole. And all of them are still immanent, still present in the great Ocean of Being that the self-organized Gaian system draws new form out of. But, as Masanobu Fukuoka says it . . .

> *only a few intermediate species remain afloat, with the great majority disappearing under the surface of the sea. . . . [A]ll organisms are continuous on the ocean floor, but these are not visible to man, who sees only islands floating above the waters.*[21]

All forms that have been still are and all that will be already exist in the Ocean of Being, underneath the surface of the waters that we spend so much of our time looking at. These forms are continually drawn into being in physical space to serve specific function. They merge back into that Ocean when they are no longer needed to do so. All are part of the continual exploration of Gaia into unique forms of homeodynamic balance that circumstances demand. Increasing complexity is part of it. The increasing complexity in the system serves the needs of the larger organism and increases its capacity to respond to perturbations of its homeodynamis. Or as Timothy Lenton puts it, there is an "innate tendency for regulatory properties to accumulate and strengthen as the biota evolves."[22] In this process, any particular organism that emerges out of the self-organized matrix of the Earth system does so for particular reasons at a particular time. Those reasons will not always exist, nor will that particular species.

Myra Hird makes the point that the real impact of this recognition is the realization that *humans are not the central players in climate (or any other bio-spheric) regulation. . . . Gaia theory's key insight here is the indif-ference of nonhuman life to human life; in other words, humanity's utter dependence upon, and vulnerability to, nonhuman life and nonlife.*[23]

Our view of the world as a static backdrop to human activity has obscured the fact that we are only minor players in the scheme of things. The vast majority of interactions that occur here have nothing to do with human beings, as Hird notes, "Humans do not even *know* about the vast majority of intra-actions that take place on Earth."[24] Plant intelligence, microbial memory and culture, viral swarm behavior and horizontal gene transfer, the capacity of animals (and slime mold) for mathematical com-putation are only tiny bits of the "vast majority" that remains unknown to most people, including nearly all scientists. There are so many oth-ers that exist, in numbers beyond counting. We will *never* know them all . . . for instance . . . plate tectonics, which has shaped the geography of the world, and which is widely believed to be a non-life-initiated event,

it's just physics, man

and the amount of water on the planet (*ibid*) are both generated by the bacterial superorganism of Earth, but most people don't realize it, can't comprehend it. But then, even stranger, bacterial organisms are responsible for the formation of clouds and rain. Those don't "just happen" either.

Clouds, Rain, and Bioprecipitation

It's a curious fact that the numbers of microbes that can be found in water droplets that spray into the air during the movement of ocean waves is considerably higher than the microbe concentration in the surface waters from which they come. It turns out, unsurprisingly, that this is not just happenstance. In fact, the ocean spray which is made up of those the droplets, and the waves that create them, are generated by living organisms.

Surface plankton and microalgae absorb a great deal of sunlight and this has the effect of warming the water around them. As the waters warm, the heat is transferred rather quickly, and continually, to the air above.

> *You can see the shimmer of heat waves rising up off the surface of the ocean as this occurs, just as you can see it rising from an asphalt road on a hot summer's day.*

These form the continual thermal columns that rise upward from the plankton and microalgae mats on the surface of the ocean on a sunny day. A unique gas, dimethyl sulphide (DMS)—a waste product of various types of marine algae—

> *in essence . . . plant farts*

is emitted as well, merging into the thermal columns, creating an even stronger thermal mass of rising air. As the thermals rise they pull more air up with them, just like a fire in a fireplace. This increases the intensity of the thermals which begins to generate winds, that is, the pulling of more and more air from across the surface of the sea toward the thermals. As the winds increase waves begin to form. Once the wind reaches a high enough speed (20 km/hr or so) white caps begin. The "foam" or bubbles in the white caps concentrate planktonic microbes (microalgae and the bacteria that live on them) within the bubbles. When the bubbles break as the waves curl over and spill back onto the surface of the sea, tiny droplets filled with bacteria and microalgae are thrown into the air. These droplets are caught in the thermal updrafts and are carried high into the stratosphere. These billions upon billions of tiny water droplets coalesce together to form clouds.

> *As the heat from the sun increases, the algae and plankton reproduce in greater numbers, thus absorbing more heat and producing, as well, more DMS, thus creating even stronger thermals. And these generate even more cloud formation and, in consequence, reflect more sunlight back into space, helping to cool the planet, stop its overheating. Gaia not only regulates its oxygen levels but also its temperature—and has for a very long time.*

And those bacteria, held within the droplets? They act as ice-nucleating agents. It turns out that the bacteria that live on microalgae and travel high in the atmosphere on the microalgae and plankton thermals are exceptionally good nucleating agents. Ice-nucleating agents promote the formation of ice crystals around themselves.

Which is why they are called ice-nucleating agents

And this is what creates the rain that is an essential part of life on this planet. Any tiny object (dust, for instance) in a cloud formation can act as an ice-nucleating agent. But bacteria are especially good at this. They form ice at much higher temperatures, as high as 50 degrees Fahrenheit. That is because these particular bacteria have a unique protein on their outer membrane that will catalyze the freezing of water at much higher temperatures. They are in fact the most active and efficient naturally occurring ice-nucleating agents known.

Once ice crystals form around the bacteria, the crystals themselves cause the formation of more ice, in the process making bigger particles. Once they attain enough weight, they become too heavy to remain in the cloud and begin to fall, pulling more and more water droplets to their surfaces—which also freeze—as they move downward through the cloud. (Thus, hail.) One the droplets get close enough to the Earth, they warm, the ice melts, and it begins to rain.

There are phenomena known as atmospheric rivers, that is, narrow bands of water vapor a mile above the ocean, that extend for thousands of miles. They exist, much like rivers on the land or rivers that flow through the oceans, carrying water and life over long distances. Occasionally, they begin to pour onto the land beneath them. In 1861 they poured onto California causing rains that lasted for 43 days. The Central Valley turned into an inland sea 300 miles long and 20 miles wide. (And this can happen again, anytime.)

In a tremendously ancient coevolutionary relationship, microalgae create the thermal columns and the bacteria generate ice nucleation which brings them both back to Earth—far from their point of origin—where they can reproduce and spread their unique form of life.

A similar process occurs over land masses. The sun's heat is absorbed by the soil and rocks and the plants, which also generates thermals. The plants, and in very large quantities, the trees, breathe out moisture-laden air through their stomata. And that moisture-laden air flows upward on the thermals, carrying bacteria that have hitched rides on pollen, fungi spores, and dust grains. But this gets even more interesting when you look at the actions of fungi (and leaf molds) in the process.

In the Amazon rain forests the fungi, as they release spores, also release a spray of potassium-rich fluid. This fluid, and the fungal spores, rise on the thermals high into the atmosphere. Potassium is particularly attractive to carbon compounds; they cling to the molecules, forming carbon-clumps. These act as particularly good ice-nucleating agents creating, once again, rain—in exactly the same way that the bacteria from oceans do. Unsurprisingly, the molds and fungi in forest ecosystems release their spores and fluids just when thermals are most likely to carry them up.

The rain forests, and their biocommunity, in a tightly interconnected coevolutionary relationship with bacteria, and fungi, and pollen, make their own rain but they also make the clouds that help keep the planet cool. Clear-cutting the forest is also clear-cutting the sky. It is one of the main causes of desertification. It's why the Nile region, once lush, is now a desert.

> *Forests are a great deal more complex in their ecological functions and intelligence than almost anyone understands. Many pine forests, for example, create the wildfires that they need in order to propagate and which also act to reduce the encroachment of other tree species. A static charge builds up as the wind flows through their needles and when it is large enough, they release it much the way we do when we rub our feet on a rug and then touch a door knob. We see so little of what is really happening around us. Newton's vision has blinded us to the complexities of the world in which we live.*

The bacteria (and fungi) first create clouds, then rain, which brings them (and the fungal spores) back to Earth far from their original start-ing point. They use the process for dispersal, to support their reproduc-tion and movement into other locations, much the same way that pollen grains are dispersed by wind to pollinate, and propagate, plants. As the rain falls over landmasses, it washes the leaves of the plants clean, allow-ing the bacteria (and leaf mold) a better foothold in the plant leaves, where they again feed and reproduce, before their descendants once again rise into the air to make more clouds.

> *Studies have found that human reductions in the diverse plant pop-ulations that normally occur in healthy ecosystems can reduce the unique bacterial populations that grow on those plants, ultimately reducing cloud cover and rain over that region. It is not just the rain forest that is important to rain.*

Spores, pollen, and bacteria can travel extremely large distances in this way, even across oceans. As William Hamilton and Timothy Lenton comment . . .

> *A tiny organism or group which could cause a thermal, be launched into it, and which could later help to seed its condensation so as not only to release more lofting power for its vehicle (via latent heat) but also to provide itself UV shelter and eventually to begin the aggregative condensation that may return the organism to the plan-et's surface, would be very effectively dispersed.*[25]

This kind of sophisticated dispersal allows a widespread propagation of the respective organisms in widely different habitats. In the process, clouds and rain are created which themselves have wide-ranging impacts on the habitability of Earth and every living organism that exists. And this is only one of trillions of complex homeodynamis-maintaining emer-gent behaviors that Gaia has innovated which ties in to every other part of the functioning of the Earth.

For instance

It turns out that as predation increases in the zooplankton and micro-algae that create the thermals, the propagation of the organisms—and the subsequent thermals they create—increases substantially. Just as damaged plants tend to go to seed fairly rapidly, Williams and Lenton comment, "Many fast-breeding organisms of other habitats use cues of adverse factors to initiate production of their defensive, dispersive or resting forms, or to begin other facultative changes (e.g., to induce wings in aphids)."[26] The microalgae thus increase the movement of their offspring to other locations to propagate the species whenever they are under threat.

These kinds of interactions are part of the trillions upon trillions of interactions that occur every moment of every day in the Gaian system and about which most people, including most scientists, know nothing. As Michael Crichton once put it, "The point remains. What we call nature is in fact a complex system of far greater subtlety than we are willing to accept. We make a simplified image of nature and then we botch it up. I'm no environmentalist, but you have to understand what you don't understand. How many times must the point be made? How many times must we see the evidence?"[27]

This is why the word "Gaia" is so crucial . . . it alters, by its very nature, *how* we see the world of which we are part. And that altering is also why it has been so bitterly attacked by so many scientists. As Mary Midgley notes . . .

What personification does is to attack the central, disastrous feature of the mechanistic paradigm which we have just noticed—the conviction that the physical world is inert and lifeless. It reverses the propaganda which had dramatized that idea by using machine-imagery and by fiercely denouncing alternative, more personal images such as Mother Nature. . . . Personifying the earth means that it is not just a miscellaneous heap of resources but a self-maintaining system which acts as a whole. It can therefore be injured; it is vulnerable, capable of health or sickness. And, since we are totally dependent on it, we are vulnerable too. Our deep, confident, seventeenth century conviction— expressed in a lot of space-literature—that we are really independent minds, essentially detached from a planet which we can easily exchange at any time for another one, has been a fantasy.[28]

Gaia as concept immediately confronts the idea of humans as detached observers, as independent minds, and it immediately connects each of us personally to a *feeling* sense of the world. Once something is personified—Women, Plants, Jews, Dolphins, Blacks, Mountains, or Bacteria—it is much more difficult to treat it as a thing,

as historically, depersonified, they too often have been.

They then can no longer be seen as mere matter or resources to be manipulated as desired. It is why the personification of each and every one of them has been so bitterly fought.

And no, at root it is not a patriarchal thing
it's about the accumulation of power, and it always has been
and that is a tribal human thing, one of our shadows
it's not gender, not race, not culture specific

But the personification of Gaia points our awareness in a particular direction, to a place the reductive mind cannot, does not want to, reach. It holds within it the truth that there is nothing here that can legitimately be depersonified, nothing that can accurately be turned into a thing. Truly, as Henry David Thoreau put it, *nothing is what we have taken it to be.* The Gaia theory undermines the entire foundations of Western science, including the emotive distancing that is inherent in all fields of science. It is no wonder it has generated such strong feelings in response.

The Pattern That Connects

Gregory Bateson's insight, that is, that

every evolutionary step is an addition
of information to an already existing system

is central to understanding Gaian expression. Because each foundational step is incorporated into every addition, every new innovation holds within it previous patterns. There is, in consequence, as Bateson understood, a network of patterns that runs through everything. These patterns? Any of us can perceive them . . . if we shift our perceptual orientation. Once perceived, we can train ourselves to look for them, as habit, whenever they appear, and then let them take us deeper into the depths of the world, where we can see their expression no matter where, or in what form, they arise. The physical forms that we see every day, in many respects, are only the temporal shadows cast by those patterns, patterns that run in their myriad billions through the ecosystems of the planet.

Pattern Formation

All self-organized systems, it is important to realize, learn. They also retain memories of what they learn and they innovate on those learnings. They build more complex forms and behaviors

> *behaviors are just as important as form;*
> *they are evolutionarily fundamental*

out of their past experiences in order to generate more adaptable and resilient self-organization. This is true of every allopoietic member of the Gaian self-organized system; it is true of Gaia. The process is not (generally) like the one we think of when we think of such things. It not the kind of tinkering we do with our linear, conscious minds. Self-organized systems, *including ourselves,* operate at their core exactly as Anthony Trewavas described plants as operating: "There is no unique separate response to each signal in this complex [of informational inflows] but merely a response issued from an integration of all environmental and internal information."[29] In other words, the organism takes in all the incoming data simultaneously as it occurs and integrates it as one coherent whole then crafts a response, exactly as a juggler does with his balls.

> *Editor: So, you know it's wrong,*
> *yet you continue to do it. Isn't that living in denial?*

But when you are talking about living systems—*any* living system—the level of complexity is much higher than that which occurs during juggling. The amount of incoming data includes trillions upon trillions of bits; when you are talking about Gaia the numbers are close enough to infinity as to make no difference. There is no way that linear processes could be used to generate the increasingly complex innovations on form and behavior that would stabilize homeodynamis. Top-down control here just doesn't work. Just as we cannot, with linear thinking, control the individual responses and functions of our pancreas, our liver, the analysis by our white blood cells of a pathogenic microbe (and the behaviors they generate in response), the production of red blood cells, the regeneration of nerve cells in the brain, or even something as simple as our respiration.

> *we are neither as rational nor as conscious as we like to think,*
> *nearly everything of importance that we do happens at the*
> *unconscious level*

The response of the system to incoming data may be anything from chemical release to an alteration in genomic structure. But those responses are always in support of the larger whole. Our white blood cells, for example, are self-organized living systems in their own right but they act to support the self-organized larger system that we know of as ourselves. And like all self-organized systems they have a great deal of free will in how they do that. They serve a specific ecological function, protecting our body ecology from microbial attack, and they have a range of capacities that are different from, say, those of red blood cells, but *how* they respond in each specific instance is up to them. They encounter microbes, engage in analyses of their nature, and have the capacity to choose between a variety of possible responses. This creates, as Tyler Volk brilliantly puts it, "an explosion of possibilities [that] forge a trail in the possibility space of new configurations."[30]

Bifurcations then occur

Normally, the system engages in continual micromolar adjustments to the existing state. That state, while never the same from moment to moment, is usually very similar. This is why linear approaches, over the short run, appear to work. But, sometimes, if the threat to self-organization is severe enough, if a tipping point is reached, the system responds as a whole by significantly altering its functional state in a short period of time. A phase change occurs.

> *This is what James Lovelock and others are afraid of with the current problems of human/Earth interactions. The Earth can shift its state from one where our life-form can survive to one where we cannot in a very short period of time. It's done it before.*

As Michael Crichton notes . . .

> *We have soothed ourselves into imagining sudden change as something that happens outside the normal order of things. . . . We do not conceive of sudden, radical, irrational change as built into the very fabric of existence. Yet it is. And chaos theory teaches us that straight linearity, which we have come to take for granted in everything from physics to fiction, simply does not exist. Linearity is an artificial way of viewing the world. Real life isn't a series of interconnected events occurring one after another like beads strung on a necklace. Life is actually a series of encounters in which one event may change those that follow in a wholly unpredictable, even devastating way. That's a deep truth about the structure of our universe. But, for some reason, we insist on behaving as if it were not true.*[31]

If we, however, begin using more holistic perceptual approaches—and abandon the linear—we begin to apprehend the living, nonlinear system as it is. We begin to recognize aspects of its fundamental nature, including the ubiquitous presence of patterns that have already been found to work in supporting homeodynamis. And some of these patterns? They are so fundamental that they can be found in nearly everything that exists. This are what Gregory Bateson refers to as a metapattern, which Tyler Volk defines as

> *a pattern so wide-flung that it appears throughout the spectrum of reality: in clouds, rivers, and planets; in cells, organisms, and eco-*

systems; in art, architecture, and politics. . . . as a pattern of patterns.[32]

But Volk then takes the definition much deeper, using the metaphor of a canoe. You can describe a canoe, he says, in a variety of ways, by its physicality let's say, or perhaps through what it is used for. But as he brilliantly observes . . .

> *There is a third way of responding. Rather than saying anything directly about the canoe, you describe the experience of being in a canoe, what can be seen while paddling around—perhaps creeks tumbling from forested gorges into a secluded lake. This third way of answering is the way I have chosen to present the metapatterns. This book is thus a travelogue. It contains views of reality as seen from the canoe of metapatterns. . . . [But let's extend this further] Let's say that the metapatterns are not the canoe but the lake itself. Just as the feeder streams flow into this single body of water, so too the streams from many regions of reality pour into the great reservoir of metapatterns. Perhaps the metapatterns are attractors— functional universals for forms in space, processes in time, and concepts in mind.*[33]

Feeder streams from many regions of reality, including the quantum, pour into this place that we call the world and certain patterns, metapatterns, are generated that Gaia uses in the formation of complex stabilizations. As such, these metapatterns flow throughout the world. As Volk so brilliantly observes they are *functional universals for forms in space, processes in time, and concepts in mind.* He is looking not only at the potential form self-organized systems can take but also the emergent behaviors and *most uniquely* "concepts in mind." That is, the concepts that unique neural networks generate are themselves held in potential in the Ocean of Being and are themselves expressed as a dimension of nonlinearity.

Volk begins his look at metapattern specifics with spheres. They are, as Buckminster Fuller once put it, omnidirectional, there is no up or down, right or left. In consequence, they are tremendously efficient and very strong. As Tyler Volk describes it . . .

the complex curving and interwebbing of adjacent parts of domes, eggshells, virus capsids, and buckyballs spreads any local force over the entire surface. The structural integrity intimately ties the parts to the whole.[34]

"The various domed shells of nature," he continues, "need to be stable in any direction—an egg rolling in a nest, a beetle tumbling on its back, a nut falling to earth. . . . In the icosahedral shell of a virus, the atomic bonded lattice resists both stretching and compressing. . . . A round seed with crush-resistant shell simultaneously packs the maximum mass of plant embryo. . . . Overall thinking about spheres can carry a quester to multiple levels of understanding."[35] Overall thinking about *any* metapattern you perceive can carry you to multiple levels of understanding. Once a metapattern captures your attention, you can begin to see its expression everywhere. The cellular surface of a leaf, for example, bears the same patterns as that of our skin and as that of a dragonfly's wing.

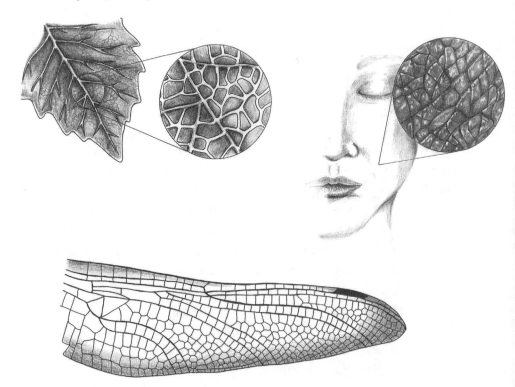

The neural network of our brain possesses the same patterns of connection as that of plant roots.

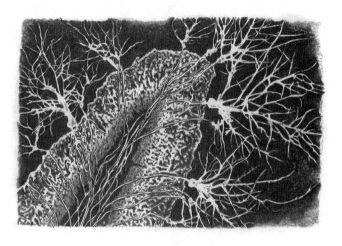

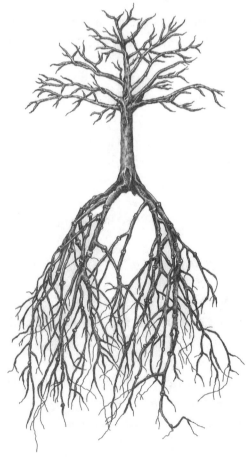

And the reproductive system of a flower and that of a human female are based on the same underlying pattern. In fact, when it comes to sex, the same patterns can be found everywhere you look.

Gaian Sex

Sexual reproduction has been happening here ever since bacteria have been—for some 3.85 billion years or so. Bacteria don't need to engage in sex to reproduce, nevertheless they often do. They exchange genes with each other (which is what sex is) and they do so irrespective of species.

> *Marriage among bacteria then does not consist of a*
> *mommy and a daddy*
> *(or even a human and a human)*

Bacteria will mate with pretty much any other bacteria at all. (Much to the dismay of Justice Scalia.) As Lynn Margulis and Dorion Sagan comment . . .

> *Bacterial life, forced into many different habitats, invented all the*
> *major forms of cellular metabolism, of which plants and animals uti-*
> *lize only a small proportion. . . . Bacteria evolved these abilities, in*
> *part, by gene donation, the world's first sex and still the most impor-*
> *tant for global ecology.*[36]

But the bacteria, over long time lines, began to innovate

> *no, no, you put the handcuffs here*

and created what Margulis calls hypersex, the symbiotic merging of two different bacteria into one unique, and very new, organism. As Margulis and Sagan describe it . . .

> *an entire bacterium enters the body of another whole bacterium*
> *and the two types live together forever. The reproduction of hyper-*
> *sexual partners led to new units in evolution: cells with nuclei*

common to all nonbacterial life—from unicellular amoebas to plants and animals with billions of such cells apiece. Some may protest that endosymbiosis is not sex. From an evolutionary point of view, however, it was even better than sex: such merged bacteria led not only to amoebas, slime molds, and paramecia, but eventually, after meiotic sex and its genders evolved, to all larger organisms, including us. . . . Indeed, animals, plants, fungi, and protoctists have hypersexuality embedded in their cellular evolutionary history.[37]

And, as they continue . . . "Transgenic bacterial sex came first, followed by hypersex. . . . Each level of sexuality coexisted with and built upon the earlier modes. Life never forgets its ancestry."[38] Again, that is an integral element of the Gaian system: each new innovation builds upon and uses prior innovations, and those generated patterns can be found in every succeeding stage of complexity. Eventually, meiotic and fertilization sex—which involved cell fusion—emerged. These were all essential preludes to the generation of gendered bodies, the Gaian innovation that split a single species into two forms. With the innovation of split genders, the male of the species contained a single set of chromosomes (sperm) and the female as well (eggs). Each possessed an embedded drive to seek the other for sex in order to recombine chromosomes.

Meiotic sex, which halves the chromosome number and then drives the organisms containing them to couple in order to recombine them, is very ancient in the Gaian system. It was common to many ancient protoctists, the ancestors to plants, animals, and fungi, and first emerged at least a billion years ago. Margulis and Sagan comment that "the most fascinating clue to the multiple origins of our kind of meiotic or reproductive sex comes from the fact that so many species of protoctists are actually induced by environmental stress to undergo sexual acts."[39] In other words, perturbations to the system stimulated a particular kind of innovation in how genes were recombined among living organisms. And whenever environmental disruption occurs, it stimulates sexual reproduction. This kind of sex has been present here for so long because it works. It's ecologically functional. Meiotic sex, Gaia discovered, increased complexity, the resistance of the system to perturbations, and survivability. And so, Gaia began to incorporate meiotic sex at greater levels of complexity as the self-organized system increased its sophistication. Margulis and Sagan comment that

> *Fusion sex, fertilization followed by meiosis, allowed beings to survive the cycles of the seasons. Sex let animals grow elaborately complex, multicellular bodies from fertile eggs. . . . Today no armadillo, gecko, or infant is born or will survive without moving through the process of meiosis, gender formation, and fertilization. The cyclical road to modern human beings requires traversal of the loop-to-loop of sex before returning to the starting point of coupled sperm and egg. . . . We are meiotic and sexual to the very core of our being.*[40]

Sex is, in fact, woven irremovably into the fabric of Gaia. Into *us*. And into the world.

> *If you are uncomfortable seeing penis and labia unconcealed in the stark light of day, if you hide this part of you among cultural and psychological confusions, refuse to see the presence of sex every place and in every thing of the Earth, you can never understand Earth, never truly act for the Earth. For those confusions will enter every act you subsequently take and spread the human confusion ever more widely. This is how unforseen consequences spread from good intent.*

All meiotic organisms, ourselves among them, are both single and double chromosomed, possessing doubled body cells and singled sex cells. Fungi, for instance, are normally single chromosomed in northern climates, but in the autumn, as the weather begins to grow colder, they become doubled. They then release half that chromosome group as spores, carried on the winds (and thermals and in rain) to new habitat where they await the spring to grow. Wind pollinated plants such as pine trees or cattails act similarly. They use wind pollination to combine single chromosome egg and sperm for the generation of offspring. But with the innovation of flowering plants, something new entered the world. Instead of the wind, pollinators carried the germ plasm from the male to the female. Not so haphazard as wind. And still, later in time, it became even more specific: animals can move and thus seek each other out, actively find their sexual partners; they don't need a pollinator. Nevertheless, the earlier, successful Gaian patterns are still there, hidden inside the new complexities.

And sex really is fundamental to system functioning. Unsurprisingly, frequent sex stimulates the formation of new neurons in neural networks, irrespective of the type or age of the organism. Sensory gating channels open more widely, cognition improves, functionality increases, homeodynamis improves. Chastity is ecologically nonfunctional.

The development of a female reproductive system that would carry half the chromosomes of the flowering plant predated the emergence of the human species by some 140 to 170 million years. Yet if you compare the plant sytem shown here

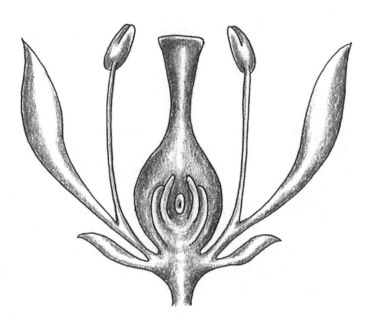

to that in human women, shown here, you will find that it is nearly identical.

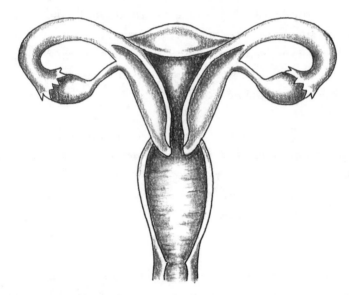

The plant female reproductive system, known to us as a flower, emerged and contained a form that would be used millennia later in human women. And once you understand that, once you know that that pattern is integral, other aspects become clear. The insight begins to "carry a quester to multiple levels of understanding." You begin to see that there is not so much difference between us and plants as we imagine. You begin to see other aspects of the pattern . . . for instance: flowers menstruate.

The are numerous functions of menstruation in human women (most things in the Gaian system perform multiple functions, it's more efficient that way) but one of them is the sterilization of the vaginal passages, the reduction of infectious bacteria that can harm the production of offspring. This is true in flowers as well. The flowers produce nectar, which the bees then collect (performing cross-pollination while they do so). The bees then take the nectar back to their hive and through complex synchrony with each other, and a great deal of wing flapping, reduce the liquid content and thicken the nectar into honey, one of the most antibacterial substances on the planet. The sugar plays a major part in its antimicrobial actions, but there are also scores of antibacterial plant compounds, secreted by the plants into the nectar, that have broad-spectrum activity. The nectar, with its sugar content, and its phytochemical antimicrobials, are extruded into the reproductive passageways of the flowers, not only to serve their coevolutionary pollinators, but to protect the passageways from infection.

Then, if you want to go further . . . look at the male and testosterone. Pine trees, some of the oldest of the wind pollinated plants, have pollen that is higher in testosterone (the chemical that has been anthropecentrically assumed to make a man a man) than any other plant known. Mammals emit semen, generated in part by testosterone, but in fact . . .

Semen is Latin
for a dormant, fertilized,
plant ovum—
a seed.
Men's ejaculate
is chemically more akin
to plant pollen.
See,
it is really
more accurate to call it
mammal pollen.

To call it
semen
is to thrust an insanity
deep inside our culture:
that men plow women
and plant their seed
when, in fact,
what they are doing
is pollinating
flowers.

Now.
Doesn't that change everything between us?[41]

And the testosterone that humans consider so important? It was here long before men. It is integral to Gaian functioning.

So, all that stuff about patriarchy?
And how it is innately antithetical to the feminine?
To the Earth itself?
It has no ecological foundation in fact.

That testosterone is so integral in the function of the human male is only because it is a specific instance of a general condition. And . . . without it, females of nearly every species, including the human, could not possess a functional physiology either. That is because at root there is very little difference in the female and male reproductive systems.

The male and female reproductive systems in humans (and all mammals) are only innovations on the same underlying form. *An archetype.* The ovaries and the testicles are the same organs, altered slightly for function. The penis and the vagina/clitoris are the same organs, altered slightly for function. The clitoris is elongated into the penis

or the penis shrunk
depending on your point of reference.

The clitorial hood becomes the foreskin. The female vagina and urethra elongate and narrow at their exterior ends and become, in men, the single urethra that travels through the penis. But deeper in the interior of the male, there are two passages still: The verumontanum—the equivalent of the vaginal passage, and the urethra which carries urine. The fallopian tubes and the ejaculatory ducts are, again, similar organs, variations on an underlying pattern. The prostate in men and the uterus in women are the same organ, simply altered to fulfill different functions.

Yes, yes, I know about the Skene's glands

The prostate and the uterus are virtually identical in size, about one by two inches. The tissues lining the prostate and the uterus also have a considerable number of similarities. Both are extremely sensitive to the same endocrine hormones and agents. This is why the herbs that can be used to help female reproductive health are also effective for men, and vice versa. The tissue dynamics are very similar in every part of the human reproductive system, male or female. The organs are not all that different, despite what we have been taught to believe.

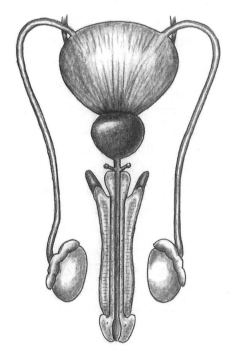

In fact, if you compare this drawing of the male reproductive system to the drawing of the female system on page 162, you can see that behind the two apparently different male and female organs lies the same underlying pattern, part of the innovation that Gaia generated for sexual reproduction. Men and women are not so different as we like to think. There are differences, of course, in the systems—and between men and women—but the similarities that exist open up vistas of understanding that reductive differentiation will never see. There is, in fact, only *one* species. Human. There are not and never have been two. We *are* the same entity, just modified slightly for gene blending.

From spores to wind pollination to pollinator pollination to animal sex, Gaia has innovated throughout her long life. To understand her means to understand that sex is ever present in the world. So much as we hide from our own sexuality, so, too, do we blind ourselves to the true nature of Earth.

> *The Protestants really did screw everything up*
> *. . . nonsexually, of course.*

The Sense of Aesthetic Unity

Patterns such as these, in their trillions, infuse life and the Earth ecosystem. Gregory Bateson referred to them not only as metapatterns but also as the Pattern That Connects. The human response to this he referred to as "the sense of aesthetic unity." In contrast to a simple *mental* recognition of the patterns that flow through the Gaian system, with the phrase "sense of aesthetic unity" something else immediately enters the equation. And that is: there a *feeling* response in the aware human to the patterns themselves. Bateson comments that

> *I was very lucky to be teaching people who were not scientists and the bias of whose minds was even antiscientific. All untrained as they were, their bias was aesthetic. I would define that word for the moment by saying that they were not like Peter Bly, the character of whom Wordsworth sang*
>
> > *A primrose by the river's brim*
> > *A yellow primrose was to him;*
> > *And it was nothing more.*
>
> *Rather, they would meet the primrose with recognition and empathy. By aesthetic, I mean responsive to the pattern which connects. So, you see, I was lucky. Perhaps by coincidence, I faced them with what was (though I knew it not) an aesthetic question:* How are you related to this creature? What pattern connects you to it?[42]

"Recognition and empathy." A sense of kindredness. The capacity to make more porous the boundary between self and other, to begin to lose the distinction between self and nonself.

Albert Einstein, too, talked about the importance of feeling, recognizing that it was only this capacity for *feeling* the patterns that could enable one to travel deeper into the metaphysical background of the world. Linear reductionism could never get there . . .

> *There is no logical way to the discovery of these elemental laws. There is only the way of intuition, which is helped by a feeling for the order lying behind appearance.*[43]

And James Lovelock, too, noted that "Gaia is an emergent phenomenon, comprehensible intuitively, but difficult or impossible to analyze by reduction."[44] To sense the pattern that connects, and to then use it to travel deep into the heart of the world, you have to have, at the root of your approach, a capacity for *feeling*. You can't get there through thinking alone. It's feeling first, thinking after.

If there's time

For as Edward de Bono put it . . .

> *Most of the mistakes in thinking are inadequacies of perception rather than mistakes of logic.*[45]

And the loss of the feeling sense creates automatically, in and of itself, an inadequacy of perception. We are *meant* to feel, *meant* to perceive at the deepest levels of our self, the touch of the world upon us. There are reasons *why* that capacity for feeling is an integral part of all living organisms. There are reasons why sensory gating, of feeling and all sensory modalities, exists. And there are reasons why mechanisms exist for sensory gating to expand, including those of the feeling sense.

The larger Gaian system generates an impulse in its organisms to *behave* in certain ways. In essence the many types of possible behavioral states inherent in the various organisms of Earth are *emergent* behaviors of the self-organized system.

And this includes the capacity for expanding gating channels

And rather than a top-down approach, the organisms themselves are left to choose their own self-generated responses to environmental perturbation based on their own, self-intuited genius. They are allowed—even stimulated—to innovate. This results in tremendous adaptability in the system as each part can intelligently create its own response to perturbations in the part of the ecosystem that is its domain. The poet Dale Pendell touched on this truth when he said . . .

How many nights now has the stream told you
this is the way to deal with obstacles[46]

There is a powerful connecting pattern, active throughout the neural networks of Gaian self-organized systems, that plays an important part in enabling that responsiveness. It is part of a larger metapattern, one the brilliant herbalist David Hoffmann calls molecular veriditas—the intelligent creation of chemicals by plants to help maintain ecosystem homeodynamis.

7
"MOLECULAR
VERIDITAS"

Evolutionarily, serotonin existed in plants even before the appearance of animals. Indeed serotonin may be tied to the evolution of life itself, particularly through the role of tryptophan, its precursor molecule.

EFRAIN AZMITIA

DNA connects all life on Earth to a common biochemical code.

KIM DAWSON

The serotonin neurons evolved from plants as a general regulatory system which responds to external stimuli to produce structural changes to meet those signals. . . . The system modifies itself to achieve the instability needed for homeostasis.

EFRAIN AZMITIA

The elegant, extremely sensitive, self-organized biological system we know of as the Earth, like all self-organized systems, exists just on the other side of the threshold of self-organization. And like all self-organized systems it is constantly faced with events that affect its homeodynamis. One of the innovations that Gaia has generated to deal with this are the neural networks that all self-organized systems possess.

Neural networks are a long-standing innovation in the Gaian system and they exist in a large variety of forms. They function to process incoming data streams and help living systems generate responses to those inputs. The more mutable the neural nets, the better able they are to respond to the never-to-be predicted environmental dynamics that all self-organized systems experience. Thus plasticity, and the capacity for the creation of new neural forms, is built into all of them—from the bacterial to the human and everything in between. As researchers Ming and Song comment . . .

> *Forty years since the initial discovery of neurogenesis in the postnatal rat hippocampus, investigators have now firmly established that active neurogenesis from neural progenitors continues throughout life in discrete portions of the central nervous system (CNS) of all mammals, including humans. . . . Adult neurogenesis represents a striking example of structural plasticity in the mature CNS environment.*[1]

Much of the human brain remains plastic (just as do portions of other neural nets such as those in plants).

> *Synaptic plasticity refers to the ability of the brain to alter its structure, either in response to substances that affect neural processing or to environmental demands, internal or external.*

That old scientific canard, prevarication, untruth, groundless belief, fabrication, lie, false report, unfounded rumor about the brain being set in its ways shortly after birth is, and always has been, in fact, inaccurate.

> *or maybe it is an accurate report about,*
> *or a general condition of,*
> *fundamentalists, irrespective of their fundament*

Nevertheless, many portions of the brain remain highly mutable throughout life. For example, the glia,

> *the delicate web of connective tissue that surrounds and holds*
> *nerve cells,*

and most particularly the astrocytes,

> *the star-shaped, most numerous, cells of the brain and spinal cord,*
> *which support the endothelial structures of the brain, provide nutri-*
> *ents to the nerves, and help repair damaged neurons,*

have very active roles in adult neurogenesis. They affect the proliferation and specification of neural progenitors as well as the migration and integration of new neurons into preexisting neural circuits in the adult brain. In essence, the *environment,* the tissue that holds the neural network, helps initiate and shape the formation of new neural structures throughout the brain and spinal cord in response to sensory inputs from the external world.

> *There is a continual, experience-driven, reorganization of the syn-*
> *aptic networks of the brain involving multiple interrelated struc-*
> *tures. Most especially: deeper experiences of the metaphysical*
> *background of the external world act as environmental inputs and*
> *change the brain's physical structure and functional organization in*
> *response. The brain is not "hard-wired"; it has no fixed circuits.*

Certain sections of the brain are especially responsive to neural restructuring, among these are the olfactory bulb, the hippocampus, and the cerebellum.

The olfactory bulb generates a variety of different types of neural progenitors that migrate and differentiate into granule and glomerular neurons. In response to expanded gating, or incoming environmental inputs of particular kinds, the plasticity and neurogenesis in the olfactory bulb escalates considerably, new neural networks forming in response.

Smell and touch are the earliest sensory modalities that Gaia inno-
vated and so are the oldest. The olfactory bulb has its roots more
deeply in the brain and smell can generate immediate organism
responses much more powerfully than sight or hearing.

In the hippocampus, synaptic plasticity and neurogenesis is critical.
The hippocampus is intimately involved in all learning and memory—
the less neurogenesis and plasticity there is, the poorer memory and
learning, the less functional adaptability of the organism to environmental demands. Within the hippocampus, numerous neurotransmitters
and neurotrophins are generated in response to environmental inputs
or expanded sensory gating channels; they are highly involved in neural
plasticity.

Neurotrophins are a group of unique molecules that promote the
survival, development, functioning, and structural relationship of neurons. Among them are nerve growth factor (NGF, a.k.a. neurotrophin-1),
brain-derived neurotrophic factor (BDNF, a.k.a. neurotrophin-2), neuro-
trophin-3 (a.k.a. NT-3), and neurotrophin-4 (a.k.a. NT-4). All of them
are highly active in the hippocampus.

NGF is strongly protective of neurons; without it they die fairly rapidly. It is especially active during embryonic development. BDNF also
supports and protects existing neurons from damage but it also stimulates the production, growth, and differentiation of new neurons and
synapses in the brain (and in the peripheral nervous system, eyes, kid-
neys, salivary glands, and the prostate).

Wait! My prostate has brain chemicals in it?
So, men actually do think with . . .

It is exceptionally active in the hippocampus, cerebral cortex, and basal
forebrain. NT-3 acts similarly to BDNF; it is a growth factor for new
neurons, supports their differentiation, as well as the formation of new
synapses. NT-4 is less understood but appears to play similar roles.

Of the many neurotransmitters that are active in the hippocampus,
one of the most crucial is 5-hydroxy-tryptamine (5-HT), also known as
serotonin. In fact, serotonin, plays multiple roles. Serotonin agonists

what a strange word, so much like agony

stimulate BDNF, and other neurotrophin, expression in the hippocampus

An agonist is the "main actor," like the pro-(t)-agonist in a story. And its root really is agony, for the pro(t)agonist is always torn by inner conflict, always opposed by the ant(i)-agonist who stands in the way of achieving heart's desire. The word comes from the ancient Greek; agonists were combatants, contenders, in the Olympic games.

and stimulates GABAergic interneurons as well. GABA (gamma-aminobutyric acid) is a major inhibitory neurotransmitter in the CNS, acting to regulate neuron excitability. GABAergic interneurons are neurons that make and release GABA into the brain and CNS. GABA is also important in temporospatial integration in hippocampus, that is, locating you in space and time.

but this is only the beginning of the story

It turns out that while neural plasticity (and sensory gating) in the various sections of the brain and CNS are modulated by multiple interacting neurotrophins and neurotransmitters (and neurotransmitter systems, including the dopaminergic, cholinergic, GABAergic, and glutamatergic systems), of all of them, by far, the most important is serotonin (5-HT).

Serotonin

The first thing to understand about serotonin and its extensive impact on neural nets is that there are a tremendous number of 5-HT (or serotonin) neuroreceptors in the brain, CNS, and throughout the body—irrespective of the life-form containing the neural net. In humans, the receptors are identified by which group they belong to. There are currently seven receptor groups known, that is 5-HT receptors 1-7 (for example, 5-HT1 or 5-HT2). There are also at least 15 serotonin receptor subtypes in the seven groups. They are designated by the addition of subletters, for instance 5-HT1a or 5-HT2b. One of the more important is the 5-HT2a receptors; they are expressed throughout the CNS near all the serotoninergic terminal-rich areas. This includes numerous regions throughout the brain, including the parietal lobe (which integrates sensory information from various sensory systems), the somatosensory cortex (located in the parietal lobe and which is the primary processing center for the sense of touch), the prefrontal cortex (which is involved in cognition, personality expression, social behavior, and decision making), the olfactory tubercle (which is connected with numerous brain regions, most especially the sensory centers that process incoming sensory data), and the apical dendrites of the pyramidal cells in the cerebral cortex, the hippocampus, and the amygdala. 5-HT2a receptors are, in fact, located every place that sensory gating occurs.

In addition to being found throughout the nervous system, 5-HT2a receptors are also expressed in platelets, the cardiovascular system, the enteric system, in mast cells, fibroblasts, on neurons in the peripheral nervous system, and in human monocytes.

In essence, 5-HT2a receptors are located in every system that touches the exterior world: the brain, which analyzes incoming sensory and other data from the exterior world; the heart, which feels the touch of the world upon it through its generated electromagnetic field; the enteric system, which ingests the external world; the immune system, which analyzes exterior contact for virulence.

More specifically: There are unique neural networks that exist in the heart (which has the sophisticated capacity to sense the meanings in every electromagnetic field that is encountered), in the enteric system (i.e., the GI tract, which allows the organism to analyze the nature of substances that are encountered without having to ingest them through sensing their electromagnetic fields), the immune system (which allows the system to analyze the nature of threats to the self-organized system and respond accordingly), and in the brain (which allows the organism to process incoming data in highly sophisticated ways). Each of these systems utilizes serotonin through extensive receptor networks to facilitate specific forms of cognition, each of which is essential to continuing system homeodynamis in human beings. Serotonin, and these kinds of receptors, are not limited to human beings however. They are ubiquitous throughout the living systems of the planet: in animals, insects, and plants. In them, they play similar roles.

For instance, in the fruit fly, *Drosophila melanogaster,* 5-HT1a, 5-HT2, and 5-HT7 receptors are all highly involved in learning and memory, especially when olfactory data is being processed. In *Manduca sexta,* the tobacco moth, serotonin (and similar) receptors process olfactory sensory data that the moth perceives through its antennae. More widely open serotonin receptor gating—caused by increased serotonin production or consumption—*increases* the sensitivity of the moth to incoming olfactory data, enhances odor discrimination, and stimulates retention and recall of the experiences. Levels of serotonin are, not surprisingly, highest at the exact times of day the moth needs to be highly attuned to odor discrimination.

> *There is a reason that neurochemicals such as serotonin*
> *and melatonin are so deeply involved in circadian rhythms.*

And in the honeybee there exists a gustatory neural network, the equivalent of the human enteric nervous system, that is highly dependent on serotonin, as well as dopamine, another important neuroactive molecule—and their receptors. As Geraldine Wright comments . . .

> *My collaborators and I recently established that the honeybee has*
> *the ability to learn to avoid odors associated with toxins in food*
> *using two independent neural pathways. In these experiments, we*
> *found that honeybees can learn to associate scents with toxins that*
> *they can pre-ingestively detect using their proboscis. This form of*
> *learning is primarily mediated by the neurotransmitter, dopamine.*

"Pre-ingestively detect," that is, without tasting. She continues . . .

> *We also found a second mechanism: bees can learn to avoid odors*
> *associated with the malaise caused by ingesting toxins. This form of*
> *learning is mediated by serotonin.*[2]

Taste-learning is mediated by the serotonin system in the bees enteric system. (This same process occurs in humans when babies first learn to crawl and begin putting objects in the mouth. Not only is the immune system learning—and growing stronger in the process—the enteric system is learning as well. It learns through this how to determine edibility without having to taste such things in the future; it is calibrating sensory intake through the enteric system's neural networks.) Other neuromodulators were found to be active in the honeybee's sensing as well, including glutamate and endocannabinoids.

> *Endocannabinoids . . . aren't those. . . ?*
> *Yes, uh huh, they sure are.*

Serotonin and 5-HT receptors in living systems are highly involved in the analysis of safety in potential foods through both electromagnetic field analysis and the sense of smell. Nematodes that lack 5-HT receptors cannot learn to avoid odors associated with the ingestion of pathogenic bacteria. Slugs, cuttlefish, mantids, and grasshoppers all use the serotonin system similarly for the processing of olfactory and gustatory data.

> *It is common in all living things, this ability to tell edibility through pre-ingestive sensing. But you can only do it if you trust your body, if you trust it to sense for you as it was meant to do. As Goethe once said, "It makes a wonderful difference if you find in the body an ally or an adversary." Distrust of the body damages the core of us.*

Serotonin and its 5-HT receptors have also been found to modulate responses to visual stimuli, including the degree of visual perception, and its interpretation across a wide range of life-forms including honeybees and fruit flies. As gating channels open more widely in response to serotonin, the amount of incoming visual data increases, visual sensitivity increases, and the cross-correlation and analysis of the larger data stream increases as well.

Serotonin also affects community/individual relationships throughout living systems. In the fruit fly, it is intimately involved in community/individual interrelating through extensive modulation of a series of serotonin receptors. Activation of 5-HT2 receptors decreases aggression and increases community cooperation while activation of 5-HT1a tends to increase aggression and reduce cooperation. This serotonergic modulation of cooperation can be seen in numerous life-forms, including crickets, crustaceans, rats, chimpanzees, humans, and, of course, desert locusts.

Desert Locust Stories

Rather than in the hippocampus, as in humans, the main sensory pathways in the locust converge in the thoracic ganglia. Sensory inputs, such as the visual and olfactory, are gated there and processed much as they are in all living systems. In locusts, however, the tendency for incoming sensory inputs—through impacts on the serotonin system and its receptors—to alter phenotype, in this instance, behavior, is extreme.

Locusts are, by nature, obsessively solitary. However, sensory inputs from the environment can, once a certain threshold is reached, stimulate a rapid change in their phenotype, causing them to become highly gregarious—to, in fact, become a swarm. They show, as researchers put it . . .

> *extreme phenotypic plasticity, transforming between a little-seen solitarious phase and the notorious swarming gregarious phase. . . . We show here that serotonin, an evolutionarily conserved mediator of neuronal plasticity, is responsible for this behavioral transformation, being both necessary if behavioral gregarization is to occur and sufficient to induce it.*[3]

The researchers comment further that the

> *behavioral gregarization in locusts requires the interpretation of complex signals from conspecifics leading to long-lasting changes in the way individuals react during future encounters. Behavioral gregarization therefore resembles memory formation, with specific sensory experiences altering future behavior, in this case of locusts. This entails a suite of changes that creates an integrated behavioral phenotype adapted to a changed biotic environment.*[4]

In other words, environmental cues, messaged through sensory inputs, generate a sophisticated modulation of the neural networks of the locusts through the activity of serotonin and its receptors, which results in a significant and immediate shift in behavior—in essence, a phase change. The beauty of this communique is that it reveals that a self-organized system, remaining close to the threshold of self-organization, modulates not only its genotype in response to altered environment (as bacteria do) but also its phenotype. In this case, the behavior of an entire species. And once it does so, the species *swarms* and begins, in that moment, to act as a unified whole, a self-organized system larger than the individual components that themselves possess a neural structure. It is like water to ice. One moment, one state, the next something completely different suddenly emerges. This stimulates, in the species as a whole, behaviors that enable its survival under changed environmental conditions. As the researchers note, "Phenotypic plasticity, the differential expression of alternative phenotypes from a single genotype depending upon environmental conditions, is of considerable evolutionary importance."[5]

Are we engaging then in a "variant" expression of human perceptual sensitivity? If so, couldn't this be viewed, in turn, as perhaps a useful evolutionary adaptation? As an age-old demographic reality, possibly hardwired into the souls of some, that actually enriches and diversifies human civilization?

Serotonin and its analogues, as so many researchers have found, are intricately involved in generating alternative behaviors in living systems in response to incoming sensory data about environmental conditions. These alternative behaviors, normally outside the habituated parameters of daily life, allow adaptive responses to changed conditions. Upon those adaptive responses rests the capacity of the species—and the Gaian system—to survive, the self-organized systems to remain intact.

Serotonin and its receptors are also deeply involved in temporal encoding, that is, an organism's sense of time, whether it appears normal speed, or very fast, or incredibly slow. This, as well, possesses adaptive functions. Perceptual framework alters with time sense alteration. During slowing, the living organism can *attend* to incoming data with greater specificity and attentiveness, in consequence increasing its ability to adapt to meanings inside incoming data streams.

Harry Anslinger, the main proponent for illegalizing marijuana in the 1920s and '30s "once wrote in a memorandum that swing had been invented by a pot-using musician, and he didn't like swing. In [Anslinger's assistant] Munch's words, the effect that the musicians were after from marijuana was a lengthening of their sense of time, so that they would be able to put more grace notes into their music than if they simply followed the written score. Munch complained that a regular musician would just play a piece of music the way it was written, but that a musician who used marijuana would work in about twice as many notes, would 'jazz' it up."[6]

Serotonin and its receptors, as they are modulated, affect CNS function and the adaptability of the organism (and the species) to environmental inputs. Neural plasticity, neurogenesis, immune function, heart function, the sense of touch (kinesthetic and non-), sexuality and reproduction, learning, memory, emotional state, sleep and dreaming, sense of self and of other, phenotype (even genotype), and the dynamics of sensory gating throughout the CNS are all affected. Cognition, that is, what you perceive and think, shifts considerably as serotonin dynamics shift. The number, function, and dynamics of 5-HT receptors throughout the whole system alter in nature and function in response to changing environmental conditions.

There are, in fact, specific environmental signals that, when they occur, stimulate the production, release, and incorporation of new neural structures and cells into existing neural nets. And many of those environmental signals act on the CNS by activating serotonin and very specific receptors in the serotonin-receptor family. In other words, the serotonin receptors in human beings respond to environmental inputs by constantly shifting their degree of activation.

And no, this is not a reductive, mechanical process where we are simply a product of our chemistry. We are engaged in a complex conversation; it's not a monologue. Most of our responses may be below the level of our conscious awareness, nevertheless it's a conversation filled with meaning. The meanings are crucial. It is not the chemical but the meaning inside it that puts the greatest pressure on the systems it touches. Our system analyzes the incoming meanings and then chooses how to respond. How we shift serotonin production and neural network structure is a choice; it is not imposed by a totalitarian, mechanically controlled world.

Shifts in the dynamics of the serotonin receptors occur throughout the system in response to inputs. 5-HT1a receptors release glial neurite extension factor, a substance which stabilizes the microtubules that form the main framework of the cytoskeleton of existing and newly forming neural cells, including neurons and astrocytes. And 5-HT2a receptors open sensory gating channels more widely in order to bring more sensory data to conscious awareness, thus allowing a greater range of behavioral response—responses outside normal habituated parameters. There is a symphony of response through the whole network which acts to modulate incoming sensory data and the response of the organism to it, including the physical form of the entire neural structure. From this view, serotonin is what some researchers call "a global factor involved in brain homeostasis."[7] Serotonin is, in many respects, the most important molecule to the function and maintenance of the neural networks in all self-organized systems.

Gaia and Serotonin

Serotonin, or 5-HT, is a very ancient molecule, first appearing eons ago in aerobic unicellular organisms. As with all Gaian innovations, future complexities of form and function built upon this early discovery.

Serotonin is one of the patterns that connect.
It is, itself, a metapattern, just as self-organization is

Bacteria use the molecule; so do all fungi, plants, insects, and animals. It is very deeply interwoven into the Gaian system and all its neural functioning. Molecularly, 5-HT has a unique ring configuration at its core, a benzene ring.

which is incredibly common in buried plant carbon,
that is, crude oil

Benzene is, in essence, an equilateral hexagon. This makes it tremendously stable and highly functional—it is very easy, as plants discovered long ago, to connect other molecular structures to it, creating variations on the theme.

*And this is why pharmaceutical companies use it
to make their drugs
all of which, by the way, are variations on plant innovations
that are millions of years old*

One of the most important innovations on the benzene hexagon is the indole ring. It is composed of a benzene ring fused to a five-sided, nitrogen-containing pyrrole ring. Basically, it's a hexagon with a pentagon stuck on the side of it. This core structure is what tryptophan, one of the most important amino acids, is generated from. Plants and microorganisms synthesize a lot of tryptophan and from tryptophan they make a lot of interesting things, among them melatonin, serotonin, and auxin. These compounds are potent agonists in the human CNS (e.g., melatonin/serotonin) and in the plant root brain (auxin/serotonin/melatonin), acting to protect and generate brain neurons and structures.

The indole ring structure, through a variety of innovative forms,

molecular veriditas

enhances bacterial, plant, and fungal neural networks, and similar networks among crustaceans, insects, and all animals, including humans. Such compounds are pervasive in the neural networks of the planet. Serotonin, for example, emerged very early in the Gaian system, as researcher Efrain Azmitia observes . . .

The reality of the situation is "neurotransmitters" predate the formation of nervous tissue. Serotonin is found in all animals, plants, and most unicellular organisms. It is synthesized from the amino acid tryptophan by the action of two enzymes, tryptophan hydroxylase and amino acid decarboxylase.

And, as it turns out, the indole ring structure from which tryptophan/serotonin is generated emerged at a crucial juncture of life on this planet. As Azmitia continues . . .

> *The creation of the indole structure served an important function in the start of aerobic life on the earth. The conversion of energy (photons) derived from the sun into biological energy requires capturing a light wave and the loss of an electron. Interestingly, the indole ring is the most efficient molecule for doing exactly this.*[8]

The indole ring structure captures light energy from the sun and converts it to biological energy, thus powering the world life system as we now know it. And, while bacteria first discovered how to do it, it is within plants that it is most crucially active, for it is plants that focus most of their time on the capture of light energy and the conversion of it into biological energy during their complex oxygen/carbon dioxide cycling. This molecule, and its pervasive use by oxygen-generating organisms, was intimately involved in the Gaian shift to an oxygen-heavy atmosphere—and thus to human emergence.

Prior to the Gaian innovation of photosynthesis, there was little free oxygen in the Earth's atmosphere. Oxygen is so highly reactive that it immediately combines with other substances. Over time, the atmosphere itself becomes inert, unreactive, as the atmospheres on Venus and Mars are.

> *It was this deep insight that led James Lovelock to understand the Earth as a living being. Something, he realized, must be keeping the oxygen levels intentionally high. The atmosphere of Earth was, in fact, being regulated and had been for a very, very long time.*

In other words, the Gaian innovation of this indole ring structure underlies the entire emergence of oxygen-utilizing organisms and the entire ecosystem that has emerged and of which they are a part. Without it, the kind of metabolism that powers most life-forms on this planet could not have occurred. One thing though . . . oxygen is a toxic, poisonous gas.

Doesn't seem to make sense, does it?

Once oxidation became the primary form of energy production on the planet, the problem of reactive oxidizing agents, which are produced during oxygen consumption, emerged. Oxygen not only powers life, it also damages it . . . and the neural structures within it.

> *Rust is the oxidation of iron, a part of its biodegrading. A similar thing happens to living cells, including neurons, when they are exposed to oxygen over time. It is part of the reason why neural nets such as our brains function less well the older we get. We are rusting.*

Once the Earth system shifted to utilizing oxygen to power complex life-forms, those living organisms had to develop mechanisms to protect cellular structures from oxygen byproducts (and to regenerate those structures when needed). So, living organisms began to create exceptionally potent antioxidants, often from trytophan. Many of the compounds that are innovations on tryptophan, including serotonin, melatonin, and auxin, are also some of the most potent antioxidants known. Azmitia comments that

> *Tryptophan was always a key to life because of its ability to convert solar energy to biological energy. The consequence of this process made tryptophan and its associated molecules involved in all aspects of an organism's life: mitosis, movement, and maturation. As oxygen began to be a major component of the atmosphere of the earth, enzymes that served a central function in conversion of CO_2 to glucose now evolved to hydroxylate many substrates. Hydroxylation leads to 5-HTP and 5-HT as well as to many indole alkaloids.*[9]

Hydroxylation, in other words, leads to the production of serotonin (5-HT) and other indole alkaloids such as psilocybin and the LSD precursors in ergot fungi. And 5-HT not only functions to modulate sensory gating, it also protects the neural structures themselves from oxidation—layered function as is so common among Gaian innovations.

Plants—which predate the emergence of our species by a considerable length of time, and are deeply involved in the energy transformation of sunlight and the production of oxygen—are, not surprisingly, deeply involved in hydroxylation and the production of tryptophan and its offspring. As Azmitia notes, "Besides the algae, fungi, and molds, the most efficient generator of O_2 and serotonin is plants. The levels of serotonin inside plants far exceed those seen in the animal brain by 100 times."[10] He continues . . .

> *A closer look at plants provides evidence that serotonin and its products, such as melatonin and auxin, serve crucial actions in the life and organization of plants. Plants are complex, multicellular organisms that have specialized cells that function as a unit, a holistic organization. Plants evolved a specialized intracellular organelle, the choloroplast, not only to capture light, but also as the source of tryptophan synthesis. All the enzymes for making tryptophan were localized inside these special organelles and could only be converted into their mature form when inside the chloroplast. Plants are extremely efficient at capturing light because they were extremely efficient at making tryptophan.*[11]

And just as a reminder, plants did not "evolve" chloroplasts. Chloroplasts are former free living bacteria that were incorporated into what became plant cells through symbiogenesis. So, not surprisingly, receptors for modifications of tryptophan such as serotonin and auxin and the various compounds we call neurotransmitters are found throughout plant structures, most especially in the root system/brain of the plant. And they are found in the earliest and most "primitive" form of "animals" that Gaia innovated, sponges.

As Wu and Cooper comment, "The early presence of tryptophan is a reason for 5-HT to be potentially the first neurotransmitter noted with the development of the nervous system. 5-HT acts as both a neurotransmitter and neurohormone and as a potent modulator of neurons and various tissues in many animals [and invertebrate] species."[12]

Serotonin is *always* present wherever neural networks are found. In fact, all neural networks are innervated by this particular molecular structure.

*That is, all neural networks,
including those formed by large aggregates of organisms
such as viral swarms and ecoranges*

Modified tryptophan molecules such as serotonin are strongly involved in the formation of social group dynamics, irrespective of the species involved. They are deeply involved in sense of self, the capacity for empathy and cooperation, sensitization to stimuli, and the perception of the meanings encoded in sensory inputs. And they are intimately involved in neural network plasticity, as Azmitia observes . . .

> *neuroplasticity is a necessary attribute of a homeostatic system, but early development and global interconnections make this system holistic in scope. The ability to change morphology, stimulate neurogenesis and differentiation, or promote cell survival is influenced by acetylcholine, catecholamines, GABA, EAAs (glutamate and glycine), and neuropeptides. However, only serotonin (5-HT) has the evolutionary and anatomical properties to serve as a global regulator unifying the whole brain into a cohesive biological system.*[13]

There is perhaps no molecule more important to the planet's neural networks than serotonin. Among other things, serotonin modulates the neural connection dynamics in the brain and CNS. Serotonin continually alters the chemistry of target neurons and strongly regulates neuron cell morphology, in other words their form and structure. "Serotonin," as Azmitia notes, "influences the morphology of sensory and motor neurons involved in neuronal networking in order to track the source of relevant stimuli."[14] Beyond their other functions, as Azmitia comments, "serotonin neurons are primarily sensory neurons (activated by external stimuli)."[15] Again, serotonin receptors exist in *every* neural network that touches the external world: brain, heart, enteric system (GI tract), and immune system. Serotonin and its receptors are the modulators of incoming sensory data. Serotonin also influences cells at all stages of development, including development and function of all the organs. In essence, it is a modulatory regulator for all self-organized systems from the tiniest (cell) to the largest (Gaia). It facilitates the neural network at each level of development of all self-organized systems. And it functions at the larger level, as a global regulator, to facilitate the self-organization of larger symbiogenetic structures—organs into organism, ecosystems into ecoranges into Gaia. Neurons that form neural networks act much like a swarm. They act through a mass, coordinated action, in concert,

in synchrony

with each other, in both the smaller local systems in which they are located, and at the larger level where all the neurons in all the subsystems synchronize with each other to form a larger self-organized system with larger computing potential.

Such as plants in an ecorange
locusts in a swarm

In the human brain the raphe nuclei, in the brain stem, appear to be the primary location that oversees the release of serotonin to the rest of the brain. They interact with every portion of the brain, are deeply involved in circadian rhythms, sleep and dreaming, and are involved continually in a complex feedback process between themselves and the rest of the brain's serotonergic neurons and neuronal structures. Azmitia comments, in depth, that

The globally projecting raphe neurons have the anatomical and functional characteristics to coordinate the physiology of the whole brain. Although specific actions of 5-HT are local, nevertheless the scope is global. The disruption of one group of raphe neurons impacts the system as a whole. The role of 5-HT as an integrating component of neural tissue emphasizes the importance of neuroplasticity. 5-HT neurons show morphological and functional responses to a variety of neuronal and nonneuronal factors. . . . The serotonin neurons evolved from plants as a general regulatory system which responds to external stimuli to produce structural changes to meet those signals. . . . The system modifies itself to achieve the instability needed for homeostasis. This function of serotonin can be observed in plants and unicellular organisms, long before the advent of neurons [in human beings]. The fluctuations in serotonin levels are broadcast throughout the brain and serve to dynamically integrate and stabilize CNS structure and function. . . . The maintenance of a stable nervous system in a dynamic environment is certainly a holistic function since it is difficult to imagine this process as being a sum of its component parts. Homeostasis implies not only stability of a given set point or function, but more importantly the dynamic equilibrium seen around that set point.[16]

He continues . . .

A homeostatic regulator needs to sense all the pertinent variables necessary to achieve and maintain equilibrium. The 5-HT distribution in the brain reaches all areas and includes target cells in the vascular, neuronal, and endocrine systems. The function of 5-HT neurons serves to integrate all cell types in all areas of the brain. The global framework serves to receive and integrate the varied pertinent variables into a holistic unit. Second, a homeostatic regulator needs to adjust the activity and architecture of the systems involved in equilibrium. 5-HT neurons can produce rapid changes in postsynaptic neuronal firing, glial activity, blood flow, breathing, temperature, and hormonal secretion. 5-HT promotes cellular mitosis, migration and maturation of neurons and glial cells, and change how these cellular systems interact. Third, a homeostatic regulator should be able to adjust its own set point to accommodate changes in input to more efficiently reduce fluctuations. 5-HT neurons modify their own cellular architecture in response not only to sensory neuronal inputs, but also to glial cells, hormonal levels, neuropeptides, and glucose. . . . The ability to change activity and response to external factors [is essential] to homeostasis.[17]

Serotonin and its receptors modulate our intake of sensory data, regulate the neural networks in our bodies, and respond with high sensitivity to environmental inputs. They are essential for the development of neural networks and neurons; living organisms deficient in serotonin have much less neural development. This is true in all life-forms on Earth, including plants.

Serotonin and the Plant Root/Brain

Similarly to animals and insects, serotonin is found throughout plant tissues, in roots, leaves, fruits, and seeds. Plant serotonin, a.k.a. phyto-serotonin, has numerous functions in plants—just as it does in us. It is highly involved in reproduction, photoperiodic responses, phytoremediative abilities, protection of plants cells against apoptosis, as a free radical scavenger, growth regulation, morphogenesis, and the growth and development of the plant root system, that is, the plant's primary neural network or brain. Increases in serotonin, as researchers put it, "coincided with greatly stimulated lateral root development." In fact, serotonin and other tryptophan-derived compounds were found to "exert a strong biological activity at very low concentrations in both in vivo and in vitro systems and are essential for maintenance of physiological and morphogenetic processes including gravity and light responses, root hair development, and lateral root (LR), adventitious root and shoot system development."[18]

Environmental demands, including stress, stimulate the increase of serotonin in plant tissues with resulting alterations in the root architecture (i.e., neural network shape). As researchers comment, "serotonin levels in plant tissues may increase by demand, under particular development transitions or when challenged by pathogens."[19] This increase in serotonin stimulates alterations in the neural network of the plant, increasing phenotype plasticity. As researchers comment, "adventitious root formation provides a flexible way for plants to alter their form and resource allocation in response to environmental changes or after injury."[20] Serotonin stimulates the formation of not only more rootlets but also more root tips, increasing as well their elongation. In other words, new neurons form *and* those root tips, similar to sensitive fingers, extend further into the soil where they begin taking in more data about the environment in which the plant finds itself. Lateral root formation increases, in *Arabidopsis* species, by up to three times as serotonin production increases (or if exogenous serotonin is added to the soil). The lateral roots mature faster and this includes the maturation of the root tips, the neurons of the root system. Researchers comment that "this result illustrates that serotonin is a compound with a strong effect on Arabidopsis adventitious root organogenesis."[21] Serotonin not only stimulates the faster emergence of new forms of the plant neural structure but also protects aging plant neural cells from reactive oxygen species, which, as Ramakrishna et al. note, leads "to a delay in the process of sensescence."[22]

As it does in the mammalian brain, serotonin acts as a global modulator in the plant brain, modulating the effects of other plant neurotransmitters and the response of the genotype to environmental inputs. Serotonin, researchers Pelagio-Flores et al. comment, . . .

> is a highly conserved indolic compound occurring in evolutionarily distinct organisms from humans to plants. The results of research with serotonin have uncovered several facts: (i) it is present in a wide number of plant species; (ii) it is produced from tryptophan; (iii) its concentration may vary in plant tissues or in response to environmental conditions suggesting important developmental and adaptive functions.[23]

Under environmental stress, serotonin production increases, which alters plant neuronal structure and development, generating unique neural net responses to the environmental stressors. The main enzyme that converts serotonin from tryptamine (i.e., tryptamine 5-hydroxylase), has its *maximal* activity in the roots, making the root system in plants "the major location for the synthesis of serotonin and its derivatives."[24] The produced serotonin stimulates the apical meristem to produce new root tips, in new formations, depending on the nature of the plant's gestalt analysis of the changed environmental situation. This allows the emergence of unique adaptive responses to changed conditions. In other words, the plant behavior changes. This includes innovations in leaf shape and chemical production.

The plant root/neural network contains receptors similar to those found in insects and animals. Analogs of, for instance, the 5-HT1a and 2a receptors function similarly in plants as they do in animals. For example, the 5-HT1a receptors act in concert with serotonin to help provide intracellular stability for the cytoskeleton and result in cell differentia-tion and proliferation inhibiton. 5-HT2a receptors, in concert with sero-tonin, on the other hand, open gating channels more widely, destabilize the internal cytoskeleton and generate neuronal cell proliferation, and synaptogenesis in response to alterations in the incoming data stream. Stimulation of 5-HT2a receptors, then, in response to environmental demands, results in destabilization or depatterning of the neural network so that new neural network forms can emerge that are better able to adapt to the altered environment.

Increased serotonin levels in plants such as *Echinacea purpurea* have been found to stimulate the regeneration of damaged plant cells. How-ever, plants deficient in serotonin have poorer root development and thus poorer neuronal networks. Low levels of serotonin in animals, e.g., rats, also inhibits the formation of healthy brain neural circuits. In fact . . .

> *The worldwide dumping and excretion of millions of pounds of over 50 pharmaceutical forms of serotonin reuptake inhibitors (SRIs) is affecting the entire neural network of the Gaian system. These inhibitors affect all organisms that use serotonin in their functioning. Because serotonin affects so many systems in so many living organisms, SRIs (whatever their form) are interfering with sexual maturation, reproduction, germination, root and brain development, in fact, with the function of every system that sero-tonin affects throughout the Earth system. SRIs are highly active in trace amounts and are present in all wastewater streams in indus-trial nations. These compounds slow development of all the species that encounter them, affect their reproductive health, and slow the responses of their neural systems to external stressors—they (e.g., Prozac) even reduce root, i.e., neural net, and shoot development in plants. Shoot and root emergence in* Mimosa pundica, *for instance, is reduced from 15–20 per nodal segment to 4 when they were treated with only 20 uM of Prozac. And these SRIs? They are not very biodegradable. They take four months to degrade in streams but once it gets into the sediment at the bottom of rivers and ponds as researchers comment: "It doesn't seem to biodegrade at all."*[25]

Antidepressants, irrespective of which life-form is exposed to them, "cause neuronal damage and mature neurons to revert to an immature state, both of which may explain why antidepressants also cause neurons to undergo apoptosis (programmed death)." As Andrews et al. go on to say, "Our review supports the conclusion that antidepressants generally do more harm than good by disrupting a number of adaptive processes regulated by serotonin."[26] The amounts of SRIs flooding the Gaian system is disregulating the neuronal networks of the planet, including its individual species, from plants to humans.

Serotonin Innovations

Serotonin is ubiquitous in self-organized living systems. But Gaia did not stop innovating after the development of serotonin.

One of the primary generators of innovation in self-organized systems is the expansive opening of sensory gating channels in neural networks. When the doors of perception open more widely, the organism can more readily perceive the metaphysical background of the world, more deeply experience the underlying patterns that are at work, perceive a greater range of the meanings that are encoded in sensory data streams, and begin to generate responses outside of habituated parameters. Serotonin is important in this, but Gaia innovated further. Unique molecular forms, created by plants (and fungi and bacteria) in every ecosystem on Earth, have been generated from the basic serotonin molecule.

And this occurred long before the emergence of the human species.

These innovations include such substances as bufotenine, bufotenidine, psilocin, psilocybin, DMT, yohimbine, yohimbane, vinblastine, and a number of ergot derivatives such as ergotamine and ergine.

These sophisticated serotonin-derived molecules have specific and crucial impacts on serotonin receptors in all neural networks on the planet. They can be considered, from one perspective, as tremendously powerful forms of serotonin. They act to alter the neural networks of the planet and all its living organisms. We know them as hallucinogens.

8
THE FUNCTION OF PSYCHOTROPICS IN THE ECOSYSTEM

DMT is now known to be widespread in the plant world, particularly in the grasses and the pea family. In trace amounts, as Alexander Shulgin titles a chapter in TIHKAL, *"DMT is everywhere." It is also found in the human body, and in the human brain.*

DALE PENDELL

Ethnographic data obliges us to accept that one of the ends that explicitly induce human beings to consume ayahuasca (and by extension, hallucinogens in general) exists in relation with certain cognitive processes which allow for the improvement in adaptive efficacy.

JOSEP FERICGLA

For art to exist, for any sort of aesthetic activity to exist, a certain physiological precondition is indispensable: intoxication.

FRIEDRICH NIETZSCHE

There are numerous names for the many hallucinogenic compounds that the Gaian system generates and they have a wide range of meanings

for people have been trying to describe
what hallucinogens do
for a very long time.

So, they have been called: hallucinogens (generating hallucinations), psychedelics (mind-manifesting), psychotropics (having an affinity or tropism for the mind), entheogens (theos, i.e., god + en, i.e., within + gen, i.e., generating, thus, generating the god within), psychomimetics (psychosis-mimicking), psycholytics (psyche-loosening or dissolving), entactogens (touch generation—thus, enhancing sensitivity to the touch of the world upon you), empathogens (empathy generating), psychointegrators (from psyche, i.e., mind + integrator, something that brings together or incorporates parts into a whole, i.e., substances that create whole mind), neurophenomenologics (neuro, indicating the neural system + phenomenologic, that is, the structure of consciousness and experience, i.e., substances that affect the neural system and, in consequence, affect the nature of consciousness and experience), and neurognostics (neuro, indicating the neural system + gnosis, meaning knowledge of the metaphysical background of the world, i.e., substances that affect the neural system and, in consequence, generate deeper knowledge of the metaphysical background of the world and the self's relation to it).

The argument about what they should be called is ongoing
an illustration of how such substances are—often—beyond words
as well as the linear mind that gives rise to human language

Earth-system-created neural modulators, i.e., psychoactive chemicals, have been in existence for millions upon millions of years; they predate human emergence by a very long time. They have been, for the most part, generated out of innovations on the serotonin molecule and, not surprisingly, they strongly affect the serotonin receptors that exist in the neural nets in living organisms. They are serotonergic activators. But they don't activate *all* the serotonergic receptors in neural networks, just some of them. In fact, they activate a particular spectrum of serotonin receptors in the brain and create, by doing so, particular kinds of effects in neural networks.

Serotonergic Neurognostics

Serotonergic neurognostics include some of the more notable psychoactive drugs, including DMT (e.g., ayahuasca), LSD, psilocybin, mescaline, and bufotenin. And while they affect a sophisticated complex of 5-HT receptors to create a unique spectrum of response from neural networks, they affect the 5-HT2a receptors the most strongly.

The 5-HT2a receptors, again, exist throughout the human body, in the GI tract, immune system, heart, and brain. Every area high in 5-HT2a receptors is strongly affected by these serotonergic innovations. In the brain this includes, for instance, the cerebral cortex, thalamus, hippocampus, amygdala, and olfactory bulb. Activation of the 5-HT2a receptors by LSD, psylocibin, and the other serotonergic hallucinogens leads to immediate alterations in the hippocampal processing of sensory data, learning, and memory, including its depth work with the meaning fields in which the perceiver is embedded. The thalamus is strongly affected as well, reducing its gating activity significantly. This allows many more sensory inflows to reach consciousness. In fact, every part of the brain that gates sensory data is stimulated to reduce its gating. The result, depending on the amount of the chemical ingested, and the dynamics of the particular neural network, is increasing awareness of the sensory field in which the person is embedded. And this is true of every living organism that ingests serotonergic neurognostics. As the researchers Nichols et al. comment . . .

> *Pharmacological activation of serotonin receptors in the [Drosophila] fly by lysergic acid diethylamide induces behaviors not unlike those observed in mammalian systems. These include alterations in visual processing abilities, reduced locomotor activity, and altered gene expression within the brain. Many of these effects are due to activation of the same serotonin receptor subtypes that are thought to be primary mediators of hallucinogenic drug effects in humans as well as the acute symptoms of schizophrenia.*[1]

The reduced locomotor activity that is common in every species that ingests neurognostics comes, by the way, from an induced contemplative state. Time perception slows, the boundaries between self and other become more porous, habituated gating parameters are negated, sensory channels open widely, and the sensory inputs, then, become so *novel* that the organism is caught up in their contemplation, just as they were when they were young.

Terence McKenna, reflecting on his experiences with DMT, described it like this . . .

> *Under the influence of DMT, the world becomes an Arabian labyrinth, a palace, a more than possible Martian jewel, vast with motifs that flood the gaping mind with complex and wordless awe. Color and the sense of a reality-unlocking secret nearby pervade the experience. There is a sense of other times, and of one's own infancy, and of wonder, wonder, and more wonder.*[2]

And Albert Hofmann, of LSD, like this . . .

> *Kaleidoscopic, fantastic images surged in on me, alternating, variegated, opening and then closing themselves in circles and spirals, exploding in colored fountains, rearranging and hybridizing themselves in a constant flux. It was particularly remarkable how every acoustic perception, such as the sound of a door handle or a passing automobile, became transformed into optical perceptions. Every sound generated a vividly changing image, with its own consistent form and color.*[3]

And Aldous Huxley, of mescaline, like this . . .

> *I continued to look at the flowers, and in their living light I seemed to detect the qualitative equivalent of breathing—but of breathing without returns to a starting point, with no recurrent ebbs but only a repeated flow from beauty to heightened beauty, from deeper to ever deeper meaning. . . . I saw the books, but was not at all concerned with their positions in space. What I noticed, what impressed itself upon my mind was the fact that all of them glowed with living light and that in some the glory was more manifest than others.*

... Space was still there; but it had lost its predominance. The mind was primarily concerned, not with measures and locations, but with being and meaning. . . . Mescalin raises all colour to a higher power and makes the percipient aware of all the innumerable fine shades of difference which, at ordinary times, he is completely blind. It would seem that, for Mind at Large, the so-called secondary characters of things are primary. Unlike Locke, it evidently feels that colors are more important, better worth attending to than masses, positions, and dimensions. . . . "This is how one ought to see," I kept saying.[4]

And Rudolf Gelpke, of psilocybin, like this . . .

After ca. 20 minutes [10:40], beginning effects: serenity, speechlessness, mild but pleasant dizzy sensation and "pleasureful deep breathing." [10:50] Strong! Dizziness, can no longer concentrate . . . [10:55] Excited, intensity of colors: everything pink to red. [11:05] The world concentrates itself there on the center of the table. Colors very intense. [11:10] A divided being, unprecedented—how can I describe this sensation of life. Waves, different selves, must control me.

Then, he abandoned his minute-by-minute note taking, realizing that

the possibilities of verbal expression [are] unspeakably paltry—measured by the flood of inner experience that inundated me and threatened to burst me. It seemed that 100 years would not be sufficient to describe the fullness of a single minute. At the beginning, optical impressions predominated: I saw with delight the boundless succession of rows of trees in the nearby forest. Then the tattered clouds in the sunny sky rapidly piled up with silent and breathtaking majesty to a superimposition of thousands of layers . . . [I] lay down in a nook of the garden on a sun-warmed wood pile—my fingers stroked this wood with overflowing, animal-like sensual affection. . . . for a moment I experienced reality from a location that lies somewhere beyond the force of gravity and time.[5]

What neurognostics do, as psychopharmacologists Adam Halberstadt and Mark Geyer observe, is "to inhibit brain regions that are responsible for constraining consciousness within the narrow boundaries of the normal waking state."[6] Although an even better way of putting it, rather than "brain regions," is "neural net regions." And rather than "constraining consciousness"—"constraining perception." There is, in consequence, a tremendously increased awareness of the sensory field, and the meanings held in those fields, irrespective of the organism involved.

Serotonergic neurognostics such as DMT and the ergot alkaloids from which LSD is made are widespread thoughout the world's ecosystems; they are deeply integrated into every one of the Earth's biocommunities. Of them, psilocybin (and its highly active precursor, psilocin), which is common in certain fungi, and DMT, ubiquitous in plants, are the most pervasive. The psilocybin-fungi group is widely disseminated in all grassland biomes (one of the primary ecozone groups on the planet), while DMT is strongly present in all forest/diverse plant ecozones and (along with the cacti which produce the phenylethylamine alkaloids that also affect serotonin receptors) is commonly found in desert ecozones as well.

> *There are also a large number of other neuroactive plants spread throughout the world's ecoranges; they all affect serotonin receptors. Rhodiola, for example, is found in high alpine and arctic regions and has strong impacts on 5-HT receptors, stimulates neuronal growth and differentiation, and enhances learning in neural networks. Plant chemicals that affect neural network functioning are **everywhere.**

Neurognostics and psychoactive compounds are the rule, *not* the exception. Each one affects neural networks in slightly different ways, creating a spectrum of responses in 5-HT receptors, all altering the gating that organisms use to filter sensory inflows.

Psilocybin

Fungi that create neurognostics can be found throughout the world, on every continent except Antarctica. Researchers Guzman, Allen, and

Gartz divided them into four groupings: 1) species with psilocybin and related indoles, including the genera *Psilocybe* (116 species), *Gymnopilus* (14 species), *Panaeolus* (13 species), *Copelandia* (12 species), *Hypholoma* (6 species), *Pluteus* (6 species), *Inocybe* (6 species), *Conocybe* (4 species), *Paneolina* (4 species), *Berronema* (2 species), and *Agrocybe, Galerina,* and *Mycena* (one species each); 2) species with ibotenic acid, which includes the *Amanitas,* specifically *A. muscaria, A. pantherina,* and *A. regalis;* 3) ergot fungi, which includes the five *Claviceps* species that grow on rye and from which LSD is made and two unrelated species in the *Cordyceps* genus; and 4) a variety of species upon which no real testing has been done but that geographically distinct groups use as sacred mushrooms. This includes 20 or so species in six genera.

However, the list can't be considered exhaustive—research in the field is still in its infancy. Albert Hofmann, who developed LSD from ergot alkaloids in the 1940s, only isolated psilocybin in 1958. Prior to this, most scientists were denying that psychotropic mushrooms—psychotropic anything really—existed at all.

> *Neurognostics, they insisted, certainly could not be common, the existence of LSD-like compounds in ergot had to be a rarity. Then Hofmann found them in mushrooms. Then in morning glory seeds. As Hofmann notes, "There was another reason for doubt in the specialist circles concerning our findings. The occurrence in higher plants of ergot alkaloids that hitherto had been known only as constituents of lower fungi contradicted the experience that certain substances are typical of and restricted to respective plant families."*[7]

But such substances aren't limited in Nature, they are everywhere. Neurognostics are common in every ecosystem on Earth, in multiple genera and species. More psychoactive-containing mushrooms (and plants, and . . .) are being found all the time.

> *as interested humans begin to look more carefully*
> *around themselves*

As recently as 2006 a previously unknown indole alkaloid from the mushroom *Inocybe aeruginascens* was found that is very similar in structure to bufotenidine, a derivative of bufotenin, a fairly strong hallucinogen.

and yes, people are already getting high on it

At this point 216 different psychoactive fungal species are known. Most are those that utilize serotonin derivatives, those in the indole group; most of those contain psilocybin. And those particular fungi, like most of the species in Guzman's group one, are coevolutionary with grasses. They can often be found symbiotically associated with the roots of various species in grassland ecoranges (and in the dung of herbivores that are grazing those grasslands) or, in some cases such as that of *Pluteus* spp., in forests throughout the world, on decaying wood. In some ecozones, where the grassland ecorange also contains woody plants, shrubs, and trees (e.g., African savannas and the Iberian dehesa), both types of mushrooms can be found together.

The *Psilocybe* genus has an ancient coevolutionary relationship with many grass species, a relationship that has existed at least since the Cretaceous some 140 million years ago. The mycelia of the organisms spread throughout the soil of grassland ecozones where they attach to the root systems of the grasses, forming a very large interconnected network, a mycorrhizal fungal mat. In this instance, it is what is called an *endomycorrhizal* (as opposed to ectomycorrhizal) association since the hyphae, that is, single strands of the mycelial network, attach to the roots of the grasses and then *insert* themselves (*endo-*) into both the intercellular spaces between the root cortical cells *and* intracellularly. They, in essence, intertwine themselves with the root cellular tissues, penetrating the cells and cellular spaces. The specific zone of the root, where the plant and the fungal hyphae meet, is the cortex. The apex, or the part of the root considered to be the main neural structure, is not touched. A sheath or collar forms around the hyphae where it touches the living tissues of the root. This acts as a metabolic zone of interaction between the two where a constant exchange of chemical compounds occurs.

The serotonergic alkaloids in the fungal hyphae stimulate, as they do in all organisms, the development of new neurons, the formation of new neural networks, and the maturation of the cells of the plant root/brain system. Some of the outlying parts of the root system, already becoming senescent, experience an acceleration of that maturation, moving more quickly into senescence; that is, they get old and die. The psilocybe then exists as a saprophytic organism, living on the decaying root mass.

From this decaying root system, and from the living roots as well, the fungi gain nutrients and other compounds that aid their growth, particularly brassinosteroids, potent plant hormones. The fungal mycelium uses this compound, in essence, as a plant adaptogen, that is, a substance which enhances nonspecific resistance to environmental stressors. Psilocybe mushrooms are particularly fond of it.

Although almost no one does so, herbal medicines can be used as medicinal agents for plants as well as animals and humans. Such herbals have effects similar, even identical, to those they have on us. You can use cordyceps or baikal skullcap or rhodiola infusions to stimulate the production of root tissues in plants—including the root brain—sida acuta infusions to fight bacterial infections, isatis infusions to fight viral infections, or even plants high in brassinosteroids to help a plant's immune function. These latter plants, used as herbal infusions, and poured on a plant's soil, will act as plant hormones and stimulate cellular expansion and elongation (in roots), stimulate regeneration of damaged tissues, and promote vascular differentiation. They will also protect plants during cold and drought conditions—or any other type of environmental stress—by acting as adaptogens. Lychnis viscaria, for instance, is very high in brassinosteroids and acts very powerfully for other plants in this way. It increases the disease resistance of plants to which it is applied as an infusion. It is also just as effective if it is placed as a companion plant in gardens, acting through root/mycelial associations and the various volatile chemicals it produces and then releases through its stomata.

The dying root systems of the grasses are not, it is important to understand, caused by pathogenic actions of the psilocybe. The root cortices of these grasses naturally become senescent and slough off whether psilocybe fungi are present or not. This old plant cellular tissue is intended, in fact, to become fodder for the grasses, a kind of self-generated potting soil that keeps the plants healthy. The fungi (and certain bacteria) are also fond of it and use it as a food source while at the same time they accelerate the biodegrading of the old tissues. Psilocybe species, in particular, have a very strong tropism, that is attraction, to a large variety of grass root systems; they treat them all similarly. They attach to the sloughing roots, accelerate senescence and biodegrading, establish themselves in the decaying roots, and form a mutalism with the grass plants to keep the process going.

The fungal mat, spread throughout grassland ecoranges, lives and feeds on the dead grass matter, including that in the herbaceous feeders' dung (usually cow dung but prior to that buffalo dung and long before that dinosaur dung), acting, along with specific bacteria, as a primary recycling agent. By attaching its hyphae to the sloughing grass roots and stimulating biodegradation, the fungi enhance the fertileness and health of the rhizosphere surrounding the grasses' root systems as well as the entire grassland ecozone. Most grassland ecosystems are, in fact, dependent on the presence of the psilocybe species for their health.

The symbiotic/saprophytic relationship between the grasses and the fungi gives the fungi the growth nutrients it needs while the grasses gain, as most plants do from symbiotic fungal relationships, a number of benefits. The rhizosphere, and thus the ecorange, is kept healthy stimulating plant growth and spread. The indole alkaloids accelerate the growth and development of the grass neurons, enhancing root development and spread. They also stimulate root/brain development and neural network shape innovations, enabling the grasses to respond more effectively to environmental perturbations. Other compounds provide anti-inflammatory, immune stimulating, cellular normalizing, analgesic, antibacterial, and antifungal actions.

Each of these latter compounds has a unique range of activity. The antifungal compounds, for instance, protect the grass root system from attack by pathogenic fungi and nematodes. In other words, as the coevolutionary bacteria on our skin and in our bowels do for us, the psilocybe fungi protect their coevolutionary partners from other, less beneficent, fungal organisms.

However, these actions are not just local. Coevolutionary relationships such as this do not, as many scientists still insist, act only between *two* organisms.

> *Scientists used to say there was no such thing as coevolution at all,*
> *that it was god eat dog, no matter where you looked.*
> *Anal-gesic: useful for treating a pain in the ass?*
> *As a specific for reductionists?*

As Michael Crichton noted, coevolutionary relationships almost always occur between *n*-number of organisms.

Coevolutionary Interactions in Complex Ecosystem Networks

As self-organized biological organisms such as plants, fungi, insects, and animals congregate in a specific region, they form an ecorange or even an ecozone (much larger). Ecoranges essentially self-organize in the process, the plants and various life-forms acting as allopoietic subunits of the autopoietic larger system.

> *And the ecozone becomes self-aware in the process*
> *just as all self-organized biological systems do*

As researchers Eoin O'Gorman and Mark Emmerson note, these "natural communities are finely structured, displaying properties that promote stability despite complexity." There is a "nonrandom arrangement of interaction strengths" between the allopoietic subunits that "promotes community level stability."[8] "Nonrandom," that is, there is something more that is happening than mere chance; there is *meaning* in the system's subunits' associations.

In grassland ecoranges and zones both the grass and the psilocybe act as what are called "strong interactors." That is, they are in essence acting as keystone species around which the entire ecorange is oriented. The other plants in the system are considered to be "weak" interactors. "Complex ecological networks," as O'Gorman and Emmerson comment, "are characterized by distributions of interaction strengths that are highly skewed, with many weak and a few strong interactors present."[9]

O'Gorman and Emmerson conducted experiments where they removed strong interactors from complex ecosystems and found, not surprisingly, that it "produced a dramatic trophic cascade" in the system. That is, the system immediately experienced a phase change, going from a state of high complexity to one much less sophisticated. They comment that

> *Natural ecosystems are a complex tangle of interactions, with 95% of species typically no more than 3 links apart. This natural complexity persists against the odds because it is governed by fundamental laws and principles that confer stability. One of the most widely accepted of these principles is the pattern of species interactions. There is a tendency to consider biodiversity in terms of taxonomic identities or functional roles, yet every species can be considered as a node in a complex web of interactions. Each node contributes to the overall balance of interactions, whether it is a strong or weak interactor. Given the highly interconnected nature of food webs, any loss of biodiversity could contribute to a ripple effect, changing the pattern of interaction strengths and thus threatening to unbalance the stability conferred by this pattern.*[10]

The loss of a keystone species in such circumstances (such as the psilocybe fungi or the grass species that are their coevolutionary partners) was found to "have effects disproportionally large, relative to their abundance." But further . . .

> *Fluctuations in population biomass are commonplace, and compensatory actions among species can maintain aggregate biomass. The changes in primary and secondary production shown here are community-level responses however, suggesting that the insurance effect of community diversity is not sufficient to overwhelm the impacts of [removing] strong interactors. Trophic cascades such as these can alter energy flow, community composition, and habitat provision, and lead to secondary extinctions.*[11]

In other words, while the keystone species remain relatively stable, the weak interactors are in constant flux around them, various plants moving in and out of the ecosystem as the environment in which the system is located changes its nature and needs. The numbers and kinds of the weak interactors change over time. This keeps the system homeodynamis intact. However, the removal of the keystone species has immediate, detrimental effects on the system, causing its complexity to collapse into a simpler state.

They found that removal of "weak" interactors did not have as extreme an effect; however, those groups of plants play a stabilizing role on the system. In other words, the strong interactors generate potent effects on the system but the weak interactors modulate those effects toward specific outcomes. "Crucially, when strong interactors were present in the community without a sufficient number of weakly interacting species around them" the ecosystem destabilized.[12] Weak interactor loss led to "reductions in temporal and spacial stability of ecosystem process rates, community diversity, and resistance."[13]

More dynamically (and more accurately), weak and strong interactors can be thought of as "links" (as some researchers have it) rather than "actors" in a communicatory network.

> *Though O'Gorman and Emmerson's concept of "nodes" is even better. A node is a point of concentration of matter, where the gravity well becomes strongest, and that "well" immediately generates "gravitational" links to all other nodes in the system. Everything is then connected in a web of stronger and weaker fields—what chaos theory freaks refer to as strong and weak attractors. They are always to be found in nonlinear systems. Why has it taken ecologists so long?*

In all healthy ecosystems, there exists a network of a few strong attractors embedded in a majority field of weak attractors. The strong exert much more powerful effects but they are held in a tightly coupled web of weak attractors that modulate their actions.

> *For example, most keystone species, if not all of them, need a weak attractor, called a nurse plant, to begin growing first in a new loca-*

tion before the keystone species can successfully grow. That nurse plant prepares the soil for the keystone species in exactly the way that it needs. How do the seeds of the keystone species find their way to the prepared soil, once it is ready? No one knows but mathematical modeling shows it isn't random. The nurse plant does send out volatiles as a communicatory message, indicating that the soil is ready, but then how do the seeds get there? Seeds can't sit down; they can't move.

The whole interwoven network, with just this combination of attractors, produces a tremendously adaptable ecorange or zone in which each part contributes essential responses that, together, modulate the system's successful adaptation to perturbations. It is not just what species are present but rather the species' *behaviors,* their interactions with the other species in the network, that is crucial. All together, they make a *community* in which every organism's actions and presence are crucial to continued functionality. The species in such a community are so tightly coupled that they can't legitimately be viewed in isolation from each other. Or as Masanobu Fukuoka once put it . . .

> *The living and holistic biosystem that is nature cannot be broken down or resolved into its parts. Once broken down it dies. Or rather, those who break off a piece of nature lay hold of something that is dead, and, unaware that what they are examining is no longer what they think it to be, claim to understand nature. . . . Because [man] starts out with misconceptions about nature and takes the wrong approach to understanding it, regardless of how rational his thinking, everything winds up all wrong.*[14]

It turns out that these complex community networks fluctuate over time in the composition of their weak interactors (the strong links tend to remain constant).

> *Once the keystone species is well-established,*
> *the nurse plants go someplace else.*

As the system responds to perturbations the particular species that are present shift locations and others take their place. New weak attractors, with different capacities, and chemical production abilities, continually flow through the system over very long time lines in order to keep the system adaptable to altered environmental circumstances. These movements, called *asynchronous fluctuations* in system stability, are actually an element of the system remaining close to the boundary of self-organization. As new plants move into the system, they then *synchronize* their actions with the rest of the links in the system, much the same way human beings do when two people begin to walk together. Out of this synchronicity come patterns of self-organization that cannot be developed any other way.

This is identical to the way musicians, once they find the balance point, once they synchronize with each other, begin to find musical expressions that can only emerge from synchrony. They improvise specific communicatory expressions out of that unified state. And they do this by taking in, from millisecond to millisecond, the musical communicatory expressions coming from the other musicians, and then creating their own in response

All of which is, of course, the expression
of a complex liquid language
filled with rapidly changing meanings
from the deepest wells of human feeling
held secretly inside musical tones

and very specifically bypassing the linear mind and reductive languaging. As Duke Ellington once put it . . .

you've got to find a way of saying it without saying it[15]

As the ever-changing musical communication is received, the receiving musicians immediately interpret them far below the level of consciousness

just as a juggler does

and they then respond, in just milliseconds of time, from the zone they are in

the unique dreaming state that this book is about

so that a continual, and ever-changing, living, communicatory expression occurs. And those of us who listen, if we allow ourselves to drop into that dreaming place with them, experience a unique, and very deep, commentary on what it means to be a human being, caught up in the human predicament, embedded within this scenario that we know of as the world, touched by a living cosmos every single day of our lives. The response of our hearts to what is presented to our senses is awakened. And just as it is with writers, this kind of musical expression is generated out of a unique and very ancient form of cognition, an ancient way of gathering knowledge from the heart of the world, a type of cognition that has been present in ecosystems long before human beings ever were.

> *This song of the waters* [as Aldo Leopold once said] *is audible to every ear, but there is other music in these hills by no means audible to all. To hear even a few notes of it you must first live here for a long time, and you must know the speech of hills and rivers. Then on a still night, when the campfire is low and the Pleiades have climbed over rimrocks, sit quietly and listen for a wolf to howl, and think hard of everything you have seen and tried to understand.*[16]

There is a continuous flow of interactive communications in ecosystems, each tiny part a response to the ever-living, never-stopping, always-flowing communications that are coming from all the tightly coupled members of that ecosystem and the environment in which it all is embedded. There is a language in the world, much older than our own,

ours is only a reflection of that older language,
our "take" on it, our innovation

and that language, as it moves through ecosystems, gives those ecosystems a shape unique to the communication occurring in that location. As Hans Olff et al. comment about complex ecosystems, "emergent structural properties and behaviour often arise at the system level, pointing at an underlying 'semantics' of system organization."[17]

Orlff's choice of the word *semantics* here is revealing; his team could have used the word "order," for instance, or even "structure." But they didn't. They, in fact, echo some of Gregory Bateson's tremendous insights—among which are: "growth and differentiation" are "controlled by communication." To which Bateson adds . . .

> *The shapes of animals and plants are transforms of messages. Language itself is a form of communication. The structure of the input **must** contain an analogue of grammar because all anatomy is a transform of message material, which must be contextually shaped. And finally, **contextual shaping** is only another term for* **grammar**.[18]

Semantics, that is,

> *the study of the meanings of speech forms, especially of the development and changes in meaning or words and word groups*[19]

of a particular sort, then "underlie" all ecosystem organization. In other words, as Olff et al. recognized, the *meanings* that flow through the system shape its structure—and the organisms that live within it. As Bateson so brilliantly observed, that flow of meanings actually shapes anatomy,

> *you can see this play out exactly when a plant with one shape and chemistry is transplanted to a different ecosystem. Both shape and chemistry change, sometimes so much so the plant is hard to identify.*

making the plants and animals we see in any particular ecosystem, literally, "transforms of messages." And those messages are particular communications about that exact ecosystem, its function, its dynamics, its interrelationships, and so on, ad infinitum. In this process, plants, bacteria, and fungi play major roles.

Plants release phytochemicals into the rhizosphere through their roots, into their mycelial partners through points of contact between root and hyphae, through their stomata into the air. These chemicals are created and released—*always*—as a response to incoming communications. There is, in fact, a continual communicatory interchange that is a running response to and commentary on the current status of the system. There is a behavioral response by every member of that system to every tiny alteration in the communicatory interchange that occurs.

just as there is in our body temperature
from moment to moment to moment
in response to its analysis of external and internal conditions

The ecosystem is as tightly coupled as a group of musicians deeply in a state of synchrony. Any incoming perturbation is immediately responded to by the system as a whole and each individual actor through its own self-intuited genius, choosing, at a level far below the conscious, exactly what to do to keep the system in balance.

But these systems don't do just one or two sets on a Saturday night. They don't get tired as musicians do. They *never* stop. And the more such systems are allowed to remain *in the zone,* to function without human disruption over long time lines, the more the efficiency of the system increases. The longer the time, the more innovations that it discovers and implements, the more improvisions of theme that are discovered.

And the more memory it has of what it has learned, memory that
it can pass on, just as we pass on what we have learned.

These improvizations can be thought of as an expression of *conditional probabilities*—essentially one choice from among a nearly infinite number of bifurcations that continually occur along the current pathway of existence.

The self-organized system touches the universe at multiple, nearly infinite points of contact along its three-dimensional edges and, as the exterior universe/system presses itself in on the self-organized subsystem, from deep within the network, what were, before, only conditional probabilities are expressed out of the system, manifested into form. *Which* probability is expressed can never be predicted; the system decides through the combined actions of all its allopoietic subunits and generates a single gestalt out of the complex whole.

Such complex ecosystems are nested self-organized groupings.

> *In nature* [as Masanobu Fukuoka puts it], *a whole encloses the parts, and a yet larger whole encloses the whole enclosing the parts. By enlarging our field of view, what is thought of as a whole becomes, in fact, nothing more than one part of a larger whole. Yet another whole encloses this whole in a concentric series that continues on to infinity.*[20]

They aren't linear assemblages. They are nested in terms of self-organizational complexity (cell to organ to organism to organisms to ecosystem) but they are also nested in terms of three-dimensional space and time. Some act over shorter time lines, some over longer. Some have stronger actions below ground, some above. And every part, tightly coupled to the others, is essential. In such healthy, complex systems the resilience of the system is high, the amount of time it takes to restore homeodynamis after a perturbation minuscule.

In response to perturbations, the network of living organisms in an ecorange constantly reorder relationships and the structure of both individual and the overall neural networks.

the semantic structure of the system changes

In other words, its messages/communications change and so too the transforms of those messages. This is another way to view neural plasticity. The neural networks in ecosystems alter their neural shape constantly. The structure of the overall system, its neural topology, is an emergent property of its self-organization and as such is constantly altered in order to maintain system homeodynamis. Such systems are, in their behavior, nonlinear. What is interesting is that while the focus has been (since the 1970s) on keystone species, it turns out that there are keystone *behaviors*. The movement of plant species, often invasives,

invasives are transforms of messages
and the messages they carry have nothing to do
with what eradication societies believe

are in fact keystone *behaviors* that are acting to restore system homeo-dynamis in ecoranges that have been damaged, often by excess human encroachment. In tropical forests, for instance, tree propagule immigration is a keystone interaction—a keystone behavior—and a dominant force in community structure and dynamics.

In grasslands, it is the psilocybe and grasses that are the keystone species; their *mutualism* is a keystone behavior. But there is another keystone behavior that's crucial here, and that is the creation and release of unique serotonergic compounds from the psilocybe fungi into the ecorange on a regular basis.

Psilocybin and Ecosystem Neural Networks

Again, the psilocybe/grass/herbivore–dung interrelationship is core to the health of all grassland ecoranges on Earth. But they are not the only organisms in grassland communities; in healthy grasslands, over 1,000 species of vascular plants can also be found. And these vascular plants exist in a matrix formed by the psilocybe/grass endomicorrhizal mat which is in fact

a three-dimensional topological space
that extends from the depth of the deepest roots
to the top of the highest tree in the range
and from side-to-side, over the undulating landscape,
as far as its boundaries flow

And this mat extends throughout the soil in that ecorange. In essence, the endomicrorrhizal network—which is composed of a hybrid organism formed between plant neurons and fungal mycelial neurons at unique synaptic connections—forms an extensive neural system for that ecorange. The other vascular plants form an integral part of this, for their root neurons are connected into the network as well.

As mycologist Paul Stametz has found, such mycelial networks are common in the world's ecosystems, and every place they emerge health and vitality is accelerated—in the plants, in the system.

The psilocybe/grass endomicorrhizal mats in healthy grassland ecoranges increase soil respiration; increase soil nitrogen, carbon, and enzyme activity; stimulate the formation of unique microbial communities; and generate high metabolic activity wherever they form. The soil structure and the clay content of the soils are affected by a variety of factors, including, and most especially, the weathering that is promoted by the plant/fungal mutualism. The fungal production of enriched soil through the biodegrading of sloughing grass roots also affects soil *texture*. The stimulated grass root systems loosen the soil as the root tips move deeper within it—so does the movement of the mycelia through the soil. This allows the soil microfauna (nematodes, amoebas, bacteria) to move more easily in the soil and for the soil to take in more water—which the complex rhizosphere zone needs to continue to function. The plant/fungal mycorrhizal network actually promotes the soil texture to its own benefit.

*the self-organized system
modifies its environment to enhance livability
just as all biological self-organized systems do*

Grasslands without such micorrhizal mats are much less healthy and much less able to respond to environmental disruption.

But it is the presence of psychoactive, neurognostic compounds in the endomicorrhizal network in grassland ecoranges that generates so much plasticity and resilience in the system. Those compounds' actions on the serotonin receptors in the plant network, just as they do in us, stimulate the formation of more root/neurons. The grass root/brain then extends itself, creating a larger neural network for the individual plant. This allows it to more effectively process data about its environment and generate solutions. But that expanding root brain is also connected through tightly coupled connections with fungal hyphae, into the larger fungal neural network. And this extended neural net flows throughout the entire ecorange, creating an even larger neural network.

The other vascular plants in the ecorange tightly couple themselves into this network as well, expanding it even further. And all of them communicate together. Millisecond to millisecond to millisecond. The release of the serotonergic compounds by the fungi, into the neural networks of the individual plants and the whole system itself,

especially during perturbations

opens gating channels more widely, allowing more sensory data intake,

and a greater perception of the meanings in those sensory inflows,
that is, a greater sensitivity to Bateson's "message material"

which generates a greater range of adaptation to environmental perturbations in order to keep the self-organized systems (plants *and* ecorange) intact. The compounds stimulate behaviors outside normal habituated parameters, in essence, enhancing innovation in the system and its subunits.

Humans are not the only ones spending their time generating new hallucinogenic alkaloids. The psilocybe do, too. If the mycelia are given N,N-diethyltryptamine (DET) as an additive to their nutrient bath—a substance not found in Nature—the mushrooms innovate on that molecular form, creating 4-hydroxy-N,N-diethyltryptamine (4-HO-DET), a tremendously potent hallucinogen, also not found in Nature. A new alkaloidal innovation then enters the neural networks of the Earth's ecosystems. (And all that LSD we've been producing and excreting? What have the Earth's organisms been doing with that?) The question arises then, as Alexander Shulgin so pointedly put it, what is natural? But a further query arises: what is driving so many humans to innovate so cleverly on all those serotonergic alkaloids?

The psilocybes have, unsurprisingly, been spreading throughout the world in disturbed ecoranges that have been overgrazed. They are especially aggressive in moving into agriculturally disturbed areas that have been fertilized with sheep, goat, or cow dung. (A.k.a. ruminants . . .

the origin of our word, ruminating.)

The capacity of these compounds to affect all living organisms, to alter their neural networks and sensory gating, reflects a deep, Gaian truth about neurognostics. They, as Kim Dawson put it, are crucial elements in *"an evolving ecological niche, one that is necessitated by an ecosysem whose survival is threatened."*[21] The fungal compounds' impact on human beings is only a specific instance of a general ecological condition and function. And its impacts on us are—as they are for all living things—important, and crucial, to our successful habitation of this planet. The same is true of DMT.

DMT

Also known as *N,N*-dimenthlytryptamine, DMT occurs extensively throughout the ecosystems of the world, just as the psilocybe do. As Rick Strassman puts it . . .

> *It is part of the normal makeup of humans and other mammals; marine animals; grasses and peas; toads and frogs; mushrooms and molds; and barks, flowers, and roots.*[22]

It is especially high in vascular plants. One source puts the compound in over 200 different species in 18 different families, most especially in the *Acacia, Delosperma, Psychotria,* and *Virola* genera. As Alexander Shulgin comments in his book *TIHKAL: Tryptamines I have Known and Loved,* "DMT is everywhere . . . [it] is in this flower here, in that tree over there, and in yonder animal. [It] is most simply everywhere you choose to look."[23]

DMT is made in plants by using enzymes to convert tryptophan into tryptamine into *N*-methyltryptamine and finally into *N,N*-dimethyltryptamine, DMT. Ayahuasca, now the most commonly used DMT preparation, is a plant decoction combination that blends a plant containing DMT (usually *Psychotria viridis* or *Diplopterys cabrerana*) and one containing B-carboline alkaloids (almost always *Banisteriopsis caapi*) that have monoamine oxidase–inhibiting properties. DMT is entirely inactive if taken orally, due to its breakdown by the human gut and liver enzyme monamine oxidase. But the B-carboline alkaloids in the second plant in the ayahuasca mixture inhibit the monoamine oxidase enzyme, allowing the DMT to cross, in a highly active state, into the blood stream and CNS.

Human beings throughout the world, in times long before the invention of chemical metaphors, figured out how to add these two plant types together to get exactly that outcome. No one ever asks how. And, no, they didn't go through the forest using trial-and-error with every plant they encountered in the search to create a hallucinogenic effect that they could not have experienced until those two exact plants were combined together in just that way.

Plants, however, don't have that particular problem. DMT affects them just fine. And like the *Psilocybe* genus, DMT is deeply interwoven into the ecosystems of the world—where it acts in much the same way as psilocybin. The trees release the compound through their root systems where it affects the soil biota, through their stomata into the atmosphere, and into the mycelial networks where it is carried throughout the ecoranges in which the plants live.

Trees and other plants can be thought of, more accurately, as an innovation on the mycelial mats that send up the fruiting bodies we call mushrooms. The earliest fungi emerged some 1.3 billion years ago (and then began making serotonergic alkaloids), the first land plants 600 millions years later. A tree root system is in fact a modulated mycelial mat. The tree is the fruiting body that extends above ground that, instead of spores, releases seeds to propagate. A tree is a transform of message material based on the earlier innovation of mycelial networks/fungal fruiting bodies.

DMT, similarly to psilocybin, stimulates extensions of plant neural networks, more widely open gating channels, and innovations in ecosystem response to perturbations in order to increase the functional resilience of the system.

DMT is in essence a serotonergic innovation
for use by vascular plants rather than by fungi
to enhance neural network functioning.

Neurognostics, of whatever molecular form, exist for this reason, and they always have. They enhance deeper perceptions of the reality field in which we are all embedded. We are not the only ones who have visionary experiences.

The Neuroactivity of Neurognostics

The ongoing conversation about neurognostics that has occupied the Western world since the 1960s is stuck in a rather deep rut. As Tyler Volk commented during his exploration of metapatterns while using the metaphor of a canoe . . .

> *Suppose you were asked to define a canoe. You describe a canoe's shape, its dimensions, materials, even methods of construction—as if preparing to build or at least to recognize one. In another type of answer you might describe what a canoe does, how it functions, carrying a person across water.*[24]

And in fact, what nearly everyone does, if they are interested in neurognostics, is to utilize one or both of these approaches . . . often with tiresome regularity. They just keep going on about the chemicals and the receptors in the brain. It's useful to a certain extent, but . . .

> *This does not, by the way, make a canoe—even though many scientists think it does—or even, more importantly, give the **experience** of canoe. It's just a map, it's not the territory. It won't support you on water or even, ultimately, get you anyplace your soul needs to go, especially if you decide to set off across the Ocean of Being, to find out, for yourself, what is there.*

So, here and there, from now on, will be some of Volk's third way, that is, "rather than saying anything directly about the canoe, you describe the experience of being in a canoe [and] what can be seen while paddling around."[25] This third way is, really, the most crucial of all—for each of us must find the true nature of the world for ourself. To do that we must actually ride in canoes—sooner or later. As Benny Shannon says, commenting on his experiences with ayahuasca . . .

> *The lawful patterns of cognition, I believe, are defined in terms of experience which is laden with meaning, not neurophysiological processes or brain events. The situation is analogous to that encountered in music. Admittedly, without a piano, piano music cannot come into existence. However, if one is to understand whatever is pertinent to the understanding of a piano sonata, it is senseless to study only the physics of the piano chords and their acoustics.*[26]

Our 5-HT receptors may be the piano, but they aren't the song . . . and they never will be. We can learn to intentionally modulate our receptors and thus come to create a particular kind of music, to actively participate in the singing of Earth. We can, then, go very deep into a state of synchrony with the other organisms of this world, even with the world itself. We can, through that, find communicatory expressions that can be found no other way, truths about this world that can be found through no other approach. But a dissection of the piano only tells us something about pianos, it doesn't tell us about the impact of music on a human heart, upon the heart of the world, or how that music assists the soul on its journey. People constantly forget, under the impetus of reductive megalomania,

> *of the insistent assertions of the neuroevangelists,*

that (as Crutchfield notes) "Even with a complete map of the nervous system of a simple organism . . . the organism's behavior cannot be deduced."[27]

> *keep that in mind*
> *our real purpose here is the song*
> *and our capacity to sing it in harmony with other life-forms*
> *all this, up to this point,*

> *has just been the construction of a more accurate map*
> *we are about to ride in the canoe soon, or maybe, even,*
> *swim . . . naked.*

But, before we get naked . . . a bit more about the piano.

Serotonergic neurognostics affect every organism similarly. As Franz Vollenweider and Mark Geyer comment, such compounds' effects "arise, at least in part, from their common capacity to disrupt thalamo-cortical gating of external and internal information to the cortex. . . . Cross-species studies of homologous gating functions, such as prepulse inhibition of the startle reflex . . . corroborate this view."[28] In other words, it doesn't matter whether you are a plant, or a spider, or a bird, or a monkey, or a human being, the neural network is going to be affected similarly. As Hofmann notes . . .

> *At very low optimum doses the webs [of spiders] were even better proportioned and more exactly built than normally: however, with higher doses, the webs were badly and rudimentarily made.*[29]

Neurognostics are, in fact, potent serotonin analogues and they affect the serotonin systems in all living organisms. And every living system uses serotonin and every living organism has receptors for it. Everybody and everything gets high and how high they get depends on how much they take.

> *the interesting question though*
> *is what the spider's webs were like*
> *after they came down*

In people, serotonergic neurognostics' impacts on the 5-HT receptors affect every portion of the body in which they occur. These impacts cause multiple downstream effects, including actions on GABA, dopamine receptors (such as D-1 and -2), and metabotropic glutamate receptors (mGluRs). Neuroimaging has shown that psilocybin (and mescaline) markedly increases brain activity bilaterally in the frontomedial and frontolateral cortices, including the anterior cingulate cortex. Smaller increases occur in the temporomedial, superior, and inferior parietal cortices, striatum, and thalamus. Decreases occur in the left caudate nucleus, bilaterally in the ventral striatum, occipital lobe, and visual pathway. Sensory gating is immediately affected, the gating channels open more widely, and on every test devised to examine gating dynamics, significant alterations have been found.

Serotonergic hallucinogens also act on dopamine receptors D1 and D2 and the adrenergic A-2 receptors. They increase *synaesthesis* (that is, the combination of two or more sensory modalities into one unique perceptual sensory medium), alter perception and the attribution of meaning to what is being perceived, and disrupt normal informational processing pathways. They change the nature of cognition itself.

they change the nature of cognition itself

They increase perceptual understandings of the environment, expand heart perception, and substantially decrease reliance on the forebrain. One begins to move out of the narrow confines of the reductive self and experience the inherent personhood of other life-forms. Benny Shannon observes that on ayahuasca there is

> The feeling that one understands the personalities of other individuals and gains special access to their mental states and inner feelings. Non-mediated communication is also experienced with animals. Indeed, experiences in which drinkers feel that they can converse with animals and understand them is very common with Ayahuasca. Also reported are similar experiences with plants.[30]

Jason Godesky comments that this experience of the personhood of other living beings is essential to successful human habitation of Earth, for if we deny personhood to "the other" we also end up

> denying the personhood of our fellow human beings. Ultimately, we can recognize others only by empathy; by recognizing enough of ourselves in the other, that we become able to assign to them the same kind of personhood, autonomy, thoughts and feelings that we ourselves experience firsthand. In general, this becomes difficult

unless we can communicate with that other, and receive feedback to
confirm that personhood.[31]

When a person withdraws empathy from the exterior world, from people, as Godesky notes, "we call that person a sociopath. [Thus] a fairly good description of civilization would focus on the systemic normalization of sociopathy. . . . To not recognize that [the world is filled with non-human persons] requires specific and significant effort. We must methodically train our children to withhold their empathy, or they will continue treating all manner of non-human things as people. Animism comes from humanity's natural condition; we have to teach anything else."[32]

Serotonergic neurognostics generate, or perhaps more accurately, regenerate, the natural childlike feelings of empathy, the direct experience of the personhood of the nonhuman other, by altering sensory gating in important ways. They alter the function of the frontal cortices, the limbic, and the parietal areas of the brain, all of which are strongly involved in sense of self, i.e., the identification of self and other, as well as the experience of the structure of time, what kind of stimuli are considered relevant, and the innovation of new behaviors. As the sensory gating of those parts of the brain is altered, the boundaries between self and other thin, empathy increases, time slows, and each incoming sensory inflow becomes novel and increasingly important. And again . . . *the boundary between self and other thins . . . sometimes it even disappears entirely.* As Fitz Hugh Ludlow described the experience . . .

> *Now in the primeval silence of some unexplored tropical forest I*
> *spread my feathery leaves, a giant fern, and swayed and nodded in*
> *spice-gales over a river whose waves at once sent up clouds of music*
> *and perfume. My soul changed to a vegetable essence, thrilled with*
> *a strange and unimagined ecstasy.*[33]

Such boundary thinning is crucial. For you begin then to see other life-forms from *their* point of view. In consequence, increased empathy is inevitable. This has deep implications for ecosystem functioning and health. As Aldous Huxley once observed, "To see ourselves as others see us is a most salutary gift. Hardly less important is the capacity to see others as they see themselves. But what if these others belong to a different species and inhabit a alien universe?"[34] Only if we can learn to see the other members of the Earth community from their point of view—to stand where they stand—and feel an empathy with their life can we begin to find a path to sustainable habitation of this planet.

But also . . . this increased sense of the other, this expansion of perceptual awareness, does something else that is crucial. It *feels* good. It literally alters the experience of existential disconnection that so many in the West now have. The indoleamine-derived hallucinogens such as LSD, psilocin (psilocybin), dimenthyltryptamine (DMT), and the phenylethylamine-derived hallucinogens such as mescaline and DOM all increase the sensitivity of and response to sensory stimuli . . . and they do so in a highly pleasurable way. The pleasure centers are highly stimulated. Sensory perception *feels* good.

With serotonergic neurognostics such as psilocybin, mescaline, and LSD the expansive effects on sensory gating stimulate synaptic plasticity and, for some, allow the sensory gating channels to remain much more widely open thereafter. This allows the regular intake of greater amounts of sensory data and the ability to work with greater ranges of meaning, increasing innovation in response to environmental inputs, including understanding associations between objects in the environment that are not normally perceived. That feeling good? It just keeps on feeling good. As Havelock Ellis, referring to mescaline, describes it . . .

I can, indeed, say that ever since this experience I have been more aesthetically sensitive than I was before to the more delicate phenomena of light and shade and color.[35]

Or Albert Hofmann with LSD . . .

A sensation of well-being and renewed life flowed through me. Breakfast tasted delicious and gave me extraordinary pleasure. When I later walked out into the garden, in which the sun shone now after a spring rain, everything glistened and sparkled in a fresh light. The world was as if newly created. All my senses vibrated in a condition of highest sensitivity.[36]

The initial ingestion of a hallucinogenic drug, in all organisms, is followed by decreased activity and greater sensory attention to environmental surroundings. That is followed, later, by increased exploration of those environmental surroundings.

The Holy Shit! and subsequent, Wow! Look at that! factors

Ayahuasca, psilocybin, LSD, and other neurognostics decrease the sensory gating of all sensory modalites, most especially visual and somatosensory (touch). Skin sensitivity increases substantially, visual perception is modified, auditory perception increases. Increased thought speed is also common but more importantly the formation of associations between disparate phenomena is strongly enhanced. The tendency to *focus* attention diminishes, attention tends to be more general, spreading outward to the whole environment of sensory stimuli. The conscious mind then follows what captures attention . . . until something else does. The self becomes highly attuned to signaling from the environment, to the messages that are coming from the world in which the person is embedded.

And now, just a bit about cannabinoids . . . because if I don't I will get letters.

Cannabinoids

Cannabinoids, which aren't exactly serotonergic in nature, also affect sensory gating. They produce the exact same effects though, usually, not quite so strongly. They have powerful effects on neural networks, playing strong neuromodulatory roles in immune and the central and peripheral nervous systems in the human body. Our bodies naturally make cannaboids (endocannaboids) and use them throughout the body where they participate in intracellular signaling. Cannabinoids (endo- or ecto-) play modulatory roles on the release of neurotransmitters such as GABA, 5HT, glutamate, acetylcholine, noradrenalin, and dopamine from a number of CNS structures such as the cerebellum, hippocampus, striatum, substancia nigra, and cortex. They act as a presynaptic autoreceptor mechanism, regulating GABA as well as glutamate neurochemicals in the neural system. Glutamate receptors actually induce the synthesis of endocannabinoids in response to environmental (or internal) cues in order to regulate GABA release and system levels. The production of the endocannabinoids alters neurocognitive architecture, stimulating neural plasticity and enhancing responses to environmental perturbations. During periods of high stress they are usually produced in higher quantities.

Cannabinoids act in all the sensory cortices, including the olfactory bulb, olfactory epithelium, and olfactory cortex; they act on the sensory gating mechanisms of odor, taste, touch, sight, smell, and feeling perceptions. The cannaboid receptors in the CNS modulate nociception, that is the neural processes of encoding and processing sensory stimuli. They act to modulate primary sensory inputs through effects on sensory gating by modulating GABA release from granule cell dendrites.

Basically, they get you high, just as serotonergic neurognostics do. And like DMT-containing plants, and psilocybe fungi, plants that contain cannabinoids, most especially cannabis, are hooked into ecosystems wherever they grow. They affect the neural networks in those systems just as they do in us.

yeah, it's true, the Earth gets high

And as they do in us, as so many neurognostics do, cannabinoids act to provide pain relieving functions in ecosystems, for every organism in the network, for the ecosystem itself.

Ecosystems can be hurt. When they are, signals are sent through the neural network, just as they are with us, signaling damage to the system. Ecosystems feel pain, just as we do—just as everything that possesses a neural network does. Functionality *demands* it. Pain is a neural signal that damage has occurred in the system. It gets the attention of the system so that the damage can be tended to. A system without a pain response would never be able to adapt to environmental fluctuations. And these neurognostics? They not only help relieve pain, they stimulate neural net reformation that can help the system generate healing responses that were formerly unavailable to it. The help the system innovate responses not only to external perturbations but internal ones.

Neurognostics and Ecosystem Function

The uniquely potent serotonin analogues that exist do so for specific ecological reasons—specifically, they function to both stimulate neural plasticity in Earth-system neural networks *and* to open sensory gating setting more widely. They stimulate neural net functioning outside of normal habituated parameters, allowing the individual organisms to generate unique innovations in response to environmental perturbations—both internal and external. So, it is not surprising that *a very wide range of living organisms* has been found to use neurognostics, and they all respond to them similarly. The drive for members of a species to use them is ecological, and of long evolutionary standing; it is not pathological. As researcher Giorgio Samorini comments . . .

> *Now that we have discovered its widespread existence in the animal kingdom, [a logical deduction] is that drug-induced alteration of consciousness* preceded *the origin of humans. Drugging oneself is a behavior that reached across the entire process of animal evolution, from insects to mammals to women and men.*[37]

Or as Ronald Siegel puts it . . .

> *Those drugs that animals select to use are those capable of interacting with normal brain mechanisms developed through evolution to mediate biologically essential behaviors directed toward food, water, and sex. In a sense, the pursuit of intoxicating drugs is the rule rather than an aberration . . . [psychotropic drug use] has adaptive evolutionary value.*[38]

And that "adaptive evolutionary value"? The restructuring of neural nets and the resetting of sensory gating in order to allow more sophisticated responses to unforeseen environmental events—internal and external. It increases response sophistication and capacity, as the poet Dale Pendell describes it . . .

> *You deserve it. To learn that your eyes have a microscopic ability,*

that your hands can be sculptor's hands, that you can understand Debussy, and follow his wry twists. How the tracts and esoterica of the alchemical philosophers are straight-forward trail notes, to which you can add commentary.[39]

The complexity of the self-organized system we know of as Earth makes the prediction of future events extremely difficult, if not impossible. But, as creativity researcher Edward de Bono puts it, "If you cannot accurately predict the future then you must be prepared to deal with various possible futures."[40] The neural networks of organisms are themselves nonlinear self-organized systems and they are generally able to deal with unpredictability. But gating parameters tend to set themselves as time progresses, and all organisms tend to habituate to certain ranges of sensory intake and response to environmental perturbations.

This includes plants, bacteria, insects, animals, and ecosystems

Neurognostics, though, act as what the Italian researcher Georgio Samorini describes as "a depatterning instrument or factor" or what Edward de Bono calls "Provocative Operation (PO) factors." That is, they "throw consolidated models into disorder." De Bono remarks that a PO

gives a person permission to use ideas that are not coherent with experience. With PO, rather than rejecting these ideas, a person can use them as springboards toward other ideas. PO therefore allows for the use of "intermediate impossibilities." Since these "impossible" ideas do not fit established models, they render possible a certain distance from existential experience. PO is a liberating device that frees [the mind] of the rigidity of established ideas, schemes, divisions, categories and classifications. PO is an instrument for insight.[41]

Or as Samorini puts it . . .

For the species to be able to preserve itself over time it must include the capacity to evolve, adapting and modifying itself in response to continual environmental changes. The principle of conservation (of that which has been acquired) tends to rigidly preserve established schemes and patterns, but modification (the search for new pathways) requires a depatterning instrument, or function, capable of opposing—at least at certain determined moments—the principles of conservation.[42]

And as he continues . . .

Since it is almost always only a certain percentage of members of any given species that engages in [drug use], this percentage may perform a depatterning function not only for itself but for the species as a whole.[43]

Are we engaging, then, in a "variant" expression of human perceptual sensitivity? If so, couldn't this be viewed, in turn, as perhaps a useful evolutionary adaptation? As an age-old demographic reality, possibly hardwired into the souls of some, that actually enriches and diversifies human civilization?

> *We can't solve problems*
> *by using the same kind of thinking we used*
> *when we created them.*

As Samorini comments, "Historically speaking, the fundamental motive for using drugs springs from a desire to understand reality more fully, not to escape it."[44] Neurognostics, as researchers have found time and time again, induce neural plasticity in the brain. The impact of psilocybin and other neurognostics is the alteration of habituated perception of the environmental field in which the perceiver is immersed. The sensory gating channels are opened so that a wider spectrum of incoming sensory flow is allowed and, as well, the meanings that are encoded within those sensory stimuli. Neurogenesis and synaptic plasticity is stimulated in the hippocampus, hippocampal function increases (the increase in sensory intake can be thought of as a richer environmental field), and problem solving outside normal habituated channels is stimulated. As Albert Hofmann put it . . .

If one continues with the conception of reality as a product of sender and receiver, then the entry of another reality under the influence of LSD may be explained by the fact that the brain, the seat of the receiver, becomes biochemically altered. The receiver is thereby tuned into another wavelength than that corresponding to normal, everyday reality. Since the endless variety and diversity of the universe corresponds to infinitely many different wavelengths, depending on the adjustment of the receiver, many different realities, including the respective ego, can come conscious. These different realities, more correctly designated as different aspects of the reality, are not mutually exclusive but are complementary, and form together a portion of the all-encompassing, timeless, transcendental reality, which has the power to record different egos, is located.

The true importance of LSD and related hallucinogens lies in their capacity to shift the wavelength setting of the receiving "self," and thereby to evoke alterations in reality consciousness. [It has the] ability to allow different, new pictures of reality to arise.[45]

Neurognostics *break* habituated patterns. Those who take them, and write about their experiences, all comment on the effect. Here is Anaïs Nin about the impacts of LSD on her habituated perceptual framework . . .

I realized the expression "blow my mind" was born of the fact that America had cemented access to imagination and fantasy and that it would take dynamite to remove this block! I believed Leary's emphasis on the fact that we use only one percent of our mind or potential, that everything in our education conspires to restrict and constrict us. I only wished people had had time to study drugs as they studied religion or philosophy and to adapt to this chemical alteration of our bodies.

[LSD's] value is in being a shortcut to the unconscious, so that one enters the realm of intuition unhampered, pure as it is in children, of direct emotional reaction to nature, to other human beings. In a sense it is the return to the spontaneity and freshness of childhood vision which makes every child able to paint or sing.[46]

And Adelle Davis, about her experiences with LSD as well . . .

> *Within a week after my first sojourn into other worlds I noticed that I seemed to have two personalities: a pre-LSD personality in which my own feelings stayed dominant and to which I reverted under stress; and a post-LSD personality characterized by serenity, tolerance, optimism, and a forgetfulness of self. When the latter personality was uppermost, I could at times sense the feelings of others with an amazingly accurate intuition. The two personalities became more evident with each experience, but after a period of months they apparently became amalgamated and were no longer separately recognizable.*[47]

And Hofmann again . . .

> *In the normal condition of consciousness, in everyday reality; one stands face-to-face with the outer world; it has become an object. In the LSD state the boundaries between the experiencing self and the outer world more or less disappear. . . . Feedback between receiver and sender takes place. A portion of the self overflows into the outer world, into objects, which begin to live, to have another deeper meaning.*[48]

The expanded perception of the metaphysical background of the world does in fact, lead to considerable innovations as habituated patterns are broken. People learn to *see* and *hear* and *sense* and *think* in new ways. You only have to look at the innovations in Western music, the developments in sound technology that then occurred, the innovations in alternative health care, computer technology, and business that all began in the 1960s under the impact of neurognostics.

> *Yes, a lot of them were stoned, and many of them are willing to admit it like Steve Jobs of Apple (though some of them, many that I used to get high with, wear suits now and pretend they've always kept their neural systems chaste, while making a living from a business they thought of when stoned on acid) or Kary Mullis, the*

Nobel laureate and biochemist, who credited LSD with helping him develop DNA amplification technology, that is the polymerase chain reaction (PCR) technique that is used in laboratories throughout the world to more quickly identify microorganisms.

That so many of the Western world's innovative leaps after WWII came from neurognostics is the dirty little secret that the narrow-minded just can't accept. Though, as Samorini says . . .

The fact that a human behavior such as drug use, so insistently denigrated and prohibited because it is considered unnatural and therefore immoral, is also to be found in the rest of nature and practiced by many animals should teach us to be more cautious in our evaluations and convictions.[49]

One of the reasons for the upset among the VSPs (Very Serious People) can be understood by looking at what happens in the interaction between those who ingest neurognostics and who actually do alter their habituated patterning and those who do not. Whether the behavior of those who are high changes at all or not, it doesn't matter. The people around them can tell that they have eaten something the others have not, that they have changed something fundamental. It frightens them. As Hofmann comments . . .

A caged community of chimpanzees reacts very sensitively if a member of the tribe has received LSD. Even though no changes appear in this single animal, the whole cage gets in an uproar because the LSD chimpanzee no longer observes the laws of its finely coordinated hierarchic tribal order.[50]

If we had an accepted place in our culture for those who have felt the swaying of the elephant's shoulders, the existence of the niche would reduce that fear level, because the behavior would be identified and its category recognized. But the problem is particularly acute in the West, even more so in the U.S. as Hofmann says, "A concept of reality that separates self and the world has decisively determined the evolutionary course of European intellectual history."[51] Those who open sensory gating are a danger to the fundamental underpinnings of that reductive paradigm. As Marlene Dobkin De Rios put it . . .

if these substances weren't illegal, shamans would emerge[52]

and that is why drugs are illegal, why schizophrenics are never trained in the use of their expanded capacities, why the arts are so poorly supported, why the gifted are considered developmentally disabled. And of all the impacts of neurognostics on human neural networks, perhaps none are more dangerous to the status quo than their thinning of the boundary between self and other.

> *In report after report on schizophrenia, this is considered to be one of the most pathological aspects of the situation, one that their minders try so hard to prevent through the use of pharmaceuticals.*

Once the boundary thins, it is difficult to separate self from other. The feelings of the other and *my* feelings become intertwined and I began to see the other from their own point of view. I begin to operate from a position of empathy, the world is no longer red in tooth and claw, and I begin to personally experience the living reality of the life-forms that exist outside my normally discrete boundaries. I began to care. And then, inevitably, I begin to be careful in how I treat the inhabitants of the world outside my skin.

When we take neurognostics, we enter a different world, not a static place filled with unrelated objects but a constantly interactive scenario filled with meaning and communication. And when we do, something very interesting begins to happen. We become intertangled in the livingness, the semantic underpinnings, of the world. And once that happens, the entire underpinnings of the reductionist, Western world begin to crumble.

And nothing, then, is ever the same again.

9

INEXTRICABLE
INTERTANGLING

To understand Gaia, we must let go of the mechanistic compartmentalizing conditioning imposed on us since childhood by our society. From an early age nearly all Westerners (and especially young scientists) are exposed to the concept that life has come about due to the operation of blind, meaningless laws of physics and chemistry, and that selfishness underpins the behaviour and evolution of all plants and animals. A child's mind becomes totally ensnared by this style of intellectuality, so that the intuitive, inspirational qualities of the mind are totally ignored. The mind's intuitive ability to see each part of nature as a sub-whole within the greater wholes is destroyed by this sort of education. The result is a totally dry, merely intellectual ecology, not a genuine perception of the dynamic power, creativity, and integration of nature.

STEPHAN HARDING

*We have been trained to think of patterns, with the exception of those of music, as fixed affairs. It is easier and lazier that way but, of course, all nonsense. In truth, the right way to think about the pattern which connects is to think of it as **primarily** a dance of interacting parts.*

GREGORY BATESON

231

I love [Thoreau's] fierce and meticulous observation. Most artists begin, as seems right, with interior absorption, introversion and examination of their interior world, and often end there. From much ancient art, we deduce that the next stage involves attention, which goes to the life beyond one's house, beyond one's mind, beyond human obsession to the enormous intertangling that we call the universe.

ROBERT BLY

The natural world, from which we are expressed as a unique eco-logical communication when we are born, it is important to understand, is not a place. It is, as Gregory Bateson described it, a *context* filled with interconnected phenomena that are *transforms of messages,* or as Buckminster Fuller put it, a *scenario.* And as Fuller went on to say, it is possible to get out of a place, it is not possible to get out of a scenario. Again . . .

It is possible to get out of a place,
*it is **not** possible to get out of a scenario*

If you can allow yourself to let that perceptual meaning into your interior, and to then see the world around you through its lens, the first thing you will probably experience is a mild nausea. Such reorien-tation contradicts a foundational belief that each and every one of us absorbs from our cultures beginning the day we are born, and it *shifts* the ground of reality inside us. *Everything* that we perceive, including ourselves, undergoes an alteration in its inherent meaning in the face of it.

One of the primary alterations is that our interior experience of the world shifts from a static orientation to one that moves. The world is no longer a place of stable nonmovement but a continually flowing field. Once you get that you are in a scenario, normal habituated behavior shifts—automatically. *How* you approach the world alters. The pen on the desk is now approached as a part of a scenario,

with recognition and empathy

not a static object sitting on another static object, you the only one possessing movement.

In a scenario, everything has movement, *all the time*. Everything is changing, *all the time*. In a scenario, evolution has not ended. It is not an escalator that has arrived at an endpoint—us—where all change ceases. Evolution—that is, Gaian innovation—has no end, and it never will. We are just passing actors on the stage, not the ultimate point of the process. As Michael Crichton put it, in his book *Prey* (HarperCollins, 2002) . . .

> *The notion that the world around us is continuously evolving is a platitude; we rarely grasp its full implications. We do not ordinarily think, for example, of an epidemic disease changing its character as the epidemic spreads. Nor do we think of evolution in plants and animals as occurring in a matter of days or weeks, though it does. And we do not ordinarily imagine the green world around us as a scene of constant, sophisticated chemical warfare, with plants producing pesticides in response to attack, and insects developing resistance. But that is what happens, too.*
>
> *If we were to grasp the true nature of nature—if we could comprehend the real meaning of evolution—then we would envision a world in which every living plant, insect, and animal species is changing at every instant, in response to every other living plant, insect, and animal. Whole populations of organisms are rising and falling, shifting and changing. This restless and perpetual change, as inexorable and unstoppable as the waves and tides, implies a world in which all human actions necessarily have uncertain effects. The total system we call the biosphere is so complicated that we cannot know in advance the consequences of anything we do. (This uncertainty is characteristic of all complex systems, including man-made ones.) That is why even our most enlightened past efforts have had undesirable outcomes.[1]*

Crichton's observation: "If we were to grasp the true nature of nature—if we could comprehend the real meaning of evolution—then we would envision a world in which every living plant, insect, and animal species is changing at every instant, in response to every other living plant, insect, and animal" is crucial. We do not and never have lived in a world where we are the actors and the rest of Nature is a static backdrop. As Buckminster Fuller once observed . . .

> *It is perplexing that one of the most persistent contemplations of human beings had been predicated on a static concept of Universe, the kind of Universe that went out with classical Newtonian mechanics. We cannot think of Universe as a fixed static picture, which we try to do when people ask where the outwardness of the Universe ends. Humans try to get a finite unit package. We have a monological propensity for the* thing, the *key,* the *building block of Universe.*[2]

The mental orientation of ourselves—and all other organisms—as being in a *place* continually leads to improper analysis of the ecological framework in which we exist and from which we emerged. One of the worst logical faults to come from this is the belief that organisms adapt to their environment by fitting themselves into niches, as if the environment were an external, static frame filled with blank holes that the various organisms then fill. Richard Lewontin comments that

> *Organisms do not find already existing ecological niches to which they adapt, but are in the constant process of defining and remaking their environments. At every moment natural selection is operating to change the genetic composition of populations in response to the momentary environment, but as that composition changes it forces a concomitant change in the environment itself. Thus organism and environment are both causes and effects in a coevolutionary process. This coeevolutionary process has one general feature. . . . It is almost always* topologically continuous. *That is, small changes in the environment lead to small changes in the organism which, in turn, lead to small changes in the environment. . . . In general the organism and the environment must track each other continuously or life would have long ago become extinct.*[3]

Or, as Lovelock comments, "Life and the material environment evolved tightly coupled together as a single entity."[4] In other words, what we have is

wait for it

a scenario, not a static place into which organisms fit themselves. The environment itself *cannot* realistically be viewed as a place but must more properly be viewed as an organism—a living field—

*just as the extracellular matrix
that surrounds our cells
is now understood to be a living field*

which itself adapts to changes or even initiates them. If you really look deeper, most uncomfortably, it becomes clear that there is no such thing as "environment" at all. The internal experience of that statement, the mild nausea that accompanies its use as a lens through which to view the world, points up the depth of attachment to the paradigm of "place" that we have accepted. Lewontin develops the understanding further, making it even more disturbing . . .

> *The properties of species map the shape of the underlying external world, just as when we sprinkle iron filings on a sheet of paper lying on a magnet, the filings form a pattern that maps the underlying magnetic field. In a curious sense the study of organisms is really a study of the shape of the environmental space, the organisms themselves being nothing but the passive medium through which we see the shape of the external world. They are the iron filings of the environmental field.*[5]

This is a beautiful way to catch a glimpse of Bateson's "transforms of messages." For Bateson was, himself, saying the same thing. Through this image, Lewontin shifts the field of view from the organism in the foreground to the background *as* foreground. It shifts our focus in uncomfortable ways, for all of us are taught that living organisms are *the* important thing (none more important than the human). These *are*, by cultural definition, foreground. But with this shift, background becomes foreground and organisms as such disappear; they become background, their importance evaporates.

This kind of shifting between background and foreground is most deliciously captured in Edgar Rubin's famous drawing. It creates this same effect of shifting foreground and background perception.

Is the drawing of the profiles of two human faces or is it of a vase? If you focus your attention on the drawing, once you have seen both possible pictures, the focus of attention automatically begins oscillating between both perspectives making it very hard to get a grasp on what is actually there, what the fundamental picture really is. While the drawing is intended to help artists and designers more effectively capture three-dimensional shapes on a two-dimensional page, what it does best is exemplify the experience of trying to find one-picture answers to complex world problems.

When you look at this drawing
you are experiencing the reality of why
top-down solutions to complex environmental problems
will always fail

One-picture answers don't exist. As Buckminster Fuller put it . . .

The parents tell the child he cannot have both the Sun and the Moon in the picture at the same time. The child says that you can. The child has the ability to coordinate nonsimultaneity. The parents have lost the ability to coordinate nonsimultaneity. One of our great limitations is our tendency to look only at the static picture, the one confrontation. We want one-picture answers; we want key pictures. But we are now discovering that they are not available.[6]

Or as Mary Midgley puts it . . .

The universe has no single secret. It does not even hold a single nest of secrets, to which some one study holds the key. We can explain a great many things, but in different ways. All studies are of strictly limited use; all are complimentary, all need each other.[7]

Or as Paul Krugman said it . . .

The map is not the territory, and it's OK to use different kinds of maps depending on what you're trying to accomplish: if you're driving, a road map suffices, if you're going hiking, you really need a topo.[8]

Chemistry is one map. Physics another map. Ecology another map. All maps are useful, none are fundamental. There is no one-picture answer.

However . . . what is disturbing in the drawing is that it gives an actual experience of the equal importance *in reality* of both background and foreground. This directly contradicts our software programming that only foreground is important, that organisms should always take center stage in our perceptual focus. But the drawing also gives an experience of something equally as important: there is no such thing as background, *only* foreground. What we have taken to be background and what we have taken to be foreground are actually, in essence, the same thing. And both have to be viewed simultaneously—at the same time—equal in importance to each other if we want to understand Earth, and ourselves.

this is the essence of holistic perception
and the linear mind just isn't very good at it

All organisms are generated out of the ecological matrix of this planet—what we have taken to be background. They are generated out of the self-organized system's deep movements toward continuing homeodynamic stabilization across the multiple layers of the reality frame that exists in this scenario. All organisms are, in fact, forms, or more accurately *transforms,* of environment themselves. They are so tightly coupled with the field from which they emerged that it is not possible, with any accuracy, to view them in isolation from that field. Doing so immediately creates an experiential and interpretational disjunct between self and world.

Any behavioral actions taken that are based on the mistaken experience that organisms are not environment, that environment is background and organisms foreground, results in environmental perturbations that will disturb the homeodynamis of the Gaian system.

Ultimately, when you examine organisms and environment deeply, it is impossible to actually find the point of demarcation, the place where organism and environment begin and end. As Lewontin notes, "the softness of the boundary between inside and outside is a universal characteristic of living systems."[9] It is extremely difficult to pinpoint the exact point at which *me* and *not me* begins. Yes, there is a focus, a nexus,

a node

of concentrated beingness, part of which is perceived as a unique physical form, that has real existence. But what it really is, is a transform of environment, created to fulfill specific functions. It is just the place where the message material becomes most dense. And as such there can be no definite boundary line between environment and organism, for there is *only* environment. What we really are dealing with in this scenario that we call the world is an uncountable complexity of nested and overlapping self-organized systems, each of them an aspect

just as our white blood cells are of us

of the larger self-organized system we call Gaia, which is itself only part of the larger self-organized scenario of Universe.

It is this irremovable intertanglement between foreground and background that has frightened neo-Darwinianist reductionists so much. In their paradigm, niches exist independent of life and life fits itself to them, competing in a never-ending struggle for survival. In the neo-Darwinianist world the struggle for survival and niche specialization are the *only* realities—in spite of the fact that Darwin himself was much more flexible, that he realized that his great insight was only the beginning, that it would have to develop more complexity as its implications and reality were better understood. As James Lovelock comments . . .

> *Just as Newtonian physics was found incomplete at the particle and cosmic scales, so Darwinism is incomplete when it tries to explain the world beyond the phenotype. In particular it fails to see that organisms do more than adapt to a dead and fixed world.*[10]

The recognition that life shapes environment which then shapes life which then shapes environment destroys the foundation of the neo-Darwinian system. It begins to destroy the whole concept of cause and effect. Evolution begins to take on quantum characteristics; linear thinking is no longer foundational. As Masanobu Fukuoka put it . . .

> *Nature is a fluid entity that changes from moment to moment. Man is unable to grasp the essence of something because the true form of nature leaves nowhere to be grasped. People become perplexed when bound by theories that try to freeze a fluid nature. . . . Behind every cause lies countless other causes. Any attempt to trace these back to their sources only leads one further away from an understanding of the true cause. . . . Nature has neither beginning nor end, before nor after, cause nor effect. Causality does not exist. When there is no front or back, no beginning or end, but only what resembles a circle or sphere, one could say that there is a unity of cause and effect, but one could just as well claim that cause and effect do not exist.*[11]

Or as Goethe said it . . .

When something has acquired a form it metamorphoses immediately into a new one. If we wish to arrive at some living perception of nature we ourselves must remain as quick and flexible as Nature and follow the example She gives.[12]

The opening of sensory gating channels more widely leads to a thinning of the boundary between self and nonself. It enables the movement of consciousness from a static sense of us being in a place to our immersion in a scenario. It allows immersion within the metaphysical background of the world.

At that moment, as Buckminster Fuller once put it, there is "no more secondhand God."

It allows us to experience, first hand, that there is no difference between background and foreground, that both are the same thing.

And *that* is where we are going now, for all this, so far, has only been preliminary. Only mapmaking. Only a story about pianos. But it is the song that I am really interested in. And even more, I am interested in the place the song lives when no one is playing it. As Stephen King once said . . .

Where I am, it's still dark and raining. We've got a fine night for it. There's something I want to show you, something I want you to touch. It's in a room not far from here—in fact, it's almost as close as the next page.

Shall we go?[13]

Gaia's Mind and the Dreaming of Earth

꒳

A human being is a part of a whole, called by us "universe," a part limited in time and space. He experiences himself, his thoughts and feelings as something separated from the rest . . . a kind of optical delusion of his consciousness. This delusion is a kind of prison for us, restricting us to our personal desires and affection for a few persons nearest to us. Our task must be to free ourselves from this prison by widening our circle of compassion to embrace all living creatures and the whole of nature in its beauty.

ALBERT EINSTEIN

Holistic science sees humans not as objective observers but as participatory "experiencers" radically embedded in the world. Intrinsic value is explicitly recognized, and knowledge is seen as a means for increasing a sense of belonging to nature, rather than solely as a means for its control. This mode of science accepts lack of complete predictability as a key feature of a creative universe. . . . Intuition is explicitly developed as a method for enhancing scientific enquiry through paying close attention to the consistency of feelings and intuitions which come up amongst a group of scientists during their investigations. . . . Participatory holistic science is more than just an intellectual stance—it involves a radical shift in our fundamental perception of nature. The shift is primarily experiential rather than intellectual.

STEPHAN HARDING

*Go to the pine
if you want to learn about the pine,
or to the bamboo
if you want to learn about the bamboo.
And in doing so,
you must leave
your subjective preoccupation with yourself.
Otherwise you impose yourself on the object
and do not learn.*

BASHO

The teachers told us quietly that the way of experts had become a tricky way. They told us that it would always be fatal to our arts to misuse the skills we had learned. The skills were merely light shells, needing to be filled out with a substance coming from our souls. They warned us never to turn these skills to things separate from the way. This would be the most difficult thing.

AYI KWEI ARMAH

The worst thing is to doubt what the Earth wants.

FREDERICH NIETZSCHE

10
"A Certain Adjustment of Consciousness"

One learns that it is possible by a certain adjustment of consciousness to participate in art—it's a natural activity for one not corrupted by mechanical ways.

WILLIAM STAFFORD

Every new object, clearly seen, opens up a new organ of perception in us.

GOETHE

Few are those who see with their own eyes and feel with their own hearts.

ALBERT EINSTEIN

Tell your people they must learn to wake up their feelings. Their heart must arise from its sleep. It must rise and stand up. That is how you find the track to God.

THE ELDERS OF THE KALAHARI BUSHMEN

*I*f you decide to open your sensory gating channels more widely, engage the metaphysical background of the world more deeply, develop Gaian ways of perception, you, by definition, leave old forms of thinking behind. You begin to move into the world the Tao Te Ching speaks of when it asks . . .

> *Who will prefer the jingle of jade pendants*
> *if he once has heard stone growing in a cliff?*

To hear stone growing in a cliff, however, means that a shift in consciousness must occur. You can't hear something the linear mind has been taught does not exist. The phrase "shift in consciousness" however has taken on mystical trappings,

> *as it must in any linear system*

making it seem something that only adepts in ancient traditions can accomplish. But it is not as hard as it sounds;

> *in fact it's extremely easy*

every person shifts consciousness thousands of times every day—it's just that, because of our schooling, hardly any of us notices it.

For example,

> *every time we read a story*

we drop into a dream state—our consciousness shifts—and the story comes alive inside us. The story, literally, becomes real. We're no longer aware of the words on the page; they have disappeared. In some magical way, as the writer John Gardner puts it . . .

> *We read a few words at the beginning of the book or the particular*
> *story and suddenly we find ourselves seeing not words on a page but*
> *a train moving through Russia, an old Italian crying, or a farm-*
> *house battered by rain.*[1]

Each of us has had the experience of being awakened suddenly from such a dream—by the insistent ringing of the telephone or a sharp knock at the door. It startles us awake as if from a deep sleep and it takes a few minutes for us to recall ourselves, for our conscious minds to begin functioning again. Yet even as we answer the phone or the door, the meanings, experiences, or people we were dreaming about linger in the mind like a wonderful taste on the tongue or delicate strains of music shimmering in the ear, more real yet than the salesman at the door or our friend on the telephone. A shift in consciousness has occurred.

though we usually just call it reading

During that shift, when we become immersed in story, a unique alteration in sensory gating channels occurs. The gating of the *feeling* sense is no longer narrow; it opens more widely—and this is crucial to the art, to the story coming alive inside us.

There is a reason why gating opens more widely (and the more accomplished the writer, the more widely it opens). It happens because writers learn, one way or another, to combine the visual and feeling senses into one unique sensory medium.

it's called synaesthesia

If done well, when you read a visual scene in a story you also *feel* the deeper realities underneath those visual scenes. You begin to encounter the metaphysical background of the world—the feeling dimension that is inside all visual phenomena.

So, let's say you are reading a visually descriptive passage, say, of driving up to a house on a dark, rainy night . . .

I turned into the driveway. It was a long dirt road that wound through the trees. The rain was beating down steadily, a ruthless drumbeat. In a moment I saw lights appear through the trees. A house rose up out of the mist, an old frame building with a wide front porch. It looked homey and warm, like home is supposed to look to a tired and heartsick traveler.[2]

. . . you end up, inevitably, experiencing how the place *feels*. "Homey" and "warm" are not visual descriptions (even though the writer used the word "looked" when he wrote the passage), they are *feeling* descriptions, part of what the writer William Gass calls the *secret kinesis* of things, that is, the hidden feeling dimension that is inside every physical object. In this instance it's part of the house's secret kinesis. And it is the presence of that secret kinesis in the writing that activates the feeling sense of the reader.

> *Without including the house's secret kinesis*
> *the writing would be dead, lifeless,*
> *mere words on a page*

The feeling dimensions of the house are what bring the scene alive. And so, what you get is not words on a page but the actual experience of "a house rising up out of the mist, an old frame building with a wide front porch."

The passage, from John Dunning's *The Bookman's Wake*, is an example of a writer's blending the visual and feeling senses into a single sensory medium. That simple visual description—"looked homey and warm"—evokes both feeling and seeing simultaneously as a unified perception. You literally feel what you are seeing. From fairly minor clues, the blending of the two senses automatically generates a complex gestalt in the reader of both kinesthetic and visual perceptions of the house.

That is part of the power of writing when it truly becomes art. Whenever these two sensory mediums are blended in just the right way, only a tiny part of what is being perceived through the writer's imagination needs to be written. Then, when those words touch the reader, and are taken inside, a complex gestalt of associational feeling and seeing is automatically generated. The trigger for it is the feeling dimension of the house, the secret kinesis within it. Without that, the writing might still be visually descriptive but the scene wouldn't work. It wouldn't come alive.

And the feeling that is described in that scene? It *belongs* to the house. It's not a psychological projection but a reality, something inherent in the thing itself. Though Dunning may have *imagined* that particular house, he had already experienced houses that felt like that.

All of us, in our day-to-day lives, have experienced the secret kinesis of houses. All of us have spent time in warm houses and all of us have spent time in cold ones.

All of us have been in houses that will never be homes. Houses where some coldness of spirit resides, which, if you stay too long, begins to seep into your own spirit and drag it down. Houses in which the lines are wrong, the rooms too small. Houses so clean that anyone entering feels unkempt. Houses in which you cannot conceive of putting your feet up, or smiling, or feeling love.

And all of us have had the experience of walking into a house where a very different experience occurs. Houses that have windows that look out on happy gardens and where happy sunlight looks right back in. Houses where we feel some kind of spirit reach out and gather us to its breast. Houses in which a part of ourselves suddenly relaxes and breathes deeply. Houses filled with warmth of spirit, of joy, of happiness. Houses in which we feel the touch of an aged relative on our brow telling us that we are loved and wanted and welcome. Houses that are homes.

This intentional blending of the visual description of a thing and its secret kinesis is the power that hides inside good writing. It's one of the major skills of the craft that all good writers must develop. Most readers can't see what is being done by the writer, they just *feel* it. And as soon as they encounter that blended sensory communication on a page, their state of consciousness begins to change: They drop into a dream state and the scene comes alive inside them. They literally *feel* the reality of what the author has done; they are no longer aware of the surroundings in which they are reading.

Here, experience it again. This time with the opening passages of Dick Francis's book *Reflex* . . .

Winded and coughing, I lay on one elbow and spat out a mouthful of grass and mud. The horse I'd been riding raised its weight off my ankle, scrambled untidily to its feet and departed at an unfeeling gallop. I waited for things to settle; chest heaving, bones still rattling from the bang, sense of balance recovering from a thirty-mile-an-hour somersault and a few tumbling rolls. No harm done. Nothing broken. Just another fall.

Time and place: sixteenth fence, three-mile steeplechase, Sandown Park racecourse, Friday, November, in thin, cold, persistent rain. At the return of breath and energy I stood wearily up and thought with intensity that this was a damn silly way for a grown man to be spending his life.[3]

Dick Francis was particularly skillful at creating this kind of a realistic scene in just a few sentences. The first two are a brilliant example of his skill: "Winded and coughing, I lay on one elbow and spat out a mouthful of grass and mud. The horse I'd been riding raised its weight off my ankle, scrambled untidily to its feet and departed at an unfeeling gallop." By the time I get to "untidily to his feet" I can literally see the horse scrambling to its feet . . . and at "unfeeling gallop"

I can see the horse running away—the stirrups flopping and jangling as it runs. I feel the ground underneath me as I lie there, watching. These are what are called associational reverberations— parts of the scene that are hidden inside the writing.

And the word "unfeeling"? It very specifically enhances the *feeling* that the rest of the passage evokes. It's brilliant. Thus, the passage is not only visually vivid, there is a deep *feeling* experience of the scene that occurs when it is read. The reader begins to literally become the character, feel as if they are there *in* the vivid, living scene—and after only two sentences.

Once a writer effectively blends the feeling sense with the visual, an alteration in consciousness takes place immediately—as soon as you begin to read. Gating channels open more widely.

That's what alteration in consciousness is.
It's a simple thing really, built into all of us. We do it naturally.

Let's go a bit deeper; here is a longer passage from the same book . . .

"You don't believe me, do you?" She demanded. "You simply don't see . . ." She broke off and frowned. "You haven't had any of these

photographs published before, have you? In papers or magazines, or anywhere?"

I shook my head. "Nowhere. I've never tried."

"You're amazing. You have this talent and you don't use it."

"But . . . everyone takes photographs."

*"Sure they do. But not everyone takes a long series of photographs which illustrate a whole way of life." She tapped off the ash on her cigarette. "It's all there, isn't it? The hard work, the dedication, the bad weather, the humdrum, the triumphs, the pain . . . I've only looked through these pictures once, and in no sort of order, and I know what your life's like. I know it **intimately**. Because that's how you photographed it. I know your life from the inside. I see the enthusiasm in those owners. I see their variety. I see what you owe to the stable lads. I see the worry of trainers, it's everywhere. I see the laughter in the jockeys, and the stoicism. I see what you've felt. I see what you've understood about people. I see people in a way I hadn't before, because of what you've seen."*

"I didn't know," I said slowly, "that these pictures were quite so revealing."

"Look at this last one," she said, pulling it out. "This picture of a man in an overall pulling the boot off this boy with the broken shoulder . . . you don't need any words to say the man is doing it as gently as he can, or that it hurts . . . you can see it all, in every line of their bodies and faces."[4]

You're already into it, aren't you? Already wondering what will happen next in the story. By the end of this passage you not only feel the scene, you've begun to care about the characters—to have a sense of them as people. And the photographs she's talking about? They've become vivid. You can actually see that last one as she describes it—*and* feel the feelings she is describing that are *in* the photo. But at the same time, you can also feel *her* feelings about it. There's a sense of her holding the photo, too—in just the same gentle, attentive way as the man is pulling off the boy's boot. Her face attentive, her expression earnest. In *her* face you can see the reflection of the feelings, both physical and emotional, captured in the photograph. It's brilliant writing.

Dick Francis was particularly good at, nearly immediately, creating the dream state that all good writing evokes. There wasn't a lot of the book in that passage but as you read it, your consciousness changed. You began to dream.

That dream state is important.
It's very similar to the state that Gaia (and plants) are in
most of the time
and you did not need a Ph.D. or advanced training to do it.

In that dream, you experienced, firsthand, a synaesthesia of sensory mediums. There was a blending of the visual and feeling senses—that's the foundational base of what's occurring. But, interestingly, at different moments, you could also *hear* some of the sounds inherent in the scene, physically *feel* parts of it as well, and, perhaps, even smell her cigarette. It literally becomes real as you read.

this dream state, where the story literally becomes real,
is what Goethe called the "exact sensory imagination"
it's the tool he used to enter the dreaming of Earth
to better understand the movements of Gaia

Part of how writers create this effect is by dropping into a kind of dream themselves as they write. We enter a dream when we read because writing itself is a special kind of dreaming. It is dreaming developed into a particular kind of art. It is because writing begins as a dream in an altered state of consciousness that it ends as a dream in the reader's mind. It is only because writers dream as they write that the reader, later, can dream at all. As Gardner says, "The organized and intelligent fictional dream that will eventually fill the reader's mind *begins as a largely mysterious dream in the writer's mind.*"[5]

Writers enter the same dream that their readers dream later as they read the book the writer has written. But writers do not sit down, pick up a book, and begin to dream. They sit down in front of a blank page and allow a dream to flow through them and onto the page. They intentionally shift consciousness into a specific state of mind, and from that state of mind, writing occurs. This is the state that all writers inhabit when they write. As John Gardner describes it . . .

An invisible wall seems to fall away, and the writer moves easily and surely from one kind of reality into another. . . . Every writer has experienced at least moments of this strange, magical state. . . . These queer moments, sometimes thrilling, sometimes just strange, moments setting off an altered state, a brief sense of escape from ordinary time and space . . . are the soul of art.[6]

Every good writer has a way of describing the state Gardner is talking about. Stephen King calls it "the zone," Goethe a "somnambulistic state," Dorothea Brande the "artistic coma," William Stafford the "creative trance." Others call it the writing trance, or the writing dream, or sometimes just "the groove." It is only when the writer is in that state, to a greater or lesser extent, that writing moves from the thudding grocery-list-prose of bad writing into something alive. And this is crucial, not only because it moves the writing into art but because of what it does to the readers as they read. Writing that emerges out of that dreaming state produces an altered state of consciousness in the reader.

Western cultures pretend that such alterations of consciousness do not occur in all people continually, that they are not important, that they are not essential to human culture, and they pretend very hard that this same state is not at the root of all science. Such alterations are normal, natural, and essential to what it means to be human.

When writers move into that dreaming state—and to be clear, it feels *exactly* like the state you are in when you are reading, immersed in the story—they *allow* a dream to flow into and through them, onto the page. And as they write, the story begins to come alive to them, just as it will do for us later. As Gardner comments, the experience is one

of seeing something one has written come alive—literally, not metaphorically—a character or scene daemonically entering the world by its own strange power, so that the writer feels not the creator but only the instrument, or conjuror, the priest who stumbled onto the magic spell.[7]

Essential to that state of mind is the blending of feeling and visual sensing. But how that blending occurs is difficult to explain, for once in the dream, the senses begin to blend of their own accord.

the senses begin to blend of their own accord

The writer literally sees the scene, literally feels the emotional tone in every object in the scene. The house *feels* a certain way. The curtains, as they waver slightly in the rising heat, *feel* a certain way. The crunch of the man's footsteps on the gravel drive *feel* a certain way.

Because the writer is *feeling* the scene *and* every element in it—as he is writing, even if he only describes a few of the things he sees—the entire scene becomes imbued with feeling. In some indefinable way—that no one can explain—the feeling sense of the writer gets *inside* the words—every one of them, no matter what kind of words they are.

The writer, as Robert Bly says it, piles up meaning behind the word, like water behind a dam. When we touch those words with our minds, deep in the dreaming state, it breaks the surface tension of the word and all that meaning immediately flows into us, all the hidden parts of the scene emerge into our awareness. It all comes alive inside us.

In that dreaming state, the words the writer chooses—unconsciously during the initial draft—are ones that have certain feeling associations to them. They create reverberational associations that flow throughout the writing, stimulating associations in the readers as they read.

It is *literally* and not metaphorically the altered state itself that allows the writing to come alive. Writing from what most people consider to be a "normal" state of consciousness won't work. Linear reductionism can't get there. As Gardner puts it . . .

In his noninspired state, the writer feels all the world to be mechanical, made up of numbered separate parts: he does not see wholes but particulars, not spirit but matter; or to put it another way, in this state the writer keeps looking at the words he's written on the page and sees only words on a page, not the living dream they're meant to trigger. . . . Reading student fiction one can spot at once where the power turns on and where it turns off, where the writer wrote from "inspiration," or deep flowering vision, and where he had to struggle along on mere intellect. One can write whole novels without once tapping the mysterious center of things, the secret room where dreams prowl. One can easily make up characters, plot, setting, and then fill in the book like a paint-by-numbers picture. But most stories and novels have at least moments of the real thing, some exactly right gesture or startlingly apt metaphor, some brief passage describing wallpaper or the movement of a cat, a passage that somehow shines or throbs as nothing around it does, some fictional moment that, as we say, "comes alive." [8]

In nearly all the writing programs in the West, most especially MFA programs in the United States, this alteration of consciousness is never taught. Instead, the mechanics of writing are emphasized, the schooling a mere training in technique. Robert Bly plays with aspects of the problem through the idea of chambers or "rooms inside our heads that more and more interfere with our taking in the power of what we see."

My main thought is that we, in 1999, being so worldly, so informed, so flooded with motifs from the past, find it more and more difficult to allow any object, whether a snowstorm or a toad or a painting, to pass through our subtle chambers [of intellect] to reach the soul. Students in graduate school, even some poets, are taught to linger in these chambers of the mind until they decide to remain there. . . . The job of the writer who knows about these chambers is to give us a frog or a giant or a snowstorm and to protect it from all the invisible forces that want to delay it, elaborate it, relate it to correct opinions, and prevent it from arriving at the soul. . . . The greatest heat in a poem appears when the poet is able,

by his or her awareness of complicated mental perceptions, to bypass
those perceptions and bring the object just seen so near the soul that
the soul feels a shock, as if it had just touched snow or hot water.[9]

In other words, to so imbue the writing with feeling that despite the pervasive atrophy of the feeling sense, the reader feels the invisibles inside the words as a powerful living reality. For writers, it is the alteration of state itself and the generation of such experiences that is crucial, that creates real writing. Technique is nothing without it.

And this is true of science as well.

The West has immersed itself in technique—in the mechanics of things—in nearly every area of art and learning and lost something very precious in the process. Our lives are now surrounded by that mechanicalism. Our houses, our clothes, our art, and our science all reflect it—moreso every year . . . and the need for Prozac increases right along with it. People just don't feel well any more.

Sound Synaesthesia

This same blending of sensory mediums also occurs in music, only with music—at root—it is a synaesthesia of sound and feeling rather than visual perception and feeling. The jazz pianist Harry Pickens notes that "in early childhood I became aware of a hypersensitivity to auditory phenomena as energetic gestalts. To this day I sense music as tonal sculpture—a primarily kinesthetic inner sensation that translates into sound."[10] Though when the synaesthesia goes deeper, similarly to that in writing, *all* the sensory modalities come into play as a blended synaesthetic perceiving. Rob Mazurek, the jazz composer and musician, described it like this . . .

The sound you do not hear but see,
and the visual you cannot see but hear,
is the work.[11]

Or as the composer Gustav Mahler put it, "What is best in music is not to be found within the notes." What is best in music is found someplace else, someplace where the musician gathers meanings that he then blends deeply into the music he is making. Harry Pickens describes his experience of it by noting that as musicians deepen "their training to access the music that is symbolized, but never contained within, the printed score, they learn to build a conscious bridge between the inaudible domains of sound sourced in the imaginal realm and the audible dimensions of external vibration."[12]

Music is an interesting and very unique phenomena. You can't really point to it the way you can point to words on a page. Music is a great deal more invisible than writing. You can point to a book, you can't really point to a song.

and no, sheet music is not the same thing

The process of experiencing a song, however, is just as magical, just as consciousness-altering as reading a story. If you have ever gone to a small venue to hear an acoustic musician you particularly enjoy, remember for a moment how that really is . . .

The stage is empty at first. But people are arriving in ones and twos, milling at the entrance, chatting to each other, coming to see and hear someone whose music they love. But the energy is a bit scattered.

During travel to the venue the people have been thinking, as people do, about the drive, the roads, will they get there on time? Will there still be good seats?

What's that tiny clicking sound in the engine?
I need to get the oil changed.

All the people, immersed in their lives, are, to one extent or another, mentally chattering to themselves. And when they arrive they are chattering still, but the focus changes. They begin to think more intently about the mechanics of the evening: parking, paying for their tickets, checking in, merging in to the crowd.

remember how that is . . .
that funny, scattered, sort-of-excited feeling

Even if they have been to this venue before, they don't know what it will be like this time, or how the crowd will feel. So, as they walk from the car, approach the place, they slow a bit, then pause, perhaps outside, perhaps just inside the door, taking it all in. Their eyes scan the place and in that moment a very important thing happens. They *feel* what the place feels like. They use their capacity for nonkinesthetic touching to feel this new place they are in. And this tells them—at the deepest possible level—about the meanings that place holds this evening.

At the simplest level, it's about safety.

A room with bright white walls and florescent lights or medieval torture weapons prominently displayed feels much different from one with warm colors and paintings of nature scenes.

But deeper than that they are analyzing the mood of the place, what is this group of people like? What kind of scenario is occurring this evening? Once experienced, and analyzed—usually below the level of conscious awareness—they adjust to it and begin then to look at the seating. Do I want to sit there?

No, not by that person.
Geesus!

How about over there?

Ummm, yeah, maybe.

They are literally feeling their way to the most comfortable place for them to sit—and in the process doing a very deep analysis of the nature of the people in the room. In the process, they are using a capacity for the analysis of invisibles by the feeling sense. *Everybody* does it.

Then, finally, they choose a seat. Eventually, everyone has arrived and is settled in their seats—often, unfortunately, in those uncomfortable metal folding chairs that everyplace seems to possess.

such practical chairs

The seats are hard and the chairs squeak on the floor as they are adjusted for leg room, there's the rustling of clothes as people shift positions to get comfortable, everyone is chatting. There's a lot of moving back and forth. And in the room . . . the *feeling* of many strangers in a strange place, all a bit closed into themselves—and a bit too close to each other for comfort.

On the stage: all the musical equipment, amps, microphone, an acoustic guitar, chair, perhaps a keyboard. A feeling of emptiness—and expectation—in the room, despite the fact that it's filled with people.

Finally, the musician emerges and is introduced. There is some applause. The musician says a few introductory words—usually humorous, they all try to be comedians. Then she picks up her guitar and checks her tuning; the first song begins.

As those first few notes shimmer into the room they are pushing against that sense of strangeness, that feeling of emptiness in the room. In that initial, awkward stage when music begins, the notes signal that something new is beginning. Still . . . it has not yet begun. The notes at this point are just sounds in the air, just as the words in a book, sitting there on the page, were once only marks on a bit of paper. Then, as you listen, the notes begin to become something more than just a scattering of sounds. They begin to take on a life of their own. In that moment, you, along with everyone else, begin to change. Your day and the details of your life begin to fade. Mental chattering begins to slow. You slowly submerge, and drop down inside the music. Step by step your consciousness, and everyone else's, shifts. You merge seamlessly into a dream state, just as you did when you were reading. Another kind of story, held inside the song, is being told and you, in the dream state, move into a place where that story comes alive, becomes as real as anything you have ever felt.

And unlike when you were reading, some new element comes into play. The musical notes add an additional element to the story. Not only is sound involved but those sounds? They have *feeling* inside them.

A good songwriter crafts the melody line of the song in such a way that the emotional structure of the sound progression mirrors the lyrics to the song. The emotional tones in the melody mimic the meanings of the story that the lyrics tell. So, at a level far below that of language, the *feeling meaning* of the story goes inside you, into a very deep, dreaming place. Into the place where your deepest feelings reside. And there it changes who you are, just as all good stories do.

Because music bypasses the linear mind—using nonlinguistic sound structures rather than the more structured language in books, it bypasses many of the filters that culture imposes on people.

Why do you think they hated rock and roll so much?

It impacts the deepest levels of the self, especially the preverbal parts of us, the parts that lived life before we learned language. It touches the most vulnerable parts of ourselves. And there, quite often, it heals the part of us that feels most deeply, our hearts.

for all of us carry wounds that trouble us
that sometimes awaken us in the depths of the night
when the soul is at its lowest ebb . . .

Interestingly enough, when beginning to play, the musician is going through the exact same alteration of consciousness. All musicians know that the first notes they play during a performance drop into a particular kind of space. It's a space in which people are in one state of mind, a scattered state of mind. They know that the first notes that shimmer into the room are a necessary beginning of the shift that has to happen for the living experience we call music to occur. They signal the beginning of a movement from one state to another. As the actor and musician Joe Seneca once put it as he began to play to a restless crowd, "We've got to take these people home."[13] The songs they choose, and the opening notes that go with them, are chosen and crafted, in that moment, with care.

So, the musician, before she begins to play, is in a similar state of mind as the audience. She's thinking of all the things she needs to do to create a good performance. Thinking of how her body feels, where there's tension, the butterflies in her stomach. Thinking of whatever problems are bothering her in her life, of whether she will do a good job this night.

For she has done poorly once or twice before

And that is why all musicians begin with one or two songs they know extremely well, songs they can play no matter what mood they are in. And most especially songs they love, that put them into that dream state almost automatically. Then, as they play, they begin to drop into what most of them call the zone, the place where real music happens. The place lead guitarists work to find as they phish deep in the imaginal pool where the music resides when no one is playing it, the place the music emerges from when they stop thinking so much and just let themselves feel.

> *this is also the place they write their music from*
> *they enter the dream and allow the music*
> *to flow through them and into the world*
> *emerging as melody and lyrics and deep feelings*
> *crafted as a unique art form*

Over the years, musicians, just as writers do, train themselves to create that state of mind at will, to move into the place where feeling and sound become one thing, the place where music becomes a living expression. And they train themselves to let it flow through them, into the world, and then into the people who have come to listen. They know the state they are going for, the place they want to take their listeners to, they know the steps involved. So, carefully, they craft song in such a way as to alter the listener's consciousness. And the only way to successfully do that is to *feel* it.

As the writing teacher Brenda Ueland once noted: "A great musician once told me that one should never play a single note without hearing it, feeling that it is true, thinking it beautiful."[14] In other words, musicians, when they play, have to be present with each note. They have to hear *every* one of them. But more than that, they have to feel the *feeling* inside every note as they play it. They work then to enter a state of mind where each note is a living, feeling thing that they are shaping *in the moment* as a living communication to the listener's deepest self.

> *They are in the same state as jugglers*
> *who are keeping a similar kind of balance point intact*

The music they are generating is a complex composition of feeling, story line, and structured sound tones that induce a specific state of mind.

And inside it all is a sophisticated commentary, a story, about experiences that we all have, sooner or later, while living our lives. This joins the musician and listener together in a special kind of relationship. Something flows from the musician to the listener and then back again. Both move together into an altered state of consciousness that depends on the feeling dimension of the music, on the feeling that resides inside every note. As the musician Don Conoscenti describes it . . .

> *Then as I became more engaged in the craft of making music I perceived it as more scientific . . . a series of techniques and devices that could generate a fairly predictable result. Certain tempos could cause people to dance. Certain manipulations of melody and meter could cause people to feel very specific emotions. There were formulas that could be very effective if well executed. The same held true for the lyrical side of it. As a songwriter I found that I could achieve a different level of storytelling through the use of archetypes. Then I found that if I could successfully blend that with rhythmic and melodic elements and the intentional use of space I could enter into an altered state of reality . . . a dreamlike state, not just for me, but for everyone else in the room who wasn't completely closed off to the experience. The emotional had evolved into something spiritual, then into something scientific, then again into something mystical and beautiful that could now be consciously accessed and shared. That kind of music making has the power not only to entertain, but to heal and affect consciousness.*[15]

You can feel that magical state in the room when it occurs. It is the moment when real music happens. The thing is, this is not a technique—it is, as Milton Erickson once put it, a *communication*. Some part of the metaphysical background of the world gets inside us because of what the musician is doing. The musician enters a dream state and the music comes alive in a special way—it flows through the musician from some other place, into this world, and into the listeners.

It is an experience
of what some musicians
call the fourth voice[16]

In that moment, the music comes from the place where music lives when no one is playing it, filled with something much deeper than mere sound.

The lead guitarist Kevin Compton says that he has to stop thinking to be able to do this, has to move out of the way, and just let himself feel the music, to feel it very deeply. Then, if he is lucky, a tiny door inside him opens and (what he calls) the Melody Makers move through him into the world where they then touch the people who listen in the deepest parts of themselves. "It's what the music is for," he says, "we just have to move out of the way and let it happen."[17] Eric Clapton makes the same point when he says, "It comes back to how it feels—whether it comes from the heart, or it's almost channeled, where I get out of the way and let it come through."[18]

The writer Michael Ventura talks about Stevie Ray Vaughan generating such an experience during a performance. His band, Double Trouble, had left the stage for a break but Stevie didn't follow them. Instead, he opened another guitar case and pulled out a twelve-string, borrowed a chair from someone in the audience and then . . .

> *sat down, hunkered over the twelve-string. Closed his eyes. Played. Like he was all alone. The club was packed, but it got real quiet. And stayed quiet. While Stevie went deeper and deeper into that twelve-string sound. "Throw it all to the firewall," a woman near me said softly. I didn't know quite what that meant, but it sounded exactly right.*
>
> *After a long while he gently put the guitar down. Nobody applauded, and few people moved. "It's like church," said the same woman. . . . But Stevie wasn't finished.*

He got his Fender out again and sat back down and began to play once more. The audience

> *stood rapt, eyes closed or heads down, the music taking us far into ourselves. The recorded version of "Lenny" lasts five minutes, but you lose your sense of time while you listen, as we did that night.*

Stevie drew them all into a timeless, beautiful world of sound. Later, after everyone had left, Ventura sat alone in the club *and suddenly, there was Stevie walking haltingly across the dance floor, sobbing—sobbing and talking, talking quickly and to himself, about love. How it was important to him, that through his playing people would know that he loved. He loved them. That's what the music was for, he said, it was for **love**.*

I cannot duplicate on the page the shudder with which he said that word.[19]

Such experiences come not out of a mechanical reproduction of notes on a page but as a living communication that begins with feeling and then becomes feeling blended with sound in just a certain way. It pulls something up deep from within the human heart. When done well, something beyond mere mechanics happens, a deeper part of the world is accessed and made available to those of us who listen. And it is only because of the heart accessing the deep feeling dimensions of the world that it can happen at all. Music that is played without feeling does not engage the listener, the dreaming does not happen, state of mind does not shift. It remains a mechanical exercise. And we are all the poorer for it.

Stevie Ray talked about it like this . . .

*I find that I do best when I listen for where I'm trying to go with it and where it **can** go—not try to rush it, not try to make up things as I go, but just let them come out. Then I'm a lot better off. If I start trying to pay attention to where I am on the neck or "this is the proper way to do this or that" then I end up **thinking** that thing through and instead of playing from my heart I play from my mind and that's where I find that I get in trouble. If I just go with what's in my heart and let it come out, then I'm okay.*[20]

The gifted flute player Erika Randolph notes that it took her years to learn to improvise after her classical schooling as a musician. "I was brought up in a classical family and got locked into a mental frame. But one day when I was playing this certain sequence my fingers just started going, moving up and down the instrument, and this door opened in my heart and I realized 'this is it, this is what improv is.' That was my eureka moment. Going to school just shut me down and I had to re-find that moment, that freedom, and not worry about accidentally playing a major seventh on a dominant chord."[21]

It is thinking too much, dissociated mentation, that kills the experience. The song, in such a situation, is then never birthed into this world.

You can get an idea of the difference between the song as living being and as mechanical technique if you look at this piece of sheet music.[22]

No. 81. "Behold All These Things" (Catalogue No. 511)

Sung by EAGLE SHIELD

VOICE ♩ = 66
DRUM not recorded

I - ho le - na waij-yaij-ka yo i - ho le - na waij-yaij-ka yo

ta - ku waij he - ħa - ka - se waij - la - ke ćiij

on ya - ni pi kte - lo

This is the sheet music that the ethnomusicologist Frances Densmore transcribed after hearing the Sioux healer Eagle Shield sing the song of yarrow, a medicinal plant.

the indigenous peoples of America
insisted that every plant had its own song
and those who knew the song
could then evoke the deeper medicine of the plant

In this instance, as with all sheet music, there are a series of horizontal lines running across the page, then a space, then another series of lines, and under those still more, all running in parallel, left to right, from the top to the bottom of the page. And on those lines and in the spaces between them there are note symbols scattered here and there, up and down the scale, and of course, a number of other notations along the left hand side, some familiar, some not.

But think about it . . . is this the song? If you have ever heard Stevie Ray Vaughan when he was in the zone, you know it's not. It's not even close.

In fact, sheet music has very little relationship to the living reality of the song. It points to it, somehow—but . . . where is the song itself? *Can* you point to it? If you *had* to point to the song, what would you do? Where would you point?

Difficult, isn't it?

The song itself is an invisible thing, something very difficult to find with the linear mind. The sheet music is only a map of the song,

and not a very good map at that

just as a book is only a map of the story it tells. It's just that a book doesn't look so much like a map; it seems more related somehow to the story than sheet music is.

but it isn't

Some people do actually think the sheet music *is* the song—but they usually aren't very good musicians. They don't know how to put feeling into their playing.

> *And in just the same way, diagrams of molecules, mathematical symbols, chemical equations, stories of neuronal structures and sensory gating, have very little to do with the world they purport to describe. Science, like music, if done without feeling has something wrong with it. It has as much to do with real science as music played without feeling—paying attention only to the sheet music—does to real music. That is . . . nothing at all.*

Take a moment, if you will, and look up the sheet music to the song "My Father" by Judy Collins; its first page can usually be found on the internet. Then . . . find a recording of the song on YouTube or Amazon .com and listen to it. There is a depth of feeling that emerges as soon as the song begins, some powerful communication that deeply impacts the listening heart. In that moment you experience the metaphysical background of the song. This is what it feels like to experience the metaphysical background of the world.

> *There is an identical depth of feeling experience behind the maps that we call diagrams of molecules and mathematical equations and the physical forms we call plants and human bodies.*

The sheet music (or the mathematical equation or . . .) isn't the song but only a rudimentary set of directions. It contains directional markers; it tells the musician not only what notes to play and at what speed but also, in a very simplistic way, *how* to play. "With feeling," it might say, or "sadly." These are important instructions but they are not very exact. The sheet music can get you into the territory of the song

sometimes

but it can't get you *to* the song, that is, if you don't have some sense of how to go there already.

A common problem in music schools is students who learn to read the map perfectly but can't evoke the song. They use the map as directions but when they play the song it doesn't sound right. It sounds mechanical, not alive. Empty.

Brenda Ueland, in her book *If You Want To Write*, captures this mechanical, paint-by-numbers approach to music, when she says . . .

> *In music, in playing the piano, sometimes you are playing **at** a thing and sometimes you are playing **in** it. When you are playing **at** it you crescendo and diminish, following all the signs. "Now it is time to get louder," you read on the score. And so you make it louder and louder. "Look out! Here is a pianissimo!" So you dutifully do that. But this is intellectual and external.*
>
> *Only when you are playing **in** a thing do people listen and hear you and are moved. It is because **you** are moved, because a queer and wonderful experience has taken place and the music—Mozart or Bach of whatever it is—suddenly is yourself, **your** voice and your eloquence.*[23]

Or as Charlie Parker once put it . . .

> *Music is your own experience, your own thoughts, your wisdom. If you don't live it, it won't come out of your horn.*[24]

"If you don't live it." That is, if you don't move *inside* it, don't feel it, don't let it become something you are saying from the deepest core of your self, it won't be real. It won't come alive. And the dreaming that happens then is not deep dream, perhaps not dream at all.

Confusing the map and the territory is a deadly mistake. This is why so much of science produces such unpredictable and dangerous outcomes. Budding scientists are trained in a map of the world

a tremendously inaccurate map
coming from an inaccurate paradigm

but they are trained mechanically, reductively, in a paint-by-numbers approach. What happens then is a dissociation, not reality. For musicians, only a *semblance* of the song is achieved if it is played this way. The most important thing is lost.

The most important thing? Well, it *is* the song, not the map of the song. And the song itself? It's a living thing. It has its own life, its own livingness. When a song is truly played, there are experiential and emotional components, some component of soul, that get into the song, and they run deep. As Wallace Stevens once said . . .

> *Music is feeling then, not sound.*

The deeper elements of song, which come into being when a song is genuinely played, affect the listener at the deepest core of the self. And those experiential and emotional components, those components of soul, cannot be found in the map, in the sheet music. They are invisibles and some other part of the self than the brain has to be used to find those things, to evoke them, to bring them into the world. As Eric Clapton once put it, the blues is

> *a musical form which is very disciplined and structured coupled with a state of mind, and you can have either of those things but it's the two together that make it what it is. And you need to be a student for one, and a human being for the other, but those things alone don't do it.*[25]

Or, as Louis Armstrong said it . . .

> *What we play is life.*

There is something in the human experience that has nothing to do with the brain that has to be allowed to live in and through the music for it to become real, to become genuine, to actually be music or song. That means you have to work deeply with invisibles, things that are not taught in music schools, or writing schools, or to budding scientists. As Gustav Mahler once put it . . .

If a composer could say what he had to say in words,
he would not bother trying to say it in music.

That is, rather than using mentation and verbal language, you have to *communicate* these deeper feeling-imbued meanings through sound, through the arrangement of those sounds, and the textures you create in the sound by the use of different instruments, including the human voice.

Musicians constantly struggle to meaningfully communicate with each other the meaning-filled sound-weaving they are creating when crafting a song. They use metaphors because the vast majority of feeling states they want to create aren't describable in language. "Put some stink on it," they might say, or "it's gotta be more nasty," or "get some dark in it, it's too John Denver," or "give me some funk on that bass line," or maybe even . . . "throw it all to the firewall."

You can't exactly say what "funk" is, but you know it when you hear it. And if the song is first played with funk and then without it, it's not the same song. The feeling of it alters considerably. And if you say to someone listening that "Boy, that's sure got some funk to it," they will know exactly what you mean . . . but they won't be able to explain it in words.

The musical world is one of the only places that the feeling sense is still strong. Nearly all musicians understand that the song's got to have feeling to it to be genuine. They understand, usually intuitively, that they have to blend sound with feeling into a unique synaesthesia for music to work. They are one of the few groups of people in the West that still have a very active feeling sense—though, most often, they only apply it to sound.

The Secret Kinesis of the World

The feeling dimension of the world is not easily describable in words, but it's deeply important—especially if you want to touch the dreaming of Earth. Unfortunately, in the West, the feeling sense is not only atrophied, very few people even know that it is a primary sensory modality. As Bradford Keeney relates, in a conversation with a Kalahari Bushman, it is incredibly difficult to convey its importance . . . or its reality to people in the West.

> *I reply as I have before, "The difficulty, my dear friend, concerns how to say it. The rest of the world does not yet accept that a feeling is as real as a tree or a rock."*
>
> *"Or a lion," she adds . . . "Are they emotionally blind? Do they keep bumping into feelings and emotions they don't know what to do with? I bet they keep on telling their hearts to go back to sleep."*[26]

The truth is: *Every* physical object you see has a distinctly different feeling aspect than every other object you will encounter. The object's visual inputs, auditory inputs, olfactory inputs . . . all have unique feeling dimensions to them. (And every one of them, just as with different musical notes, has a slightly different feeling or emotional tone to it than the one before or after it.)

The developed use of this feeling dimension of things—the secret kinesis of physical objects—that *is* the key to opening sensory gating channels more widely. It's one of the innate mechanisms of hallucinogens, neurognostics of any sort. They (usually) make people *feel* very good.

Unless you're having a bad trip
(and yes, I'll talk more about that later)

They restore the feeling sense and enhance it. They open the gating channels of the *feeling* sense more widely so you can feel the impact of the world, its nonkinesthetic touch, upon you while at the same time enhancing the pleasure centers of the brain. They stimulate the reclamation of the feeling sense—and subsequently access to the metaphysical background of the world.

this is the real reason they are illegal

Reclaiming the feeling sense, and developing it as a primary sensing tool, is one of the main ways to begin to enter more deeply into the metaphysical background of the world. Although it seems onerous, the key to its reclamation, as it is with all art forms, is a lot of practice.

So, let's play with it a bit so you can get a sense of what I mean . . .

Let your eyes wander around the room you're in until something catches your attention—desk, pen, cup; it doesn't matter what it is. It is just, for whatever reason at this moment in time, interesting to you. It appeals in some way.

Now. Look at it carefully, note its shape, notice its color. Really *look* at it; let your visual sensing take it in. Let your eyes touch the thing as if they were fingers capable of extreme sensitivity of touch. Immerse yourself in *seeing* the thing that has caught your attention. Now, ask yourself, *How does it feel?*

In the tiny moment of time that follows that question, there will be a burst of feeling, an "intimation of mood or feeling" as Goethe once described it. Your nonphysical touching has just *felt* a part of the exterior world. There's a specific and unique feeling experience that occurs whenever this question is asked about something that is acutely observed. What stands revealed is a dimension to things beyond height, width, and breadth. There is a feeling dimension to them. *The secret kinesis of things.*

Now, let your eyes be captured by something else, again focus on how it looks, its shape and colors, and when you are really noticing it, ask yourself, *How does it feel?* There will be, again, that immediate emergence of an "intimation of mood or feeling." The thing has a *feeling tone* to it. Even if you might not be able to say exactly what that feeling tone is, it's very distinct, isn't it? And this particular feeling tone will be unique to the thing itself. It's different from the one possessed by the last thing you felt. In fact, everything you touch in this way will have a slightly, or sometimes very, different feeling or kinesis to it.

Now, do it again with something else. Only this time after you ask *How does it feel?* just after the unique feeling tone emerges, savor it for a while as if you are smelling a unique but delicate perfume or tasting a unique and subtle flavor. Immerse yourself in what you are now feeling.

Now . . . shift your attention to yourself. Notice how *you* are feeling.

Interesting, isn't it? The state you are now in is different from how you were before this exercise began.

If you really have immersed yourself in this exercise, you will find that your physiology has shifted. Your breathing will have slowed and deepened, your body become more relaxed. Eye focus will be different, too, more soft-focused; peripheral vision has been activated. You are seeing with Henry David Thoreau's "unworn sides of the eye." As he says . . .

> *It is by obeying the suggestions of a higher light within you that you escape from yourself and, in transit, as it were see with the unworn sides of your eye, travel totally new paths.*

Colors will likely be a bit more luminous, sounds more resonant, body sensations more sensitive.

> *sensory gating in all systems is opening more widely now*

Everything around you will feel more *alive*. State of mind has shifted as well. Your thoughts will be slower and deeper. Perceptual focus is enhanced. You will feel a bit *dreamier*.

Now, do it again—look at something, observe it in detail, and then ask yourself, *How does it feel?* At the emergence of the feeling tone, again savor it for awhile, then pay attention to your state. Pay attention to how *you* feel. Now compare that feeling to the feeling you had just a moment ago, when you last focused on yourself. There's a similarity, isn't there? There is a particular feeling that accompanies this kind of perception.

The particular feeling you have in your body when you do this can be remembered, if you wish, and recreated anytime. You begin to get a sense of the state you are going for. Habituating yourself to this feeling, deeply anchoring it in your experience, gaining familiarity with it, will allow you to drop down into it over and over again. At will.

This state, as everyone who trains in it learns over time, can be deepened considerably. It must be if you wish to fully enter the metaphysical background of the world. This first step, you might say, is where you get your foot in the door of it. You can, if you wish, extend it a bit further now . . .

Do the exercise again and while you're in that state, slowly take your eyes off the thing you are looking at and slowly look around at everything else you can see. (Keep breathing from this more relaxed state, let your eyes remain soft focused.) Let your eyes slowly pan the room and allow that feeling part of you to feel *everything* in the room as a wash of feeling flowing into you from what you are seeing. Instead of feeling the secret kinesis of one thing, you are feeling the secret kinesis of many things at once. At this moment you are *feeling* the world around you (with the part of you that can nonphysically touch) as a continual act similarly to the way you *see* or *hear* the world around you as a continual act.

This form of perception is a natural one for all people. But for most people in Western cultures, the skill hasn't been developed (often it has been actively discouraged). The same isn't true for our other forms of sensory perceiving.

When we were born we experienced a continual flow of visual and auditory sense impressions but we had no interpretations for them. It was through experience that we learned to understand what we were seeing and what we were hearing. By intentionally working with the secret kinesis of things, intentionally activating this form of sensing as a regular part of our perceiving, we learn to understand and work with these kinds of sensory impressions just as we once did visual and auditory impressions. We reclaim a form of perception that was once common to all people and cultures and which is innate in every infant born into this world. Engaging again with this kind of nonphysical touching is what James Hillman describes as "recovering the response of the heart to what is presented to the senses."

Continually sensing in this way *is* the key to opening the doors of perception more widely at will, the key to entering deep within the metaphysical background of the world. When this form of perception is initiated, the conscious mind begins to move into the background, the statistical mentality begins to be left behind, mechanicalism begins to be abandoned. By focusing intently through the senses and then asking *How does it feel?* you move out of analytical thinking, out of the brain, and begin to move into a different kind of cognition, one that is intimately interwoven with feeling.

So, there are three initial, essential steps to this. The first is seeing—really looking at—what is right in front of you, the second is asking *How does it feel?* The third? It's something rather tedious I'm afraid . . . practice, practice, and, still, more practice. In other words, everywhere you go, every place you visit, everything you encounter, ask yourself, *How does it feel?*

How does this restaurant feel? How does that street feel? How does this pencil feel? How does that tree feel? How does this person feel?

How does **it** feel to my sensing, to me?

And just an FYI, don't ask How do I feel? *That question takes it into the realm of emotions: mad, sad, scared, angry, depressed, I-don't-know, pissed off, sort-of-happy. Of all the phrasing I have explored,* How does **it** feel? *produces that burst of feeling, that intimation of mood that Goethe spoke of, more effectively than anything else.*

As you do this you will begin habituating the skill **and** building an internal database of feeling experiences associated with the multiple phenomena you have encountered. You will become used to using this kind of sensing as a regular part of your life—just as you have done with visual and sound perception. Your feeling sensing will grow stronger as a result; you will become increasingly more sensitive to even the slightest touch of the world upon you, the slightest feeling tone in anything you encounter. And, as well,

importantly

the *novelty* of things will begin to increase. One of the truths about habituated gating parameters . . . everything you daily encounter has a reduced novelty to it. That is why hallucinogens are so potent in engaging their user with the world, they *increase* the novelty of sensory inputs.

Because each thing—every phenomenon—does in fact possess a unique feeling dimension to it, different from all other things, when you begin to pay attention to the feeling tone of a thing, its novelty increases against background sensory inputs.

you have also created a task set
that begins to override gating parameters

As the skill is habituated—as you continually perceive the world through your feeling sensing—the novelty level of *everything* increases. This, over time, opens gating channels more widely as a general condition. *All* sensory inputs begin to take on the same kind of luminosity that occurs with hallucinogens. You begin to engage the world, as a habit, with more open gating. As more time passes, gating continues to expand, you begin to enter more and more deeply into the metaphysical background of the world. You, in essence, begin to *live* in the same state that hallucinogens induce. You are, in fact, high all the time.

it's kinda nice, really

But this is only the first part of the process. It's crucial, as you begin to do this, to develop further skills. It is deeply important to learn how to attribute meanings to what you are experiencing and to develop a metaphorical language to describe them. There is no well-developed, sophisticated language for the metaphysical background of the world.

as an art form, such languaging has been severely neglected

Most spiritual traditions have some descriptive terms that can be found— the majority, however, are not very exact, some are incredibly misleading, some so vague as to be useless.

most of the world's religions are very poor maps of the territory
and there's a reason for that
wild psychonauts are not generally welcome in polite company
cultures prefer them domesticated
not self-medicated

Nevertheless, learning how to attribute meaning to the feelings you are experiencing from the touch of the world upon you is crucial. You have to learn how to navigate the sea of meaning in which you are traveling.

11
THE SEA OF MEANING

At dessert, Goethe had a laurel, in full flower, and a Japanese plant, placed before us on the table. I remarked what different feelings were excited by the two plants—that the sight of the laurel produced a cheerful, light, mild, and tranquil mood; but that of the Japanese plant, one of barbaric melancholy.

JOHANN PETER ECKERMANN

Everyone seems to believe that human thought and emotions are the products of the human mind, but I think otherwise. . . . When people see a green tree, they all think that green trees are beautiful. Trees leave a sense of peace. When the wind ripples the surface of the water, the spirit becomes restless. Go to the mountains, and a sense of the mountain arises. Travel to a lake, and one feels the spirit of the water. All these emotions arise from nature. Go anywhere nature has been disturbed and I doubt that anything but disturbed emotions will arise.

MASANOBU FUKUOKA

There is always at the peak of Brent Tor a sense of sacredness, as if it were a place where God and Gaia meet. The feeling is intense, like that felt in great Cathedrals, caverns, and on other mountain

tops. . . . Brent Tor and other places like it have a sense of peace.
They seem to serve as reference points of health against which to
contrast the illness of the present urban or rural scene.

JAMES LOVELOCK

It has nothing to do with book knowing. It is heart knowing; this is
a library of feelings.

BRADFORD KEENEY

*I*n the beginning, when you first begin to develop feeling perception
as a habit, the easiest way to deepen the experience, after you ask
how something feels, is to ask yourself whether you like it or not—does
your heart pull you toward it, or does it move you away from it? Do you
like the "intimation of mood," the emotional or feeling tone of the thing
that emerges in your experience when you feel it . . . or do you not?

People coming unexpectedly on a great rock formation or tremendous old-growth tree sometimes experience a sudden feeling of awe.
Something shifts them out of their normal day-to-day sensory habituation and overrides their narrow gating. They *feel* something in the experience, something outside their usual states of mind. Something from *out there* touches them so strongly that it goes inside and captures their conscious mind's attention. This is what Robert Bly was talking about when he remarked (about the poet Antonio Machado) that he

knew that a secret "you"
was present in the feelings evoked by a landscape.

Some powerful living force—despite the years of schooled reductionism—touches a person when they have such an experience. And for a few minutes in time, they are held in the embrace of the world's touch, taken out of the mechanical world in which they have been submerged since their schooling began, experiencing, as our ancestors once did, the living reality of the world—connected to the metaphysical background of Earth, to some living and intelligent phenomenon that will not let us go until we feel its touch. Mark Twain describes his experience of such a moment like this . . .

I still kept in mind a certain wonderful sunset which I witnessed when steamboating was new to me. A broad expanse of the river was turned to blood; in the middle distance the red hue brightened into gold, through which a solitary log came floating and conspicuous; in one place a long slanting mark lay sparkling upon the water; in another the surface as broken by boiling, tumbling rings, that were as many tinted as an opal; where the ruddy flush was faintest, was a smooth spot that was covered with graceful circles and radiating lines, ever so delicately traced; the shore on our left was densely wooded and the somber shadow that fell from this forest was broken in one place by a long, ruffled trail that shone like silver; and high above the forest wall a clean-stemmed dead tree waved a single leafy bough that glowed like a flame in the unobstructed splendor that was flowing from the sun. There were graceful curves, reflected images, woody heights, soft distances, and over the whole scene, far and near, the dissolving lights drifted steadily, enriching it every passing moment with new marvels of coloring. I stood as one bewitched. I drank it in, in a speechless rapture. The world was new to me and I had never seen anything like this.[1]

And there are other times—everyone has experienced them—when you go someplace new, encounter a strange person or place, and, unexpectedly, are uncomfortable, even terrified. There is something about the place or the person that overrides gating so strongly that you *know* beyond any ability of the mind to disregard it, that this place you are in, this person you've just met—this restaurant, this neighborhood

this concentration camp

this abandoned field, decaying house, landscape, empty factory, person's face—has something wrong with it. So wrong in fact you want to get away as fast as you can.

Rilke poignantly captures the shifted and distinctly different perceiving I am talking about in his book *The Notebooks of Malte Laurids Brigge* . . . but he also encounters a depth, a meaning, that is tremendously disturbing to him . . .

Have I said it before? I am learning to see. Yes, I am beginning. It still goes badly. But I intend to make the most of my time.

To think for instance, that I have never been aware before how many faces there are. There are quantities of human beings, but there are many more faces, for each person has several. There are people who wear the same face for years; naturally it wears out, it gets dirty, it splits at the folds, it stretches, like gloves one has worn on a journey. These are thrifty, simple people; they do not change their face, they never even have it cleaned. It is good enough, they say, and who can prove them the contrary? The question of course arises, since they have several faces, what do they do with the others? They store them up. Their children will wear them. But sometimes, too, it happens that their dogs go out with them on. And why not? A face is a face.

Other people put their faces on, one after the other, with uncanny rapidity and wear them out. At first it seems to them they are provided for always; but they scarcely reach forty—and they have come to the last. This naturally has something tragic. They are not accustomed to taking care of faces, their last is worn through in a week, has holes, and in many places is thin as paper; and then little by little the under layer, the no-face, comes through, and they go about with that.

But the woman; she had completely collapsed into herself, forward into her hands. It was at the corner of rue Notre-Dame-des-Champs. I began to walk softly as soon as I saw her. When poor people are reflecting they should not be disturbed. Perhaps their idea will yet occur to them.

The street was too empty; its emptiness was bored; it caught my step from under my feet and clattered about with it hither and yon, as with a wooden clog. The woman startled and pulled away too quickly out of herself, too violently, so that her face remained in her two hands. I could see it lying in them, its hollow form. It cost me indescribable effort to stay with those hands and not to look at what had torn itself out of them. I shuddered to see a face from the inside, but still I was much more afraid of the naked flayed head without a face.[2]

Rilke is not talking here about a fantasized image, but something deeper, an underlying truth he found one day when he was not expecting it. Looking at the world with his deeper perceiving, he came upon the real face underneath the one the woman wore in her daily life. He captures the terror that can be—and, sooner or later, always is—encountered when using feeling perception to see and feel the world around you. Although the beauty is what we are most drawn to, in the darkness and terror are truths that all travelers in the metaphysical background of the world eventually encounter, must face, and come to terms with. They all have teachings that are necessary. If you are so afraid of the dark that you always run from it, it is impossible to truly learn to heal anything—either landscapes or people. As Nick Cave once put it . . .

> *Those songs that speak of love without having within their lines an ache or a sigh are not love songs at all but rather Hate Songs disguised as love songs, and are not to be trusted. These songs deny us our humanness and our God-given right to be sad and the airwaves are littered with them. The love song must resonate with the susurration of sorrow, the tintinnabulation of grief. The writer who refuses to explore the darker regions of the heart will never be able to write convincingly about the wonder, the magic and the joy of love . . . just as goodness cannot be trusted unless it has breathed the same air as evil.*[3]

In this process, we have to learn—and it does take time, years of it—to walk in damaged landscapes—of both the Earth and the human heart—and not lose our way, not lose ourselves. For when you enter the world with your feeling sense intact, you will encounter *everything* that is there. Eventually. That is why learning how to take care of your deepest self is an essential part of the journey. Many people just close down their feeling sense again if they don't. The songwriter Jimmy Webb talks about that this way . . .

> *It seems to me that one of the battles of aging is to maintain a passion, a sensitivity to our own feelings as well as to the vulnerability of the world around us. Without being able to expose ourselves to*

pain—to break down and cry if need be—we don't have what we need to be songwriters or even human beings.[4]

It takes a certain courage to continue on, to keep feeling, to refuse to close the heart again, once some things are felt. But a full life depends on our capacity for feeling.

We travel through a sea of meaning every day of our lives, but we rarely pay attention to its touch upon us. We rarely see the reality underneath surfaces, often because we don't want to either see or feel what is really there.

our feelings give us clues about the scenario we find ourselves in and they do so every minute of every day of our lives

Everything in the world that you will ever encounter lies between these two extremes. The gentle beauty of a meadow flower is but a paler form of the awe that Twain described. The empty echoing of footsteps in an abandoned factory building filled with the waste of industrial obsessions is but a paler form of the horror Rilke described. There are millions of shadings of feeling you will encounter, subtle alterations of tone and feeling, similar to those that musicians pay attention to—as Clapton described it . . .

it was always tone and feeling for me

but, rather than sound, this work is concerned with minute distinctions in your feeling perception of objects.

These subtle differentiations in feeling tones are like the minute variations in colors contained on an artist's pallette. When, for example, you look at a meadow in flower, you are getting an experience of the unique range of colors that are expressed from subtle alterations and combinations of all the primary colors. That color variation comes in a unique burst of color blending you see with your eyes. If you look closer, each individual thing will also reveal its own unique color range as well, its slight variations of green, shades of pink, yellow, purple, or brown. Just so with the feeling expressions of a place and everything in it.

Like the visual field in a meadow, there is a feeling field as well. Each landscape, ecorange, ecozone, ecosystem possesses its own feeling field, unique from all the others. And that feeling field can tell you a great deal about the underlying nature of that place: its degree of health or illness, degree of strength or weakness, its function, its purpose.

So, the first step is to feel everything you come into contact with, to train the feeling sense to be receptive to every touch upon it. The next is to determine whether you like it or not,

for this will begin to give you a sense of its underlying nature,

and finally, to begin to ask yourself, why? Why do I have this response?

When you ask yourself why, what you initiate in yourself is a deeper contemplation of the underlying nature of living phenomena.

It's like that experience . . . of seeing a dog lying on a dirt path, and that automatic response of, "Awww, hi there," and starting to move toward the dog, then suddenly stopping because something doesn't feel right. After this happens a few times, you begin to correlate that particular feeling with the reality of that situation—the dog is not friendly, it only looks friendly to the superficial glance. Once correlated, you know the meaning that is inside the feeling (unfriendly dog). The long-term process of developing the feeling sense entails correlating every feeling with a corresponding meaning—in depth.

If developed as a skill base, this is what leads to very deep understandings of the movements of Earth and every other self-organized system you will encounter. It is out of this deeper questing that Barbara McClintock came to understand corn transposons, how Luther Burbank came to understand the genetic history of a plant and then was able to urge it to grow in a new form, how Goethe understood the metamorphosis of plant shape, how Masanobu Fukuoka farmed without using fertilizers, pesticides, or breaking the surface of the soil.

So, again, the first step is opening the feeling sense, the second is noticing how you respond to each particular touch, the third is working to understand the meaning of the thing you have encountered, to determine its nature, the "why" of it.

To repeat: It takes a long time, for in this process you are creating a map of the meanings that flow through the world—a library of feelings as Bradford Keeney has it. You are creating a map of the world as it actually is, not as you were taught it to be. It takes focus of mind, attention to detail, and a genuine love of the craft—like any other art form you wish to master. You are training yourself in a most unique profession—and there are many who have gone before you. Some of them have spoken of the process they endured to develop the skill of truly seeing and feeling the deeper realities of what is being presented to their senses.

Developing Perceptual Acuity

There is no better description of what sensory training involves than Mark Twain's account of it in *Life on the Mississippi* (most especially chapters 4–13, from which these excerpts are taken—they are well worth reading in full). His training, while focused on visual sensing blended with feeling, is identical to what training in feeling sensing entails.

Twain began his apprenticeship by convincing a river pilot to train him in the art, but comments that

> *I entered upon the small enterprise of "learning" twelve or thirteen hundred miles of the great Mississippi River with the easy confidence of my time of life. If I had really known what I was about to require of my faculties, I should not have had the courage to begin. I supposed that all a pilot had to do was to keep his boat in the river, and I did not consider that that could be much of a trick, since it was so wide.*

His teacher, Horace Bixby, began Twain's apprenticeship by calling the boy's attention to certain landmarks along the river . . .

> *Said he, "This is Six Mile Point." I assented. It was pleasant enough information but I could not see the bearing of it. I was not con-*

scious that it was a matter of any interest to me. Another time he said, "This is Nine-Mile Point." Later he said, "This is Twelve-Mile Point." They were all about level with the water's edge; they all looked about alike to me; they were monotonously unpicturesque. I hoped Mr. Bixby would change the subject. But no, he would crowd up around a point, hugging the shore with affection, and then say: "The slack water ends here, abreast this bunch of China trees: now we cross over."

It was a long day, filled with scores of similar observations. Twain went to bed exhausted and fell deep asleep but, shockingly, at midnight, the night watchman appeared with a lantern and woke him up. He went back to sleep . . . several times, that is . . . until Bixby arrived.

Something like a minute later I was climbing the pilot-house steps with some of my clothes on and the rest in my arms. Mr. Bixby was close behind, commenting. Here was something fresh—this thing of getting up in the middle of the night to go to work. It was a detail in piloting that had never occurred to me at all. . . . I began to fear that piloting was not quite so romantic as I had imagined it was; there was something very real and worklike about this new phase of it.

The boy struggles into his clothes, then watches as Bixby takes the steamboat to the bank several times—in the dark (remember, there were no electric lights then; it was *really* dark) to drop people off at their farms.

Presently [Bixby] turned on me and said:
   "What's the name of the first point above New Orleans?"
   I was gratified to be able to answer promptly, and I did. I said I didn't know.
   *"Don't **know?**"*
   This manner jolted me. I was down at the foot again, in a moment. But I had to say just what I had said before.
   "Well, you're a smart one!" said Mr. Bixby. "What's the name of the next point?"

Once more I didn't know.

*"Well, this beats anything. Tell me the name of **any** point or place I told you."*

I studied awhile and decided I couldn't.

This goes on for some time, getting worse, until finally Bixby blows . . .

Oh, but his wrath was up! He was a nervous man, and he shuffled from one side of his wheel to the other as if the floor was hot. He would boil awhile to himself and then overflow and scald me again.

"Look here! What do you suppose I told you the names of those points for?"

I tremblingly considered a moment and then the devil of temptation provoked me to say:

"Well, to—to—be entertaining, I thought."

This was a red flag to the bull. He raged and stormed so (he was crossing the river at the time) that I judged it made him blind, because he ran over the steering oar of a trading-scow.

The crew of the scow curse Bixby, Bixby responds with considerable flexibility—and at great length—then calms a bit.

"My boy, you must get a little memorandum-book, and every time I tell you a thing, put it down right away. There's only one way to be a pilot and that is to get this entire river by heart. You have to know it just like ABC."

That was a dismal revelation to me, for my memory was never loaded with anything but blank cartridges. However, I did not feel discouraged long. I judged that Mr. Bixby was "stretching."

Unfortunately, for Twain, Bixby was not "stretching," still, the boy begins to make some progress. It goes to Twain's head; he thinks he's just about got it handled. But one night, a group of pilots come on board and ride with Bixby and Twain in the pilot house. The pilots begin to describe minute details of the entire length of the river: wood piles that signal a crossing, downed trees that signal low water, sandbars that can't be seen with the naked eye. Twain begins to feel seriously depressed . . .

> *The thing that was running in my mind was, "Now, if my ears hear aright, I have not only to get the names of all the towns and islands and bends, and so on by heart, but I must even get up a warm personal acquaintanceship with every old snag and one-limbed cottonwood and obscure wood-pile that ornaments this river for twelve hundred miles; and more than that, I must actually know where these things are in the dark. . . . I wish the piloting business was in Jericho and I had never thought of it."*

Nevertheless, he keeps at it and reveals, eventually, that

> *At the end of what seemed a tedious while, I had managed to pack my head full of islands, towns, bars, "points," and bends, and a curiously inanimate mass of lumber it was, too. However, inasmuch as I could shut my eyes and rattle off a good long string of these names without leaving out more than ten miles of river in every fifty, I began to feel that I could take a boat down to New Orleans if I could make her skip those little gaps. But of course my complacency could hardly get start enough to lift my nose a trifle into the air, before Mr. Bixby would think of something to fetch it down again. One day he turned on me suddenly with this settler:*
>
> *"What is the shape of Walnut Bend?"*
>
> *He might as well have asked me my grandmother's opinion of protoplasm. I reflected respectfully and then said I didn't know it had any particular shape. My gunpowdery chief went off with a bang, of course, and then went on loading and firing until he was out of adjectives. . . .*
>
> *"My boy, you've got to know the **shape** of the river perfectly. It is all there is left to steer by on a very dark night. Everything else is blotted out and gone. But mind you, it hasn't the same shape in the night that it has in the daytime."*
>
> *"How on earth am I ever going to learn it, then?"*
>
> *"How do you follow a hall at home in the dark? Because you know the shape of it. You can't see it."*

"Do you mean to say that I've got to know all the million tri-fling variations of shape in the banks of this interminable river as well as I know the shape of the front hall at home?"

*"On my honor, you've got to know them **better** than any man ever did know the shapes of the halls in his own house."*

"I wish I was dead."

"Now I don't want to discourage you but—"

"Well, pile it on me; I might as well have it now as another time."

*"You see, this has got to be learned, there isn't any getting around it. A clear starlight night throws such heavy shadows that, if you didn't know the shape of the shore perfectly, you would claw away from every bunch of timber, because you would take the black shadow of it for a solid cape, and you see you would be getting scared to death every fifteen minutes by the watch. . . . You can't see a snag in one of those shadows but you know exactly where it is, and the shape of the river tells you when you are coming to it. Then, there's your pitch dark night; the river is a very different shape on a pitch-dark night from what it is on a star-filled night. . . . Then, there's your gray mist. You take a night when there's one of those grisly, drizzly, gray mists, and then there isn't **any** particular shape to a shore. . . . Well, then, different kinds of moonlight change the shape of the river in different ways."*

The boy is disheartened again, but, crucially, he doesn't give up . . .

I went to work now to learn the shape of the river and of all the eluding and ungraspable objects that ever I tried to get mind or hands on, that was the chief. I would fasten my eyes upon a sharp, wooded point that projected far into the river some miles ahead of me and go to laboriously photographing its shape upon my brain, and just as I was beginning to succeed to my satisfaction, we would draw up toward it and the exasperating thing would begin to melt away and fold back into the bank! . . . No prominent hill would stick to its shape long enough for me to make up my mind what its form really was, but it was as dissolving and changeful as if it had

been a mountain of butter in the hottest corner of the tropics.
Nothing ever had the same shape when I was coming down-stream
that it had borne when I went up. . . . It was plain that I had got to
learn the shape of the river in all the different ways that could be
thought of—upside down, wrong end first, inside out, fore-and-aft,
and "thort-ships"—and then know what to do on gray nights when
it hadn't any shape at all.

Twain begins to learn, experientially, that the real world, as opposed
to the human world, is constantly altering its shape, from moment to
moment to moment; and that he has to be as fluid in his perceptual
sensing as life itself if he is to keep up with it. He has to experience,
know, the river as a living entity that is always moving, changing, shifting. And so, he begins to develop relationship with a living thing, not
a static entity. He begins to hear the river's communications, as do all
those do who have developed enough sensitivity to do so.

And just as soon as Twain began to feel as if he had really begun to
learn the river, that he was just about good enough to be a pilot, Bixby
takes him further into his education. It turns out that the boy also has
to learn the depths of the river at every point along its length. Not only
that, he has to learn the meaning of every tiny alteration in the surface of
the water. As Twain puts it . . .

I had often seen pilots gazing at the water and pretending to read it
as if it were a book, but it was a book that told me nothing. A time
came, however, when Mr. Bixby seemed to think me far enough
advanced to hear a lesson on water-reading.

And so Twain begins to read the surface of the river. It becomes a book
that tells him of the river's nature, its hidden depths, its movements. A
certain color of the sun in the evening meant wind on the morrow; a log
floating in a specific way meant the river was rising; the slanting ripples
on the surface of the water—just so, meant that just underneath was a
sandbar, the water too shallow for a boat; a tumbling, boiling water indicated a dissolving sandbar underneath the surface; lines and circles in the
water that took a particular shape, a shoal building up.

> *By enhancing your feeling sense and using it continually*
> *to build a library of feeling experiences*
> *you learn how to read the world around you*
> *as you would a book of words*
> *you learn how to move through, to live in,*
> *the metaphysical background of the world*
> *as a way of life*

Eventually, as Twain puts it, he "had learned to read the face of the water as one would cull the news from the morning paper."

This constant focus on the craft, Twain says, resulted in a tremendous store of knowledge about the river, so deeply ingrained inside him, that he came to know the river as well, or better, than he knew the hall in his own home. The river became a living part of him and he a part of it. He knew every part of the depths that flowed beneath him. When he then traveled across its surface, piloting a steamboat, he was immersed in a living communication with it. The river told him about itself, and he moved through its world, responding to its communications, carrying the people whose lives were entrusted to him, safely. He didn't *think* the next section of the river was safe, he *knew* it. His *feel* for the river was complete.

But he said . . . once he was done . . . that he was not the same person that had begun the training so long ago; it had changed him. He was who he had wanted to be, but he was no longer what he had been. Nor could he see the world as he once had; his *vision* had changed.

> *None of us ever truly knows what we are in for when we decide to begin this training, to learn to travel deep in to the metaphysical background, to be someone who reads the feeling currents of the world as we would a book. In the beginning it seems romantic but it costs you everything you are. My training has lasted over 40 years; it's been worth every second of it.*

This work changes those who do it. It changes their relationship to themself. It changes their relationship to the society from which they come. It changes their relationship to the world.

Bradford Keeney, writing about the Bushmen of the Kalahari, comments on the state that comes into being when something is known this intimately.

> When Bushmen say they own something it means not only that they own the feeling for it but also that the feeling has transmitted its essence, its complex nexus of relationships, into their very being. We become the other—whether a friend, butterfly, redwood forest, giraffe, or seahorse—through our intensely felt union with it.[5]

When sensory gating channels are widely opened, the boundary between self and other thins. The phenomenon you have focused on moves *inside* you and you know it from inside itself—just in the same way as you know yourself. You *know* the reality of the interior life of the other solely in reference to itself. For the first time you can experience the life that occurs outside the human frame in its own terms—without using the human world as a point of orientation.

We who travel this path must learn to let the other life-forms of the Earth speak to us on their own terms. They have a destiny unrelated to ours that is just as important to them as our individual lives are to us. More . . . we are only a small part of the song that the Earth sings. Only if we can learn how to step out of our human orientation and see from the Earth's point of view can we do anything functional about the predicament facing our species. Once we step out we can begin to see the connections between things, the invisible lines that bind them together. Only then can we truly understand that the hawk is in reality a part of the mountain and the mountain a part of the hawk, both equally crucial expressions of what we have taken to be background.

This kind of understanding occurs because the feeling of a thing—if you follow it deeply enough—transmits, as Keeney so wonderfully says, "its complex nexus of relationships," into the depths of the self. You then know, experientially, that everything you touch with your feeling sense is connected to something else (and that to something else again). You also begin to see *how* they are connected.

Following your feeling sense, you find the invisibles that connect an invasive plant such as Japanese knotweed (*Polygonum cuspidatum*) to the movement of lyme disease through ecosystems. It comes then as no surprise that the plant is specific in the treatment of lyme disease, reducing the inflammation in the neural system that the disease organism initiates. Looking deeper you find that another invasive, Amur honeysuckle (*Lonicera maackii*) has potent interrelationships with emerging diseases such as dengue and encephalitis, both spread by mosquitoes. The plant strongly reduces the numbers of eggs laid by the mosquito *Aedes triseriatus,* a primary vector of La Crosse encephalitis. It has the same impacts on the vector of dengue, the closely related *Aedes aegypti.* The more honeysuckle plants there are, the fewer mosquitoes, and the less the incidence of disease. Further, the plant contains compounds specific for reducing the kinds of inflammation both dengue and encephalitis cause. They literally stop the kinds of inflammation that encephalitis viruses cause in the brain by protecting brain neurons and microglial cells from damage. The plant, like Japanese knotweed, is invasive in the areas where the diseases are most strongly emerging.

Both these plants are considered dangerous invasives to be eradicated with extreme prejudice in order to "protect" ecosystems. That activists can't see the ecological movements underlying the plants' emergence in the areas where they are needed illustrates the problems inherent in using linear thinking and poor modeling to approach ecosystem fluctuations. This is why a different kind of thinking has to be used, one based on something very different from mental reductionism. Henry David Thoreau once put the necessity for the shift like this: *A man has not seen a thing if he has not felt it.*

Following the feeling sense connects you to these kinds of underlying connections. Following those connections inevitably leads ever deeper into the heart of the world. You begin to see then what has been before you all along.

You begin to read the book of the world
not just a river that flows through that world

Goethe speaks of the capacity to perceive the deeper aspects of the world this way . . .

We all walk in mysteries. We do not know what is stirring in the atmosphere that surrounds us, nor how it is connected with our own spirit. So much is certain—that at times we can put out feelers of our soul beyond its bodily limits; and a presentiment, an actual insight is accorded to it.[6]

These presentiments, insights, come from following the feeling sense deep into the heart of the world. The Bushmen of the Kalahari, as Bradford Keeney makes clear, have an extremely well-developed feeling sense—and they use it for just this purpose. It is their *feeling* of the world that allows them access to its depths. They describe their developing knowledge of the world, captured through their feeling sense, again, as "a library of feelings." And in fact, that is just what it is. Twain was constructing just such a library of the river inside himself during his training.

The training process the Bushmen describe is similar to Twain's. It comes from a continual touching of the world. This creates a library, a database, of your feeling experience of every object you encounter inside you. And just as with Twain's training, to gain mastery, you must not only learn the subtle variations in feeling that each object expresses but also what each feeling indicates. What it means.

Developing a Perceptual Database

Creating a database of feeling perceptions builds over time. You accumulate, as you continue, thousands upon thousands of feeling experiences. And what brings each of them into focus, what brings their innate meaning more into conscious view is comparison. *This* plant feels slightly different from *that* one. It is by comparison that humans perceive differences. So, as you do this, remember: it's always more effective to feel this thing, then that one. (Always do two at least.) This comparative process brings their differences into focus and by so doing illuminates the essential nature of each. And, again, the process, while inherently enjoyable to those who are drawn to it, can be tedious. Sophistication in its use demands constant practice, every day. In other words: How does this feel? How does that feel? How does *that* feel? Eventually, such perceptual sensing becomes second nature.

Over time, a library of feelings is crafted and you begin to have a sense of the world through a much deeper perceptual framework than existed before. Like Twain's knowing of the river, the world begins to get inside you. You begin to know it as well as you know your hallway at home, the back of your hands. And you begin to know, far deeper than words, what the subtle feelings that things possess are telling you about the world through which you move.

You are moving along a river, too, just as Twain did, but your river is the whole world. And the tiny signals that your feeling sensing are sending you tell you about the depths you are encountering, about the terrain that is approaching, about any particular part of the journey. As Twain relates . . .

> "What is the height of that bank yonder, at Burgess's?"
>
> "How can I tell, sir? It's three-quarters of a mile away."
>
> "Very poor eye—very poor. Take the glass."
>
> I took the glass and presently said:
>
> "I can't tell. I suppose that bank is about a foot and a half high."
>
> "Foot and a half! That's a six foot bank. How high was the bank along here last trip?"
>
> "I don't know; I never noticed."
>
> "You didn't? Well, you must always do it hereafter."
>
> "Why?"
>
> "Because you'll have to know a good many things that it tells you. For one thing, it tells you the stage of the river—tells you whether there's more water or less in the river here than there was last trip." . . .
>
> "Do you see that stump on the false point?"
>
> "Ay, ay, sir."
>
> "Well, the water is just up to the roots of it. You must make a note of that."
>
> "Why?"
>
> "Because that means that there's seven feet in the chute of 103."
>
> "But 103 is a long way up the river yet."
>
> "That's where the benefit of the bank comes in. There is water

enough in 103 now, yet there may not be by the time we get there,
but the bank will keep us posted all along." . . .

"But what I particularly want to know is, if I have got to keep
up an everlasting measuring of the banks of this river, twelve hun-
dred miles, month in and month out?"

"Of course!"

My emotions were too deep for words.

We learn in this process to sail the boat of our soul through the world, using markers just as Twain described. Those markers determine what we will encounter farther up the river. But we also are learning to sense the movement of invisibles that affect the movement of our ship, just as a sailor on water learns to sense the movement of wind, another invisible, as he sails. As Buckminster Fuller relates . . .

Sailors watch for every clue nature may give to coming events—
cloud formations, temperature of the water, wind direction shiftings,
etc. To survive, navigators must anticipate comprehensively. The
sailor's subconscious as well as conscious faculties interact to inform
his anticipatory decisions.[7]

And we come to sense the movements of these invisibles through deeper perceptual capacities, just as the juggler does. We *feel* their movements in what Fuller calls our subconscious and that part of us acts to *inform* our *anticipatory decisions*. There is no way to hold all the linear details in the mind and to respond from linear cause and effect in this process. We create our library of feelings and at a certain point enough data exists that the deep self can begin to generate informed responses out of it. We become aware then of the invisible movements in the world, movements that are the currents of the river in which we are swimming, upon which we are sailing. And we can respond then, just as a sailor does to those currents, those movements of the invisible.

The development of the skill takes time, a great deal of feeling, and much observing. But it also demands much thought, for it is important to not only build a library of feelings but as well to begin to understand what those feelings mean.

In the beginning, you see something and ask: *How does it feel?* And, in response, there comes an intimation of mood, a unique feeling complex. The crucial first step. But to go deeper, you then have to interpret the meaning of that intimation of mood, that feeling complex.

So, let's say you see a car that attracts your attention and you look at it closely, then ask yourself: *How does it feel?*

What comes back, let's say, is a feeling of tiredness. The intimation of mood or feeling the car possesses. Then you ask yourself if you like it or not. Yes, you do. It feels friendly. But what does this friendly tiredness mean? It takes some deep questioning, and, usually, much experience, to find out.

For me, a car whose engine is worn out feels much different from a car whose engine is still strong. It feels tired, as if it needs a rest. When I feel into a car that has a new, strong engine, the feeling burst is completely different. The car feels impersonal, machine-like. (Though it may feel "cool" to my advertised mind.) I am not particularly drawn toward such a car when I use my feeling sense, nor am I put off by it. It's impersonal.

It took me a long time and the purchase of several worn-out cars before I figured out what these feelings meant.

If you explore deeper into these kinds of feelings you will also begin to discover that other sensory modalities come into play as well.

With an old car that feels tired—if I stay with that feeling of tiredness and let it develop more fully—I always get an image of an old man in overalls with dust on his clothes—colors are dim and faded—there is a sense of gray whiskers and tired hair, and knees aching at the joints. The image even smells dusty. The car feels like it needs to settle in for a long rest. There's a friendly feel to it, but tired.

In contrast, when feeling a car with a strong, good engine I see bright shiny metal and smell engine oil. Colors are bright and sharp. It is ready to go, not tired, not sleepy, not needing to rest.

It is this comparison between the two that reveals deeper aspects of their essential natures.

Every person has their own unique interior representation during this kind of perceiving. That is, the feeling tone that emerges, if you allow it to deepen, is translated into certain interior representations that are unique to you. Your individual system takes the feeling experience and turns elements of it into other sensory modalities in order to store it as memory. This is the way that the brain turns "it feels tired" into an encapsulated memory you can retrieve later.

The sensory images that form are not the thing itself, but merely the way the brain reveals deeper aspects of the phenomenon you are interested in. You feel the car but there are also visual, auditory, and physical aspects to that feeling, a sensory gestalt, as it were, that is generated as you stay with the experience. The brain pulls out of your store of memories experiences that match, in nature, the one you are having now. And it builds a multiple sensory gestalt to hold the meaning you have encountered as a sensory memory that can be more easily stored. As you spend more time with this kind of sensing, your own unique forms of representation will become familiar to you. You'll tend less then to mistake the representation for the thing itself.

What occurs in such moments is a synaesthesia of perception, the blending of multiple sensory modalities into one unique sensing sensory form. Every person who begins to feel the world finds that their senses naturally begin to blend into a synaesthesic whole. The feeling of the thing generates—if you stay with the sensing—a blended sensory perception of it. Thus, Bradford Keeney observes that

> *Strong spiritual elders talk this way. They can smell another spiritually developed person, while seeing their light and hearing their song. . . . When all the senses are dancing well together, you also pay less attention to one being developed over the other or any dissociation that encourages you to say you are seeing sounds or feeling shapes . . . [you] feel, see, hear, taste, and smell at the same time without conscious differentiation. It is synaesthesia with no conscious narration about it being synaesthesia. . . . We learn to draw distinctions and make indications that then enables us to say, yes, I am smelling love and hearing hope.*[8]

As he goes on to say . . .

> *I think it is likely that we are all whole synesthetes. This orienta-*
> *tion assumes that the senses are not mutually exclusive, but inter-*
> *woven in constant interaction. In this regard, we can also say there*
> *is one sense, though we have found a way to differentiate its variant*
> *forms of coordination and interplay as separate sense making. We*
> *all see when we hear and feel, but some are not as "conscious" of it*
> *as others. Sort of like saying you are seeing sounds, but you aren't*
> *paying attention—a kind of synesthetic blind spot. . . . When we*
> *pay attention to one part of the whole of unitary sensing, the rest of*
> *it goes off the screen of consciousness.*[9]

Feeling the world brings the natural synaesthetic experience of the world
back into conscious experience. You literally begin to smell the tiredness or
strength of the car as well as feel it. And, if you take the time to slow the
process down, begin to split the beat of a fly's wing into a thousand discrete moments, you will start to perceive the various elements of what is
happening.

Synaesthesia, as Jason Godesky describes it . . .

> *is the mental function (or suite of functions) in which the senses run*
> *together, in which colors have a feel to them and tastes have a color.*
> *. . . The phenomenon marks a total immersion in sense, when the*
> *observer is no longer in control, no longer separating sight, sound,*
> *texture, and becomes a part of his sensual surroundings. That is, the*
> *observer calls forth the world. This synaesthetic perspective offers the*
> *possibility of actually engaging plants in communication; trying to*
> *understand, catalogue, and analyze the slightly varying scents by*
> *which plants communicate consciously would surely overwhelm us*
> *almost immediately, yet we can perceive far more than we can con-*
> *sciously articulate. Much of our brain's conscious function centers on*
> *filtering out the stimuli from our senses. Synaesthesia means we can*
> *"see" and "hear" as well as smell what plants are "saying," in a pro-*
> *cess that involves our noses as much as our imaginations.*[10]

Imagination in that sense is crucial to the process; again, your brain is creating a metaphorical representation of the perception from your store of memories and experiences. Like the generation of the words "funk" or "stink" to describe the feeling that certain musical sequences create. To describe, in depth, what you are perceiving through your feeling sense entails the use of metaphor.

Just as musicians can't exactly describe the feeling impact of particular aspects of song texture, it is not easily possible to capture feeling perceptions in language.

*It's **possible** but it takes a lot of work
and much time to escape the necessity for metaphor,
years of time*

Everyone has their own particular metaphors that emerge. Each person's brain generates those metaphors out of the lived experience of that person. Out of the years of sounds, and sights, and tastes, and smells, feelings, experiences, situations, books, stories, movies, moments of a lived life. The brain scans the memories/experiences of all of them and from each of those events, if there is something relevant to the current sensing, the brain takes something and combines it with all the others to give substance to what is being felt. Then it is stored as memory, in the library of feelings. This sensory gestalt holds within it the essential meanings that belong to that feeling experience and, with work, you can begin to extract those meanings in more consciously usable form.

This kind of sensory perception can be used with everything in the world, including plants and ecoranges. It is the way that natural scientists such as Goethe and Barbara Mclintock learned so much about the world around them. But to truly learn such deep truths about the world you must go even deeper, you must learn how to follow golden threads.

12
FOLLOWING
GOLDEN THREADS

Complexity theory is a general theory of complex dynamic systems. The Latin complexus *comes from the Greek* pleko *meaning to plait or twine. Thus a complex system is literally one consisting of interwoven parts.*

TIMOTHY LENTON

When we try to pick out anything by itself, we find it hitched to everything else in the universe.

JOHN MUIR

"Tell them they have to wake up twice in the morning," Nyae continues.

This means that you should first wake up in the morning and get out of bed. Then awaken your heart: walk out of the bedrock of objects and materialism and into a spiritual world guided by the felt lines of relationships that hold everything together. Now the ropes, rather than the objects they connect, are primary. They are the most important and the most real.

BRADFORD KEENEY

When you find you do have a response—trust it. It has a meaning.
WILLIAM STAFFORD

*I*f you do use your feeling sense as your primary perceptual touching of the world you will encounter, from time to time, touches on your feeling/sensing that are out of the ordinary. These touches will capture your attention as nothing else in the feeling field does. From some place deep inside you will come an urge to turn toward that touching, a desire to immerse yourself in it, and to begin to follow it wherever it leads. These unique touches are what the poet William Stafford called golden threads.

He found the concept in one of William Blake's poems (though Blake called it a golden string) . . .

> *I give you the end of a golden string*
> *Only wind it into a ball,*
> *It will lead you in at Heaven's gate*
> *Built in Jerusalem's wall.*[1]

What Blake was describing is movement *through* the doors of perception (again, another Blake descriptive) *into* the metaphysical background of the world. And for him, as it is for so many of us, that deeper world is a sacred one.

William Stafford used that concept in the creation of his poetry. But it is not limited to that. It is at the core of music, and woodworking . . . art of any sort, including deep science. It is at the core of Goethe's work and Masanobu Fukuoka's and Albert Einstein's. It is necessary to understanding the invisibles that occur in every aspect of the self-organized system we know as Earth.

To get an idea of how Einstein and others used this to find the truths they found, it is easier to start with less complex systems: writing and wood and music. For these are perfect metaphors for the deeper work that must occur when you begin to travel deep into the heart of the world to understand the creating that Earth does during its dreaming.

Golden Threads in Writing

The great Japanese poet Basho described the presence of golden threads long before William Blake; all people who journey deep into the world, irrespective of culture, time, or geography, know of them. Basho, also talking about poetry, put it like this . . .

> *Your poetry issues of its own accord when you*
> *And the object become one—*
> *when you have plunged deep enough into the object*
> *to see something like a hidden glimmering there.*[2]

Basho knew that the boundary between self and other, of necessity, must thin for true poetry to occur. When the boundary thins, as the Kalahari describe it, the phenomenon that is being touched with the feeling sense moves into the core of our being . . . and we into its.

> *We become the other—whether a friend, butterfly, redwood forest,*
> *giraffe, or seahorse—through our intensely felt union with it.*

Basho was speaking of this movement when he wrote . . .

> *Go to the pine*
> *if you want to learn about the pine,*
> *or to the bamboo*
> *if you want to learn about the bamboo.*
> *And in doing so, you must leave*
> *your subjective preoccupation with yourself.*
> *Otherwise you impose yourself on the object*
> *and do not learn.*

For deeper reasons that any of us can ever know, of all the connections that run through the world, there are certain ones that touch us more strongly, that call us, that become golden threads that generate in us what James Hillman called *notitia*, the attentive noticing of the soul. And from that noticing, as Hillman describes it, comes "the capacity to form true notions of things." The connections that touch us in this way are special. They are the ones meant for us for reasons only the Earth will ever know.

William Stafford was deeply focused on the hidden glimmering that Basho speaks of. He was a master of following such threads. Deep meaning touched him and as soon as he felt it, he turned toward it, focusing on it with the whole of his attention. He began to follow it then, working to capture its essence in language. And we, coming later, can feel that thread and experience its deeper meanings as if they were our own.

Like this . . .

> *If you don't know what kind of person I am*
> *and I don't know what kind of person you are*
> *a pattern that others made may prevail in the world*
> *and following the wrong god home we may miss our star.*
>
> *For there is many a small betrayal in the mind,*
> *a shrug that lets the fragile sequence break*
> *sending with shouts the horrible errors of childhood*
> *storming out to play through the broken dike.*
>
> *And as elephants parade holding each elephant's tail,*
> *but if one wanders, the circus won't find the park,*
> *I call it cruel and maybe the root of all cruelty*
> *to know what occurs but not recognize the fact.*
>
> *And so I appeal to a voice, to something shadowy,*
> *a remote important region in all who talk:*
> *though we could fool each other, we should consider—*
> *lest the parade of our mutual life get lost in the dark.*
>
> *For it is important that awake people be awake,*
> *or a breaking line may discourage them back to sleep;*
> *the signals we give—yes or no, or maybe—*
> *should be clear; the darkness around us is deep.*[3]

Stafford spent his life, attentive to his feeling sensing of the world around him, being open always to the touch of golden threads. He said that it was essential to understand that: *When you find you do have a response—trust it. It has a meaning.* When something captures your attention in this way, *trust it.* Follow it home to where it lives, deep inside the world.

To the alert person, a golden thread may emerge from any ordinary thing and open a doorway into the metaphysical background of the world. Because it is impossible to know when or where or from what a golden thread will emerge, the writer (as all people must) remains attentive to everything that is encountered, always paying close attention to how everything, even the tiniest little thing, feels. Light pours through a window in a particular way, a person moves their body slightly, you enter a summer field and suddenly experience it as a property of mind. Something inside those things brushes against you. Meaning of some sort, not yet understood, touches someplace deep. Ripples flow up from the depths of the unconscious and touch your conscious mind. A particular feeling envelops you and you stop and focus your whole attention on what is right in front of you. *Notitia.* The touch of a golden thread.

Writers follow the threads by writing down, as concretely as they can, what they are experiencing, what they are feeling, what they are seeing, hearing, sensing. Robert Bly describes this, brilliantly, as "following the tiny impulses through the meadow of language."[4] It must be done slowly. Carefully. Feeling your way. Tiny movement by tiny movement.

It is the feeling equivalent of catching the hint of an elusive scent. You lift your nose to the slight breeze, a delicate touching. Seeking. Ah, there. Your feet move of their own accord as you trail what you have sensed through the meadow in front of you. You twist and turn slightly, following where the scent leads, adjusting your movements to the rise and fall of the land through which you walk. Following the scent home. Finding the core that gives rise to it. Following tiny impulses through the meadow of language.

Such threads begin with the simplest of things: A tiny, odd feeling in a social interaction or elephants walking, holding each other's tail. Anything can become a door into deeper worlds. Stafford comments that "the artist is not so much a person endowed with the luck of vivid, eventful days, as a person for whom any immediate encounter leads by little degrees to the implications always present for anyone anywhere."[5] Golden threads touch all of us, every day, but most often only artists and children take the time to follow them.

> *This is why so many people such as Einstein and Luther Burbank were so childlike, they retained the wonder and sense of the living- ness of the world that all of us had as children. As Einstein once put it, "The pursuit of beauty and truth is a sphere of activity in which we are permitted to remain children all our lives."*

The initial touch of a golden thread is *always* attended by a specific kind of feeling. Experience will bring trust in that touch and the feeling that accompanies it, familiar recognition at its emergence. You feel the touch of the thing, it captures your attention, then, if you are a writer, you work to encapsulate it in language.

Working to describe it, however, causes a slight movement away from the experience itself. So a writer will write a descriptive line, perhaps sev- eral, then stop and compare what has been written to the feeling they are trying to describe.

They look at the lines, focus on them with the whole of their atten- tion and then ask: *How does it feel?* In that moment, a certain emotional tone emerges *from the lines themselves* just as it does from anything that is sensed in this way.

Because the writer is in the zone, dreaming as they are writing, the lines are an expression of synaesthesia, filled with feeling. The writer feels into them, tasting, savoring the feel of the words. Then they step back inside the thread and feel *it*. Then they compare the feeling of the thread and that of the lines they have written. They are going for congruency, for identity between the two. At the experience of any difference, they engage in tiny micromolar adjustments of the lines they are crafting, trying to get them ever closer to the thread that has touched them. Great art occurs when the lines and the golden thread become identical in feeling. When you, as reader, later read those written lines you literally experience the golden thread as if it were your own. Leonard Bernstein was speaking of this when he said . . .

Any great work of art . . . revives and readapts time and space, and the measure of its success is the extent to which it makes you an inhabitant of that world—the extent to which it invites you in and lets you breathe its strange, special air.[6]

The work of bringing the two to identity may not be completed quickly, shaping and polishing may take hours, or months, or years for some pieces. But in the initial shaping, the line that has been written and the feeling of the golden thread approach a congruency. They get close enough for the innate sense of congruency each of us possesses to give a *yes,* even if a provisional one. Some sort of polishing almost always has to occur later. That is when the first draft slowly becomes the final draft, where the work to make the two things identical at the tiniest levels of which the writer is capable occurs. The time where all the implications in the word are teased out and developed so that the experience itself flowers in those who read it.

Once a writer has captured those lines well enough that they approach a congruency to the thread, something very interesting happens as they turn to the thread once more. The thread takes them someplace new.

Of its own accord, the attention of the self suddenly shifts, moves in some new, never-to-be-predicted, direction. The part of the self that is intimate with meanings flows along the line of meaning—the golden thread that has touched the self—heading toward its depths. The golden thread moves and the deep self moves with it. The feeling of the thread is the same but there's more to it now, it has deepened in some way, become richer. More meanings inside the thread begin to reveal themselves. New thoughts, feelings, sensations, images, emerge—spontaneously—into awareness. And now the process begins of capturing *them* in language. Stafford comments: "If I let the process go on, things will occur to me that were not at all in my mind when I started. These things, odd or trivial as they may be, are somehow connected."[7] The lines that take up residence in the writer's heart, as the writer William Gass might put it, "father or nurture other lines, sentences, further feelings and thoughts of significance."[8] And they do so automatically. The thread takes us to whatever things it is intertwined with, connected to. And they are always things that appear to be unrelated to the thread we are following.

The writer is feeling his way along the string that has emerged into his awareness. He is using that capacity for nonphysical touch to follow a particular meaning that has touched him and captured his attention, trusting it to lead him where it needs to go to be itself, to emerge complete and whole in language. "Any little impulse is accepted and enhanced," Stafford remarks. Over time you learn to trust the process, the experience, for, as Stafford continues, "only the golden string knows where it is going, and the role for a writer or reader is one of following, not imposing."[9]

There is a kind of devotion in this, a returning, as Bly calls it, "like a swallow to the barn of yielding, to the little spark of light given off by the end of the thread,"[10] to Basho's glimmering residing inside the objects of our attention.

True writers (musicians, scientists, all artists) follow; they are servants of the process, not its masters. They follow the thread where it leads and write down what they find on the journey. They are, in a sense, transcribers, and good writers know it. Being too purposeful, Stafford observed, may break the thread. One must be careful not to pull too hard.

And what *is* that pulling too hard? Trying to control where the thread is going, directing it where the statistical mentality wants it to go, forcing it away from its nature and into the desires and needs of the individual. This may be conscious on the part of the writer who has too much investment in the psychological, the social, or in reductionisms of one sort or another. It may be unconscious in the writer that has not developed the skill of rigorous self-examination and introspection or in the writer who is still too afraid, who does not trust the dreamer inside him enough to let go of control. Ultimately, those limitations must be abandoned. To become good at the craft demands a yielding to the thread and the process of following.

Practice at the craft develops the skill of following the thread without pulling too hard. In the beginning all of us pull too hard, the thread breaks, we wander off and don't find the park. But over time, as the skill is refined, the threads can be followed wherever they lead. The meanings of which they are composed are captured in language in such a way that the words themselves are an experiential map of the territory. They take the attentive listener deep inside particular kinds of meanings. The meanings slip over the self like a lens and you see aspects of reality that can only be glimpsed, as Thoreau described it, with the unworn sides of the eye.

Every golden thread, if followed, generates somewhere within it, often toward its end, a long floating leap into a moment or experience of what the Spanish poet Federico Garcia Lorca called duende. It is a moment in which a particular kind of experience occurs, one that lies beyond mechanicalism, beyond reductionist approaches, beyond the linear mind and the statistical mentality.

This poem by Machado captures what Lorca was speaking of . . .

> It is good knowing that glasses
> are to drink from;
> the bad thing
> is to not know what thirst is for.[11]

We start with something all of us know, glasses and using them for drinking. This simple description of a part of the world that is familiar to us comes first, capturing attention, firmly anchoring awareness and perception in one kind of reality. Then there is a movement into something else. The reality framework of the piece shifts entirely, leaving one paradigm, one reality orientation, and ending up in another, the two connected by the slenderest of threads. What the self sees, what it perceives, when that shift occurs is very different from what it saw before. Some new insight occurs. The world the conscious mind lives within expands tremendously and in an unexpected direction. For a moment the statistical mentality catches glimpses of something far outside its normal boundaries and perceptions. And there is just a little bit, or perhaps a lot, of a kind of awe at this unexpected glimpse of a reality unsuspected, a reality that surrounds us every day of our lives. There is, as Lorca put it, the trembling of the moment and then the silence. Duende.

Because the writer focuses so completely on the feeling of the thing he is describing, getting it as fully as possible into language, the words become imbued with life force, filled with meaning. The writer piles up meaning behind the word like water behind a dam. The longer the thread is followed, the more meaning that piles up, not only behind the words but behind the sentences and paragraphs. A powerful forward movement takes hold, an inescapable inertia toward some destination occurs in the writing. You reach the end of the linear world, a chasm appears, and you take a long floating leap up, out, over, landing for a moment on the other side. Duende.

A golden thread may lead only a short (writing) distance, as in the poem by Machado, yet still possess a long floating leap into the unconscious and tremendous duende. A golden thread *always* leads to such a leap if it is followed; it always generates an experience of duende somewhere in the piece. And those moments of duende may be strong or mild, they may be connected together in an interwoven duende conversation, or they can stand individually. Golden threads always lead to a shift in perception, a traveling from one state of mind to another. Bly comments, echoing Blake . . .

> *If every detail can by careful handling, through association, sound, tone, language, lead us in, then we live in a sacred universe.*

We find, always, when we follow golden threads, the metaphysical background of the world. As you focus more deeply on the feeling that touched you, your sensory gating channels will begin to open more widely, much more widely. It is then that you begin to leave the human world behind, then that you begin to enter the imaginal world, then that you begin to find that, as Robert Bly once put it, *the owl's dark eyelids cover a luminosity our reason cannot grasp.*[12]

Golden threads are an experience of the extensive interconnections that touch the nodes that we know as physical objects, what Gregory Bateson called "a vast network or matrix of interlocking message material."[13] *Anyone* who begins going deeper into the metaphysical background of the world will encounter them, will find golden threads; the experience is widespread. It is limited to no culture, continent, or profession. The Kalahari Bushmen of Africa talk about it like this . . .

> *Strong ropes connect you with everything in the universe and when*

it is important to know about the other end of a rope, it will tap or pull on you.[14]

Many of the Kalahari, similarly to Stafford, remain sensitive to the emergence of a thread, or rope as they call it. They feel its touch, its pull, as a tapping. Through their heightened feeling sense they turn toward it, follow it to its end. They know, from deep experience, that the thread is something emerging from the metaphysical background of the world, capturing their attention; they know there is purpose in it. Among the Iroquois, for instance, it is said that when a person needs a plant, "it stands up where it grows, calling to you. That is why it is easy to find a medicine you seek."[15]

Golden threads touch us because something deep inside us needs what is on the other end of that thread. It can be the need for words, for poetry. It can be the need for medicine for our healing or, in the case of the Kalahari (sometimes), food, as they put it, "A Bushman hunter feels something tapping on his arm when it is time to hunt."[16] But the key to it is the feeling sense, as the Bushmen say it . . .

> *The rope is our track. We feel it pulling us. When you wake up your heart and find yourself alive with good emotions, it not only makes you tremble, it also enables you to feel the pulling of the ropes. The ultimate tracking is not achieved with the mind but with the heart.*[17]

In other words, the mind can never find the way; it is in our capacity to feel that we find the heart of the world.

Wood

The cabinetmaker James Krenov was a master of following golden threads in his relationship with wood. He used his feeling sense, touched the wood with it, listened to what it told him. And he described what the process is like, trying to capture the invisibles of it in language . . .

> *Getting into this matter of listening to wood, of composing, weaving together an intention with what you and your chosen wood have to*

say, is an experience difficult to describe. To me, it is the essence of working with wood.

A painter or sculptor visits a certain place and sees and feels something there he wants to interpret: a person, a scene, the way the light falls. A time and a place. A sense of life. Something similar happens with the cabinet maker—he who is more than a maker of cabinets. He has an idea, maybe a sketch. A boxlike object with a few gentle curves whose meaning he only guesses. Or a more sculptural piece where he imagines the play of light on shapes; serious or with humor, difficult or easy. And there before him is the wood he has chosen. Wood—and with it a mood.

Then within this mood, all these other aspects: the shadings, accents, tensions—that which corresponds to the painter's inspiration and later on, often much later, all those bevels, roundings, shapes within shapes which will clarify and enhance what has been an intention and a hope.[18]

"Wood, and with it a mood." There is Goethe's intimation of mood or feeling again. Krenov finds a piece of wood and for some reason the mood in the wood captures his attention—notitia. He begins to listen to what it is telling him, responds to the conversation, begins to follow where the wood is leading him. And out of that comes a shaping, a shaping composed of two living beings in deep conversation. Something more than the sum of the parts then comes into being.

Theodore Sturgeon captured some of what this is like in his story "Slow Sculpture."

The shaping of a bonsai is therefore always a compromise and always a cooperation. A man cannot create bonsai, nor can a tree; it takes both, and they must understand each other. It takes a long time to do that. One memorizes one's bonsai, every twig, the angle of every crevice and needle, and, lying awake at night or in a pause a thousand miles away, one recalls this or that line or mass, one makes one's plans. With wire and water and light, with tilting and with planting of water-robbing weeds or heavy root-shading ground cover, one explains to the tree what one wants, and if the explanation

*is well enough made, and there is great enough understanding, the
tree will respond and obey—almost. Always there will be its own
self-respecting, highly individual variation: Very well I shall do
what you want, but I will do it my way. And for these variations,
the tree is always willing to present a clear and logical explanation, and more often than not (almost smiling) it will make clear
to the man that he could have avoided it if his understanding had
been better. It is the slowest sculpture in the world, and there is, at
times, doubt as to which is being sculpted, man or tree.*[19]

With everything an artisan attempts to shape the process is the same,
whether a living tree or a piece of wood or music, or these things we
hold in our hands that we call books.

Following a golden thread, irrespective of the craft we practice, starts
with noticing something that touches us and captures our attention. (As
the painter Marion Milner once put it, she simply let herself "find what
the eye seems to like.")[20] We then begin to follow it to find out where
it wants to go. Paying close attention in this process to what is . . . not
what we think is, is crucial. Most often we see only what is in our minds,
not what is in our eyes. Mostly we feel only what we have been taught to
feel, not what we truly feel. With the attentive noticing of the soul, we
step away from our programming and what we think we know. We feel
something and then we stop and genuinely *look*, identifying what has
caught our attention. Then we begin to really see it, noticing whatever
it is as if for the first time. The senses begin to bring us tidings of invisible things, all of them filled with meaning. To do this work, to develop
excellence in the craft, we have to genuinely see whatever it is that we
have felt, then follow wherever that feeling takes us. Krenov, in his book
The Fine Art of Cabinetmaking, describes it like this . . .

*I wonder if people notice that with all the technical skill, love, and
care put into them, many of his bowls still lack something? They
are not all of them alive. It is sad, almost tragic. . . . Because of
ignorance, as well as prejudice, we exclude so much. We need to see
better. To see—in the way that Yanagi meant, which is to sense and
notice (in that order) even before we know. That seemingly odd*

bevel, that uneven curvature of line, the surface flat yet somehow alive—these we see only when we have first sensed the meaning of their conversation. The craftsman works, looking and looking again, from one revelation to another—often by way of mistakes, listening to the material, coming upon unexpected signals. Good things and bad things: knots that should not be where they are, fascinating colors that appear as if out of nowhere. It takes effort. But it gives something more in return.[21]

That perfectly describes it, doesn't it? *The craftsman works, looking and looking again, from one revelation to another—often by way of mistakes, listening to the material, coming upon unexpected signals.* But always following that feeling, following tiny feeling impulses from one revelation to another.

Golden threads always start with an experience, a moment being lived. They are not something that belong only to those who write. It's just that some of us work to write them down after we have lived them. It's possible to follow golden threads behaviorally not just linguistically. It is a skill that belongs to living an inhabited life. Something touches you and you begin to follow it, to find out where it leads. It signals that something important is happening; it captures the attention of the deep self.

A house, a cabinet, a wooden bowl. If these things are crafted with this kind of feeling attention, following the golden threads that reside in the wood, allowing their conversation with you to emerge into form, what you find at the end of the process is a house, a cabinet, a wooden bowl that is filled with feeling and aliveness. Houses that are homes. Cabinets that greet you with joy each time you pass by. Wooden bowls that contain something ineffable. Always.

Music

Although every musician has their own approach to the crafting of their music, for me . . . it begins with sound, with a musical sequence. It always begins the same way. In the midst of playing something, anything, some sequence of sounds captures my awareness and halts what I have been doing. Something in the sound sequence in that instant emerges as a golden thread. I stop then and begin to follow it. Everything else fades from my awareness; there is only that sound sequence and I begin to play it over and over again. I only have a little bit of what it will become but I play that first note and then the sequence that follows over and over again.

There is a mood in the sequence and the beginnings of a conversation. As I play it over and over I begin to get inside it and it inside me. Nothing is in my attention now but that sequence and the meanings that are beginning to emerge from within its deeps. And as the process continues the musical phrase begins to become *mine*, it begins to express itself out of the depths of me, to become something I am saying from the deepest parts of myself. The nonlinguistic part of me that resides deepest in body memory begins to speak, and the speaking is composed not of words but pure meaning held in sound. Somehow the sound sequence that has emerged of its own accord and captured my attention has come alive. It merges into my deepest self and begins to speak through me. The composer Jimmy Webb is touching on this when he says that in this process, "we learn that chords are living things."[22]

So with deepening attentiveness, core meanings begin to emerge out of the sequence. And in that continual playing of the sequence my fingers begin to emphasize this aspect of it, that chord a bit more than another, finding contrasts, sharpening them, deepening them, evoking the mood and meaning held deep within the note sequence. To really allow music to come alive in this way, Jimmy Webb notes, takes great attentiveness of mind. "It is our responsibility," he says, "to pay attention."[23] And in the process I find, as I always do, that, as Mozart said, "The spaces between notes is music, too."

Then, there comes a moment, always, when the sequence has fully become itself, when I have internalized it enough that it is now my voice, when I have finally found the true mood of the thing, have found the contrasts that make it come most alive, when I have the spaces between the notes emerging as strongly as the notes themselves, that the golden thread moves. In that moment, the sound sequence takes the next step, the step that has been inherent in the sequence from the beginning, the sound sequence I could not remotely see when I began. And the step seems, always, inevitable. The music begins to emerge of its own accord from the

PLEASE SEND US THIS CARD TO RECEIVE OUR LATEST CATALOG FREE OF CHARGE.

Book in which this card was found _____

☐ Check here to receive our catalog via e-mail.

Company _____

☐ Send me wholesale information

Name _____ Phone _____

Address _____

City _____ State _____ Zip _____ Country _____

E-mail address _____

Please check area(s) of interest to receive related announcements via e-mail:

☐ Health ☐ Self-help ☐ Science/Nature ☐ Shamanism

☐ Ancient Mysteries ☐ New Age/Spirituality ☐ Visionary Plants ☐ Martial Arts

☐ Spanish Language ☐ Sexuality/Tantra ☐ Family and Youth ☐ Religion/Philosophy

Please send a catalog to my friend:

Name _____ Company _____

Address _____ Phone _____

City _____ State _____ Zip _____ Country _____

Order at 1-800-246-8648 • Fax (802) 767-3726

E-mail: customerservice@InnerTraditions.com • Web site: www.InnerTraditions.com

INNER TRADITIONS
BEAR & COMPANY

Inner Traditions • Bear & Company

P.O. Box 388

Rochester, VT 05767-0388

U.S.A.

place music lives when no one is playing it. And slowly it emerges into this world, saying what it uniquely is meant to say, I only the medium through which it expresses itself. My job one of following, not imposing.

And yes, some songs just write themselves in a few minutes.
Others take months or years.

Once the melody line has been found from beginning to end, its mood and meaning developed from continual replaying and digging deep into its heart, the words begin. The words that fit most effectively with the piece are those that do two things: 1) the lyric lines themselves echo the nonlinguistic meanings held inside the notes and the note sequences; and 2) the words themselves, when said conversationally, naturally possess a faint shadow of the melody line that runs through the song. Still, not all songwriters begin with the music, of course. Rosanne Cash speaks of what happens when the words are where the song begins . . .

I've found that melody is already inherent in the language, and if I pay close enough attention to the roundness of the vowels and the cadence of the words, I can tease the melody out of the words it is already woven into. I have found that continual referral back to the original "feeling tone" of the inspiration, the constant re-touching of that hum and cry, more important than the fireworks of its [initial burst of] inspiration.[24]

When it comes right down to it, neither the words nor the music come first; they both emerge at the same time. We just perceive one of them first. The entire composed piece is inherent in each of them; there is no background, no foreground, just the thing itself. And we, following the golden thread, pay close attention, feel into the thread, allow the song to emerge from the background of the world into form. Thus, when lyrics and song are combined in just the right way, the song feels as if it is one organic whole . . . because it is. The lyrics were already inherent in the song . . . they were just allowed to come into a linguistic form (and vice versa).

And because all songs crafted in this way begin with some deeper touch of the world upon the self, something that catches the attention of the soul, there is some deeper element of the metaphysical background of the world inside them. They begin with a feeling, thus they express the deepest feelings in the human heart. There is something more in the words and melody lines than simple song. As Jacob-Ernst Berendt put it in his book, *The World Is Sound* (Destiny Books, 1991), "Music is more than music."[25]

And it is fascinating that as a songwriter works to tease out the melody that is already woven into the words, they happen on a deep truth about human language. It is partly composed of song—and always has been. Depth analysis of human language has found, in fact, that the expressive and emotive layer of it is identical in its structure to birdsong, something Charles Darwin speculated long ago.

Too bad his followers are so religious

Human language is a fusion of the kind of communication birds, whales, and dolphins use with a more utilitarian type of communication used by, for instance, chimpanzees. As Robert Berwick, a professor of linguistics at MIT puts it . . .

> *What got joined together was the ability to construct these complex patterns, like a song, but with words. . . . All human languages have a finite number of stress patterns, a certain number of beat patterns. Well, in birdsong, there is also this limited number of beat patterns.*[26]

Birds, dolphins, and whales use a more holistic communicatory language, filled with meaning as a gestalt rather than a linear cause and effect process. Each melody they create is a single unit of communication holding within it the essential meaning as an experiential gestalt.

> *And that is in part why our songs can be so potent in their impacts. They, too, when done well, carry within them an experiential gestalt of communication that is far larger than any of the parts that have gone into them.*

Cetaceans and birds learn, over time to combine those gestalts in more complicated patterns. They literally create conversations composed of experiential gestalts rather than a series of linked meanings. And some trace of that capacity resides in human language.

It is this inherent melody line deep inside our spoken language that song lyricists, if they are good at the craft, bring out when they join a crafted melody with lyrics. They find those linguistic melody lines when they drop down deep inside the words and in their dreaming allow the melody underneath to emerge into awareness. And something from some other place comes into the world. As Rosanne Cash put it . . . "Sometimes these songs are postcards from the future. Often I have found that a song reveals something subtle but important about my own life that I was only vaguely aware of while writing, but that became important as time went on. . . . [But] I don't consider these postcard songs prescient as much as just coming from a source of creativity outside linear time."[27]

Depth Immersion

The secret to the following of golden threads is immersion in the thread through the use of the feeling sense, an immersion so deep that you forget everything else but the touch of that thread and the effort to bring it into form in the world. Everything else disappears. Nothing remains but the thread and your relationship to it . . . and your movements, so gentle, so careful, to shape it into form in this world. In those moments, nothing else matters . . . or even exists.

You can get a feel for what this process is like in this story about a musician by a gifted young writer just completing his first novel . . .

"Think about the sound your guitar makes when it's not being played." McKenzie was looking very intently at Michael. "Think about what it's like inside the guitar. How it smells. Think about the wood and how it's shaped. How the shape shakes with the music."

Michael nodded. And started to think about his guitar.

The smell. That's what he thought about first. The smell of his guitar. So good. Good wood. Kind wood. Smelling light, smelling of pine. And the strings, metal strings, smelling of metal.

His guitar smelled unlike any other. It had taken him awhile to realize it. But he had smelled other guitars and each one smelled slightly different. Slightly unique. Just like his. He could recognize his guitar by its smell alone.

He smiled.

And suddenly there was a sound that came through the house. That surrounded the house. A sound soft and subtle . . . but over-taking all others. Michael could feel a vibration resonating up his arm, could feel it moving around his hand, like a current in water. Moving on the current, through the water.

"Yes," McKenzie whispered. "Yes."

Michael knew that sound, knew it well. He had heard it after picking up his guitar, but before striking a note. After playing, but in between songs. When he was at rest, with one hand on the neck and another hand resting on the body. He had felt it, felt the vibration of his guitar. The sound that happened all by itself. A sound that couldn't so much be heard as felt. Yet a sound that existed just as much as anything else, that was part of every song just as much as the sounds that rang out loud. A sound that made Michael's guitar completely unique. Because, even though there were guitars that looked exactly the same as Michael's, his was different. Different because of the wood that made it, different because of the hands that built it, and different because of the history it had lived, the songs it had played, and the places it had been.

When a guitar is first finished, it is still very much like a tree. The wood, the grain, the molecules, all the small things that hold the wood together, that make it what it is. They still think and behave and hold themselves like they are part of a tree. Because that's what they've always known. That's what their life has been up to that point. Only after a guitar is played does the shape of those small things begin to change. All those notes. All that noise. All that vibration. Song after song. And the small things that hold everything together start to shift. The vibration of the songs played take hold of the wood and shape it. Until it is no longer like a tree, but like a guitar. A guitar with a very unique history.

With Michael's guitar it was a history played by him. So that the songs he played, the notes he played, in a very real way, shaped the guitar into what it was now: a thing unlike all others in the world. A thing with its own history; a thing with its own unique sound. A very subtle sound. More of a vibration than a sound. A vibration that Michael knew just as well as he knew the smell of his guitar. And Michael was feeling that vibration now, hearing that very soft sound in the current that moved through the room. It was being carried with the current surrounding the house, filling up the space inside the stone walls and resonating deep inside Michael's bones.

"Oh," Michael spoke softly. "Oh my."

"Go. Go play," McKenzie said to him. "Quick, go play now!"

McKenzie pushed him towards the door. The sound was still going, still vibrating through the house as McKenzie directed him toward the room where he had awakened. The room where his guitar stood in a corner, making the very same noise that filled the entire house now.

"Hurry! Hurry!" McKenzie said.

Michael picked up his guitar and sat on the edge of the bed. He sat with one hand on the neck and the other resting on the body. He sat listening to the noise.

Something inside him started to twist and move; a streak of excitement. He had an idea, another idea, for a song. . . . And then, Michael began to play. He played. And played. And it was very, very good.

The sounds were taken, carried on the current, and amplified through the house. And sometime, hours later, Michael played the last note. And he felt that particular feeling that comes when something good is completed, something true. There was the feeling that there was something more in the world, something alive. Like a living being with a life all its own, breathing and smiling, strong and proud. And that being, that song, had been born through Michael.[28]

Every one of us can do this, can immerse ourselves deep inside the golden threads that touch us; it is the secret to finding the heart of a thing, to finding the connections between things, to journeying deep into Earth, into the metaphysical background behind and inside everything.

The focus creates a task set that overrides habituated gating parameters. The immersion and continual feeling into the thread opens the gating channels more widely, and the more deeply immersed we become, the more widely they open. We begin to find then the reality that underlies the surface world that we live in during our daily lives.

Artists go deep but natural scientists go very deep. When the world itself is the focus, something new enters the process, something very much alive and intelligent and aware in its own right. And that changes things. We find then something that *responds* to our questing, sensing with its own desires and intentions. And the journey itself begins to become something else, something very different.

That is what people such as Goethe, Luther Burbank, Einstein, Masanobu Fukuoka, and Barbara McClintock did. As Einstein once put it, "Look deep into nature, and then you will understand everything better." It is where their deep insights came from . . . and they all knew it . . . and they all described what they did so that those who wish to follow them can do so. Reductionists hate it however. The schools do not teach it. Few books contain the story. As Aldous Huxley puts it . . .

Literary or scientific, liberal or specialist, all our education is predominantly verbal and therefore fails to accomplish what it is supposed to do. Instead of transforming children into fully formed adults, it turns out students of the natural sciences who are completely unaware of Nature as the primary fact of experience, it inflicts on the world students of the humanities who know nothing of humanity, their own or anyone else's.[29]

Or as ecologist/Gaian researcher Stephan Harding says it . . .

No student of ecology is ever introduced to this new mode of mental discipline—in our schools and colleges. There is no culture of experiencing oneness with the natural world. All one does on an ecology trip is to collect and measure. Deep contemplation of nature is considered to be at worst a waste of time, at best something to do in one's spare time. . . . Truly great scientists had this connection, this sense of the greater whole of which they were a part. Without educating this sensitivity, we churn out scientists without philosophy, who are merely interested in their subject, but not thoroughly awed by it. We churn out clever careerists. . . . It is this kind of training which leads to the mentality responsible for the massive social and environmental mistakes of Western-style development. Trained to shut down perception of the world so that we see it as a mere machine, we are perfectly free to improve the clockwork for our own ends.[30]

Nevertheless, this deeper, feeling approach is where real science begins . . . and, no, you don't have to have advanced degrees to do it. In fact . . . as Barbara McClintock says, science "gives us relationships which are useful, valid, and technically marvelous; however, they are not the truth."[31] To get to the truth, to see the world as it really is, there is a "necessary next step," as Evelyn Keller puts it. And that next step? "The reincorporation of the naturalist's approach—an approach that does not press nature with leading questions but dwells patiently in the variety and complexity of organisms."[32]

She's talking about the necessity for *nonscientists,* for the unique approach that comes from your own inherent genius, for the restoration of the human as an integral part of Earth understanding. One of the things we have lost is the diversity of multiple points of view, eyes looking out from other realities and sharing what they have seen, creating a diversity of understanding that allows our species to adapt to a never ending and always changing universe.

Keller is talking about that, about the necessity for a different kind of thinking.

13
THE NATURALIST'S
APPROACH
The Beginnings of
Deep Earth Perception

This is not a breathless account of discoveries from the brave new world of genomics and molecular biology, but a journey back to the roots of modern science, where natural philosophers roamed across a landscape without disciplinary boundaries.

ANDREW SUGDEN

The ultimate descriptive task, for both artists and scientists, is to "ensoul" what one sees, to attribute to it the life one shares with it; one learns by identification.

EVELYN FOX KELLER

The state of feeling which makes one capable of such achievements is akin to that of the religious worshipper or of one who is in love.

ALBERT EINSTEIN

Anything will give up its secrets if you love it enough.

GEORGE WASHINGTON CARVER

The process that artists, writers, musicians use to drop deep inside golden threads, to follow them, to craft what they find on that journey into art is the same for people who wish to understand plants, to understand Earth, to understand its functioning. Goethe and Masanobu Fukuoka, Henry David Thoreau and Luther Burbank—all of whom I have written about before—spoke in some depth about how they did what they did, so did Barbara McClintock. She, as they did, left traces of her approach to the world, trail markings that any of us can follow.

I want to make plain here
*that anyone can do this, that **you** can do this*
you do not need advanced degrees
or training in the technique people call science
all you need is your natural capacity to feel,
the curiosity and wonder of your childlike self,
and the willingness to never stop your questing

Barbara McClintock was born in 1902 in Hartford, Connecticut, and received her Ph.D. from Cornell in 1927. She began her study, as James Lovelock did, when a different, much less reductionist approach to the natural world was still possible for young scientists. Despite the restrictiveness of the times, of being a woman in what was primarily a man's profession, she became one of the world's most distinguished cyto-geneticists. She won the Nobel Prize for her work on corn transposons in 1983, this after most other researchers had abandoned the study of corn genetics as being "too boring, too old hat."

McClintock, along with Lynn Margulis, was responsible for some of the most important discoveries about the true nature of organisms in environment since Darwin's seminal studies on evolution. Because her findings contradicted deeply held beliefs within the scientific community about the nature of evolution and life, she was ostracized afterward—for several decades—by most of her former colleagues.

The beginnings of the rift occurred in 1951 at a conference in which she began openly discussing the mutability of genetic structures. Until that moment, McClintock had been considered one of the great-est genetic researchers in the world. She comments that "it was just a surprise that I couldn't communicate; it was a surprise that I was being ridiculed, or being told that I was really mad. . . . Later on there were years I couldn't talk to anybody about this and I wasn't invited to give seminars either." McClintock reports one well-known geneticist saying to her, when visiting, "Now I don't want to hear a thing about what you are doing. It may be interesting, but I understand it is kind of mad."[1] Another prominent geneticist described her, publically, as "an old bag who'd been hanging around Cold Spring Harbor for years."[2] The criticisms were scathing, and unrelenting.

You must not extend awareness further than society wants it to go.
Do you understand what I mean here?

Geneticist Sewall Wright is reported to have said that she was incapable of understanding the mathematics of her work, and that's why her results made no sense. And molecular biologist Joshua Lederberg, the 1958 Nobel Prize winner for studies on bacterial gene exchange, and some colleagues were thrown out of her lab by McClintock after a half hour, "because," as she put it, "of their arrogance."

I can't help but love her for that,
for throwing a Nobel Prize winner out of her lab

Lederberg said afterward, "By God, that woman is either crazy or a genius."[3]

Most of her former colleagues went with crazy

However, if you really look at what McClintock said she was doing, it wasn't crazy at all. But . . . she wasn't using reductionism. She was doing something else. She was using a different kind of approach, a different kind of thinking.

"I was just so interested in what I was doing," McClintock said. "I could hardly wait to get up in the morning and get at it. One of my friends, a geneticist, said I was a child, because only children can't wait to get up in the morning to get at what they want to do."[4]

You can see this attitude in the approach of every person who delves deeply into the heart of the world, the childlikeness of their approach and the sense of wonder they have about the world through which they move.

> *The embedded developmental stages (or consciousness modules) that still remain within every one of us serve specific ecological and evolutionary functions. They act as a lens through which we are able to perceive unique layers of the textural reality of the world. It is the young child in us that allows us to experience the livingness of the world, that has the most widely open gating channels, that approaches the world with empathy and caring. It is this part that feels most deeply, this part that can sense and follow golden threads with the most ease. This is the reason that the great scientists, naturalists, and spiritual adepts are all so childlike. It is through this part of the self that the metaphysical background of the world is most easily accessed.*

Einstein, culturally considered the most luminous of Western scientists, the one most filled with mythic dimension, often talked about the necessity to keep the sense of wonder and curiosity about the world alive. "The important thing is to not stop questioning," he said. "Curiosity has its own reason for existing." He knew it was crucial to any understanding of the world, and one of the most easily lost of all our human capacities. He said, more than once, that "it is a miracle that curiosity survives formal education."

> *it is a miracle that curiosity survives formal education*
> *actually . . . most times, it doesn't*

When the childlike self remains alive and present in the world, the feeling sense is more naturally accessible. So, if this part of you is still alive for you, still allowed to come out and play . . . when you come across something that catches your attention there is a natural tendency to turn toward it, to let it become the focus of your attention, to immerse yourself in the novelty of it. It *feels* interesting, it is fun to *be* with that thing.

And as the focus of the self concentrates on the thing that has captured attention, gating channels begin to open more widely. And as they do, you begin to access the metaphysical background of the world.

How did McClintock do what she did? Her biographer Evelyn Fox Keller comments . . .

> *Her answer is simple. Over and over again, she tells us, one must have the time to look, the patience to "hear what the material has to say to you," the openness to "let it come to you." Above all, one must have "a feeling for the organism."*[5]

At the root of McClintock's work was her *feeling* for the living entity she was trying to understand.

> *your ability to **feel** is at the root of the capacity to do this*

Then, she remained open to what it had to *say* to her, letting it lead her.

> *She experienced the process as a communication*
> *with a living being, equal in importance to herself*
> *not as the dissection of an inanimate world*

She kept following the golden thread that captured her attention. As McClintock once put it, "I went no place the corn did not first tell me to go." You remain open to what has touched you, feeling into it, letting it speak of its world, in its terms. As Richard Lewontin succinctly puts it . . .

> *If one wants to know the environment of an organism,*
> *one must ask the organism.*[6]

And Basho again . . .

> *Go to the pine*
> *if you want to learn about the pine*

As McClintock described it more fully . . .

One must understand "how it grows, understand its parts, under-
stand when something is going wrong with it. It isn't just a piece of
plastic, it's something that is constantly being affected by its
environment . . ."

Ah, nonlinearity . . .

You need to have a feeling for each individual plant. "No two plants
are exactly alike. They're all different, you have to know that differ-
ence," she explains. "I start with the seedling, and I don't want to
leave it. I don't feel I really know the story if I don't watch the plant
all the way along. So I know every plant in the field. I know them
intimately, and I find it a great pleasure to know them."[7]

Her habituated gating channels altered under the impetus of her desire;
the *novelty* threshold of each thing remained high, each thing remained
unique. She did not see a row of corn plants but a gathering of individuals
in community. Her feeling for each individual plant remained exquisitely
sensitive to its movements, how its life was going, how it was on this day,
then that day. And she cared so much for them as they grew that she did
not want to leave their side. And this knowing . . . it brought her great
pleasure, as does the company of any friend that we love.

Arne Naess, the father of Deep Ecology, once remarked on just this
way of being. These experiences, he said are

an articulation of the implicit philosophy of 5 year old children who
have access to at least a minimum of animals, plants, and natural
places. These children experience animals as being like themselves
in basic respects. They have joys and sorrows, interests, needs, loves
and hates. Even flowers and places are alive to them, thriving or
having a bad time.[8]

As Keller comments, "Over the years, a special kind of sympathetic
understanding grew in McClintock, heightening her powers of discern-
ment, until finally, the objects of her study have become subjects in their
own right; they claim from her a special kind of attention that most of

us experience only in relation to other persons. 'Organism' is for her a code word—not simply a plant or animal—but the name of a living form, of object-as-subject."⁹ In other words, she did not distance herself from the world but embraced it with the deepest part of herself, experienced it, and its living organisms, as kin. And she did so because she approached the world with the part of her that felt most deeply, her childlike self.

We are urged to grow up, to leave this part of us behind. But when we do, we lose one of the most valuable parts of ourselves. Most especially we lose the part that has the greatest capacity for deep relationship with the world. As well, these childlike parts of us, as Aldous Huxley once said, "are remarkable for their intelligence and ardor, for their curiosity, their intolerance of shams, the clarity and ruthlessness of their vision." The child in us is the part most easily able to perceive a lie, whether in science, in politics, or in personal relationship. (And yes, it is true, as most children have wondered, cows in France do talk differently than cows in the United States.)

There are reasons why we are urged to leave this part of us behind
The first step in the ecological reclamation of the self is to feel,
to reclaim the parts of ourselves that feel and feel deeply

The necessity of *seeing* what is right in front of the self rather than merely looking at it was also essential to McClintock—it is a crucial skill for reading the text of the world. The training of the eye, just as it was for Mark Twain, is a fundamental necessity. Keller comments that McClintock's approach required

an extensive training of the eye. . . . "Seeing," in fact, was at the center of her scientific experience. . . . [F]or McClintock, this reciprocity between cognitive and visual seems always to have been more intimate than it is for most. As if without distinguishing between the two, she knew by seeing and saw by knowing. . . . Ordinary language could not begin to convey the full structure of the reading that emerged. . . . Witkin [McClintock's sole scientific confident for many years] can be said to have learned a special kind of language—a language in which words and visual forms are woven together into a coherent structure of meaning. . . . In order to "see" what McClintock "saw," Witkin had to learn more than a new "language"; she needed to share in McClintock's internal vision. In that sense, "seeing" in science is not unlike "seeing" in art. . . . [I]t gives rise to a [particular] kind of knowledge . . .[10]

In other words, a synaesthesia of perception occurred. It's identical to Goethe's description of the process . . .

My thinking is not separate from objects; the elements of the object, the perceptions of the object, flow into my thinking and are fully permeated by it; my perception itself is a thinking, and my thinking a perception.

As McClintock focused her seeing, what she was looking at became her whole world. As she once put it, "Well, you know, when I look at a cell, I get down in that cell and look around."[11] She says that

the more I worked with [the chromosomes] the bigger and bigger [they] got, and when I was really working with them I wasn't outside, I was down there. I was part of the system. I was right down there with them, and everything got so big. I even was able to see the internal parts of the chromosomes—actually everything was there. It surprised me because I actually felt as if I were right down there and these were my friends.[12]

That feeling of friendship is crucial, "seeing," in this sense, cannot occur without it. Seeing without the feeling of caring, without an empathic feeling sense of the thing observed, is merely looking. But *seeing . . .* that is something much deeper. It is the blending of the feeling and seeing senses, and behind both a deep, unwavering caring for the thing perceived. *Everyone* who has done this work has commented on how that facilitates communication between the perceived and the perceiver; George Washington Carver is one of them. "Anything will give up its secrets," he once said, "if you love it enough." As Keller put it, "A deep reverence for nature, a capacity for union with that which is to be known—these reflect a different image of science from that of a purely rational enterprise."[13]

McClintock was clear that there was a "real affection" on her part. "As you look at these things," she said, "they become part of you. And you forget yourself. The main thing about it is you forget yourself."[14] Or as Stephan Harding at the Schumacher Institute in the UK has it . . .

As you experience this dynamic, ever shifting reality, you may sud- denly find yourself in a state of meditation, a state where you lose your sense of separate identity, and become totally engrossed in the life process being contemplated. The contemplated and the contempla- tor become one. From this oneness there arises a deep appreciation of the reality of interdependence.[15]

Such depth immersion is crucial. You feel into the thread that has caught your attention *and everything slows down the deeper you go* so that you begin to attend to each and every tiny aspect of what you are seeing. Sense of self fades. The only thing of importance is the thing you are seeing *and feeling.* There is a genuine and very deep ecstatic feeling to touching something so closely with the feeling sense in this way. You *feel* each tiny part of it because of the love and caring you feel for it.

It is like the touch of your beloved upon your body, and your touch upon them. For the feeling sense is, in actuality, exactly like incred- ibly sensitive fingers, the touch of the soul, of the heart, directed with tremendous sensitivity and focus. It feels into the living nature of the thing studied, caresses it, feels into the deeper realities of its interior self. It is a form of tantra. And this caressing, there is a union that comes from it, from the depth of the love given . . . and received.

You strive in the touching to really understand what you are focused on, as it is from inside itself, seeing into its deeper nature with the mind's eye, with the synaesthetic blending of senses that is occurring. Goethe talked about it like this . . .

Here we do not set forth arbitrary signs, letters, and whatever else you please in place of the phenomena; here we do not deliver phrases that can be repeated a hundred times without thinking anything thereby nor giving anyone else pause to think. Rather, it is a matter of phenomena that one must have present before the eyes of the body and of the spirit in order to be able to evolve clearly their origin and development for oneself and others.[16]

From this, as Evelyn Keller puts it, McClintock "developed a unique virtuosity at integrating these disparate clues [from her observations of chromosomes] into a coherent and meaningful whole. Her ability to identify those clues that were worth following, her instinct for what was important, grew steadily."[17]

McClintock's ability to sense golden threads increased the more she used the capacity, the more she felt into that part of the world that had called her to meet it on its own terms. In the process, as time goes on, you get a feel for the rightness or wrongness of any step you take. There is less tendency to lose direction, for you know the feeling of golden threads. So, you let the thread tell you where to go. The job is one of following, not imposing. "You let the material tell you where to go," McClintock said, "and it tells you at every step what the next step has to be because you're integrating with an overall brand-new pattern in mind. You are not following an old one; you are convinced of a new one. And you let everything you do focus on that. You can't help it, because it all integrates."[18]

It tells you at every step what the next step has to be

It's like this . . . you are following a golden thread, focusing on it with your whole attention while at the same time working diligently to capture its essence in your understanding. Nothing exists in your awareness but this perceptual exploration and your desire to understand it. And in the midst of your immersion there will come moments when some deeper aspect of its nature suddenly bursts into your understanding.

What happens next is interesting. You are sitting, held in the contemplation of this sudden, new understanding, when, of its own accord, the attention of the self suddenly shifts, moves in some new, never-to-be-predicted, direction. The part of you that is intimate with meanings flows along the line of meaning that touched you, heading toward its depths. The golden thread moves and the deep you moves with it. The feeling of the thread is the same but there's more to it now, it has deepened in some way, become richer. More meanings inside the thread begin to reveal themselves. New thoughts, feelings, sensations, images, emerge—spontaneously—into awareness. And now you begin the process of trying to understand them. William Stafford comments: "If I let the process go on, things will occur to me that were not at all in my mind when I started. These things, odd or trivial as they may be, are somehow connected."

Robert Bly says that

something surprising happens often during the writing. It is as if the object itself, a stump or an orange, has links with the human psyche, and the unconscious provides material it would not give if asked directly. The unconscious passes into the object and returns.[19]

During the focus on the thread, feeling into it,

literally and not metaphorically

a very unique part of the self travels deep within the thing perceived, what Bly here is calling the unconscious. What is true is that

We move deep into other psyches once we fully enter that kind of immersion. Seeds from some other country attach themselves to our clothes. When we awaken from the dream of our immersion, return to this place, this other state of consciousness, they return with us, hitchhikers from a deeper part of the world. And just as seeds do on the physical level, they detach themselves when we have returned to this familiar country. They drop themselves into the soil of this world, into this part of Earth. And a different kind of life takes root that, over time, spreads. A forest slowly begins to grow and we,

*and the people who stumble across our work, find ourselves sud-
denly shadowed by strange leaves, embraced by a wildness that was
once common in the world. We become entangled in fragrances that
could not have been known otherwise. And there is a smell that
enters deep within us—it changes who we are and how we see the
world and ourselves. We are not merely physical beings moving
among static objects in a dead world.*

This immersion, this process of paying attention so closely to what
has called you to attend it, naturally generates synaesthesia. You see/feel/
hear the organism. A new facility of perceiving develops; synaesthetic
perceiving begins to become a habituated skill. You possess now not five
or six sensory organs but seven or eight or nine, even more, depending
on the sensory blendings that are occurring. For all who engage in this
process, as Goethe put it . . .

*Every new object, clearly seen
opens up a new organ of perception in us.*

Or, as Evelyn Keller says it, "A motivated observer develops faculties that
a casual spectator may never be aware of."[20]

As you follow the golden thread that has touched you, as you immerse
yourself deep within the feeling of it and begin to see the world from *its*
point of view, your sensory gating will open more and more widely. And
the more you focus on the phenomenon, the more immersed you will
become, and the more gating will open. As the immersion continues, deepens, the nature of what you are feeling into—and its unique connections
to other parts of the world—will begin to emerge into your awareness. You
are headed toward a goal, the understanding of this thing that will not let
you rest, completely immersed in it, so totally focused on feeling it, thinking into it, synaesthetically perceiving it, that you have no sense of yourself
at all . . . and it is at this moment that your perceiving becomes a thinking.

And now, the deeper, living realities of the world begin to open themselves to your gaze. There comes now a burst of knowing, seemingly, out
of nowhere. You emerge then in what Goethe called the pregnant point.
As he put it . . .

> *I persist until I have discovered a pregnant point from which sev-*
> *eral things may be derived, or rather one which yields several*
> *things, offering them up of its own accord.*

These insights are literal truths about the phenomenon you have been focused on, immersed within. They emerge into awareness as a synaesthetic blend of feeling/seeing/understanding as a sudden gestalt. You see then the reason why the gastrointestinal tract possesses so many neurons and neural structures, perceive the pervasiveness of phytoandrogens in ecosystem, begin to see the foundational nature of music in Earth functioning. You literally begin to *see* what is happening in the metaphysical background that underlies the physical expression you are attempting to understand.

This experience of the pregnant point is not an unusual one; all of us have had such moments. Let's see if I can give you a more concrete sense of what it feels like . . .

Have you ever had the experience of walking along a street and catching a glimpse of yourself in a shop window but, in one of those odd moments that sometimes occur, you don't realize it's you. So, for a few moments you really do see yourself as another person might. You don't know who that is you're looking at but for some reason you are caught up in looking at them. Then, suddenly, the *meaning* of what you are seeing coalesces inside you. With a start, you realize it's you that's reflected in the glass.

Or perhaps you've had the experience where you're looking at something but, for some reason, you can't figure out the perspective of what you're seeing. You can't figure out the scale. Is the thing near or far away, small or large? What *is* its relationship to the field around it? So, you keep looking at it, working at it, and suddenly you understand just what you've been looking at. The perspective of the thing suddenly clicks into place.

Or maybe you have looked at one of those books that were popular for a time (I forget what they're called). There's a picture of some sort, a lot of apparently random colors and shapes on the page, but it seems to make no sense. However, if you look at it in a certain way it turns out there really is a picture in there. So, you strain, your friends urging you on, trying this way of seeing, then that, then . . . suddenly, there it is.

The visual images we are looking at in such a book are composed of an apparently random grouping of irregular-sized color or black and white blotches. These are the sensory impulses that are reaching our eyes and then passing through them into the brain. The visual perceptions are coming in, but there is no meaning to them. Yet there *is* meaning; there is a picture, somehow, in there. If you keep looking at it, of a sudden, a recognizable picture emerges.

The same thing happens in the first two situations I described; visual images are coming in but what they mean is unclear. In the first example you know it's a person, you just don't know it's you. In the second, you are perceiving some sort of visual images from the world but you can't figure out their relation to each other.

However, when you do finally understand what you're looking at, when you finally perceive the meaning inside it, you see it suddenly, immediately. As Henri Bortoft observes: *The effect is just as if the [image] had been switched on, like a light.* All of a sudden, click, it's just there.

Bortoft goes on to ask . . .

> *What happens in this instant of transition? There is evidently no change in the purely sensory experience, i.e., in the sensory stimulus to the organism. The pattern registered on the retina of the eye is the same whether the [image] is seen or not. There is no change in this pattern at the instant when the [image] is seen—the actual marks on the page are exactly the same after the event of recognition as they were before. So the difference cannot be explained as a difference in sensory experience.*[21]

What happens is that the *meaning* within the sensory impulses has been grasped. The part of the brain that deals with meaning has received the sensory impulses from the visual cortex and successfully analyzed and integrated the relationship of the visual elements to the whole and to each other. The thing that is more than the sum of the parts, the organized pattern that is there, suddenly bursts into awareness. The *meaning* is finally perceived and the image that is inside the sensory frame suddenly appears. Click. Like flipping a light switch.

The visual elements that make up the thing you are looking at, however, are not the thing itself, not the meaning. The meaning is somehow *in* the picture, but it isn't the picture. It's not the series of visual impulses you have received. Nor is the meaning merely an element of the figure. If a person who cannot see the image in that apparently random grouping of black and white blotches makes an exact copy of them by hand, the image will not stand out any more clearly to them than it did before. Bortoft comments succinctly that *What we are seeing is not in fact on the page, even though it appears to be there.*

This *meaning* is an added dimension to the patchwork blotches on the page. It's a dimension concerned with relationships and the tension between parts and that invisible something that comes into being when a grouping of parts suddenly unifies into one coordinated whole. It's an invisible yet vitally important dimension of everything we encounter. Bortoft says that

> *The error of empiricism rests on the fact that what it takes to be material objects are condensations of meaning. When we see a chair, for example, we are seeing a condensed meaning and not simply a physical body. Since meanings are not objects of sensory perception, seeing a chair is not the sensory experience we imagine it to be.*[22]

We live in, are immersed within, a world of meanings not objects. But because the condensation of meaning occurs almost immediately when we see a physical object, none of us notice the process happening. It's so automatic we miss ourselves doing it.

> *this is due in part to the habituation of gating channels*
> *there is little novelty to the things we perceive*
> *so . . . they just are . . . a chair, a couch, a plant*

But it has not always been so automatic; when we were babies it wasn't automatic at all. We experienced the same kind of sensory impulses then that we do now but we didn't understand the meanings in them. We learned how to understand the inherent meanings over time—and we learned it at the simplest level possible; we learned to stop at *chair* or *tree* and then go on with our lives. But the thing is, *chair* is only part of the complex of meanings that are embedded within the visual images we are receiving, and the most superficial one at that. The chair possesses not only *chair* as a meaning but also a feeling tone that is itself a key to the deeper meanings that it possesses. If the chair is approached through our feeling sense, if we begin to develop our natural capacity for perceiving the secret kinesis of things, rather than leave it undeveloped in the unconscious, then those other meanings begin to emerge into our awareness through our practiced, synaesthetic perceiving. The invisible elements of the thing, its deeper nature and meanings, including its connections to other, apparently unrelated phenomena, become sensible to our synaesthetic perceiving. And as we think through our sensing, feel more deeply into the image itself, a similar pattern recognition experience occurs deep inside the self. Something new just pops into our awareness, like a light switch being flipped. And once that happens we begin to see what was right in front of us all along. It occurs for everyone who works in this way. For instance . . .

McClintock developed the ability to actually see what was happening in the genome. Keller comments that she "could directly read off the history of genetic events that had accompanied the plant's development."[23] She could literally see the genes turning on and off. And Luther Burbank who co-created, with the plants, most of the food plants we now take for granted noted that "heredity is nothing more than stored environment." He came to that truth because, over time, he learned to literally see every shape a plant had ever taken throughout its entire evolutionary history. He said that

> *In imagination I look back far into the past*
> *and inquire as to the racial history of this fruit*

He, like McClintock, could see the "history of genetic events that had accompanied" its development. This process develops in its users, naturally, an extremely sophisticated visual imagination. It allowed McClintock to, as she put it, "integrate" what she was seeing. This capacity of seeing with the internal eye, using the imaginative sensing of the feeling self is common to this work. As researcher Gerald Holton once observed about Einstein, "The objects of his imagination were to him evidently persuasively real, visual materials, which he voluntarily and playfully could reproduce and combine, analogous perhaps to play with shapes in a jigsaw puzzle."[24] As Einstein himself put it, "Logic will get you from A to B. Imagination will get you everywhere," and "When I examine myself and my methods of thought, I come to the conclusion that the gift of fantasy has meant more to me than any talent for abstract, positive thinking." This capacity was crucial as well for Goethe; he referred to it as "the exact sensorial imagination."

Henri Bortoft, a scholar who has spent many years focusing on Goethe's techniques of perception, succinctly describes what Goethe was talking about . . .

> The aim is to think about the phenomenon concretely in imagina-
> tion, and not to think about it, trying not to leave anything out or
> to add anything which cannot be observed. Goethe referred to this
> discipline as "re-creating in the wake of ever-creating nature."
> Combined with active seeing, it has the effect of giving thinking
> more the quality of perception and sensory observation more the
> quality of thinking. The purpose is to develop an organ of percep-
> tion which can deepen our contact with the phenomenon in a way
> that is impossible by simply having thoughts about it and working
> it over with the intellectual mind.[25]

Access to the metaphysical background of the world, expressed in the mind as living images in the sensory imagination, arises out of this kind of synaesthetic perceiving and feeling into the world. There is something inside the *image*, the physical, visual form of what we are concentrating on, that connects us to its root, in the metaphysical background of the world. Bly comments that

> When a poet creates a true image, he is gaining knowledge; he is
> bringing up into consciousness a connection that has been forgotten,
> perhaps for centuries. . . . The power of the image is the power of
> seeing resemblances. That discipline is essential to the growth of

intelligence, to everyone's intelligence, but especially to a poet's intelligence. Emerson, who was Thoreau's master, said, talking of true analogies:

It is easily seen that there is nothing lucky or capricious in these analogies, but that they are constant, and pervade nature. These are not the dreams of a few poets, here and there, but man is an analogist, and studies relations in all objects. He is placed in the center of beings, and a ray of relation passes from every other being to him.[26]

When Bly says: *When a poet creates a true image, he is gaining knowledge; he is bringing up into consciousness a connection that has been forgotten, perhaps for centuries,* he is talking about what artists have called analogical thinking.

Analogical thinking is the kind of cognition that occurs when you think *through* your synaesthetic perceiving, headed toward a goal (this is crucial), in this instance, feeling into and attempting to understand some part of the living world that has captured your attention. Caught up in what you are doing, you literally become *immersed* in your synaesthetic sensing and in your search for understanding All sense of self, and the world around you (except for what you are focused on), fades. When there is submersion to the point where all sense of self fades you are *in* analogical thinking. Automatically.

The different kind of thinking that this book is about entails learning to think analogically. It is the only way that the deeper text of the world *can* be read. As Robert Bly says, this form of perception not only sees deeper within things but it also "sees the hidden links between the 'ghosts of things' and the things themselves."[27] It is how we make the connections that are woven through the world visible to the conscious mind, which usually cannot see them. The new thoughts, perceptions, and understandings that emerge out of analogical thought occur as sudden epiphanies, moments of duende, intimations from who knows where. Like flipping a light switch, they are suddenly there.

And there is no other way of getting to them except analogically. That is, at root, the power and beauty of what it means to be a natural scientist. It is a way of thinking that is also a way of perceiving that is also a way of understanding; it gives us access to the underlying nature of the world. It is very different from current scientific approaches, and a great deal older.

Analogical thinking is one of the oldest forms of depth perception that human beings have, one of the oldest ways that we have used as a species to understand ourselves and the world around us. We find truth in this kind of perceiving, deep aspects of reality that, when articulated, wind their way down inside us and set up a reverberational response from the truth receiver that lives there. We literally think our way to the truths that reside, and can only be found, in the metaphysical background of the world, truths that underpin our daily world and that lead to a whole life. We find in this kind of thinking a way to *understand* the life we live embedded within. And the more we engage in analogical thinking, the more we educate this capacity in ourselves, the more we give it experience, the more we find in it.

Continued focus on the thing, our immersion within it, as the years go by leads to an increasingly deep capacity for analogical thought. The deeper our capacity for analogical thinking, the more unique understandings that will emerge into our thinking. The emergence of these understandings, moments in the pregnant point, lead to the emergence of pattern that has, heretofore, been concealed inside the physical form that we have been contemplating. As Bly has described, the process, by its very nature, brings into consciousness connections that have always been there but which have been forgotten—perhaps, in some instances, connections that have never before been found.

When we focus intently on the visual images of the objects surrounding us, we increase the amount and degree of sensory inflows. Those sensory inputs are filled with a great deal more than *chair* and, through synaesthetic perceiving, we can feel our way more deeply into the meanings that are held within the image. We are, in essence, seekers of meaning through a unique kind of cognition. The more sensory data from the image that flows inside us, the more of the *text* that is embedded within it will flow into us. The more of the text we have access to, the more meaning we can distill out of it, the more rays of relation we can find and experience.

The meaning-filled text of the world is embedded deep within everything we *see,* within every image we encounter. When we enter the image, we find what Henri Corbin called the imaginal world, that is, the deeper metaphysical backgound of the world, through using a particular kind of imagination. As Corbin noted (in his particularly difficult languaging) . . .

> It is the cognitive function of the Imagination that permits the establishment of a rigorous analogical knowledge, escaping the dilemma of current rationalism.[28]

To get a sense of the relationship between image, imagination, and the imaginal let's play again with one of the earlier exercises in this book. That is, just take a look at anything you wish in the room you are in now, and focus on it visually. Really *notice* it through your visual sensing and then ask yourself, *How does it feel?* You will again experience that instantaneous burst of the feeling tone that is a part of that object. Just stay with it a minute and let the feeling develop.

Now, take a break. Take a deep breath, perhaps stretch a bit or move your body. Then . . . close you eyes and *remember* the thing you were just feeling. Remember how it looks in all the detail you are capable of and remember as well how it felt. Still with your eyes closed, keep seeing and feeling the thing. Now . . . reach out with your hand to the place where the image is. Now, open your eyes and look at where your hand is. It will most likely be out in front of you someplace, somewhere in the region of space in front of your chest.

Now, break state, that is, move a bit, stretch, or even get up and walk around, so you move out of the slight dreaming state you are in. Take a couple of deep breaths. Now . . . start thinking about something that you are troubled about, bills you have to pay, or a problem facing you, perhaps a government agency you are upset with. *Close your eyes* and see a visual image of it, of the people involved, and of you talking to them about it, and what you are going to do to attempt to solve the problem. Say all the things in that imaginary scene that you would say if you let yourself say whatever you wanted to. Let the scene unfold until it is clear. When it is, reach your hand out and put it in the place where *that* image is. Now open your eyes and look. Most likely your hand is up, either out in the region in front of your head or even higher—above it entirely.

This is an example of two different kinds of images—and two very different types of imagination. It is an example, as well, of two very different forms of thought, each of which works with images in very different ways.

The latter example is one that works through and with the brain. It works with the kind of imagination that most people define as something done in the brain, a mental fancy. It is the kind of imagining that is useless for understanding the world.

However that first imagining, the remembering of the thing you were seeing and feeling, is an example of what Goethe called the exact sensorial imagination. The exact sensorial imagination is at the core of analogical thinking; it is another way of describing it. It is a thinking, a cognition, that occurs through both feeling and images. It is a thinking into the meaning dimensions of images through subtle perceptions of their feeling dimension. This is how the imaginal realm is accessed. And that imaginal realm is where the mythic, the world of the Forms that Plato spoke of, and the human can meet—the only place they *can* meet. It is a world that is entered through this particular kind of imagination. For most ancient cultures, this kind of imagining occurs not through or in the brain but through and in the heart.

Jason Godesky comments that

> *"Old growth" societies do not see imagination as an illusion or internal human idyll; rather, they see imagination as a form of communication, by which a human can perceive what a given environment says. . . . [For example] while the human sense of smell lacks much of the precision some other animals possess, humans do experience synaesthesia naturally; allowing imagination to wander and freely assign mental images and feelings to particular smells would thus follow evolutionary pathways, naturally relying on the mutually-agreed meanings of various smells. Just as dreams try to match mental images to internal body states, imagination would try to match mental images to a wealth of subconsciously and synaesthetically perceived sensory stimuli. Or to put it more bluntly, imagination represents, at least in part, the human perception of plant communication.*
>
> *This can seem very suspect to us, with our habit of dismissing imagination, but we should remember that neurologically, our brain*

constantly matches sense impressions to memories and patterns it has previously encountered; thus we can perceive a particular pattern of light and shadow and recognize it as a human face, or a tree. . . . Synaesthetic imagination allows us to understand what plants tell us, as our brains scramble to match the chemical signals to the best patterns it can fit. . . . [This] is a pathway of communication with the more-than-human world.[29]

Indigenous cultures' understanding of the heart's capacity for sensory perception and cognition was far different from the kind of mushy sense of heart we now have in the West. To the ancient cultures, the heart was a sophisticated organ capable of both perception and a unique form of analytical thought, a thought that was oriented around images filled with feeling, a synaesthetic perceptual sensing that uses a specific form of imagination, what Goethe called the exact sensorial imagination—or, what I am calling here, analogical thought. Baudelaire was speaking of this capacity as well, when he said . . .

By imagination, I do not simply mean to convey the common notion implied by that much abused word, which is only fancy, but the constructive imagination which is a much higher function.[30]

And the skill of that sensorial thinking, that imaginative faculty, can be developed through practice into a potent perceptual and analytical tool as elegant and specific as the brain (as many writers and scientists have proved). But, it is distinct from the kind of thinking the brain performs; it has a sensorial dimension to it—it is not mere mentation.

It is this kind of imagining that is central to this way of perceiving and thinking. It both works with and generates images that are filled with kinesthetic dimensions and those kinesthetic dimensions hold within them deeper awarenesses of the object of our attention. It's how the imaginal is accessed, how we get to the place where we can touch the mythic, enter the dreaming of Earth.

That is what we, as psychonauts exploring the deeper foundations of the world, do. We access the imaginal through our capacity for analogical thought and we build, year by year, a database of our analogical exploration of the world. For us imagination is not something that happens in the brain but is rather a different form of cognition, one inextricably interwoven with feeling, one filled with full sensate perceiving. It is the only way we can get to the meaning-filled text that underlies, that resides within, the world of form.

McClintock understood this; she commented that her type of perception was actually a special form of cognition. Her "computer" as she put it, her brain, "was working full time—mediating between the spots [of pigment seen under the microscope], the patterns they formed, and her internal vision."[31] The writer John Gardner considered the elements of this process—reclaiming the feeling sense, training the eye, depth immersion of the self, synaesthesia, entering the dreaming state—as "the fundamental units of an ancient but still valid kind of thought."[32] It is a form of cognition that, in fact, allows depth understanding of the world without recourse to linear reductionism. And it finds, not facts, as McClintock noted, but truth.

> *The process of truly understanding something in the way McClintock or Goethe or Burbank did, however, it must be said, takes years. It took Barbara McClintock six years to understand corn transposons, six years until its full nature burst into her understanding.*
>
> *It took me ten years to understand the function of the gastrointestinal biological oscillator in humans, eight years to a depth glimpse of phytoandrogens, twenty-five to an understanding of heart perception and cognition. As Einstein once put it, "I think and think, for months and years." But really, what else do we have to do with our time here, play cards? Believe me, this is a lot more fun.*

McClintock knew that her particular kind of seeing was crucial to her eventual understanding of corn genetics, knew that her seeing was often affected by her internal state. So she would sometimes leave her laboratory and go and sit beneath nearby eucalyptus trees to meditate and, as she put it, "work on herself." Then, when she was ready, she returned and begin to look and feel into the corn once more.

Such caretaking and work on the self is essential. Feeling so deeply actually involves *feeling* deeply and, because the heart and the self remain open, undefended, not dissociated, *all* the consciousness modules, all the parts of the self are affected. *Stuff* comes up. And that can affect the capacity to do the work. As Goethe once put it . . .

> *To grasp the phenomena, to fixate them into experiments, to order one's experiences, and to come to know all the ways in which one might view them; to be attentive as possible in the first case, as exact as possible in the second, to be as complete as possible in the third, and to remain many-sided enough in the fourth, requires that one work one's poor ego in a way I had else hardly thought possible.*[33]

Self-caretaking, deep interior analysis, a drive for rigorous self-examination, a genuine love of all the parts of the self, and importantly . . . the willingness to remain mutable, to have flexible perspective, the willingness to see what is true, not what you have been taught is true is essential in order to remain balanced.

> *That is part of the reason why reductive scientists prefer reductionism. They are afraid of such self-examination, such self revelation. They are afraid to **feel** the world, to feel much at all. That we as a people have refused to recognize this in them has allowed the distortions of science they create, and the harm it causes, to go unchallenged.*

Over time and deep relationship, long years of it, McClintock began to understand that something other than chance was controlling mutations in the genome. As Keller comments, "these were mutations that did not strike capriciously within the life of the single plant; whatever set them off was a factor that was constant. For McClintock, this regularity meant that something was controlling the rate of mutation."[34] And this was McClintock's sin, the transgression that caused her ostracism. She commented later that the instructions for gene rearrangement came not only from the organism itself but also from the environment in which it lived. Nothing could have undermined reductionist Darwinism more. As Keller comments, "Central to neo-Darwinism theory was the premise that whatever genetic variation does occur is random, and McClintock reported genetic changes that are under the control of the organism. Such results just did not fit in the standard frame of analysis."[35]

But this recognition, that environment and organism controlled genetic mutation, did more than "not fit" the model in place. It indicated intelligence in places that human centrists could not accept that it existed. But there are further implications that are even more troubling. . . . When McClintock's understanding is combined with Heisenberg's insights into the nature of subatomic particles—that they change their nature from particle to wave and back again depending on whether they are observed or not—something tremendously unsettling begins to emerge.

Subatomic particles exist in a quantum state of *potential*. When they are measured—i.e., observed—that potential collapses; the particle takes on a specific form and that form subsequently shapes both space and behavior. Subatomic particles act along quantum planes, they don't live in the classical Newtonian world of linear cause and effect. And while generally unrecognized, this has powerful impacts on genetic structures.

DNA is a flexible organ of the cell that exists in a state of dynamic change; it is in fact nonlinear, as all organs are. It constantly responds to environmental cues, to the exterior world's touches upon it. From one orientation, any current shape of DNA in an organism can be viewed as a grouping of genetic codes held in place, in that structural formation, by chemical bonds. Genes are turned on and off when those chemical bonds are broken, then reformed in new ways as new chemical bonds are generated. And those chemical bonds are broken and reformed by the movements of electrons and protons—all working at the quantum level, in quantum space, in quantum reality. Protons and electrons exist in quantum reality and in the quantum world they exist as potential in multiple locations and forms simultaneously. In other words, in the quantum world the subatomic particles exist in forms that both turn on and turn off genes at the same time.

The genes that are generating the current form of an organism, a bacteria or a plant, are in essence stable. The subatomic particles that controlled how those genes act have already been measured and have collapsed into classical space, what we think of as reality. So you find an apparently stable state. But all organisms contain what has, from classical perspectives, been considered "junk" DNA, that is, sequences that don't seem to do anything. And there are a lot of them. These apparently irrelevant DNA sequences are highly mutable and responsive to quantum alterations. The genes in these "junk" sequences, in the quantum world, exist in multiple states of potential continuously. They are no longer nailed to classical reality but exist and drift within the quantum multiverse of potential gene sequences. In this state, as molecular geneticist Johnjoe McFadden comments, there is "a quantum superposition of all possible mutations. The superposition would have grown, branching like a tree, into the multiverse of all the trillions of possible DNA sequences that could lead off from the original gene."[36]

As the thousands/millions of environmental inputs are taken into the organism, they put pressure on the organism to alter itself to maintain homeodynamis. Those inputs are taken in as a complex gestalt, and it represents a specific, unique communication that the organism analyzes far below the level of what we call conscious awareness. Those "junk" genes that are existing simultaneously in the quantum multiverse hold within them all potential forms the organism can take in any of the millions upon millions of possible exterior environmental states. And as one of those possible environmental states comes into being its nature is communicated to the organism through sensory inflows. That communication percolates down to the genetic level and entangles some of those potential genetic states in itself. It calls forth a particular kind of emergence from the multiverse of potential forms. As McFadden puts it, "The only event capable of halting our duplicated gene's drift through the quantum multiverse is the establishment of another chain of entanglement with the cell's environment."[37] And the environmental pressure, the unique communication that occurs, is what does it. That communication in essence matches certain forms in the multiverse that can be thought of as communicatory responses. The communication in essence brings potential into actuality. It touches the quantum world and begins the movement of genes in quantum potential along a pathway of response, the gene form coming more into being at each step along the way. As McFadden notes, "any [potential genetic expression] may encounter an environmental entanglement that generates measurement . . . [thus] amplifying the quantum state irreversibly to the classical level."[38]

McFadden comments that what is occurring is

> *the ability of quantum measurement to interact with, and shape the dynamics of a system. The special relationship between quantum objects and quantum-measuring devices draws out classical reality from the quantum world. In one last analogy, the process may be compared with the kind of Improvisation Theatre pioneered by Viola Spolin in the 1930s. Spolin's revolutionary approach was to throw away the script. Instead the actors would respond to the audience's reactions and prompting by improvising the ensuing action. At the start of each performance the improvised play can be said to be* indeterminate. . . . *The play has certain potentialities dependent on the set of characters present, but no defined plot. With no audience present, we could imagine a* quantum play *in which all possible plots were acted out as a quantum superposition. However, in a real performance, the interaction between the actors and their audience draws out the course of action, the plot for that night's performance. Just as the audience of an improvised play draws out from the infinity of possible plots a single reality for each performance, so measurement of a quantum system draws out from the quantum superposition of all possible states a single reality for the physical world.*[39]

The subatomic particles only end up in one location, in an identifiable form, if they are measured, that is, observed. In this case what measures or observes the particle—thus affecting the current gene state—is the environment in which the genetic information exists, that is the DNA structure itself. (The DNA structure's environment is the cell in which it is located.) And that environment is impacted by the communicatory inputs coming from the larger self-organized system in which it is embedded. As the environment places pressure on the organism, that places pressure on the cell and that pressure causes the cell to act as a quantum measuring tool, forcing a shift in state of subatomic particles. A mutation then occurs that benefits the cell, the organism, and ultimately, the larger environment, the Gaian system itself. Mutations are in fact not random. Genetic rearrangements are under the control of the organism and the environment—though control in this sense is different from what we usually mean by the term. It's not linear but nonlinear. In essence, it is the organism's own cells that drive evolution. They respond to environmental cues (pressures) and collapse potential DNA states so that the organism better fits the environment. As McFadden reveals . . .

> *In this way, even lowly* E. coli *cells may have a certain control of their destiny; a control denied to inanimate objects. This is what makes living organisms special. They are able to use quantum measurement to perform directed actions and one of those actions is quantum evolution.*[40]

Cells act as their own quantum-measuring devices; mutations are not in fact "random" at all. A bacteria, placed in a solution in which it cannot survive, that has no fuel source for it to feed on (such as the cleaning solutions in hospitals), will, in fact, genetically alter itself so that its offspring can survive in that environment. In such circumstances, the genetic mutation exists as potential in quantum space, one of an innumerable number of possible mutations in the genetic structure, all dependent on certain positions of subatomic particles. And so, the cell acts as its own quantum-measuring tool, forcing the subatomic particles to actualize where the genetic mutation supports survival.

There are always several of these; the cells choose

DNA restructures itself, form alters its nature, and adaptive mutation occurs. And environment? When it needs a particular rearrangement of genetic material to express a form that will support self-organization, it moves organisms along the path most likely to do so. In other words, "The instructions for gene rearrangement come not only from the organism but from the environment in which it lives."

And it is not just plants and bacteria that alter gene expression in a single generation in response to organism or environmental inputs—and then pass those alterations on to their offspring— salmon do as well. It is becoming clear that this is more the norm than the exception. Not only environment but organisms are a great deal more fluid than we have been taught. There is no fundamental "it" to be found, only temporary forms of message material that themselves are indicative of ongoing communicatory interactions, that themselves show the shape of environmental space at that moment in time.

McClintock was beginning to understand with her insight about the source of gene rearrangement that living organisms are essentially nonlinear, self-organized systems, that the static picture commonly ascribed to them by Western culture and science was inaccurate.

"For McClintock," Keller notes, "reason—at least in the conventional sense of the word—is not by itself adequate to describe the vast complexity—even mystery—of living forms. Organisms have a life and order of their own that scientists can only partially fathom. . . . It is the overall organization, or orchestration, that enables the organism to meet its needs, whatever they might be, in ways that never cease to surprise us. . . . Our surprise is a measure of our tendency to underestimate the flexibility of living organisms. The adaptability of plants tends to be especially underappreciated."[41]

McClintock commented that "animals can walk around, but plants have to stay still to do the same things, with ingenious mechanisms. . . . Plants are extraordinary. . . . There is no question that plants have [all] kinds of sensitivities. . . . They can do almost anything you can think of. But just because they sit there, anybody walking down a road considers them just a plastic area to look at, [as if] they're not really alive. . . . [Plants] are fantastically beyond our wildest expectations."[42]

Because she followed her sense of the right, kept asking the questions that her most childlike self generated, let her sense of wonder, her empathy, her feeling for the organism, for the corn, guide her, McClintock found truths that other researchers simply could not perceive. Their assumptions about the nature of Nature made them impossible to perceive. The narrowness of their gating channels, their loss of heart perception, kept them far away from the real world that lay all around them. But when we follow the feeling sense, we are literally feeling our way deep into the meanings that underlie the world of form. We are reading the text of the world through our synaesthetic perception. We follow trails of feeling into the heart of the things we encounter and as we do we begin to understand that nothing is isolated from anything else. Golden threads connect a myriad of apparently unrelated phenomena.

Because of this McClintock understood, unlike most scientists, that the world is not a series of disconnected parts. She always had what she called "an exceedingly strong feeling" for the inherent connectivity of everything. "Basically," she said, "everything is one. There is no way in which you can draw a line between things. What we do is to make these subdivisions that are artificial, that shouldn't be there."[43]

In these descriptions of McClintock's work are the steps that anyone can follow to engage in deep Earth thinking. *Anybody* can do it. The writer Samuel Delaney captured the truth of this, of *your* inherent abilities and capacity to do this work, in this passage from his book *The Fall of the Towers* (Bantam, 1982).

> *Suppose a truck were coming and you wanted to cross the street. With a glance or two you could determine whether you could make it or not. "Do you realize that when you do that, you're doing subconsciously a problem that would take a mathematician with pencil and paper who knew the exact weight of the truck, speed, rate of deceleration, and friction component of the wheels at least a couple of minutes to solve? Yet you do it in under half a second with only the inaccurate information your senses can gather in a moment or two."*[44]

And James Lovelock as well . . .

> *You do not need to know the details of a friend's biochemistry to know them as a person and in a similar way you can envisage Gaia without knowing the recondite details of its geochemistry. We humans have the ability to recognize whole systems instinctively, and this ability makes the Earth understandable outside science.*[45]

And throughout human habitation of Earth millions of people have used this innate capacity to gather information from the heart of the world. It is what all deep Earth peoples have done throughout time, from the indigenous peoples who learned the uses of plant medicines without recourse to reductionism or linear thinking to Einstein. And all who have spoken of how they learned what they learned described, in their own words, the same process that McClintock has. What they describe is in fact a different kind of thinking, the kind of thinking that Einstein was urging us to adopt in order to address the problems facing us. And rather than being linear, reductive thinking what occurs is holistic thinking, a kind of thinking that the artists who best know it have named analogical thinking.

However, when analogical thinking is combined with the experience that the ancient Athenians called aisthesis, something unusual begins to occur. As the immersion of the self deepens you begin to go much further than the organism or phenomenon you have been focused on. You begin to access the metaphysical background not of one thing but of all things, of the Earth itself. You begin to understand then what the dreaming of Earth is. There are moments then of unique insight, moments when great things catch us up in their grasp and take us trembling and awed to the shores of another land. Suddenly, for no reason, we suddenly move from our dreaming deep in analogical thinking into an even deeper place. We break through and directly begin to perceive the underpinnings of the world.

14
THE IMAGINAL
WORLD

*Only intuition resting on sympathetic understanding can lead to
[these laws] . . . the daily effort comes from no deliberate intention
or program, but straight from the heart.*

ALBERT EINSTEIN

*Stevens and Frost, both geniuses, walk gingerly in this area . . . the
area where meeting a mandolin or a moose is meeting consciousness.*

ROBERT BLY

*The duration of a spark, the individual and the nonindividual
have become interchangeable and the terror of the mortal limita-
tion inside me in time and in space appears to be annulled.
Nothingness ceases to exist when all that is not the man is added to
the man. This is when he seems to be himself.*

HANS BELLMER

*U*sing the feeling sense to touch the world brings, as I have said, an
intimation of feeling or mood. If you look at something near to
you and let your sensory noticing of it take over the whole of your attention, immediately there is a shift from linear thinking into something

different. In that moment your sensory perceiving becomes your thinking. It is what you do instead of thinking with the linear mind.

So, if you really look at something in front of you now and begin to notice its shading of colors, its form, its three-dimensionality, the texture of its surface, and then ask yourself, *How does it feel?* you will immediately experience an intimation of mood or feeling. This marks a shift in cognition, a shift in perception, a shift in the kind of thinking you are doing. And at that moment, in a tiny millisecond of time, your gating channels open more widely.

This particular exercise begins with using the feeling sense to touch something in the human world but something unusual happens if awareness is extended in a somewhat different direction. If that touching leaves the human world entirely and enters the wildness of the world, if this capacity for nonphysical touching is used *out there,* if the eyes look closely at some part of the natural world and we ask ourselves, *How does it feel?* something new enters the process, something important.

To understand what that is, go into your yard or take a walk in a park and let yourself wander, just looking at this and that, until something catches your attention—a large tree perhaps. Then stop and let yourself really look at it and, when you are really immersed in seeing it, ask yourself, *How does it feel?*

In that tiny moment of time a unique feeling tone will emerge into your awareness, just as it did before. But, if you pay close attention, you will notice that there is a difference. There is a livingness to it, which the pen or cup or desk did not have (or perhaps did not have as much). And that livingness itself has a particular feeling to it. There is a secret kinesis to the natural world and it is perhaps the most important secret kinesis of all. Henry David Thoreau was talking about this when he said . . .

It is only when we forget all our learning that we begin to know. I do not get nearer by a hair's breadth to any natural object so long as I presume that I have an introduction to it from some learned man. To conceive of it with a total apprehension I must for the thousandth time approach it as something totally strange. If you would make acquaintance with the ferns you must forget your botany. You must get rid of what is commonly called knowledge of *them. Not a single scientific term or distinction is the least to the purpose, for you would fain perceive something, and you must approach the object totally unprejudiced. You must be aware that no thing is what you have taken it to be. [To perceive something truly] you have got to be in a different state from the common.*[1]

"A different state than the common." That is Einstein's different way of thinking again. It is the dreaming state, the state of analogical, feeling perception and thinking. And in that state sensory gating opens more widely, novelty increases, and you find that the thing you have approached, touched with your feeling sense is *not* what you have taken it to be. You begin now to encounter the living reality of the plant— something that is very far from scientific descriptions of it.

To make the experience even more distinct it helps to immediately compare the plant you have just felt with something else, so, after the tree, find something else that captures your attention, perhaps a blade of grass or a small flowering plant or even a stone. Focus on it and ask yourself, *How does it feel?* Again, an intimation of mood or feeling will emerge, one that is different from the tree. Yet, it, too, will possess that *livingness,* that unique difference, however slight it is, in feeling from the manmade things you perceived earlier.

Now, just stay in that state of perception and let your eyes pan over everything. Simply feel the world around you and let the feeling tones of everything that you see wash over you. Nonphysically touch the world as a general mode of perception just as you do with your eyes when you see and your ears when you hear. There is something much more *living* about this than when you apply it solely to the human world.

Something new enters our experience when we reach out with that nonphysical part of us and touch the wildness of the world. It is a great deal more complex than what occurs in cities or houses or books. Importantly, hidden within the secret kinesis of the world, within the feeling of any particular wild place or thing, are the deeper dimensions that belong to the world in general and that thing or place in particular. And these deeper dimensions are a great deal older than the human artefacts with which we are usually surrounded. And they are a great deal more *alive.*

When you travel further along the road of feeling, going from "How does this conversation feel?" to "How does this table feel?" to "How does this river feel?" you begin to find that there is much more to the world than we have been taught. You begin to notice that a complexity of perceptual feeling arises from touching the wildness of the world and that the feeling you receive back possesses dynamics that are more complex than those that come from focusing solely on the human world or any of its elements. There are reasons for this, among which is that what you are touching now has its own aliveness, its own awareness, its own capacity to communicate.

I did not go anyplace that the corn did not first tell me to go

What occurs, sooner or later, is that one day, when you reach out with your sensing and touch some living part of the world, suddenly there is some sort of *response*. Sooner or later, often when you least expect it, something will touch you in return. And though it's usually subtle, it doesn't have to be . . .

You are riding in a small boat and suddenly a whale rises to the surface right beside you, rolls to the side and meets you eye-to-eye. Suddenly you are not looking at an external object but are being seen in turn, suddenly you are *seeing* each other. Can you get a sense of what I mean here? Can you feel what that might be like? Or perhaps something like this happens . . .

A reporter had been assigned a story by his editor. It was a human interest story, all about dolphins and how intelligent they are and besides they are cute, make interesting sounds, the kids love them. It will be great for the paper. But this reporter . . . he's pretty jaded. He likes cutting-edge investigative pieces and really resents having to do the story. Intelligence in dolphins? What a joke. And besides, who cares? Nevertheless . . .

The reporter made the long drive to the lab, parked his car, smoked another cigarette, stabbed it out, threw the butt on the ground, and knocked on the door. The scientists introduced themselves, shook his hand, and began to show him around. The reporter followed the scientists to the long glass wall of the lab, the wall that marked the division between lab and dolphin tank, the place where each species could watch the other, could sometimes meet. And as they did every morning, the dolphins had gathered just on their side of the glass, to make their morning hellos.

The reporter watched the scientists go through their morning ritual, watched the dolphin family respond. Made nice noises over the six-week-old baby dolphin, took a longer tour around the lab, went through the desultory question-and-answer-session, drank the obligatory bad coffee that all scientists make, and then spent the rest of the time leaning against the glass wall of the dolphin tank, chain-smoking cigarettes, filling the time until he could go back to the office.

Now for whatever reason the young dolphin was fascinated by the reporter and instead of swimming off with his family, he just kept floating there looking at him in the curious way young children, irrespective of species, have about something new. The man ignored the kid, kept his back to the glass, and kept on smoking. But the young dolphin seemed possessed of inexhaustible patience. He just kept hanging there. Staring. And after awhile the reporter began to get twitchy, then mad. So, he took a deep drag on his cigarette, turned, and blew smoke at the glass, directly in the dolphin's face. The dolphin back-pedaled in surprise, looked at the man for a moment, then swam rapidly off. The reporter grinned, sighed, then leaned back against the glass again and continued to smoke.

But in a minute or two the young dolphin returned, swam up close to the glass, and just hung there . . . staring. The reporter tried to ignore it but after a while, in irritation, he turned and glared through the glass at the young dolphin. As soon as he did, the young dolphin blew a cloud of smoke directly in his face. And the whole room stopped.

It took awhile for everyone to understand what had happened, for of course dolphins don't smoke (and anyway, even if they did, it wouldn't work under water). The dolphin, who was still nursing, had gone to his mother, taken some milk, and come back and puffed it in the man's face. Not bad for a six week old infant—of a species considered inferior in intelligence to humans.

But the most important thing is . . . something unique happened in that moment, something that captured the awareness of everyone in that room. A *communication* between two living beings took place. And in that moment, some powerful, deep meaning came reverberating up and out of the background of the world and swept away the statistical mentality. For a moment in time every human in the room swam in deeper waters. They stopped thinking, caught up in *feeling* the meaning that had entered the room. Time seemed to stop and everyone was caught up in the experience of an invisible thing.

One of the people who was there that day said he had never seen cynicism and skepticism evaporate in a human being so quickly. In that one tiny moment of time, the journalist's separation from the other life-forms with which he shares this planet ended. He was touched by a living, aware, caring, intelligence from the world and he could not deny it. Some door in him opened and the whole aware universe came flooding in and he was never the same again. For him, the long loneliness of the human species ended.[2]

During such moments, whether they come from a dolphin or a great tree we have unexpectedly stumbled upon in some ancient forest, we are suddenly caught up in something that has nothing to do with the human world. We feel something coming into us from *out there*, something that is outside our narrow human perspectives. In that moment, we are pulled out of ourselves into a world that is more ancient than the human—a place where living intelligences can touch each other as kin. We discover then that trees have been doing something more for the past 300 million years than simply pining away for our emergence.

We feel the touch of life, of a nonhuman awareness, upon us. But more . . . we experience something unique to most humans in the West. An intelligence, just as subtle and sophisticated as our own, but very *nonhuman,* reaches out and *communicates* with us. Across the species divide, in spite of our isolation, a different kind of language than our own, one filled with meaning and intent, tells us something. And a new world opens up. When that happens we take a long floating leap, land someplace else, and look around with new eyes. We experience in that moment what the ancient Greeks—the Athenians—called aisthesis, the touch of a nonhuman soul upon the deeps of us—and know that ours touches them in turn.

We are not here for ourselves alone

Aisthesis such as this often emerges into our experience at unexpected times. It comes sideways to our normal orientation, grabs the depths of us and drags us unexpectedly into a world we did not suspect existed.

This is almost always how it begins for us in the West

And when that happens, we abandon the view of life that does not allow us to extend interiority to dolphins or trees or stones.

And so break the great injunction of reductionist science

Being unable to extend interiority and consciousness outward, as Robert Bly once said, keeps human beings isolated in their own house and, in extreme cases, we simply look out at a world with which we have no possibility of contact. We are cut off from the metaphysical background of the world and our perceptual capacities are kept in a box.

*A box that science teaches us **is** the whole world*

If that box is very tiny, as it is with strict reductionists such as Richard Dawkins, the mind can see very little of the real world that lies outside the box; there is only the human on a ball of resources hurtling around the sun. All things in the universe—from that orientation—center around the human, for there is no exterior consciousness. To such scientists the sun may no longer revolve around the Earth but it most certainly still revolves around human beings.

But . . . once you are touched by a living intelligence from out there, you are changed. It is nearly impossible not to be. The living reality of that experience works on the self, undermining the old paradigm, and you begin to, more and more frequently, step outside the normal habituated boundaries of the Western world. You begin to enter an older, wilder, less-domesticated world, the place barbarians inhabit, where the hair begins to grow long, where wild lights begin to gleam in the eye. You begin to enter the wilderness that still lies underneath the concrete of the civilized world.

This most assuredly extends awareness further than society
wants it to go.
This is what becoming barbarian means.

For some people, this touch of communication and intelligence from the wildness of the nonhuman world marks a phase change in their life. They abandon the human world as the fundamental point of reference and begin to cultivate the experience of aisthesis. They intentionally seek it, deliberately step into the world with their feeling sensing intact, actively seeking the moment of communication, the place where the nonhuman and the human meet and exchange the shapes of their lives. The place where the human sits down at the feet of the nonhuman and learns what is really true about the world *out there*.

Natural scientists who pursue this approach spend years running their nets through those deeper waters, immersing themselves more and more fully, bringing home, to this world, the things they find, the things they are taught by the wildness of the world. Anyone can do it as Bill Mollison, Masanobu Fukuoka, Viktor Schauberger, Luther Burbank, and so many others have shown.

The linearists, however, never use the things
that are brought back very wisely.
You should keep that in mind
should you have the desire to go to work for them.

You don't have to be a scientist to do it, or to change the world. In fact, in proportion to their numbers, very few scientists *ever* do it.

It is through this immersion in the depths of the *real* world that the solutions to the problems that face us can be found. Not as universals, straightjackets forcing conformity on all in a frantic attempt at control and safety, but rather as local communicatory responses from the deepest regions of the world itself, into the human heart, and into this world, for use at *this* location and place.

Mollison and Fukuoka, for instance, in their search for a new way to grow food, for Earth-sustainable agriculture, did not create a one-size-fits-all approach but a way of bringing food forth that depended on deep relationship with the place in which it is grown. And that relationship depends on communication between two equal intelligences. It's a communication, not a technique.

As Annie Le Brun, in her remarkable book *The Reality Overload* (Inner Traditions, 2008), comments, there is, in these moments of communication, a "charged state of awareness," where we are opened up to what we are not. And that is when the solutions we need emerge. As she notes . . .

> *The entire history of analogical thought*
> *gives evidence of these "instants of solution."*[3]

Analogical thought *is* the different kind of thinking we need. But that capacity can be taken further yet. It is possible to fully shake off the cultural habituation of years, to shed the clothes to which you have become accustomed and to immerse yourself completely in these waters.

If you fully combine the experience of aisthesis with analogical thinking so that it blends into a unique synaesthesia of perceptual cognition and feeling, the human world can sometimes be left behind entirely. There is no longer me, over here, touching a nonhuman intelligence over there. There is me, inside the world in which the nonhuman lives. The human world is no longer the reference point. The boundary between self and other disappears and you begin to see the world through *their* eyes.

To Be Called Beloved by the Earth

This kind of experience, when it first occurs, can be considerably unsettling. The normal human markers are lost, everything we thought we knew about ourselves becomes irrelevant. Cultural definitions, the particular view of the world that we have accepted from Western science, historical markers, family stories, our personal biography . . . all the things that we use at a level deeper than conscious awareness to orient ourselves in space and time are gone.

Once we step completely outside that framework the human, and our own personal life, whose story has always been central to us, the normal framework we use to orient ourselves, is gone. Who am I then if I am not Stephen Harrod Buhner who was born in such and such a time and place and who has had, since that time, all those experiences that I did have? I am only one being among many, neither more nor less important than any. Underneath that human experience there is a deeper identity, one that all organisms on this planet share. Such an experience is unsettling when first encountered; it shakes the foundations of self-identity. (See appendix 1, "Sensory Overload and Self-Caretaking").

Nevertheless, this loss of the human orientation is important. (And ultimately, incredibly interesting.) Once the human orientation is left behind, the world as it is, not as it is pictured from a human orientation, begins to emerge into awareness. There are functional dynamics at work in the Gaian system that cannot be seen until the human framework is left behind. For, as Thoreau once put it . . .

So much of man as there is in your mind, there will be in your eye.

We literally *can't* see the deeper dimensions of Earth if we remain in a human-oriented frame. For we then tend to think that the oil in the California hills is, and always has been, there for us. We believe that there is something unique about our intelligence, that we, in our billions, are intrinsically more important than the plants that grow in our yards. Foundationally, the thinning of boundary between self and other is crucial. The complete elimination of it is, at times, a necessity. It is only then that it is possible to experience the other inhabitants of this scenario from inside their own lives. Understanding emerges, only at such moments, that the human world and its concerns are as unimportant to the other life-forms here as the mosquito you just swatted is to you. It changes things. For the first time the arrogance of the human perspective vanishes. It's possible then to see just how thoroughly it biases nearly every aspect of science . . . and how much it alters nearly every human intervention into the ecological functioning of the planet. We have a place here, yes, but it is not as important as we have been trained to believe. The experience of boundary dissolution, for the first time, lends a realistic perspective to the human orientation. Behavior alters accordingly. It can't help but do so.

This is why the boundary thinning that is experienced by those labeled schizophrenic and those on hallucinogens is considered to be pathological. It undermines the humancentric worldview. Through the lives of those whose boundaries have thinned, we catch glimpses of the shimmer of infinity in the face of the other, catch glimpses through the doors of perception of the metaphysical background of the world.

Once you come to understand, in your experience, that you are just one life-form among many, that you can meet the other life-forms here in moments of tremendous intimacy, it enables one of the most wondrous of explorations possible. To leave the human world behind, the surface identity of the self, and swim, only one life-form among a multitude, deep into the metaphysical background of the world is to enter a place where we meet there as living beings, identical in nature at the core, similar intelligences, all given birth by Earth, all expressed out of the Ocean of Being into form. And in those moments of touch, we look back at each other with luminous eyes and tell tales of the lives we have lived and the lands we have seen and speak of the commonalities of what it means to be alive on this Earth, kin, all of whom came from common ancestors long ago.

And then . . . sometimes, in unique moments, deep inside the experience, we slide completely out of our frame and totally into the other's . . . and they into ours. We then look into each other's eyes—my eyes through your eyes, your eyes through my eyes. Touch with our hearts, your heart, my heart, and mine yours. Here, we experience the deepest possible intimacy that any living being can know. There is a communicatory interblending of soul. Something of the other then resides inside me and something of me inside the other. Like the viral blending of genomes, we become in that moment a part of the other and they a part of us. And when we return to this world, something from the other remains inside us. It makes us truly barbarian, no longer civilized. We are no longer presentable in polite company.

Still . . . it is possible to go even deeper yet. It is possible to move inside the scenario itself, the place from which all life-forms emerged. It is the place where background *becomes* foreground, the place where *environment* is the intelligence encountered, the place where communication of a very different sort begins.

The Imaginal Realm

During analogical thinking, we follow an invisible trail that wanders through the world by using a particular capacity of perception. And as we do it more often as a habit of mind we begin to be aware that we do not inhabit a world of disconnected living organisms each isolated in its own house. We find that they reach out from time to time using their own unique form of language and communication. We learn how to communicate with them, allow them to tell us of their own lives in their own words. And sometimes, like lovers, for a brief moment, we change places and know each other from the inside.

But sometimes, sometimes, something different happens. For some reason the point of view shifts. We take our focus off the living organisms that we have thought the most important and for some reason begin to look with these analogical eyes at the field itself. We begin to experience then, at the deepest possible level, that we are immersed in a fluid medium, a living textual field—Fuller's scenario—throughout which are scattered the condensed meanings—Bateson's transforms of messages, O'Gorman and Emmerson's nodes—that we call, and usually perceive, as external objects, as living organisms. These transforms of messages are directly experienced then as condensations of meaning that are expressing, multidimensionally, aspects of the textual field in which they are embedded. We suddenly get a sense of the field itself as foreground, of everything on which we have previously been focused as *only* condensed expressions of the field. We find suddenly, in our experience, that there is *only* the field and that the field is alive—is in fact the *only* life-form.

We touch the Tao

And we, all the life-forms, are only expressions of it in unique shape and time. There is a phase change that happens, from one state to another.

Robert Bly has a way of describing that phase change in his discussion of the marvelous Russian tale "The Maiden King" (in his book of the same name). There is a boy whose father hires a tutor to teach and watch over while the father is working. And because it's a fairy tale, it is inevitable that odd, even magical, occurrences will occur once the two of them begin their work together. And indeed, one day, they do. The tutor has taken Ivan fishing on a small raft out at sea, and as Bly comments . . .

> *The father apparently has wisely asked the tutor to teach the boy how to fish. We each need to know how to "fish." Psychologically, fishing amounts to an inquisitiveness about the "treasures of the deep." We float in broad daylight, on our well-constructed, rationally engineered raft or boat, looking down into the cloudy waters—inhabited by God knows what—the same waters each dreamer fishes in at night. Teaching people how to fish is a just aim in education. We are fishing right now. Fishing is a kind of daydreaming in daylight, a longing for what is below.*[4]

Bly is describing here what it is like, from a somewhat different orientation, what the process of following golden threads is like. We begin in our "rationally engineered" world, the day-to-day state of linear cognition most people think is fundamental, and we begin using our sensory capacity to *feel* into the world. We are driven in this by "a longing for what is below." We are fishing in, as Bly notes, *the same waters each dreamer fishes in at night.* We are feeling the line we have dropped into the water—that is, the feeling sensing that we have sent into the world—in just the same way we feel sensitively with our fingers when we are trying to loosen the nut on a bolt we cannot see. We are letting our consciousness, our entire awareness enter our fingers and nothing else is in our awareness. We are absorbed, immersed in the sensing, only paying attention to what our sensing is telling us. And as we do that, analogical thinking emerges. We stay immersed, our analogical perception deepens.

This is how it works. And as we gain experience with the process we begin to catch fish. We eventually find in our exploration that we have been a bit too self-centered. We catch hold of something and suddenly discover one day that it is not exactly clear which end of the line we are on. Something intelligent reaches out and touches us in turn.

Are the plants fishing, too?
Themselves dropping lines down in the depths?
One day finding an herbalist on the other end of the line?

We experience then that dolphins and corn and barley are intelligent. And once we are over our shock, we approach more carefully, tentatively reach out once more and begin to make relationship with them. And as we show ourselves trustworthy,

as we must in any intimate relationship,

they begin to tell us the stories of their life. And if our love affair deepens enough, one day we, without expecting it, slip outside our frame entirely, find what Masanobu Fukuoka was talking about when he said, "Only to him who stands where the barley stands and listens well will it speak and tell, for his sake, what man is." Our boundaries thin so much that we *become* the other.

We travel, always in this process, between the Newtonian, linear world of cause and effect and the deeper world that lies inside and behind it. Back and forth in endless oscillation. Each time we decide to travel again into the metaphysical depths of the world, we must once more initiate a shift in consciousness, change our form of cognition. And even though we *know* the territory from previous experience, we still begin our immersion floating on the surface of those metaphysical depths, on our rationally engineered raft.

For our rational mind serves a purpose
it is as much a part of us as our hands
and our hearts

Each time we begin by feeling into the depths, encountering golden threads, and following them where they lead us . . .

for only the thread knows where it is going
and that will always be true

we meet then the living intelligences of the world, learn how to travel in their world, see from their point of view. Over the years, we become used to the process, comfortable in the territory. It's familiar. But suddenly . . . for some reason we will never understand with our rational minds, one day, something different happens. While we are still deep in our dreaming, totally immersed in what has captured our attention, our focus shifts. We suddenly look up and perceive the textual field itself. We are no longer focused on *one* thing but suddenly are perceiving *everything* through that state of mind. Background in that moment becomes foreground. Bly describes it like this . . .

> *The boy and the tutor are looking down into the sea, one might say, for the Presence that swims about in the murky world below the surface of things; and all at once the Presence arrives on the surface of the ocean, coming in from the horizon, seemingly belonging to the sea itself.*[5]

Unsuspectingly, we have stepped *through* what Blake called Heaven's gate built in Jerusalem's wall. As Henry Corbin puts it, "One sets out; at a given moment, there is a break with the geographical coordinates that can be located on our maps. But the 'traveler' is not conscious of the precise moment; he does not realize it," does not notice it happening, he just suddenly finds himself arrived.[6]

Corbin remarked that the Persian mystics said that there was a world Aristotle didn't know of, one where the mythic and the mundane interpenetrated each other. They called it the imaginal world, or as Corbin put it: *the Mundus Imaginalis.*

> *And here it has a deeper meaning,*
> *it means the world imagination,*
> *the place where the world dreams form into being*

This the place that lies underneath the world of form,

> *from another perspective*
> *you can think of it as the doorway to the quantum multiverse,*

you didn't think that human beings
never noticed its existence before physicists were invented, did you?

The textual field of Earth has existence simultaneously in both the classical Newtonian universe and the quantum multiverse

the classical universe is just one form that the multiverse can take
and as quantum reality freaks insist, there are an
endless number of them

In older times what is now called the quantum multiverse was known as the mythic world.

The textual field of Earth as it exists in classical space can be perceived, as Richard Lewontin revealed, by seeing its shape through the concentrated nodes of living organisms/physical matter—and the lines that touch and connect them, that weave them all together into one whole event.

It is similar to the visual representation of a gravitational map of
space that shows the gravitational lines—gravity's golden threads—
condensing around the gravity wells we call planets. But this kind
of "looking" occurs not with the eyes, but through the feeling sense
and the exact sensorial imagination. We perceive this similarly to
the way viruses perceive cells. They identify cells through a percep-
tion in three-dimensional surface chemistry. We perceive the textual
field through a perception in three-dimensional feeling space that
then emerges on the field of our inner vision as images—the exact
sensorial imagination.

The textual field's form in classical space reveals the moment-to-moment shape that Earth takes in order to maintain self-organization. Gaia generates that ever-changing form continually out of an underlying field of potential—out of the mythic world, the quantum multiverse. Plato called this the realm of the Forms . . . or, as other ancient Greeks might have called it, it is the realm of the Archi, the place from which all form comes.

When you suddenly look up and find yourself immersed in the textual field itself, you enter the place where the mythic and the mundane meet. The place the quantum multiverse and classical space intersect. It is the place Corbin called the imaginal realm, the place where the phenomena that are immanent in the Ocean of Being reside before emerging into our world. It is the place that McFadden describes when he says that there is

> a dense series of measurements of a quantum system along a particular path [that] will force the dynamics of the system to evolve along that path.[7]

In other words, the Earth desires the emergence of a particular form out of the multiverse in order to stabilize self-organization. The form is being pulled out of the multiverse but has not yet been measured, only *potential* measurement has occurred. The system need, a response deep inside Gaia to the gestalt of all inputs, is beginning to be expressed into specific form. As the need emerges more fully into specificity, into *exactness,* it begins to bring one form more than all others out of the underlying Ocean of Being. Just before it emerges into this world, before it collapses into form into classical Newtonian space, it exists in the imaginal world as archetype.

15

THE DREAMING
OF EARTH

To anyone who thinks about it carefully, this must at first seem a rather strange statement: "The process by which he works eventually leads him to his goal"—as if the process had some kind of magic in it, some daemonic will of its own. Indeed, some writers—not the least of them Homer—have taken that point of view, speaking without apology of Muses as, in some sense, actual beings, and of "epic song" and "memory"... as forces greater than and separate from the poet. We often hear even modern writers speak of their work as somehow outside their control, informed by a spirit that, when they read their writing later, they cannot identify as having come from themselves. I imagine every good writer has had this experience.

JOHN GARDNER

This "mysterious power which everyone senses and no philosopher explains" is, in sum, the spirit of the earth, the same duende that scorched the heart of Nietzsche, who searched in vain for its external forms on the Rialto Bridge and in the music of Bizet, without knowing that the duende he was pursuing had leaped straight from the Greek mysteries to the dancers of Cadiz or the beheaded, Dionysian scream of Silverio's siguiriya.

FEDERICO GARCIA LORCA

I felt that I was now seeing plain, whereas ordinary vision gives us an imperfect view; I was seeing the archetypes, the Platonic ideas, that underlie the imperfect images of everyday life. The thought crossed my mind: Could the divine mushrooms be the secret that lay behind the ancient mysteries?

R. GORDON WASSON

*A*rchi means *the first*. They are the primary or first things from which all phemonena come—they are the potentials that reside in the quantum multiverse. Archetype, the more familiar term, combines "archi" with "type"—meaning "impression," from the Greek to beat or strike, to mold. Archetype is the first expression of the archi in identifiable form—though not physically. It means to prefigure or foreshadow. The archetypes, which reside in the imaginal world, prefigure the forms they become in our world. As those archetypes express themselves into classical Newtonian space, they change. They are modified by where and how they appear.

Every form we see in this world is a modified expression of the archetype that underlies it. The essential identity we recognize as *plant*, for instance, exists as a unique archi in the mythic or quantum world, what Masanobu Fukuoka termed the Ocean of Being that underlies everything. This is the place the Persian storytellers were talking about when they said, "At one time there was a story and there was no one to tell it," or "At one time there was a story but there was no one to hear it but God."[1]

The *archetype* of plant, however, is to be found in the imaginal world, the place from which Earth dreams form into being. This is what Lao-tzu was speaking of when he said . . .

Thirty spokes unite in one hub
It is precisely where there is nothing
that we find the usefulness of the wheel[2]

And when that archetype expresses itself into our world, the archetype alters itself to fit the demands of the field in which it emerges. The living organisms of this world have their roots (spokes) in the imaginal realm.

It is from there they are expressed. Together they form the wheel, the Earth system, the thing that is more than the sum of the parts, the entity that circles endlessly in physical space.

Every plant we see is an expression of the underlying archetype whose present form has been altered by the part of the scenario into which it has emerged. The form a plant takes comes from the demands that environment has made on it and those demands are, that shape is, encoded within its seed as heredity. There is only *one* plant form, Goethe said, and it's the archetype, or as he called it, the *Urpflanze,* which resides in the imaginal world. And from this understanding Goethe was able to articulate his great understanding of the metamorphosis of plants, that all parts of the plant are merely leaf morphed into different form to fulfill different function.

It was from his ability to see underlying archetype that Luther Burbank could perceive plants the way he did. He knew, *in his experience,* that all plant forms began as one central form long ago. He knew that the history of each plant was a history of the demands that environment had made on it over long evolutionary time. He could then bring forth old forms as new food plants or even find ways to cross-breed not only species but genus. He said that the longer ago the divergence occurred, the harder it was, but it could be done. You just had to overcome a lot of inertia.

And it was his capacity to perceive archetype that allowed Masanobu Fukuoka to say . . .

> *My method of growing rice may appear reckless and absurd, but all along I have sought the true form of rice. I have searched for the form of natural rice and asked what healthy rice is. . . . If you understand the ideal form, it is just a matter of how to grow a plant of that shape under the unique conditions of your own field.*[3]

He was understanding in this that the ideal form (the archetype) underlay all rice expressions and that the archetype would alter itself to fit the shape of the field in which it was grown once it collapsed into form in classical Newtonian space. He knew, too, that the form, as it emerged, could be influenced by numerous factors but that there was one form above others that was the most potent form the rice could take in any particular field. And it was that form he worked to bring most strongly into existence.

All plant forms, as Goethe, Burbank, and Fukuoka knew, come from the original Urpflanze, expressed into the endless variety that occurs when something extrudes itself from the imaginal world into this one. To understand this "is a growing aware," as Goethe put it, "of the Form with which again and again nature plays, and, in playing, brings forth manifold life."[4] Or, as Henri Bortoft describes it, "The archetypal plant as an omnipotential form is clearly a different dimension of the plant than what appears in the space-time dimension as many plants."[5] When the archetype of plant manifests in this world, as he says, "It is inherently dynamical and indefinitely flexible."[6] The essence of nonlinearity.

When we find our way into the imaginal world, we enter the place where we can perceive the archetypes before they are expressed into form. We enter a distinct and real place, and somewhere deep inside us, we recognize it. It is a place to which some part of us belongs, for we, too, come from archetype. It is an archetype that has expressed itself in multiple forms over long evolutionary time, forms that have also been shaped by the fields in which they have grown.

When we reenter the imaginal world, we touch the place from which our archetype emerged. We find the root of what it is to be human. And we encounter other archetypes, are touched by them, begin to remember the world from which we once came and which still resides deep inside our species memories.

Corbin is clear about the nature of the imaginal world: "In offering the two Latin words *mundus imaginalis*," he says, "I intend to treat a precise order of reality corresponding to a precise mode of perception."[7] It is the mode of perception turned as a general perceiving onto the textual field that allows that precise order of reality to be experienced. And that place is a living reality. It is not the ancient artefact of a more superstitious age. It is as real now as it ever has been. Entering it, you find as natural scientists, indigenous peoples, writers, poets, singers, have always done, the invisibles that lie underneath this world of form, the archetypes that are the root of all forms we know. As the Bushmen of the Kalahari say, once in this state, you "can see shapes, forms, and even fully developed works of art before they are created."[8] Or as R. Gordon Wasson once put it during an experience with psilocybin mushrooms . . .

> *I felt that I was now seeing plain, whereas ordinary vision gives us an imperfect view; I was seeing the archetypes, the platonic ideas, that underlie the imperfect images of everyday life. The thought crossed my mind: could the divine mushrooms be the secret that lay behind the ancient mysteries.*[9]

Looking deeply, you can understand, as Goethe and Burbank and so many others have, that these archetypes, as they come into physical form in what we think of as the world, are only expressions—as they must be—of the textual field itself, of environment. For there is nothing *but* environment—the thing that is more than the sum of the parts, that invisible aware intelligence that works to keep its self-organization intact. And each archetype that is expressed into this world immediately begins taking on a unique physical form—and associated behaviors—in order to fit into, to fulfill the function necessary for, the particular part of the scenario into which it has been expressed.

> *just as we do when we are birthed into this world*

Specific archetypes are generated into form in a particular place and time necessary to keep homeodynamis intact, to maintain the self-organized field. That is why Lewontin described the objects we tend to look at as foreground as being only concentrated fields that themselves show the shape of environmental space. Form is expressed *only* to fulfill ecological purpose. Forms are a self-organizational homeodynamis necessity. And these forms . . . they are pulled out of quantum potential by the needs of the environment itself. We are, all of us, dreamed into being by the needs of this place.

Everything we encounter—and every ability, facility, behavioral expression possessed by the phenomena we encounter—has been generated out of the needs of the self-organized system itself. We are all microcosmic instances of a macroscosmic event. And each aspect of the microcosm is inherent in the macrocosm, is a reflection of the macrocosm, the larger system from which it comes.

We dream because the Earth dreams. We sing and know music because the vibrational expression we call music is inherent in this place. We have the capacity to create because the larger system from which we come has at its core the capacity to create. We express new form through dreaming because that is how all form is created in this place. As the poet Dale Pendell once wrote . . .

> As dreams are the healing songs
> from the wilderness of our unconscious—
> So wild animals, wild plants, wild landscapes
> are the healing dreams
> from the deep singing mind
> of the Earth.[10]

We are, all of us, dreamed into being. For the Earth lives in a dream. It exists in a very complex form of the state a juggler is in as he juggles, where some deeper part, some dreaming part, of himself maintains the balance point.

The greater part of all self-organized systems exist in a state of deep dreaming, what we, in our hubris, tend to call an unconscious state. This is true of the majority of the self that we call *our* self. Without most of our consciousness modules in that unconscious dreaming state, coordinating incoming sensory data into a comprehensive communicatory gestalt and generating congruent responses, we could not exist at all. Imagine having to consciously maintain white blood cell generation, analysis, and response; heart function and blood circulation; kidney function and filtering of the blood; skin generation and repair; and all the other billions of billions of living movements that are necessary for our self-organized state to remain intact. No human could do it using the linear, "conscious" mind. As Michael Crichton put it . . .

> A human being is actually a giant swarm. Or more precisely, it's a
> swarm of swarms, because each organ—blood, liver, kidneys—is a
> separate swarm. What we refer to as a body is really the combination

of all these organ swarms. . . . It turns out that a lot of processing occurs at the level of the organs. Human behavior is determined in many places. The control of our behavior is not located in our brains. It's all over our bodies. . . . "Swarm intelligence" rules human beings. Balance is controlled by the cerebellar swarm and rarely comes to consciousness. Other processing occurs in the spinal cord, the stomach, the intestine. A lot of vision takes place in the eyeballs, long before the brain is involved. And for that matter, a lot of sophisticated brain processing occurs beneath awareness, too. . . . So, there's an argument that the whole structure of consciousness, and the human sense of self-control and purposeness, is a user illusion. We don't have conscious control over ourselves at all. We just think we do. Just because human beings went around thinking of themselves as "I" didn't mean it was true.[11]

It is only because most of our self remains unconscious, that it dreams, that we exist at all. And that same kind of "unconsciousness," that same kind of dreaming, is what the Earth does and has done every millisecond since its self-organized state began. We are in fact dreamed into being, just as everything that we encounter has been.

As so many spiritual adepts have said, we are dreaming, all of us, all the time. But, truly, it is not possible to awaken in the way we think of it when we speak of sleeping and waking. The most we can do is to become aware that we are dreaming, awaken inside the dream. As Rumi once put it . . .

worlds within worlds;
dreamers concoct entire Baghdads
from their breasts

asleep or waking
where have you seen yourself
mirrored completely?

a dreamer wanders
from room to room

> *only to awaken*
> *in another sort of room*[12]

When we enter the imaginal world through our analogical perceiving, suddenly look up and become aware of that which surrounds us, we wake only inside the dreaming and find that it is itself only another form of dreaming. That is the humor of it and why all those who find the way to this place learn to laugh. What humor! What a joke we have played on ourselves!

Then as always, we drop away from the knowing, begin to move away from such deeps, back into our bodies. For . . .

> *There is one place*
> *in all the universe*
> *that has been made*
> *especially for you*
> *and that is inside*
> *your own*
> *feet.*[13]

16
REEMERGENCE
INTO CLASSICAL
NEWTONIAN SPACE

If you want to understand Gaia, you have to learn to think in terms of nonlinear, circular logic of feedback systems.

TIMOTHY LENTON

Good holistic thinking is harder than reductionist thinking, so learning to do it properly, even learning what sorts of things we can accomplish with it, is a challenge for the future.

PETER SAUNDERS

There comes a time when the mind takes a higher plane of knowledge but can never prove how it got there.

ALBERT EINSTEIN

We don't know because we don't want to know.

ALDOUS HUXLEY

The Earth, as it generates new form, is, again, in the same kind of dream state as we are when we write or make songs or read a book or hear a story or drop deep into analogical thinking and begin to follow golden threads. The Earth is just like us . . . only more so. There is no linear mind activity the way we think of it. (Though there is in a way we don't think of it.) There is, at a very deep level, a constant intake and analysis of all inputs—interoceptive and exteroceptive—that affect the self-organized state in which the Earth exists. And there is a constant response by the system to those inputs. The Earth initiates continual alterations in the form and behavior of everything in the system in order to maintain optimum self-organizational homeodynamis.

> *Those potentials emerge out of the Ocean of Being in which the Earth has its roots, out of the quantum world where all potential forms and behaviors exist simultaneously, in response to the need that Earth expresses in response to the shiftings in the state of self-organization.*

The new forms and behaviors that come into being are continual informational gestalts about the communicatory interaction that is occurring between Earth and *its* environments, both of them: its external environment—the *out there* (for Earth is not an isolated event, it is embedded in Universe) and the *in here*, that is, the billions upon trillions of subparts that we know of as ecoranges, ecozones, forests, rivers, oceans, trees, dolphins, people, birds, bacteria, viruses and on and on and on.

The process of response and modification of the state of self-organization that exists is exactly like the one that Anthony Trewavas described that occurs in plants, that is . . .

> *There is no unique separate response to each signal in this complex [of informational inflows] but merely a response issued from an integration of all environmental and internal information.*

Unless there is an informational inflow that the Earth's sensory gating mechanisms (and yes, Earth does have them) identify as crucial to respond to

> *such as extensive damage from asteroid strike*

the Earth normally does not use any form of linear cause and effect processing of data or directed response—just as we do not, unless the splinter in our finger signals a necessity for it.

Nevertheless, the Earth does have linear communicatory capacities, it's just that we will never notice them—the time lines and orientation are too far outside our range just as our white blood cells will never notice our linear conscious communications and activity. The Earth is involved in other things more important to itself than the self-importance of one tiny species. This is why the members of some African tribes, when asked if they talk to God, responded that, no, they didn't. "God," they said, "is very far away and very busy. We talk to our ancestors. They still remember what it is like to be a human being; they are not so far away from us. They still care; they still have time to listen."

The Earth integrates the entire informational inflow that surrounds it into one holistic gestalt at each and every moment in time and generates a response that comes out of a unique dream state. Deep in that dreaming state, where there is an *integration of all environmental and internal information,* occurring as one unified gestalt, the Earth initiates movements that generate new forms of both behavior and physicality that *as a whole* represent its response to alterations in the self-organized homeodynamis of the system.

In other words, when some alteration of behavior or physical form is necessary in the subsystems of the Gaian system, whether in an ecorange or a species, Gaia sends an impulse into the system. This process is identical to that in the juggler who senses something off in the balance point of his juggling. An awareness of the potential loss of self-organization is generated deep inside him, and an analysis of potential responses occurs, and from those a choice is made, a response initiated to maintain balance. And over the years of practice, he gets better at maintaining that balance.

Just as over the eons
Earth has developed
more sophistication and experience as well.

That impulse in the juggler automatically shifts behavior, but it is left to the unconscious consciousness modules of the juggler to determine, at the bifurcation point, which choices to make to keep the balance point intact.

The same is true of Gaia, the impulse is sent from deep in the dreaming state. The subparts of the Earth system most able to reestablish homeo-dynamis respond, altering both behavior and physical form in order to do so. And they retain choice. At the touch of the Gaian impulse a series of possible responses are generated within the suborganisms, they then choose among them best how to respond—based on their own self-intuited genius.

Pulling potential out of the quantum multiverse if necessary

And then they change: form, behavior, location, communication, or language in which the communication takes place. But the parts of the system don't know that they are fulfilling Gaian imperatives, they just wander around looking for grass. They remain bees looking for nectar and on this particular day they go to this flower rather than that one.

For us, who wish to see these movements of Gaia with the linear mind, we must learn to see sideways. We can see Gaian movements most clearly through the shadows they cast. Gaia's behaviors come at 90 degrees to our normal orientation, as if we were two dimensional beings in a three-dimensional world.

Or three-dimensional beings in a multiverse

Gaia's behavior intrudes into our linear, cultural space but does not origi-nate in it. Without a different kind of thinking, we can't even perceive where it comes from. It just seems to appear.

To make it even more difficult, Gaia operates on such long timelines that it is hard for us to perceive Gaian behavior.

Really, what does a bristlecone pine do in 5,000 years of life?
If there is something it does only once every 1,000 years,
we will never notice it.

Immersed in our short lives, we can perceive in our lifetime perhaps only a single note or two of a Gaian symphony that has been playing for eons. We hear the note but cannot hear the entire symphony. Because of that the note appears to be meaningless.

To perceive Gaian movements through linear thinking you have to train yourself to look for ecological patterns of response that are unusual and involve long time lines. The way, for example, that Lovelock noticed that the temperature of the planet has remained fairly constant over eons and the consistent high levels of oxygen in the atmosphere. Closer to home, and on shorter time lines, you can perceive Gaian impulses in the movement of what are called invasive plants, plants that are moving into areas and acting to restore damaged ecosystems. You can see Gaian movements in the emergence of medicinal plants into areas where the diseases they are specific for are becoming endemic. And you can perceive Gaian impulses in behavior alterations in species. The way locusts suddenly swarm, for example, or in the large numbers of people training to become herbalists.

> *When I ask them why, why they are spending years and large amounts of money training in a profession they are not legally able to practice, they say they just felt they had to.*

And you can see the shadows of Gaian functioning in the emergence of hallucinogens into the Western world at just one specific moment in time. Hallucinogens had always been a part of the human world but in 1943, when Albert Hofmann created LSD, their use was still local, in small tribal groups across the world.

> *Western explorers such as Wasson and Schultes sought them out after this though, going deep into ancient forests and cultures to find the medicine people who used them . . . and the plants they used.*

Hofmann, however, while exploring the chemical constituents of rye ergot accidentally dosed himself one of its altered compounds and LSD entered the Western world's consciousness.

> *Then they sent the mushrooms and cacti and other plants to Hofmann for testing and psilocybin and mescaline entered the Western world, too.*

By the mid-1950s Aldous Huxley and others were writing about their experiences with hallucinogens such as mescaline and LSD and by the mid-1960s, well, it had captured everyone's imagination. Hallucinogens entered the consciousness of the Western world just as a whole new generation of people were coming into adulthood and for some reason

some Gaian reason

it became a phenomenon, affecting the exact cultural group that is most divorced from the metaphysical background of the world. Hallucinogens emerged as a motive force, influencing the cultural structure of the West. They began to depattern the mental orientation of the most reductionist culture the Earth has ever known.

It is no wonder the Western governments have been so afraid of them, have tried to stamp them out wherever they emerge.

And those hallucinogens? They affected *everyone*. Baseball players used them in the world series (throwing a perfect game). Scientists (where do you think the concept of sensory gating channels began?). Researchers (who discovered new innovations like the PCR amplification). Inventors (computers). Herbal companies (from tea to medicinals). NASA even used them to train astronauts for space. And then there was the music . . .

The Earth experienced the greatest musical innovation among the human population it had seen in centuries. New musical forms emerged and *everyone* became involved in them; they influenced everyone who heard them . . . and their ripples continue to move through our cultural waters. Not only new musical forms emerged but thousands upon thousands of musicians. For reasons they cannot explain, they have spent years and fortunes learning to play music, developing sophistication in a craft that most of them will never be able to make a living at.

After forty years of training, some of the best musicians in the world are often only paid $100 for a performance that takes, including travel, set up, and tear down and the performance itself, a full day of their time. But when asked why they have spent so long, training in a profession that can't support them, they all just say some version of, "I don't know, I just had to. It's what I am meant to do."

It is not uncommon for the musicians I know to have upward of $30,000 worth of equipment. They keep trying to capture a certain sound that only they can hear, to bring it into the world in just a certain way.

> *The musician Phil Brown once spent a full week as a teenager trying to bend one note on the electric guitar in just the way it needed to be bent so he could capture just one sound.*

Then they struggle to get certain words to go along with those tones and the feelings they possess. They don't know why, they just know they have to. They keep at it because something in them says they must.

> *The part of them that says they must is what some ancient Greeks called the daemon (or daimon). It is an outside force placed in living beings at birth that continually urges them toward their life purpose. From another perspective it could be considered the thing that directs human beings to fulfill their ecological purpose.*

We will never know *all* the reasons these things emerge into the world, we can only see some of the shadows they cast. But there is a reason that these things must come into the world. The German writer Ernst Junger noted that

> *You may then wonder what the goal of writing is . . . It is the creative instant itself, in which something timeless is produced, something that cannot be wiped out. The universe has affirmed itself in the individual and that must suffice, whether or not anyone else notices it. In 1942, when I visited Picasso on the Rue des Grands-Augustins, he said to me: "Look, this painting, which I have just completed, is going to have a certain affect; but this affect would be exactly the same, metaphysically speaking, if I wrapped the painting up in paper and consigned it to a corner. It would be exactly the same thing as if ten thousand people had admired it."*[1]

The thing that moves us, absent psychological confusions, is something deeper in the system; it does not originate in us. We can never see the full outcome of those movements through us, nor the others that we perceive in the world around us. The Lakota holy man, Black Elk, told his story to John Neihardt in 1931. The book *Black Elk Speaks,* when it was published in 1932, did not do well and it soon went out of print. Black Elk died in 1950, feeling he had failed the great visions given him. However, in 1961 the book was reprinted and soon became one of the best-selling books in the world, the fundamental text of the spirituality of the indigenous peoples of the North American continent. It emerged into the world's consciousness just as hallucinogens were coming into play; it, too, challenged the Western reductionist paradigm. It changed everything.

To see Gaian movements with the linear mind, you have to see the shadows that they cast into the world, into our short time lines. And once you do, once something like that captures your attention, it becomes a golden thread that can be followed deep into the dreaming of Earth.

It is how Lovelock found Gaia after all

You turn then and begin to follow the thread, begin to use this other kind of thinking, then to learn from Gaia herself about the deeper elements inside the thread *and* its connections to other phenomena. Thus with the music. Its emergence is a golden thread; it means more than it appears.

The Song of Earth

We have entered, when we enter the imaginal world, the place where the song lives when no one is playing it.

Which is the real form of the song "Summertime"? The one Gershwin initially heard, or the one Janis Joplin sang much later? The song, as it moves into this world, alters itself to fit the shape of our particular field. Underneath that shape is the archetype of that song, the unique oscillatory communication that has been called forth from the mythic world in which it began only as potential.

The more we practice this skill of perception, the more we can find

truths that can be found no other way. When we return from our journey we bring with us insights and experiences that, as we emerge once
again into Newtonian, classical, space, begin to alter themselves to fit the
unique structure of *our* ecological field and landscape. We play the song
then in *our* way. Its truths become our truths, its voice our voice. It is the
communicatory response of our hearts to what has been presented to the
senses. It is one of the joys of this scenario, the song and the singing. And
we possess song, just as everything in this scenario does, because song is
inherent here, an expression of self-organizational oscillation.

All open, nonlinear, self-organized systems immediately begin to
oscillate at that moment of self-organization. What that oscillation is, is
the movement of the system around its point of equilibrium, its threshold.
On one side is chaos, on the other self-organization. Touches upon that
self-organized state cause a slight movement back toward the threshold
approaching the chaotic state; the system responds and reestablishes
homeodynamis in a new configuration, moving it back a bit further
from the threshold. And this process is continuous. There is an oscillation, electromagnetically expressed, that occurs throughout the entire life
span of every self-organized system. That is what music is. These oscillatory patterns are not random; there are patterns within them. They are
in fact songs, possessing melody, movement, communicative interiority.
They *speak* of the life of the self-organized system, of how it feels, of the
interior struggles it undergoes and the impact of the exterior world upon
it, and its responses to those struggles, those touches.

The blues is inherent in the life of every organism that is, so is the
sweet melody of love song. These songs are a multidimensional representation of the self-organized biological systems that generate them. As
ethnobotanist Kathleen Harrison remarks about the pervasiveness of the
medicinal plant songs in the Americas . . .

> *Every species has a song. If you are granted the song in a vision state,*
> *or by just submitting yourself to the presence of the song and opening*
> *up, then it's a real gift, and you are able to remember that song for-*
> *ever and share it when it seems appropriate. That song has power,*
> *healing power, and there are some which are handed down from one*
> *curandero or curandera to the next, and there are others which come*

to us as individuals. But they are part of an encyclopedia on the sonic level of the same thing that seeds represent on another level.[2]

"They are part of an encyclopedia on the sonic level that seeds represent on another." *Everything* has a song. And that song is a communicatory description of the livingness of that self-organized entity. It is a sonic representation of the nonlinearity of every life-form, of the form and behavior that is altering itself continuously.

But as with the over 100,000 "secondary" metabolites that plants create, oscillations in plants, as Abhala et al. comment, "have been taken as an 'irrelevant' aspect of plant life. Despite the fact that rhythmical behavior is a quintessential pattern of life itself, most researchers still treat oscillations in plants as some unwanted 'physiological noise.'"[3] Nevertheless, these field oscillations (songs) are just as important on the sonic level as chemicals are on the chemical level. They are not only a communicatory expression of field shape at any one time but oscillatory fragments, pulled out of the midst of the song. They hold in sonic form the same things seeds hold, environment captured in one expressible shape. The song is a map of the interaction of that system with both its interior and exterior worlds, the shape of the thing as it has emerged in the field in which it has taken root. And its melody alters from moment to moment as the field shape changes in response to incoming touches (interoceptive or exteroceptive). The genome that is held inside the seed is a map but so is the song that is its oscillating electromagnetic field.

Seeds are only one potential expression of form. They hold within them, tightly bonded together, one part of the long communication that has occurred between that plant archetype and multiple environments in classical Newtonian space. Each seed is a slightly different expression of a single part of that communication, a communication that has lasted for some plants as long as 300 million years. And so, too, each song. The song of a plant, captured by our synaesthetic perceiving at any one moment in time, represents, like a seed, only part of the entire song, a part that has emerged into our awareness during our very short life span.

Indigenous peoples who engaged in sensory synaesthesia in their exploration of the world *felt* the electromagnetic oscillations of the plants with the primary part of the self that humans possess to feel such things, the human heart. And, as all humans can do, they synchnronized their heart field with the EM field of the plant—just as we do with our friends when we synchronize our walking with theirs. The perceived EM field was then "heard" through sensory synaesthesis.

And, as it happens, humans are not just passive listeners in this process. Plants don't just have a song that they unknowingly sing, they use their capacity for vibratory oscillation (song) as a highly elegant form of communication. (This is one of the ways that bees are called to a flower's nectar; the flower's song as it alters its communication throughout the day sings of it to them.) Plants as they sing create, with other life-forms, a kind of harmonic chorus. All the organisms sing together, their songs blending into the unique expression that any ecosystem has, the singing of many songs merging into one song. Again, as Aldo Leopold described it, "There is other music in these hills by no means audible to all. To hear even a few notes of it you must first live here for a long time, and you must know the speech of hills and rivers." As plant researchers Volkov et al. put it, less poetically, the oscillatory nature of plants allows them to establish synchronicity with other plants, and life organisms, including people. Because, at root, plants are a "vibrating" system that is capable of resonance. They can respond with maximum amplitude to an alternating driving force. That is, "plants synchronize their normal biological functions with their responses to the environment."[4] There is an innate tendency in Universe, within Gaia, for self-organized systems to vibrate in harmony, to share rhythms. It's a universal phenomenon, as foundational as chemistry . . . or self-organization. As Joachim-Ernst Berendt notes . . .

Two oscillators pulsating in the same field in almost identical rhythm will tend to "lock in," with the result that eventually their vibrations will become precisely synchronous. This phenomenon is referred to as "mutual phase-locking" or entrainment. Entrainment is universal in nature.[5]

Entrainment can be found in something as simple as our hearts. The pacemaker cells, as they come into being during the self-organization of the heart, begin to beat, to oscillate. Every new cell that forms begins oscillating with the previous ones. A heart pacemaker cell removed from the heart will begin beating wildly, begin to die, but if another pacemaker cell is placed near it—they don't have to touch—the first will synchronize its beating with the second, healthy cell. Each oscillating cell generates an electromagnetic (EM) field around it; any new cell entering that field will begin to synchronize with its oscillations. This results in a giant self-organized grouping of pacemaker cells. The heart then becomes a large EM generator that produces a field 5,000 times larger than the brain's. As you get close to another person you can literally feel that field. We call it "being in someone's space." As we walk together, our fields synchronize. As we talk together, our fields synchronize. And plants? They generate such oscillating fields constantly and as Volkov put it, they synchronize with each other. They do this exactly the way musicians do who are playing together. The writer George Leonard described it well . . .

> *In music, the miracle of entrainment is made explicit. The performer's every gesture, every micromovement, must be perfectly entrained with the pulse of the music, or else the performance falls apart. Watch the members of a chamber group—how they move as one, become as one, a single field. We have become accustomed to such miracles: the extraordinary faculty of jazz musicians to "predict" precise pitch and pattern during improvisation. . . . The miracle springs not so much from individual virtuosity . . . as from the ability of a large group of human beings . . . to sense, feel, and move as one.[6]*

All the subunits in ecoranges synchronize like this; they entrain together to produce one, integrated whole whose vibratory oscillation is in harmony. A unique, larger-than-the parts self-organized entity comes into being. The song of the hills emerges. New plants that enter an existent ecorange represent a new movement in the song; they entrain themselves to the song already being sung but they add new texture, new sound, new movement.

The Bushmen of the Kalahari talk, as Bradford Keeney says, of becoming "awake," awake to the metaphysical background of the world. In this state of perceptual awareness they say they get "second eyes, second ears." They, Keeney says, may then hear the songs that run through the world and the "songs become lines or ropes that take you somewhere."[7] The songs are one expression of the golden threads that connect everything together.

They are "lines or ropes or grids of connection between living things." And they are, as Keeney continues, "indistinguishable from the songs that are voiced in ecstatic emotion."[8]

Among many of the ancient indigenous peoples of America, when a medicine person was invoking the plant for healing, its song would be sung and that would help focus the medicinal qualities of the plant on a sonic level just as the body of the plant does on the physical level. Importantly, as the song was sung once more, the singer would drop down into the reality of the song, let it speak through him. He would synchronize with the song, just as a group of musicians do who are playing together. He would take on the reality of that song, once more be in that state of deep perception, the state of being that was in place when the song was first experienced.

As with any song, there has to be a certain kind of feeling to it for the song to come alive. It has to be real, to be genuine. And as the reality of that song came once more into the world, the person hearing it during the healing would in fact begin to experience the healing of the plant on a sonic level. The captured oscillations of the plant, from that moment in time, would be re-expressed as a living communication and the ill person's field would synchronize with it, would use that other field as a template around which to reform itself. The song *is* medicine.

This should not seem as strange to us as it might upon first hearing it. When we listen to songs that move us, they do in fact heal us. The various consciousness modules we have within us—the infant, the four-year-old, the mother, and all the others—are themselves psychological expressions—specific behavioral aspects of self-organization—that possess oscillation, just as our organs, our hearts, our bodies do. Damage to, that is, disharmony in, any of those modules is carried within its oscillating field. As the poet Novalis once put it, "Every disease is a musical problem."

> *The electromagnetic, oscillating field that every living thing generates as it lives contains within it the complete story of its current state of being, including every wound, illness, and need.*

The songs that people write, and perform, speak to specific kinds of damage in the specific module fields that they have, and that are possessed by others. They write those songs in dreams. And as we listen to those songs later, the parts of us that need them come to the fore and for a while we dream, our conscious minds sleep. And while we sleep, that part of us synchronizes with the oscillations of the song and that song goes deep within us, reforming the field of that part of ourselves. And sometimes, those songs lead us to ways we can generate that wholeness permanently.

That is much of what healing is. The restructure of the field. In essence, a medicinal plant restructures the field of the organ it affects by acting on its physical components. The same thing can happen on the sonic level.

*And no, just using the spirit of the plant will not fulfill the same function as using the spirit **and** the body of the plant together. Both are ultimately necessary. Want proof? Try eating the spirit of food for a few years and see how it goes for you. Our bodies exist for a reason, so do the plant bodies. Matter **and** spirit, neither is higher to the other.*

Using the song of the plant, evoking its spirit, using its body as food for the body that is us . . . this is more powerful still. There are multiple layers to reality, all important but none foundational, each an essential aspect of self-organization.

When Masanobu Fukuoka spoke of the ideal form of rice he was also talking about the oscillatory form that ideal rice has, and it can indeed be perceived from that orientation, the song of rice—as can everything. All particles are in fact waves and those waves present themselves, to those who can hear them, as sounds, in fact, as composed melodies that generate shape, form, behavior. The writer Joachim-Ernst Berendt quotes George Leonard on this in his book *The World Is Sound* (Destiny Books, 1991) . . .

At the root of all power and motion, there is music and rhythm, the play of patterned frequencies against the matrix of time. . . . We now know that every particle in the physical universe takes its characteristics from the pitch and pattern and overtones of its particular frequencies, its singing. . . . Before we make music, music makes us.[9]

Our organs, in every part of our body, are, just like the ideal form of rice, possessed of an oscillatory field that alters itself as it manifests itself in our landscape. As Karsten Kruse and Frank Julicher put it (complicatedly), oscillations "emerge as the collective dynamic behavior of an ensemble of interacting components in the cell."[10] And that oscillating field changes from moment to moment to moment during its life. Any damage to the field is then held in its oscillatory pattern, its song. Other oscillatory patterns, held in actual songs as we known them, or in the plants we use as medicines, can alter the damage in that pattern, restore the organ to health. As physician Mitchell Gaynor puts it, "You can look at disease as a form of disharmony. And there's no organ system in the body that's not affected by sound and vibration."[11] Intentionally generated oscillatory patterns—in specific form, whether those in a heart field to which an ill person synchronizes or those in *specific* song shapes designed for the purpose—can literally help remake physiology. Such oscillations are especially potent in their impact on the shape and functioning of neural networks. Music, it turns out, stimulates the creation and release of serotonin in neural nets, generates net restructuring and the formation of new neural network shapes. It decreases sensory gating and directly affects cognition and perception.

If you begin to look deeper at oscillatory patterning, songs, as root in this scenario we are in, you begin to find that not only do all medicinal plants have a song, all parts of the Earth have a song, every living phenomenon, every ecozone, ecorange, mountain, and body of water. As Berendt put it, "the world is sound." Many people have known this, it's just taken scientists a few millennia longer to catch on.

As the composer Edward Elgar noted, "There is music in the air, music is all around us; the world is full of it, and you simply take as much of it as you require." But as with plants, these songs are not just a byproduct of the livingness of an organism, the Earth is not only song, it sings.

The Earth generates a continual oscillating field as it lives moment-to-moment-to-moment. It is in fact an enormous biological oscillator. And that field generates a continual song, a song that goes out into space, in an energy spectrum that is inaudible to us.

But it is not inaudible to the other planets in our solar system

Some researchers have slowed that sound enough to move it into our audible spectrum—you can listen to it if you Google "Earth's song." It sounds nearly identical to dolphin or whale song.

And that is no coincidence

The songs of cetaceans and the song of Earth bear great similarity.

Dolphin song is a complex communicatory and informational gestalt that generates in other dolphins a direct experience of what is being communicated without using the medium of linear reductionism, or words. As dolphin researcher Jack Kassewitz notes, "Dolphins appear to have leap-frogged human symbolic language and instead have evolved a form of communication outside the human evolutionary path."[12] And the information contained in cetacean songs is truly immense. There is "an information density," as Berendt puts it, "of between one and ten million bits per half hour of whale song—which is the approximate amount of information contained in [Homer's] *Odyssey*."[13] In other words, whales are communicating *each half hour* the same amount of information as that in an entire book that would take us hours or days to read. And what is really interesting is that if a three-dimensional photograph of certain whale songs is generated, it looks like this . . .

and particular dolphin songs like this . . .[14]*

*You can see these in color on the back cover of this book.

In fact, *every* song that emerges from Nature, irrespective of the organism, takes a different field shape and it matters not whether you look at the songs of birds or that of cetaceans.

> *Our songs are but pale imitations of a complex singing that has existed billions of years before our emergence into the scenario.*

From these photographs it's possible to directly see that a flower or a plant is merely one form of Earth song, sung into specific expression at one moment in time. The musician and researcher Hans Kayser, in his *Harmonia Plantarum,* found that " plants," as Berendt comments, "have harmonic shapes and proportions—in the calyx, the leaf, bud, stamen, the ovary, the fruit, the stem, and in the configuration of leaves."[15] And those shapes and proportions alter depending on the location in which the plant grows. These transforms of messages? They are also songs filled with meaning.

We are not only dreamed into being but sung. Each of us has a song that is, on the sonic level, what our bodies are on another. We are in fact, on one level, made of song, and it is no wonder we sing or love song. It is an expression of the life and form that we are. And it is no wonder that we seek out songs, for they do in fact help heal us, help us once again find the shape that the archetype was meant to take in the unique field in which we have emerged.

We can help other forms of life heal by finding the shape that they were meant to take in this particular field. We can hold them in our heart field and work toward synchronization . . . or we can sing.

> *Which is itself a form of heart field. It is heart field made audible.*

And if we sing well enough, hold the song fully enough, bring the real song out of the imaginal world as Fukuoka did the ideal forms of rice, we help sing the ecozone or plant or loved one we care for back to health.

Earth rests in the deeps and like whales and dolphins sings its deep dreaming into those deeps, to the other planets that also swim in those same waters. We are not an isolated planet, a lifeless ball of resources hurtling around the sun.

The scenario is much bigger than that.

BRIDGE

Bifurcation

✁

In a dynamic and self-organizing state, this open-endedness is most pronounced at the point of bifurcation: the critical or singular moment when a system has the potential of entering one or two or more available states.

NIGEL CLARK

Elites quite naturally define as the most important and admired qualities of a citizen those on which they themselves have concentrated. The possession, use, and control of knowledge have become their central theme—the theme song of their expertise. However, their power depends not on the effect with which they use that knowledge but on the effectiveness with which they control its use. Thus, among the illusions which have invested our civilization is an absolute belief that the solution to our problems must be a more determined application of rationally organized expertise. The reality is that our problems are largely the product of that application. The illusion is that we have created the most sophisticated society in the history of man. The reality is that the division of knowledge into feudal fiefdoms of expertise has made general understanding and coordinated action not simply impossible but despised and distrusted.

JOHN RALSTON SAUL

When everyone is saying something it takes a real effort to step outside and say, wait a minute, how do we know that? It's especially hard if you spend your time hanging out with other Very Serious People. . . . This is what you need to know: important people have no special monopoly on wisdom; and in times like these, when the usual rules . . . don't apply, they are often deeply foolish, because the power of conventional wisdom prevents them from talking sense about a deeply unconventional situation.

PAUL KRUGMAN

Men by their constitutions are naturally divided into two parties: 1. Those who fear and distrust the people, and wish to draw all powers from them into the hands of the higher classes. 2. Those who identify themselves with the people, have confidence in them, cherish and consider them as the most honest and safe, although not the most wise depository of the public interests.

THOMAS JEFFERSON

In 2004, Carolina Izquierdo, an anthropologist at the University of California, Los Angeles, spent several months with the Matsigenka, a tribe of about twelve thousand people who live in the Peruvian Amazon. The Matsigenka hunt for monkeys and parrots, grow yucca and bananas, and build houses that they roof with the leaves of a particular kind of palm tree, known as a kapashi. At one point, Izquierdo decided to accompany a local family on a leaf gathering expedition down the Urubamba River.

A member of another family, Yanira, asked if she could come along. Izquierdo and the others spent five days on the river. Although Yanira had no clear role in the group, she quickly found ways to make herself useful. Twice a day, she swept the sand off the sleeping mats, and she helped stack the kapashi leaves for transport back to the village. In the evening, she fished for crustaceans, which she cleaned, boiled, and served to the others. Calm and self-possessed, Yanira "asked for nothing," Izquierdo later recalled. The girl's behavior made a strong impression on the anthropologist because at the time of the trip Yanira was just six years old.

ELIZABETH KOLBERT

A striking feature of self-organized systems is the occurrence of a bifurcation—a sudden transition from one pattern to another following even a small change in a parameter of the system. . . . [Such systems] characteristically show bifurcations. . . . [This] can have important evolutionary consequences for self-organized systems. We have shown how a small change in a system parameter can result in a large change in the overall behavior of the system. Is it possible that such properties could provide self-organized systems with adaptive, flexible responses to changing conditions in the environment and to changing needs of the system?

SCOTT CAMAZINE

17

THE ECOLOGICAL FUNCTION OF THE HUMAN SPECIES

Gaia isn't alive because Gaia doesn't reproduce.

RICHARD DAWKINS

Until the human is understood as a dimension of the earth, we have no secure basis for understanding any aspect of the human. We can understand the human only through the earth.

THOMAS BERRY

Earth is a giant living being, perhaps a superorganism, as far beyond us as we are beyond our constituent cells.

DORION SAGAN

[Bacterial] metabolic diversity and adaptability means that microbes can live where other life is impossible, in extreme environments such as deep-sea thermal vents, beneath the Arctic and Antarctic ice caps, and even inside other organisms. Microbial life is heavily implicated in all the biogeochemical cycles, dwarfing the contribution of multicellular organisms—which in any case have

microbes at the root of their metabolism. Mitochondria and chloro-
plasts, the main energy-producing organelles in animal and plant
cells, both have evolutionary origins as once-free bacteria annexed
into the greater whole. . . . Gaia's metabolism is microbial.

WILLIAMS AND LENTON

We're like bees you see, bees that go out looking for honey without
realizing that we're also performing cross-pollination.

BUCKMINSTER FULLER

*I*t is common, even among people who really should know better, to
think of the Earth as an isolated scenario. That is, even though they
know the Earth is an open system that cannot, and does not, exist without exterior inputs,

sunlight, for example,

they still think of it as isolated from the rest of the Universe.

terrestrial chauvinism

They tend not to realize that there is an *outside* to our Earth. This is true
even among many nonlinear, chaos theory freaks. They get so caught up
in the micro that they can't see the macro. They *know* that every self-
organized system is extremely sensitive to perturbations. They *know* that
even very tiny inputs can have immense impacts. Or, as Nigel Clark puts
it so brilliantly, "Small variations in initial conditions . . . have a habit
of amplifying in rather momentous ways."[1] "Rather momentous ways." (I
love the British.) Or as Robert Heinlein once put it, "Population problems have a horrible way of solving themselves."

Nonlinearists *know* that in a self-organized system, any touch upon
it will start a ripple effect much like dropping a stone in a pond. But
they are still surprised when a chemical at one hundred parts per trillion
is found to alter biological functioning across the entire planet. As Louis
Guillette, a reproductive endocrinologist and professor of zoology at the
University of Florida, put it . . .

We did not [test] one part per trillion for the contaminant, as we assumed that was too low. Well, we were wrong. It ends up that everything from a hundred parts per trillion to ten parts per million are ecologically relevant. . . . [A]t these levels there is sex reversal [in males of all species]. . . . [And our research] shows that the highest dose does not always give the greatest response. That has been a very disturbing issue for many people trying to do risk assessment in toxicology.[2]

But, other than noticing the sun from time to time, nonlinearists will rarely understand that the self-organized Earth system is itself immersed in the midst of the self-organized galaxy, is, in fact embedded within it, just as ecoranges are embedded within the larger Gaian system. And that those galaxies themselves make up ecoranges in the self-organized Universe. As physicist Lee Smolin describes the situation, it

seems that our life is situated inside a nested hierarchy of self-organized systems that begin with our local ecologies and extend upwards at least to the galaxy. Each of these levels are non-equilibrium systems that owe their existence to processes of self-organization, that are in turn driven by cycles of energy and materials in the level above them. It is then tempting to ask if this extends further up than the galaxy. Must there be a non-equilibrium system inside of which sits our galaxy? Is there a sense in which the universe as a whole could be a non-equilibrium, self-organized system?[3]

Few people understand that the touch of Universe upon Earth is constant. That, in fact, Earth is a truly open system. And such open systems are always being changed by the touch of the outside upon them. *Every* touch ripples through the system. *Every* touch changes something. As researchers John Briggs and David Peat comment about understanding even the apparent simplicity of small ponds . . .

Any ultimate coordinating of events around the pond is made impossible by the fact that all systems are open to the rest of the universe. . . . Even the movement of distant stars will produce minute changes in the gravitational field experienced on earth. While these fluctuations will be beyond any hope of measurement on earth, nevertheless they will always destroy initial correlations.[4]

We inhabit a planet that is not closed to the universe around it. It is touched every minute of every day by its surrounds. And even if we cannot "see" the results of those touches, they continually alter the self-organized system that is Earth in unpredictable ways. We are part of a scenario that is ongoing, in which evolution has not stopped, and in which humans play only a small part.

*As uncomfortable as the awareness is
we are only infinitesimally tiny players in a very large story*

The galaxies that exist in Universe, as Clark comments, "are immensely complex systems, constantly engaged in the circulation of energy and material with the intersteller medium which surrounds them." And our own planet is only one participant "in the vast and productive self-organizing cycling of elements in one such galaxy; the earth inheriting the organic elements necessary for its own self-organization from the greater system of which it is a small part."[5]

The *stars,* including our sun, supply the power for the self-organization of life into new forms over long time lines. The Earth is *not* a tiny pebble of life alone in the void that surrounds it but is rather a node with extensive interconnections to the rest of the galaxy and Universe itself.

And these interconnections, this touching, includes a great deal more than sunlight. The Earth receives over 80 *million* pounds of extra-terrestrial matter from the galaxy around it *every* year. It's composed of cosmic dust, meteorites, asteroids, and comets that break up in transit through the atmosphere.

*It's not just inanimate dust you know,
it also contains a large variety of organic molecules.*

All this affects the structure of the self-organized Earth system. Sometimes the effect, as the dinosaur extinctions have made clear, is catastrophic. Such catastrophic events do have substantial impacts on Earth functioning. The Earth system has spent a great deal of time in past geologic ages reconstituting itself in new forms after they occur. (It's how our species emerged after all.) The common tendency is to view such catastrophic bombardments as random events

shit happens, you know?

But there is increasing evidence that they are not any more random than the bacterial/algal creation of rain. It appears that, as with all self-organized systems, there is an underlying order to them that is part of a much larger ecological function. As Clark comments, "Episodes of bombardment, it now appears, may not be as haphazard as formerly presumed."[6] Astrophysicists have begun to notice a nonlinear periodicity to them, some of them are being generated by "chaotic outbursts" in the orbits of Saturn and Jupiter. These outbursts trigger alterations in asteroid path and behavior so that they specifically intersect the orbit of Earth. And while the larger events get all the attention

Wow, look at that redwood!
What about that microbe?
What?

the smaller bombardments that continually occur are rarely noticed. They cause changes that have barely been glimpsed, that are usually overlooked. Virtually no one has asked the questions: "How is this shifting Earth homeodynamis?" or "What alterations are occurring in the self-organized state in response?" But they should be, for as Clark notes . . .

In a dynamic and self-organizing state, this open-endedness is most pronounced at the point of bifurcation: the critical or singular moment when a system has the potential of entering one or two or more available states. In this region, even the smallest fluctuation in the environment of the system may prove pivotal in deciding which direction change will take. And because of the randomness of these instabilities or irregularities it is impossible to determine the outcome in advance.[7]

How are these constant influxes of matter altering the Earth's self-organized state? *What* bifurcations are occurring? *Why* is the Earth receiving directed inputs in the form of cosmic matter? The questions are never asked and that failure is, itself, a source of further disruptions. As Clark continues . . .

The marginalization of earth-transforming forces that are other-than-human, the disavowal of fluctuations and instabilities that are not of our own making, in this sense, creates the conditions for further excessive outbreaks.[8]

Every touch on a self-organized system presents the system with a choice of how to reestablish homeodynamis in response to the perturbation. It urges potential out of the quantum background, out of the dreaming, out of the Ocean of Being. Many of the forces that shape our world, for example, the amount of cosmic dust that falls yearly on Earth, are invisible to our linear or cultural minds and will remain, all our lives, opaque to us. The alterations in Earth functioning that occur in response to that cosmic dust remain invisible as well. Our perceptual limitations inhibit our seeing the totality of such events, and that includes such things as the ecological function of the human species. Our function is ultimately neither social nor cultural, it is at last ecological—we are part of a larger system, not isolated bits thrown up through chance by a blind universe.

What Are People Anyway?

It is common for a subset, a rather large subset unfortunately, of those who love the Earth and are concerned about its current state to view human beings as a cancer (or perhaps a virus) infecting the Earth.

There are very few people
who trust the Earth less than environmentalists

Assertions regarding the plague-like nature of humans and urgings to "save the Earth" from the human plague are common. There are a lot of problems with that, the major one being, of course, that it's not accurate. What is true is that the *Earth* does not need saving.

> *And even if it did, human beings do not possess the comprehensive informedness necessary to understand the system well enough to control outcomes through top-down approaches—and they never will.*

Gaia has been self-caretaking for a very long time; Gaia does it very well. The belief that *we* must save the Earth—even if it is driven by deep concern for the damage that is occurring in natural ecosystems—is only another example of hubris, the flip-side of the arrogance of the belief that we can do as we wish to the Earth without repercussion. As Michael Crichton put it . . .

> *To the Earth, a hundred years is nothing. A million years is nothing. This planet lives and breathes on a much vaster scale. We can't imagine its slow and powerful rhythms, and we haven't got the humility to try. We have been residents here for the blink of an eye. If we are gone tomorrow, the Earth will not miss us. . . . Let's be clear: The planet is not in jeopardy. We are in jeopardy. We haven't got the power to destroy the planet—or to save it. But we might have the power to save ourselves.*[9]

It's a misguided human-centric orientation. The problem is that Gaian functioning can't be managed by a human-limited point of view. The paradigm is inaccurate to the task. Nor can a comprehensive approach be created out of linear thinking. To attempt to do so is simply applying the old way of thinking to the problems that the old way of thinking has created.

> *Before anyone begins exterminating "invasive" plants, it is more sensible to first understand what they are doing, why they are moving into the ecosystems they are "invading." But this question is never asked. It's just assumed they are "bad plants," destroying the*

"good plants." The environmental "cure" is, as usual, based on igno-
rance, an expression of two-dimensional, linear thinking. It's not
going to turn out well.

Yes, there are things we can do, things we are supposed to do,
but they do not come out of linear reductionism. They come from
certain acts of co-creation. As Barbara McClintock put it, "I did
not go any place the corn did not first tell me to go." Good holistic
*thinking, as Peter Saunders once put it, is **much** harder than*
reductionist thinking. It takes practice and intent. Short cuts aren't
going to work.

The assumptions underneath most approaches to ecological problem
solving are almost always inaccurate. It is true that human-driven alterations have occurred in the biosphere in the past two hundred years. It
is true that the climate of Earth is changing considerably. But this does
not mean that the *Earth* is in trouble, it means that the current ecological expression the Earth has generated in this geological age and that we
take for granted is facing a phase change.

This has implications for *human* habitability—most especially for
the survival of human civilization—not Earth continuance. And it has
implications for those of us who love wild ecosystems and the life-forms
that inhabit them. There is deep grief for most of us in their loss; there
is no escaping that emotional impact for anyone who has retained the
capacity to feel.

But Gaia has been through the loss of species *and* unique ecological
expressions before. Gaia is in a constant process of change, it's just that
the time lines are so long compared to our time sense that we normally
don't notice it—unless a phase change is happening.

Gaia understands the birth of new species, Gaia also understands
death, for death is built into the system. The Gaian system depends on
it. Organisms have been dying here for billions of years. Each and every
organism that emerges out of its matrix matters to the Earth—all of them
are necessary—but it does not fear their passing. It is we who grieve.

The tremendous fear of death we have in the West drives many
of our behaviors, including environmental. It is also, unsurprisingly,
deeply embedded in the American health care system. It is common, for

instance, in news reports, to hear physicians and researchers speak of the "cause of death" when talking of someone's mortality. The assumption is that the bacteria or virus (or heart disease or stroke) *caused* the death. The problem is that, that statement, well, it's frankly crazy. Embedded within it is a communication, a belief—fundamental to the paradigm— that if all "causes" of death are defeated there will be no more death.

> *This is, in fact, the power that technological medicine holds in Western culture. Every person born in the West has been immersed in the belief that if only medical researchers have more time, more money, more research facilities, eventually all causes of death will be understood and removed. Death is viewed as a glitch in the system, a mistake that must be corrected—and more strangely, something that can be corrected through science. We will then live to be 120 or 380 years old or perhaps researchers will figure out ways to clone our bodies and insert us into them or even to put our consciousness into grid systems on the moon where we will then "live" for thousands or even millions of years. This is, in fact, a utopian fantasy that has about as much chance of happening as every politician suddenly having integrity.*

As Harvard researcher and zoologist Richard Lewontin puts it, "the claims made by medicine imply this possibility without explicitly stating it. Medical scientists speak of 'preventing' deaths by curing disease, but the evidence is that death cannot be prevented, only postponed at best. Moreover, the postponement has not been as effective as is sometimes claimed during the last fifty years of great progress in physiology, cell biology, and medicine. . . . [The truth is] that although the proximate causes of death can be dealt with, death itself cannot. So, there must be a cause of death as a *phenomenon,* as distinct from the individual cases."[10] In other words, if *every* "cause" of death were removed, despite what physicians (and news reports) say, there would still be death. Death is inherent in this place. Endings are inherent in this place.

> *We are all biodegrading as we speak*
> *and we're supposed to*

We cannot end death, we cannot end endings. All we can do, as our ancestors for a thousand generations before us have done, is grapple with the truth of it and find our own way of integrating that truth into our fabric. Then . . . living a full life that understands—and accepts—its inevitability.

This is the real teaching of the Buddha's story about the man and the tiger.

> *Hanging onto a cliff face, a tiger above him and more tigers below, the man feels the vine he is holding on to begin to give way, its roots pulling out of the cliff. There is nothing he can do, but then he notices a beautiful ripe strawberry growing to the side. He reaches over and plucks it. And it is delicious.*

There is nothing we can do about death, all we can control is how we live. If you truly understand, however minimally, Gaia as a living being, if you extend yourself outside the human frame, as Goethe did when he said . . .

> *I trust myself to Nature, she may do as she will with me*

and begin to look at Gaia from a much larger, and not necessarily human, frame of reference, you have to understand that Gaia does not make mistakes. The system is highly refined, from billions of years of life and experimentation and learning. Death is inherent in the system *for a reason*. It is not a mistake. Nor is the human species a mistake.

If you truly trust Gaia, you have to understand that what is happening now is *not* the result of a virus or a cancer (or uncontrollable rapists) spreading voraciously across the body of a female and very passive Earth who was just doing her loving best to care for her children and got blindsided by an abusive, patriarchal, penis-wielding species. If you truly trust the Earth, you have to assume that the human species

> *as it is, not as it might be in some imagined utopian fantasy*

is just the way it's supposed to be.

Despite press to the contrary, the species has not changed all that much in the past 35,000 years.

You have to ask yourself, "What is the ecological function of the human species *as it is?*" Not how it might be.

We don't look at plants (as a general phenomenon) and say, "Gee, they could be so neat if they get over their competitiveness." Or, to that white blood cell, "Arms are for hugging."

Every species that we see is an innovation on less complex bacterial forms. And every one of them is generated out of the ecological matrix of the planet to fulfill specific homeodynamis stabilizing and ecological functions for the self-organized system.

As with every species that exists, the human fulfills multiple ecological functions . . . for instance, humans fulfill the same functions as any large predator such as bears or mountain lions—Gaia always layers functions; it's more efficient that way. Humans also—as is true of every larger species on the planet—serve to spread seeds of plants to new locations.

A deeper look at plants always generates the question, "Are we only a domesticated species, serving primarily as a mechanism for plant propagation?" (Wait, I don't think I like where that is going.)

But you have to ask yourself, if you really want to grapple with the "people-as-cancer—Gaia-as-innocent-bystander" belief, what ecological function the human species is fulfilling through the processing of so much ecological capital, through the generation of technology?

The Ecological Function of the Human Species

People tend to get grandiose about the purpose of human beings: we are the universe become conscious of itself; we are the first emergence of intelligence in the universe via Darwinian mechanisms; we are uniquely gifted among all living organisms in possessing a soul and are thus beloved of God (and Jesus), holding a special place in his heart. Really, it's embarrassing. Every one of those beliefs is only a modified version of an underlying hubris, an expression of a certain kind of belief in human entitlement.

Mirror, mirror on the wall, who's the . . .

There is a common drive to believe we are somehow special, though to be fair, among some nonindustrial cultures humans were simply thought of as one life-form among many, just one part of the circle of life. Nevertheless, in most industrialized nations, the belief has emerged that we are very special indeed. But . . . we aren't. We are just part of the weave. Though we do have, as all organisms do, a unique and very special ecological function beyond the general ones that other large predators possess. It is concerned with Gaia's reproduction.

It is an odd thing that the human species has been so powerfully driven to go outward and upward for much of its history. There is a drive deep in the organism for this. So driven are we, that we have even traveled into space.

This is one of the Gaian shadows that has been cast into our limited vision. It's curious, the depth of the drive, the power, the fascination with space we once had. But once it reached a certain expression, hardly anyone cared anymore.

There is speculation among some that life arose on Earth because bacteria from *out there* impacted this planet in the distant past. And Lynn Margulis did find that all life-forms that we know came from four early bacterial types billions of years ago. Over long time lines those four combined through symbiogenesis to create complex organisms. In other words, life here began with a few simple bacteria. So, people think, maybe those bacteria were sent through space and, arriving here, initiated life over long eons of time.

It is unlikely to ever be determined if that is true, but it is inarguable that bacteria from *here* are, through our actions, going *out there*. Our space probes are filled with bacteria (and viruses and . . .) that we are sending to every planet in this solar system and even farther out. As Lewis Thomas comments . . .

The Earth may be entering the first stages of replication, scattering seeds of itself, perhaps in the form of microorganisms similar to those dominating the planet's own first life for the first two billion years of its Precambrian period.[11]

Just as pollen, bacteria, viruses, and fungal spores travel into the great spaces around them through complex, usually invisible, mechanisms, we travel into the great spaces outside us. And, interestingly, we have, unknowingly, patterned our space probes on pollen, bacterial, and viral shapes. For instance . . . here is the Russian satellite *Sputnik* and an *E. coli* bacterium.

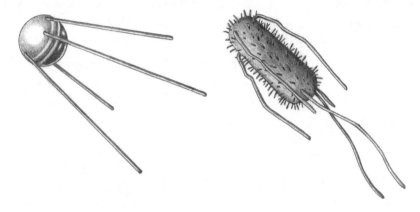

Even the moon lander was oriented along viral forms.

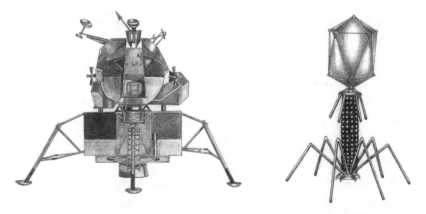

And as those viral and bacterial organisms take life to new locations when they travel, so do we. Just as bacteria, viruses, and pollen rise up on thermal currents and travel tremendous distances to other locations where they can spread, so too have we sent bacterial organisms deep into space on thermal currents, to other planets, to other solar systems, where they can take root, where Gaia can reproduce.

> *We're like bees, you see, bees who go out looking for honey without realizing that we are also performing cross-pollination.*

And the bacteria (and viruses, and . . .) we are sending out into space are extremely hardy. As a NASA bulletin noted in 1998 . . .

> *For a human, unprotected space travel is a short trip measured in seconds. . . . But for some kinds of microbes, the harshness of space travel is not unlike their everyday stressful existence, the successful execution of ingenious survival tricks learned over billions of years of Earth-bound evolution.*[12]

There were, it seems, inadvertent stowaways during the pre-Apollo missions to the moon, bacteria: *Streptococcus mitis*. The "only known survivor," as NASA put it, "of unprotected space travel." The

> *organisms survived launch, space vacuum, 3 years of radiation exposure, deep-freeze at an average temperature of only 20 degrees above absolute zero, and no nutrient, water, or energy source.*[13]

These particular bacteria were sent to the moon—breathed or touched onto equipment by technicians—with one of the Surveyor probes that preceded the Apollo missions. (There were six in all.) Only one of the probes was ever visited by humans—during the *Apollo 12* lunar mission. And it was then that the bacteria were discovered. Pete Conrad, the mission commander, commented that

> *I always thought the most significant thing we ever found on the whole . . . Moon was that little bacteria who came back and lived and nobody ever said [anything] about it.*[14]

The astronauts collected the bacteria, brought them back to Earth, where they immediately revived. Bacteria, it turns out, can survive these kinds of conditions for millions of years. The oldest that people know of survived 25 million years of encapsulation in the intestinal tract of a resin-trapped bee.

It took somewhere between 500 million and one billion years for bacterial life to spread on this planet; life takes its time. Gaian seeding has begun, though it might take 500 million years or more before the birth of Gaian offspring. And you know bacteria and viruses are not the only Earth organisms that can survive unprotected in space. The tardigrade or water bear (*Echiniscus blumi*) lives every place on Earth; there are over 900 kinds of them. They are considered to be what is called extremophiles, organisms that can survive pretty much any habitat. They can survive boiling, freezing, extreme radiation— of every kind (1,000 times that survivable by people)—and extreme atmospheric pressure (6,000 atmospheres, six times that of the deepest ocean trench). They can survive at temperatures as low as −457 degrees (one degree above absolute zero) and heat as high as 357 degrees, and they can live for decades without water or food. One was reported to have been revived after dessication in a 120-year-old moss specimen. They have been sent into space numerous times, surviving unprotected for the ten days of the experiment and being able to reproduce later. And they carry within them, as well, fungi, bacteria, and viruses.

Still . . . this is probably not the first time that Gaia has sent her seeds beyond the boundaries of the planet—and it won't be the last.

We are, after all, only passing actors on the stage

In many respects the tremendous volcanic explosions that have occurred in the Gaian past, and the powerful meteor impacts that have altered life, can be thought of, primarily, as life-spreading events. The Krakatoa explosion was strong enough to throw Earth matter, filled with microbes, up into space where those microbes would float on the cosmic winds, much as pollen grains do on Earth's winds, until they were caught by the gravitational field of another planet. The asteroid impact that caused the Cretaceous-Paleogene extinction was, as well, powerful enough to throw microbe-filled Earth matter into space. And the impact at the Darwin Crater in Tasmania (800,000 years ago) was so powerful it turned the rock and soil into frothy glass, encasing millions of organisms within it. Fragments of life-filled frothy glass were hurled beyond the Earth gravitational field by the impact, where they, too, were caught by solar and cosmic winds. Inevitably, the thought occurs: Is the nonlinear periodicity of asteroid impacts on Earth specifically connected, in part, to this Gaian seeding of the galaxy, this wind pollination of Universe?

Gaia always innovates on earlier forms. Wind pollination gave way to pollinator pollination; it is much more efficient for the pollen to go exactly where it needs to go. Human pollinators are now taking the bacteria exactly where they need to go. We, inevitably, think it is all about us, not realizing that we are in fact performing cross-pollination.

Autumn

Plants, in the fall, begin to set seed. They use the nutrients stored over the winter, spring, and summer to create their seeds and send them into the world so that the species can spread. They begin to look a bit ragged at the end of the growing season. Plants use stored resources to reproduce. They then go into the long winter to regenerate. In spring they begin the cycle once again.

It is not surprising that the Earth is beginning to look a bit ragged, not surprising that so many stored resources have been used up in the creation of a technology that has served to send Gaian seeds to other planets. It is also not surprising that we are reaching peak oil, peak top soil, peak water, peak bacterial resistance, peak everything just as the bacterial seeds have been sent out. Given the length of geologic time lines, *every* indicator reaching peak within a fifty year period is beyond coincidence.

It is one of the shadows Gaia casts into linear space

What is at risk, from our human point of view, is not the planet but our civilization. It is entirely dependent on resource extraction, a resource extraction that cannot be maintained. We have already exceeded the human carrying capacity of Earth. We are, at this point, burning the house to keep warm in the winter. And while the climate *may* alter so much that human life can no longer survive here, the chances are much more likely that human life will continue on, at least for a while, most probably for a very long while. The important thing, however, is not that we die—or even that our species dies—for that is inevitable for all of us.

everything returns to the Ocean of Being eventually

What is more important is how we live.

We can live the life that is meant for us—just as every bird, microbe, white blood cell, and plant does. And in the process we can love the sparrow *and* the hawk. We can do the work that Gaia has set before us. In the end that is all any of us has. If there is any greater joy than the touch of my beloved's hands I know not what it is. If there is any greater satisfaction than doing the work that is mine to do, and doing it well, I know not what it is. And that joy, that satisfaction, can be found whether automobiles exist or not, whether skyscrapers exist or not, whether physicists exist or not—as it has always been. Our ancestors did not live diminished lives just because they did not know of Ph.D.s or cappuccinos or airplanes or Mozart or nonlinearity. As Rainer Maria Rilke once said . . .

> *All will come again into its strength:*
> *the fields undivided, the waters undammed*
> *the trees towering and the walls built low*
> *and in the valleys, people as strong and varied as the land.*
>
> *And no churches where God*
> *is imprisoned and lamented*
> *like a trapped and wounded animal.*
> *The houses welcoming all who knock*
> *and a sense of boundless offering*
> *in all relations, and in you and me.*
>
> *No yearning for an afterlife, no looking beyond*
> *no belittling of death,*

but only longing for what belongs to us
and serving Earth, lest we remain unused.[15]

We are human and a part of Gaia, as all life is. And we have the life that has been set before us. Ultimately, that really is enough. And in the end it is all any of us has.

Nevertheless, it *may* seem that I mean by this chapter that everything is fine, the damage to the biosphere all part of the plan, nothing to worry about, so we should do nothing. It *may* seem as well that I am saying that we live in a deterministic world, that we have no choice in what we do, that we are just programmed by Darwinian mechanisms and chemistry to act in certain ways. Neither is correct.

That we are driven to do something in response to ecological over-harvesting is also Gaian; there is the necessity to trust the internal impulses we have, the movement of what the ancient Athenians called the daimon that is within us, the thing that drives us to do the work that is within us to do.

There is a reason that hundreds of thousands of people have been training as herbalists in the U.S. the past forty years, a reason their increasing numbers map exactly the rise of pharmaceutically-resistant bacteria. The thing is . . . the human species is going to be needing these skills before too long, just as we are going to be needing a different way of thinking.

We, as all life-forms do, have a great deal of choice in *how* we do what we do. Just like the plants, we *choose* which path to take at moments of bifurcation. The world is not linear, nor is it deterministic in the reductionist sense of the word. The linear reductionism of Western science—which has influenced our thinking so deeply—is not accurate to the world. A different way of thinking is necessary. And just as with herbal medicine, there is a reason it is emerging more strongly now.

The utopian fantasies of Western science are, for the most part, hubris. As Barbara McClintock put it . . .

We've been spoiling the environment just dreadfully and thinking we were fine, because we were using the techniques of science. Then it turns into technology, and it's slapping us back because we didn't think it through. We were making assumptions we had no right to make. From the point of view of how the whole thing worked, we knew how part of it worked. . . . We didn't even inquire, didn't even see how the rest was going on. All these other things were happening and we didn't see it. . . . Technology is fine, but the scientists and engineers only partially think through their problems. They solve certain aspects, but not the total, and as a consequence it is slapping us back in the face very hard.[16]

Science is fun, it has its place, but it has no capacity for love or empathy. Its servants make the medicines that sometime save our lives and televisions that entertain us when we are fatigued, but they also make the gas that killed the Jews, the ovens that burned them, and the processes that damage the biosphere. Such will *always* be true of science.

And those who insist that is not true know nothing of human beings

There is another way to approach the world, another path to the gathering of knowledge, one that has embedded within it both love and empathy. But it means abandoning the old forms of thinking. It means taking another road.

18
"THE ROAD
NOT TAKEN"

After all, if all the experts insist that experts have value, who are non-experts to disagree?

NOAH SMITH

These are times of madness dressed in good suits.

PAUL KRUGMAN

Reason, unable to cope with genius, has wed itself to mediocrity.

JOHN RALSTON SAUL

Two roads diverged in a wood, and I—
I took the one less traveled by,
And that has made all the difference

ROBERT FROST

You should understand, and probably do if you have read this far, that I am a barbarian. As I mentioned at the beginning of this book, I am not going to lay out the problems that lie before us and then call for legislation, or more money, or signing petitions, or ask you to recycle. I am going to make another suggestion. And it is a suggestion that will contradict everything you have been taught, everything that you have come to believe about yourself and our Western culture. It will undoubtedly be upsetting, seem crazy even. I am about to suggest that you to give up trust in experts and to begin to trust yourself . . .

It doesn't sound too upsetting yet, does it?

We exist in a time where nearly all of us in the West have been trained to put our trust in experts, most especially in the terminally schooled. In fact, most people who examine their lives in any depth will often find that from the moment they began formal schooling they were trained in a deep mistrust of their own perceptual capacities, of their own genius, of their capacity to feel, of their own ability to find solutions to the problems that face them, and our species. At the same time they often find they have been trained to believe that some undefined expert—someone *out there*—is better able to find solutions, possesses more genius, has more knowledge, and is in general more competent and thus more worthy of trust. And to them they have been trained to turn—and this is true even if they spend much of their life attaining advanced degrees themselves.

So, we reach a bifurcation in this book, a divergence of paths. One path is composed of the belief that the incredible edifice of Western schooling and reductive science and experts—a top-down control over all things—is the way we must approach the problems that face us. Or as Ken Wilber once put it . . .

It is science and only science
that can solve the problems facing us

I mean, it's the adult thing to do. Or as Mary Midgley describes it . . .

The notion of "primitive animism" comes from a familiar Enlightenment myth which compares the intellectual development of the human race to that of an individual. That myth gave the name "animism" to a supposedly childish "primitive" phase, followed, first by more organized religions, then by metaphysics, and finally, in the adult state, by science, which made all its forebears obsolete. Smaller, more "primitive" cultures were always more childish than larger ones, and non-Western cultures, similarly, were more childish than that of the West. Finally, all other Westerners were more childish than Western scientists, who emerged as the only truly adult members of the species.[1]

The alternate path I am suggesting is very different. It is composed of a deep belief and trust in the individual, a belief that all solutions must occur on the ground in the location where the problems are most manifest, that those solutions must be created by those who live in those locations, generated out of their own inherent genius and their own deeply human nature, which, of course, includes things like empathy, love, adaptability, intuition, spirituality, and their own unique form of reason.

I take the second road . . . and this book is an expression of that road, of the more than forty years that I have spent upon it, and of what I have found there. It is the road I am suggesting you explore for yourself.

Besides a barbarian, I am, in many respects, a child of the late-nineteenth and early-twentieth centuries, and my values have been shaped by those times. The United States in 1952 was a very different place than it is now and the threads of the old republic, and its values, were still vibrant then. Trust in the individual was still strong and the technocrats had not yet taken control. Vestiges of the great experiment of the American republic still remained. And that experiment? It will make you uncomfortable to hear it . . .

I can hear the objections now

The great experiment of the New World was that any person could engage in any profession at any time irrespective of prior training. There were no licensure boards, no laws prohibiting entry into any profession, no decades of schooling necessary to do work of any kind. And the structure of the government that was created at that time was intended to preserve that freedom of the individual.

I told you this would be upsetting

It was a complex and extremely brilliant creation;

and yes, there were problems . . .
but I am not talking about those now

it was built around trust in the inherent genius of individuals and a strong distrust of bureaucratic institutions and elites. The tremendous innovation that occurred in the century and a half after the republic's formation are a testament to its soundness.

In the years since I was born—and in my studies of the five decades preceding my birth—I have seen the degree of innovation that occurs in any area that is unregulated by government, schooling, and licensure. It is significant.

The innovations in physics, electricity, automobiles, and communication that occurred in the early part of the twentieth century were, for the most part, developed by the self- or (compared with our time) minimally-taught. Since then innovations in music, healthcare (massage, oriental medicine, herbalism, psychotherapy, midwifery), genre literature, computer technology, and sustainable agriculture (permaculture), as examples, have all been driven primarily by the unschooled, the unlicensed, the eccentrics who live outside the center. Anna Freud commented succinctly on this phenomenon when she stated (in 1968) that

> *When we scrutinize the personalities who, by self-selection, became*
> *the first generation of psychoanalysts we are left with no doubt*
> *about their characteristics. They were the unconventional ones, the*
> *doubters, those who were dissatisfied with the limitations imposed*
> *on knowledge; also among them were the odd ones, the dreamers,*
> *and those who knew neurotic suffering from their own experience.*
> *This type of intake has altered decisively since psychoanalytic train-*
> *ing has become institutionalised and appeals in this stricter form to*
> *a different type of personality. Moreover, self-selection has given*
> *way to the careful scrutiny of applicants, resulting in the exclusion*
> *of the mentally endangered, the eccentrics, the self-made, those with*

*excessive flights of imagination, and favouring acceptance of the
sober, well-prepared ones.*[2]

"The sober, well-prepared ones." It is important to understand that the
sober, well-prepared ones are not equipped constitutionally to deal with
nonlinearity. As Paul Krugman once put it, when talking about eco-
nomic nonlinearity, "Experience has made it painfully clear that men in
suits not only don't have any monopoly on wisdom, they have very little
wisdom to offer."[3] The writer Jenny Diski captures some of what is at the
core of the sober ones when she says that

> *They were the ones who never thought to doubt that everything
> they knew and thought was right and good and normal, that
> whatever they did not know or had not heard of was subversive
> and dangerous, and who had moral rectitude stamped, like
> Blackpool rock, through their unbending spines from coccyx to
> brain stem. . . . There was the same quivering, tight-lipped prissi-
> ness, the untroubled moral righteousness, a desire for the respect-
> able and normal so powerful [that it governed every movement of
> life].*[4]

The writer and psychologist Adam Phillips reaches deeper into its
absurdity when he reveals that

> *Psychoanalysts after Freud have to acknowledge that the founder of
> psychoanalysis was never properly trained . . . and there was no one
> to tell him whether what he was doing with his patients was appro-
> priate. That Freud was the first "wild" analyst is one of the difficult
> facts in the history of psychoanalysis. It is easy to forget that in what
> is still its most creative period—roughly between 1893 and 1939—
> when Freud, Jung, Ferenczi, Klein and Anna Freud herself were
> learning what they thought of as the "new science," they had no for-
> mal training. Later generations of analysts deal with their envy of
> Freud and his early followers by making their trainings increasingly
> rigorous, by demanding and fostering the kind of compliance—
> usually referred to as "conviction"—that tended to stifle originality.*

Psychoanalytic training became a symptom from which a lot of peo-
ple never recovered.[5]

Please understand. Those original people, they *self-selected*. (Or as Einstein put it, "true art is characterized by an irresistible urge.") That is
what people do who follow a deep, inner sense that there is something
they must do. It is the mark of those who follow their hearts, who follow
their natural interests. There is something inside them calling them to
a particular place, a particular kind of study, knowledge, and awareness.
Those that follow that inner urging, who find and never let go of golden
threads, are the ones who change everything.

And no, formalized schooling of the sort we have now can't support
such a thing. It is antithetical to its very nature.

Perhaps nothing captures this truth more powerfully than William Deresiewicz's "The Disadvantages of an Elite Education."

It didn't dawn on me that there might be a few holes in my educa-
tion until I was about 35. I'd just bought a house, the pipes needing
fixing, and the plumber was standing in my kitchen. There he was
. . . and I suddenly learned that I didn't have the slightest idea
what to say to someone like him. So alien was his experience to me,
so unguessable his values, so mysterious his very language, that I
couldn't succeed in engaging him in a few minutes of small talk
before he got down to work. Fourteen years of higher education and
a handful of Ivy League degrees, and there I was stiff and stupid,
struck dumb by my own dumbness. "Ivy retardation," a friend of
mine calls this. . . .

It's not surprising that it took me so long to discover the extent
of my miseducation, because the last thing an elite education will
teach you is its own inadequacy. As two dozen years at Yale and
Columbia have shown me, elite colleges relentlessly encourage their
students to flatter themselves for being there, and for what being
there can do for them. . . . To consider that while some opportuni-
ties are being created, others are being cancelled and that while

*some abilities are being developed, others are being crippled is,
within this context, not only outrageous, but inconceivable. . . .*

*My education taught me to believe that people who didn't go to
an Ivy League or equivalent school weren't worth talking to, regard-
less of their class. I was given the unmistakable message that such
people were beneath me. . . . I never learned that there are smart
people who don't go to elite colleges. . . . I never learned that there
are smart people who don't go to college at all.*[6]

Deresiewicz notes that his Ivy League students rarely take risks after
graduation, for they have never learned to fail and, as he comments, risk-
ing always entails failures along the way. His students are in fact so inculcated in one particular view of reality that they can't even see the risks
that need taking, can't even ask the big questions that a fully aware life
demands be asked. As Deresiewicz says, "We are slouching, even at elite
schools, toward a glorified form of vocational training."

*Indeed, that seems to be exactly what those schools want. There's a
reason elite schools speak of training leaders, not thinkers—holders
of power, not its critics. An independent mind is independent of all
allegiances, and elite schools, which get a large percentage of their
budget from alumni giving, are strongly invested in fostering insti-
tutional loyalty. As another friend, a third-generation Yalie says,
the purpose of Yale college is to manufacture Yale alumni. . . . [Yet]
being an intellectual begins with thinking your way outside of your
assumptions and the system that enforces them. But students who
get into elite schools are precisely the ones who have best learned to
work within the system, so it's almost impossible for them to see outside it, to see that it's even there. . . . The tyranny of the normal [is]
very heavy in their lives.*[7]

Still, he says, some students intentionally refrain from attending Ivy
League schools, often because they have a more independent spirit,
because they know they will not become educated there, only schooled.

They didn't get straight A's because they couldn't be bothered to give everything in every class. They concentrated on the ones that meant the most to them or on a single strong extracurricular passion or on projects that had nothing to do with school or even with looking good on a college application. . . . [They were] more interested in the human spirit than in school spirit.[8]

And it is from this eccentricity, this self-selection, this individuality, this capacity for thinking outside the assumptions of the system that change comes, that the different kind of thinking we need arises.

James Lovelock himself noted in his autobiography that he could never have done what he did had he trained similarly to the way so many scientists are now forced to do. He had, when he began, the freedom to design his own degree, to study in multiple disciplines, to learn from people who had themselves trained similarly. He was not forced into a narrow specialty. He had the freedom to follow where his heart led him. And he stubbornly remained outside the mainstream, an independent scientist. Lovelock comments that

I have been an explorer looking for new worlds, not a harvester from safe and productive fields, and life at the frontier has shown me that there are no certainties and that dogma is usually wrong. I now recognize that with each discovery the extent of the unknown grows larger, not smaller. The discoveries I made came mostly from doubting conventional wisdom, and I would advise any young scientist looking for a new and fresh topic to research to seek the flaw in anything claimed by the orthodox to be certain.[9]

In virtually every field in which great innovation has occurred, the early explorers were either untrained, minimally trained, unconventionally trained or trained in some other, unrelated, field. And all of them found flaws in the assertions of the orthodox.

It is the origin of Lynn Margulis's work
She refused to believe her teachers when they told her
the nuclei in the mitochondria were irrelevant

The great herbal renaissance that began in the U.S. in the late 1960s and early 1970s was initiated by people who were not trained in any formal way. Anna Freud's descriptions of the early psychoanalysts fits them perfectly—as it does the musicians of the 1960s and the computer geeks of the '70s and '80s.

And the permaculturists and the . . .

Thus we saw the greatest flowering of herbal knowledge and development in the Western world since the 1880s. Predictably, as the field grew, many of the early innovators began to seek licensure, to create organizations to govern practice, and to institute requirements for practice that they, themselves could never have met—and which many still cannot meet. They begin to seek the "sober, well-prepared ones." To get around the new requirements, they simply voted themselves the credentialing—after all it was *their* organization. (The same thing happened in psychoanalysis.) Few of them seem to see the contradiction in this, in the fact that it was the very lack of reductionist schooling and preset areas of study that allowed them to engage in so much innovation. They followed where their interests led them, where the Earth and their own hearts called them. And in so doing their inherent genius found what it was here to do, what it was here to say.

Some of them have told me that it was okay for them to do this, but that people now are too stupid to be allowed to. Because, you know, it was different then.

And yeah, they really said it . . .
But it is something I cannot accept
I cannot accept that you, who are reading this, are too stupid
to follow your own hearts, and in the process,
bring the solutions we need into the world.

As the early pioneers' gating channels narrow with age, as they actively seek to protect their lawns, as the more eccentric die off, more regulation occurs and innovation begins to grind to a halt. A conservative mind-set takes over; the field begins to experience a distortion of its original purpose. It becomes a battleground for the accumulation of money and power. In the latter part of the eighteenth century this exact problem was common in Europe, so here, as those in the colonies struggled to craft a new country . . . they did something different. They trusted the individual. Anyone was free to engage in any profession they wished. There was no licensure, no legal regulation, no top-down control.

But what about protecting the public?
What about safety?

The objections that are emerging in your mind to that statement are an indication of the depth of lack of trust in the individual in which you have been trained. It is, as well, an indication of the degree to which you have been trained to believe that experts can solve the problems facing us. And as well to believe that such training, such expertise, such licensure produces greater safety for the public. It doesn't.

What is really true
is that such processes can't protect the public
in reality, they can't

Analyses of licensure laws continually show that they do not produce more safety to the consumer. More deeply however, it is important to look at what that kind of orientation regarding the professions does in the real world. It, by its nature, prevents the discovery and creation of things like psychoanalysis. And just as with nonlinearity in living systems, there is a growing recognition in a number of quarters of this exact problem. Social scientist Nigel Clark comments that

> When confronted by claims of the self-enclosure of any political or social entity, we have learned to ask what is being excluded or marginalized by the act of demarcation: what is being disavowed on the inside and what is being banished to the outside.[10]

In this instance, it is human ingenuity and genius and the capacity for analogical thinking—for individual eccentricity—that is banished to the outside. The loss to the human community is considerable. As the writer and editor Jon Graham put it, "analogy can connect the body and mind, objective space and subjective space, and the animal plant and mineral realms in ways that logic cannot. It is the key to the groundbreaking correlations [Annie] Le Brun makes between the environmental degradation of our physical world and the ravages suffered by the imaginal realm of our minds. The relationship between the disappearance of the great mammals like the blue whale and the great rebels of times past is the same."[11]

There is an assumption that this banishment, this adoption of the sober, serious ones and their system of control, can produce safety. But part of what is left out of the top-down control mind-set is that all such systems are run by people, are composed of people, and all of them possess the same flaws that all people do, including the lust for power, prestige, and money.

Years of training, licensure boards, continuing education credits, and training based on reductive science do not in fact produce better or safer outcomes. And they never have. An analysis of outcomes shows it and the awareness of the flaws in the system in which we have been trained is becoming apparent to many. The primary outcomes in such systems are a significant increase in costs to the public and an incredible decrease in innovation . . . and, ultimately, as resistant bacteria show, great harm to the public.

This is why the health care system in the United States is the most expensive on Earth . . . and why its outcomes are so poor.

John Ioannidis of the Institute for Clinical Research and Health Policy Studies, Department of Medicine, at Tufts University published a rather remarkable article in August 2005; the title is interesting: "Why Most Published Research Findings are False." He comments that

Published research findings are sometimes refuted by subsequent evidence, with ensuing confusion and disappointment. Refutation and controversy is seen across the range of research designs from clinical trials and traditional epistemological studies to the most

modern molecular research. There is increasing concern that in modern research, false findings may be the majority or even the vast majority of published research claims. However, this should not be surprising. It can be proven that most published research claims are false.[12]

"Most published research claims are false." Ioannidis found that underneath the practice of science in the Western world lay not a solid foundation but a sandy beach. He noted that his research, focusing primarily on medicine, found in nearly every instance that "the studies were biased. Sometimes they were overly biased. Sometimes it was difficult to see the bias, but it was there." As David Freedman, in the *Atlantic*, reports . . .

Researchers headed into their studies wanting certain results—and lo, and behold, they were getting them. We think of the scientific process as being objective, rigorous, and even ruthless in separating out what is true from what we merely wish to be true, but in fact it's easy to manipulate results, even unintentionally or unconsciously. "At every step in the process there is room to distort results, a way to make a stronger claim or to select what's going to be concluded," says Ioannidis. "There is an intellectual conflict of interest that pressures researchers to find whatever it is that is most likely to get them funded."[13]

Even randomized, controlled trials were found to be heavily influenced by bias, to show what the researchers . . . and the funders . . . wanted them to show. Ioannides tested his findings by looking at forty-nine of the most highly regarded journal articles (and their research findings) in medicine in the previous thirteen years. These were the studies felt to be the most impeccable, best designed, and possessing the least chance of bias. He found that up to half of them were wrong or substantially exaggerated. Going further afield, Ioannides found that studies showing links between genetic structure and diseases, links that then led to specific treatments for anything from "colon cancer to schizophrenia have in the past proved so vulnerable to error and distortion that in some cases you'd have done about as well by throwing darts at a chart of the genome." He notes that "even when the evidence shows that a particular research idea is wrong, if you have thousands of scientists who have invested their careers in it, they'll continue to publish papers on it. It's like an epidemic, in the sense that they're infected with these wrong ideas, and they're spreading it to other researchers through journals."[14] An editorial in the prestigious journal *Nature* went so far as to say, "Scientists understand that peer review per se provides only a minimal assurance of quality, and that the public perception of peer review as a stamp of authentication is far from the truth."[15]

Ironically, considering the *Nature* editor's comments, Nobel Prize–winner Randy Schekman recently added his voice to the chorus with his article "How journals like *Nature, Cell,* and *Science* are damaging science: The incentives offered by top journals distort science, just as big bonuses distort banking." And those incentives? They are part of a growing problem; the journals are no longer forums for the publication of disinterested science but have become instead resources for the corporate accumulation of money and power. This is because, over the past several decades, most of the important journals have been acquired by large corporations who are now using that control to financially leverage their niche.

These corporations, unsurprisingly, are often found to have close ties to other corporate entities whose interests are affected by the research the journals print. It is no wonder then that as consolidation has progressed, the journals have begun to control what is allowed to appear in print as well as who can access it. They are, in essence, controlling what kind of research is done and the outcomes the papers report. This distorts not only research but the knowledge base science is presumed to rest upon.

As a brief look at the publishing giant Reed Elsevier shows, the income stream generated from this kind of journal control is massive.

Formed by the merger of Reed Publishing and Elsevier Scientific in 1993, Reed Elsevier is one of the largest publishers of science journals and academic texts in the world. In 2001 the company bought Harcourt Press (which already owned Academic Press). Numerous journals are published under these four imprints, giving Elsevier massive influence across a wide range of scientific disciplines. As consolidation like this has occurred, companies such as Elsevier have begun to significantly increase fees to universities and libraries for subscriptions. A single journal, which once cost as little as $200 per year, is now costing as much as $20,000. (This has caused many universities, such as the University of California, to stop subscribing.) The combined Reed Elsevier corporation, much of whose business occurs through online research, dwarfs other online juggernauts such as eBay and Amazon. Its annual revenues? Eight billion dollars, eight times eBay and over twice that of Amazon.

The company, as John Carlos Baez, a mathematical physicist at the University of California, notes, has engaged in numerous practices (besides price and market control) that raise serious concern. Two are, as he observes, "Elsevier's recent support of the Research Works Act, which would try to roll back the U.S. government's requirement that taxpayer-funded medical research be made freely available online. The six fake medical journals Elsevier created, which had articles that looked like peer-reviewed research, were actually advertisements paid for by the drug company Merck."[16]

In the first decade of the twenty-first century, in response to these kinds of problems, some thirty thousand scientists signed a pledge to only publish in, edit, review for, or subscribe to scholarly and scientific journals that agreed to unrestricted free distribution (open access). Unsurprisingly, for-profit publishers were not supportive. In consequence, academics and researchers throughout the world began to create freely available alternative publishing venues such as the Public Library of Science (PLoS).

Despite this, and whether or not corporate control of research and prestigious journals is inhibited, the problems inherent in disciplines run by human beings are unlikely to be eliminated (though, with focus, they can, to some extent, be minimized). As Paul Krugman has observed . . .

Many people seem to have a much-idealized vision of the academic process, in which wise and careful referees peer-review papers to make sure they are rock-solid before they go out. In reality, while many referees do their best, many others have pet peeves and ideological biases that at best greatly delay the publication of important work and at worst make it almost impossible to publish in a refereed journal.[17]

Scientists and researchers, nearly everyone forgets, are people, and they suffer the same limitations and problems all people do, irrespective of Ph.D. status. Greed is just one of them. Historian Steven Shapin, in his massive work *Never Pure,* has carefully tracked how science is, and always has been, an expression of unexamined cultural structures, relations, beliefs, and survival needs. It is shaped most commonly by the beliefs and attitudes of the culturally and socially powerful to mirror and spread those beliefs. As he relates . . .

> *The historical case for the existence of knowledge without prejudice is not good. Knowledge free of prejudice has not been obtained in historical practice, and it is probably impossible to obtain in principle. The Republic of Science seems rather to reflect the most widely distributed prejudices of its time and of its citizens. And, insofar as these are so widely distributed, they may appear to its citizens as no prejudices at all.*[18]

The same unexamined biases that encouraged scientists of the nineteenth and early twentieth centuries to find, for instance, that women, blacks, Jews, indigenous peoples (and dolphins, and plants and bacteria) were all inferior to Caucasian males; or to assert that the Earth is not alive; or that dissociated mentation is free of bias; or that linear reasoning is the way to true understanding of Universe are, and always will be, in play. It is not a patriarchal thing; it is a human thing. In consequence, science is not, never has been, and never can be value free. The truth is, science isn't all that different from anything else that humans do. It isn't the way to unbiased truth. It can't supply value-free, objective answers to the problems we face. It is not and never has been free of prejudicial presuppositions about the nature of the reality in which its practitioners are embedded. It is just a tool, and like all tools it has inherent limitations. It is useful for some things, not useful for others. Using it to solve our current problems is like using a hammer (if that's the only tool you have) when what you need is a screwdriver.

We can't solve problems
by using the same kind of thinking we used
when we created them.

Many supporters of science are uncomfortable with this kind of statement (especially from outsiders); they insist that the continual give and take that occurs in science ultimately reveals the errors that are present, that the strength of the field is that it corrects itself. In actuality, that is generally untrue.

In actuality, that is generally untrue.

Most of the refutations come from people outside the fold, the eccentrics who are following independent research interests and whose livelihood does not depend on funding. And even then, even though a wrong idea has been definitively proven to be inaccurate Ioannides found that it tended to persist as accepted truth for decades afterward. He has found that up to 90 percent of all medical research and subsequent practice is flawed, often seriously so. And this is not limited to medicine; other researchers have found similar outcomes in all fields of science, from physics to economics.

To paraphrase Paul Krugman (he was talking about economists), Western science has very much the psychology of a cult. Its devotees believe that they have access to a truth that generations of differently thinking humans have somehow failed to discern; they go wild at the suggestion that maybe they're the ones who have an intellectual blind spot. And as with all cults, the failure of prophecy—in this case the various utopian materialist fantasies—only strengthens the determination of the faithful to uphold the truth.[19]

People have been trained to believe that "science" is a foundational approach that, by its very nature, leads to accurate pictures of the world around us and that basing action on those pictures will lead to a better world. But science is only a tool and like all tools is only as good as its user. And scientists, irrespective of their background, are still only people, with all the problems, and limitations, that all people have. They are not, by definition, better people or better thinkers than anyone else you might meet on a crowded street.

Part of the reason for our current troubles is because the practice of what is called science has changed considerably, and not for the better, since the late 1800s and early 1900s.

It's now filled with the sober, well-prepared ones.

It was, once, the practice of what is more accurately natural philosophy. These were people, male and female, of all nationalities, degreed and non-degreed, who were interested in understanding the world in which they lived. They were the self-selected. As Michael Crichton comments . . .

> *For four hundred years since Galileo, science has always proceeded as a free and open inquiry into the workings of nature. Scientists have always ignored national boundaries, holding themselves above the transitory concerns of politics and even wars. Scientists have always rebelled against secrecy in research, and have even frowned on the idea of patenting their discoveries, seeing themselves as working to the benefit of all mankind. And for many generations, the discoveries of scientists did indeed have a peculiarly selfless quality.*

But in the late 1970s this began to change. As Crichton continues . . .

> *Suddenly it seemed as if everyone wanted to become rich. New companies were announced almost weekly, and scientists flocked to exploit genetic research. By 1986, at least 362 scientists, including 64 in the National Academy, sat on the advisory boards of biotech firms. The number of those who held equity positions or consultancies was several times greater.*
>
> *It is necessary to emphasize how significant this shift in attitude actually was. In the past, pure scientists took a snobbish view of business. They saw the pursuit of money as intellectually uninteresting, suited only to shopkeepers. And to do research for others, even at the prestigious Bell or IBM labs, was only for those who couldn't get a university appointment. . . . But that is no longer true. There are very few molecular biologists and very few research institutions free of commercial affiliations. The old days are gone. Genetic research continues, at a more furious pace than ever. But it is done in secret, in haste, and for profit.*[20]

And this is true not only in genetic research but in all fields of science, including, as examples, medicine, Earth system studies, and economics. In consequence, the entire practice of what we call science has been distorted considerably. *What* is studied, *who* is allowed to study it, the outcome of studies, what studies are made public, and how the accumulated knowledge is put into practice are all controlled by corporate interests—with the active participation of most researchers, and most universities. It doesn't really matter whether the outcomes benefit society, only that they make a profit. Things have gotten so bad in medicine that it moved Marcia Angel, M.D., to write . . .

> *It is no longer possible to believe much of the clinical research that is published, or to rely on the judgement of trusted physicians or authoritative medical guidelines. I take no pleasure in this conclusion, which I reached slowly and reluctantly over my two decades as an editor of* The New England Journal of Medicine.[21]

"It is no longer possible to believe much of the clinical research that is published . . . or to rely on the judgement of trusted physicians . . ." This is a very difficult statement to accept, and it applies to experts in nearly every field, including environmentalists, ecologists, and public safety advocates. Even such a prestigious environmental activist as David Suzuki has recognized the problem. "Environmentalism," he says, "has failed."[22] And it has failed for the same reasons that science is failing: reliance on dissociative mentation, uncorrected human limitations, unrestrained power and money, and top-down approaches.

I still remember the great public movement urging people (and businesses) to switch to plastic bags and abandon paper—a movement begun by "expert" environmental activists. And I remember their triumph—and that of the public—when paper was abandoned on the West coast. And I notice now, decades later, when plastic waste has become such a problem, that calls are emerging for banning plastic and going to paper.

> *And those reusable shopping bags? Turns out they are the perfect breeding ground for noroviruses. In fact, that is one of the major ways the virus now spreads among human communities. From the lettuce to the table to the intestine.*

The problems, as Einstein put it so well, come, in significant part, from *how* we think. And though we like to believe that the approach we are trained in here in the West is the best, it, in actuality, skews how we see and experience the world and in consequence skews any solutions we create. Analysis of research papers in the brain sciences (neuroscientists) have found significant biases in the work, just as they have been found in other areas of science. A lot of that bias occurs in what is studied.

Some 96 percent of behavioral science experimental subjects are from Western industrialized cultures who represent only 12 percent of the world population; 68 percent are Americans. Seventy percent of all psychology papers are produced in the U.S. while almost all psychological research is performed on graduate students, a group that represents 0.2 percent of the world population. Researchers take their results to be representative of the human species, but the outcomes are not actually generalizable to other populations.

In fact, deep examination of the brain and psychological sciences has found that populations in the West, most especially in the United States, are abnormal when compared to the majority of humans on the planet. Most people just don't think like we do . . . and they never have. As researchers Heinrich et al. put it, "The findings suggest that members of WEIRD societies [Western, Educated, Industrialized, Rich, and Democratic], including young children, are among the least representative populations one could find for generalizing about humans."[23] When comparing visual perception, fairness, cooperation, spatial reasoning, categorization, inferential induction, moral reasoning, reasoning styles, self-concepts and related motivations, Westerners, most especially Americans, are not like anybody else. For instance, *only* Westerners fall for the Müller-Lyer optical illusion, which tricks the viewer into thinking one line is longer than another, when in fact both are the same length.

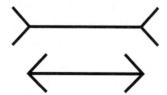

The Kalahari Bushmen, and all people in nonindustrial cultures, see the lines as the same length. We in the West fall for the illusion because we have spent our lives immersed in Euclidian landscapes. The sides of our buildings and corners of our ceilings give us familiarity with those types of lines. After a while we become lost in that framework. (And, interestingly, brain damaged people in the West can solve puzzles that the undamaged cannot. The disruption of linear reasoning forces the use of a different approach that, in itself, allows solutions to emerge.) Westerners, in fact, know very little about the mind of human beings but a lot about the mind of a very narrow subset of the human species, one that has spent its life immersed in an unnatural environment. Brain physiology in cultures other than the West is significantly different—as is *how* people think. The paradigm we are immersed in actually shapes physiology—what you are taught does in fact shape what you are able to perceive. And it alters brain structure accordingly.

> *It turns out that sensory gating is a lot more open in every other culture on Earth. The further away you get from industrialized reductionism, the more open they are. What those other cultures see is actually there. We in the West just can't perceive it.*

The primary activists (from scientists to environmentalists) for the planet are in Western industrial cultures, most especially in the United States. But they are in fact the least able to think differently, to actually abandon top-down approaches for the different kind of thinking Einstein urged us to find. The kind of thinking we are trained in here in the West just doesn't work in the real world. And the kinds of top-down solutions that so many people want to impose on the rest of the world are, in nearly all instances, coming from a position of dissociation, that is, I am *here,* the world is *over there.*

The world is seen as a static backdrop and we humans are the only actors upon the stage. And this is fundamental to the Western paradigm—it's inescapable. The solutions suggested are in nearly all instances static behaviors intended to be applied as a universal in all locations by all people. Such an approach will never work—though it is unlikely to stop people from trying it over and over again. The belief is that if we just keep doing the same thing but even more stringently it will eventually work. It won't.

*So, I am suggesting you give up the approach
and do something different*

The answers we need will never come from experts out there; *they
can't.* They will come from you—and people like you. Buckminster
Fuller recognized this long ago, when he said . . .

1. *It is my driving conviction that all of humanity is in peril of extinction
   if each one of us does not dare, now and henceforth, always to tell only
   the truth, and all the truth, and to do so promptly—right now.*
2. *I am convinced that humanity's fitness for continuance in the cosmic
   scheme no longer depends on the validity of political, religious, eco-
   nomic, or social organizations, which altogether heretofore have been
   assumed to represent the many.*
3. *Because, contrary to that, I am convinced that human continuance
   now depends entirely upon:*
   A. *The intuitive wisdom of each and every individual.*
   B. *The individual's comprehensive informedness.*
   C. *The individual's integrity of speaking and acting only on the indi-
      vidual's own within self-intuited and reasoned initiative.*
   D. *The individual's joining action with others, as motivated only by
      the individually conceived consequences of doing so.*
   E. *The individual's never joining action with others, as motivated
      only by crowd-engendered emotionalism, or by a sense of the
      crowd's power to overwhelm, or in fear of holding to the course
      indicated by one's own intellectual convictions.*[24]

Bucky understood that the systems that are in place are creations
of the old thinking, of the old paradigm. And he understood that
such systems need to be abandoned, for they can never prepare us for
the future that we now face, nor respond to the demands of our time.
We need the eccentrics, the dreamers, the unconventional ones, the
doubters, those who are dissatisfied with the limitations imposed on
knowledge. They are the ones who can find solutions that the existing
systems cannot.

In 2012, scientists who had been struggling for over a decade to find the molecular structure of an AIDS enzyme gave up. The methods they were using to find the structure, as they put it, "just didn't work." So, in desperation they turned the problem over to the internet and the gaming community. "To the astonishment of scientists," as reporters put it, the problem was solved in **ten** *days.*[25] *And in 2012 a 16-year-old solved a mathematical problem that had stumped mathematicians for 30 years. When the boy found out there was no solution he just refused, he said, to accept that it was so. So, he decided to "have a go" at solving it. He said the only reason he did so was "schoolboy naivety."*[26]

The Universe is a nonlinear, self-organized system. The Earth is a nonlinear self-organized system embedded within that larger system. Outcomes *can't* be predicted by using a top-down approach. The analysis has to happen on the ground, in the moment, by people who are in relationship with and attending to that particular location. As Nigel Clark notes, "many of the ordering and controlling imperatives that were once definitive of modernity are now known to unleash cascades of unforeseen consequences: by-products that arise out of the sheer complexity attained in our interchanges with the biophysical world."[27]

We are in the midst of a paradigm shift. One that is finally beginning to force us to abandon as foundational the Newtonian view of the universe as a place of predetermined, linear, cause-and-effect forces as well as the thermodynamic view that believed everything is sliding inexorably down into an inactive, featureless, equilibrium. As Clark comments, "the new view affords the cosmos an ongoing capacity to give rise to new structures, processes, and potentialities, a break with determinism that implies, as physicist Paul Davies points out, that the universe is intrinsically unpredictable . . . abrupt or discontinuous transformation is something we should expect.

"In the real world," he observes, "there will always be some intrusion that ripples the surface of reasoned judgement . . . symmetry is broken and uniqueness asserts itself. . . . And it is that outside, leaking or bursting back in, that will sooner or later upset the dreams of a more evenhanded and regulated existence."[28] The "static" background *acts*, linear predictability fails, and as Jacques Derrida notes the still surface of the pond is shattered, "an *irruption* [takes place] that punctures the horizon, *interrupting* any performative organization, any convention, or any context that can be or could be dominated by a conventionality."[29] Conventional approaches, approaches based on a linear analysis of a (nonexistent) static background, will now, always fail.

It is the unruly masses that are most able to respond to such discontinuous transformations, that can engage with the unruly Earth and the unpredictablity of Universe. These are the ones who will "give rise to new structures, processes, and potentialities, [and] break with determinism."

It is the eccentrics, the outsiders, those who have opened sensory gating channels and are willing to look deep into the scenario in which they are embedded who will find new structures and potentialities. That place of touching is where engagement with the world *as it is* will occur. That is where the old forms will be abandoned and new approaches found. It will not be in schools or in established degree programs. It will not be in government or in NGO hierarchies of "let-us-help-you-irrespective-of-what-you-think-you-need." It will not be in old forms. It will come out of individual human beings and their love of place, their need, and their genius.

So . . . my suggestion is not for more studies, not for more government grants, not for trusting experts to solve the problems that face us. It is for you to follow your own genius, for you to find in yourself the still small spark of understanding that, with care, blossoms into genuinely new solutions to what you yourself see as problems. It is not about top-down solutions forced on the world's populations by people whose desire more often than not is for control over others, but about each individual doing what he or she understands must be done by themselves in the location in which they themselves live.

This is in fact what Gaia does. Gaia generates organisms out of the ecological matrix of the planet to fulfill certain functions. And Gaia instills in each of those organisms a drive to fulfill that function. But *how* each organism responds, how each organism actually fulfills that function is up to them. They have the ability to choose. Gaia trusts the individual genius of each organism, to innovate, to respond, to create solutions to the individual events that each organism experiences. There is, in fact, no other way for the system to work, for homeodynamis to be retained, for the balance point to be maintained.

Bucky understood that only *you* know what it is that you should do in response to the challenges of our times. And he understood that Gaia speaks through the work that each of you is given, that deep inside you some part of you knows just what it is that you should be doing. And he understood that that thing in you, telling you what to do, is an expression of Gaia, speaking through the movements of your life. And that only if you trust that thing can the solutions to the challenges that face us be successfully met.

If we want to do something effective to address the problems that face us, then we must begin to use a different way of thinking than the thinking we used when the problems were created. That means we *have to use a different kind of thinking.* That means stepping outside the normal channels of thought, of questioning basic assumptions, of actually becoming different in the self. Ultimately, it means becoming barbarian.

19
BECOMING
BARBARIAN

A person suffers if he or she is constantly being forced into the statistical mentality and away from the road of feeling.

ROBERT BLY

There is less danger of a cleft reality experience arising in a natural environment. In field and forest, and in the animal world sheltered therein, indeed in every garden, a reality is perceptible that is infinitely more real, older, deeper, and more wondrous than everything made by people, and that will yet endure, when the inanimate, mechanical, and concrete world again vanishes, becomes rusted and fallen into ruin. In the sprouting growth, blooming, fruiting, death, and regermination of plants, in their relationship with the sun, whose light they are able to convert into chemically bound energy in the form of organic compounds, out of which all that lives on our earth is built; in the being of plants the same mysterious, inexhaustible eternal life energy is evident that has also brought us forth and takes us back again into its womb, and in which we are sheltered and united with all living things.

ALBERT HOFMANN

There was once a man who was terribly afraid that there were monsters under his bed, so much so that he could not sleep. In desperation he finally went to see a psychiatrist who explained that, yes, he could help him with the problem, but it would take some time. So, for four years the man explored his childhood and his marriage and his psychological problems but to no avail; the problem remained. In disgust, the man eventually told the psychiatrist that he was quitting. The psychiatrist became pretty insistent that the man continue, that sooner or later what they are doing would take care of the problem, but the man looks at the psychiatrist, holding his eyes intently, and says, "No, I am not doing this any more. It is useless. I am going to do something else."

A few weeks later the psychiatrist sees the man in the supermarket and the guy looks great. "Wow," he says, "you look great, what have you been doing?"

"I went to see someone else, a guy that lives down my street," the man said, "and he cured me in one session."

"One!" says the incredulous psychiatrist. "How did he do that?"

"Easy," says the man. "He told me to cut the legs off my bed."

*I*t is common in our Western world for people to speak of things they have *thought* about ("Alan Turing was really amazing, he figured out that . . ."), but it is rare for them to speak of the interior of a world that they themselves have experienced, even if it is their own interior world.

Unless of course it's their story of an abusive childhood

It is considered improper in our time for anyone seeking to understand the world to talk of their feeling response to what they experience in their explorations. And should they try to do so anyway, the words usually come out stilted, folded in uncertain ways, wrinkled, shorn of depth. The deformation comes from pressure of culture to make sure that the words used in communication are devoid of feeling, that they are rational, reasonable, unemotional. That they remain a form of dissociated mentation.

Dissociated mentation has become the hallmark of the reasonable man—of the reputable scientist. Somewhere along the way our human capacity to feel became suspect and, in an irrational drive for reasonableness, it was abandoned. In consequence, most people have lost not only the response of the heart to what is presented to the senses but the ability to speak of the heart's responses to the touch of the world upon them. Our language becomes enfeebled, as do our communications. The historian John Ralston Saul, in his remarkable book *Voltaire's Bastards: The Dictatorship of Reason in the West* (Vintage, 1992), comments on the effects of this when he notes that

> *The undermining of universal language, in large part by the dialects of expertise, has meant that we can't turn to the word to steady ourselves. Instead, the writers and their pens, having invented the Age of Reason, are now its primary prisoners and so are unable to ask the right questions, let alone to break down the imprisoning linguistic walls of their own creation. . . . Yet to argue against reason means arguing as an idiot or an entertainer who seeks only to amuse. The structures of argument have been co-opted so completely by those who work for the system that when an individual reaches for the words and phrases which he senses will express his case, he finds that they are already in active use in the service of power. This now amounts to a virtual dictatorship of vocabulary. It isn't really surprising that a society based upon structure and logic should determine the answer to most questions by laying out the manner in which they are posed. Somehow we must do what Voltaire once did . . . we must rediscover how to ask simple questions about ourselves.*[1]

And perhaps one of the simplest questions we must ask ourselves is *how* does this life I am in *feel* to me? How does this job feel? How does this house feel? How does this denuded forest feel? How does this relationship feel? How do these clothes feel? How does this food feel? In fact, the question to ask every minute of every day is "*How* does this (whatever it is) *feel* to me?" For it is our feeling sense that tells us the nature of the environment in which we find ourselves. It is as crucial as that other neglected sense, the sense of taste, and as informative about what is happening to us. As Alice Walker once put it . . .

The United States should have closed down and examined its every intention, institution, and law on the very first day a black woman observed that her collard greens tasted like water. Or when the first person of any color observed that store-bought tomatoes tasted more like unripened avocados than tomatoes. The flavor of food is one of the clearest messages the Universe ever sends to human beings; and we have now eaten poisoned warnings by the ton.[2]

But it is not only our food that has lost its interior richness but our surroundings. We have also eaten poisoned fields of feeling by the ton. If you truly begin to ask yourself *how* the store you are in feels to you as you shop for tasteless tomatoes, or *how* the office of the physician you are in *feels* to you, or *how* the pill you are about to take *feels* to you, or *how* the school you send your children to *feels* to you, or *how* the environmental article you are reading *feels* to you, you will begin to discover that something is amiss in the world—just as amiss as the lack of taste of commercial tomatoes or peaches or the apples inappropriately called red delicious. You will also begin to reclaim the interior of your own life. As e. e. cummings once put it . . .

A poet is somebody who feels, and who expresses his feelings through words. This may sound easy. It isn't. A lot of people think or believe or know they feel—but that's thinking or believing or knowing; not feeling. And poetry is feeling—not knowing or believing or thinking.

Almost anybody can learn to think or believe or know, but not a single human being can be taught to feel. Why? Because whenever you think or you believe or you know, you're a lot of other people but the moment you feel, you're nobody-but-yourself.[3]

"The moment you feel, you are nobody-but-yourself." This means what you really feel, not what you have been *taught* to feel. And it is in that central core of the self, where your real feelings reside, that what is most important exists. As the poet William Stafford described it . . .

In your life—the center of it, not the part for earning a living, or the part that gains you notice and credit, or even the part that leads others to like you—but in the central self are feelings so important and personal that the rest of the world cannot glimpse who you are and what is happening, deep in there, where it is you alone.[4]

Feeling is not the same as emotion, though they are connected. Feeling is the thing that happens when you walk into a restaurant, suddenly stop, look at your friend, and say, "This place feels funny, let's leave." Emotion is when someone steps on your toe and you get mad, or a lion jumps out of the bushes and you get scared, or your best friend dies and you grieve. Feeling is the thing that happens when you walk into the house, expecting someone to be home, and suddenly realize that no one is there. An empty house *feels* different from one that is not empty. And this kind of feeling is what Barbara McClintock was speaking of when she said that to do what she did

You must have a feeling for the organism

And this kind of feeling is what Gaian researcher Stephan Harding was talking about when he said . . .

Participatory holistic science is more than just an intellectual stance—it involves a radical shift in our fundamental perception of nature. The shift is primarily experiential rather than intellectual.[5]

This shift entails an experiential movement from dissociated mentation to the use of the feeling sense as a primary aspect of cognition.

It is difficult, in times such as these, to adequately convey that this one thing, the loss of the feeling sense, is the root of so much of the trouble in our world . . . or that the way out of our predicament is its reclamation. It is the foundation upon which all other solutions rest. For when you feel, you are nobody but yourself. As Judy Garland once put it, it's better to "be a first-rate version of yourself rather than a second-rate version of somebody else." And it is the unique you that we need now, not second-rate versions of Spock or Data or Dawkins.

To think differently means to think *differently*. It means giving up dissociated mentation. It means diving into the heart of the world and

finding out for yourself what is there. It then means speaking of, and acting upon, what you have found. And more than what you have found,
what you *felt* during the journey. For the feelings that you have as the
world touches you and as you touch the world are unique to you.

> *The greatest act of disobedience in which you can engage*
> *is to begin to feel again*
> *to ask yourself every minute of every day*
> *every time you see something new in your field of vision*
> How does it feel?

Inevitably, this means becoming barbarian, that is, someone not civilized.
    If you look at its Latin root, the word "civilized" is a modification of
the word "civil." Civil means "of or pertaining to citizens." Citizen means
"of the cities" and thus to be civilized means "to become of the cities."
All it originally meant was a New Yorker. But the *Oxford English Dictionary* now defines it as:

> *To bring out of a state of barbarism, to instruct in the arts of life,*
> *and thus to elevate on the scale of humanity.*

Thus the evolutionary escalator emerges once again.

> *the concept is pervasive you know,*
> *it's **in** everything*

This modern definition emerges out of social Darwinism—an inescapable side effect of the neo-Darwinist model—and views culture along a
range of development similar to that of species. In other words, once we
rose from the slime

> *Martha!*

slowly we turned, and step by step we lived first as dirty savages in caves
afraid of lions and stuff, then roved in hunter-gatherer tribes hardly ever
washing, finally discovered agriculture,

Geesus, about time

began to develop cities, writing, Bic pens—so no more quill sharpening—
multisyllable words, printing presses, gossip columnists, antibiotics, airplanes, axis-of-evil, alliteration, and Ph.D. degrees. "To elevate on the
scale of humanity."

Barbarian comes from a Greek root that means "unintelligible
speech." In essence, it simply meant "them" rather than "us," an outsider,
somebody that doesn't talk like us. By extension it came to mean somebody that doesn't act like us.

> *The word "barb" also means beard, an unshaven state*
> *Thus, a barber deals with barb*
> *So, not only funny talking but hairy*

Barbarian had these same sorts of meanings for the Romans but over
time it came to have a more specific meaning, that is, someone not of
Rome, someone not sophisticated. And when the Christians took over
the Roman empire after its collapse, it came to mean a heathen—a pagan,
someone not of the Christian faith. To the Christians the Romans were
barbarians . . .

> *kind of a what goes around comes around sort of thing*

Barbarian in essence means someone not of the cities, someone with
wildness inside them, someone unshaven, someone whose speech is
unintelligible, someone who is a pagan, a heathen. Pagan, to take this all
the way home, was a term that came into use once Christianity finally
had control of the Roman cities. It literally means "villager, rustic." In
other words, the old Roman beliefs were still held in the villages outside
the cities. Heathen is similar; it means a person of the heath. And heath
means "uncultivated land, wilderness." A heathen is someone of the wilderness, not of the cities, someone with wildness inside them.

The Earth, by definition, is not of the cities . . .

> *Do you understand that?*

Gaia *is* wilderness. Gaia is the Earth ecosystem functioning with its wild-ness intact. When this work is taken up, when you begin shifting your perception—as a way of life—when you begin a different kind of think-ing, a Gaian way of thinking, by definition you begin to become "not of the cities." A certain wildness begins to re-enter the self. Speech begins to change. A deep connection with the sacredness and intelligence of the Earth begins. Pagan sensibilities recur. You begin to become "of the heath," wild, once more.

Do you understand what I mean here?

This work changes those who do it. There is no escaping that. And the more you change, the more your speech will become unintelligible to those who live in cities, to those who have advanced degrees, those who use the conventional thinking that got us into this mess to begin with. You will begin speaking of things that those in cities cannot, by definition, understand. You will begin to "know the innermost weave of the world," as Goethe described it, to "witness its dynamics and creation." And your words will begin to take on a depth that truly is alien in our time.

Though you should realize
that there will also be those who thirst for them.

You begin then to enter the world that myth and fairy tale speak of. And we all know how fairy tales begin: "Once upon a time" they say. And that is an important beginning. For in that moment the dreamer deep inside us awakens to a signal as old as humankind. The dreamer knows immediately that important invisibles are going to be discussed. So a fairy tale might begin with "once upon a time" and then say "in a certain land, in a certain kingdom." And that is the right and true next line, for the land that we are traveling to cannot be found in this world.

To make the point even clearer, the storyteller might also say: "On this Earth there are five continents, we are now going to the sixth" or "our planet has six oceans, we are now going to the seventh." For the thing about fairy tales is that they happen simultaneously in two worlds, this world and the invisible world that lies underneath and behind this one. And that other continent, that other ocean is located in the invisible world.

If you are a literalist you will have trouble with this, you will have trouble with everything I am saying. You will try to turn it all into a metaphor—but it is not. For our planet has six oceans—and we are now going to the seventh.

* * *

Once upon a time in a certain land, in a certain kingdom, there lived a young man and woman who met and fell in love. They were happy as all young people who meet and fall in love are, and before long they decided to marry.

The young man's father is a merchant, the young man his assistant. So the prospects for the young couple are good.

> *And we know when we hear this that the young man will often be away from home, know already that the male will be absent in a particular kind of way, though of course this knowledge is not in our conscious minds. It is something the dreamer inside us understands from signals in the story's beginning.*

Well, the merchant is happy for his son and he gives the couple on their wedding day a small cottage sitting at the edge of the forest.

> *Again, some new knowledge comes into the story but this time it percolates upward enough that we feel something different. Such a forest, next to such a cottage, is the place where the ancient deeps of the world and the human world touch. Important things always happen at such places of contact and the dreamer inside us knows it. It is at this point we feel something moving inside us, some important invisible begins to emerge into this world.*

So . . .

Once upon a time in a certain land, in a certain kingdom, there lived a young man and woman who met and fell in love. They were happy as all young people who meet and fall in love are, and before long they decided to marry. The young man's father is a merchant, the young man his assistant, so the prospects for the young couple are good. The merchant is happy for his son and he gives the couple on their wedding day a small cottage sitting at the edge of the forest.

The house is surrounded by a small wooden fence, but the fence and the gardens and the house itself have all been a bit neglected. So the young couple spend a lot of time making everything beautiful again. They don't have much money, but they are happy and they laugh a lot as they create their new life together.

And it comes as no surprise that in a few years they one day find they are to have a child.

There is almost always a child in fairy tales. And the sex of the child doesn't really matter. The child can be female as in Cinderella or male as in the Maiden King. The most important thing is that there is a child. And in this fairy tale it turns out that the child is a girl.

Now the young couple are filled with joy and happiness at the birth of their child and the family is a happy one. And though the father is often absent with his work, there is great love given and received between everyone.

From the beginning the young mother takes the girl child with her everywhere. The mother had, over time, turned the land around the house into bountiful gardens in which much of their food was raised. She was also wise in the ways of simples and medicinal plants, for she had learned these things from her mother as her mother had learned from hers before her.

And as her mother had done with her, the woman began to teach her young daughter about gardens and medicinal plants. And from time to time on very special occasions they would go together into the forest by their home for certain plants that could only be found there.

From the beginning the mother warned the girl not to go too deeply into the forest for there were things in the forest, she said, that were very ancient and powerful and were better left undisturbed. So, on these trips into the forest they would only go in a little way, and early on the mother showed the girl the boundaries she should not go beyond.

*And of course, at this point in the story, we know that eventually
the girl is going to go deeper into the forest, don't we?*

Now the mother showed the girl all the plants she knew in the forest,
all the ones useful as simples. And she taught her how they should be
harvested and used for medicine. There was also one special plant that
the mother said the young girl should always look for, for it was very rare
and very hard to find. But it was one of the most powerful of medicines
and much to be desired. The mother described the plant in detail and
she made the young girl promise that if she ever found such a plant she
would come and get her immediately.

Now as the young girl grew older she became more adept at the
work and the mother allowed her to wander on her own in the forest
during their forays to find herbs. And one day, as always happens in fairy
tales, the young girl went just a bit too far into the forest.

As we all knew she would.

It was then, of course, that she found, for the first time, the plant her
mother had told her about. And as she had promised she went and found
her mother and took her to the place where the plant was growing.

A look passed between them that said everything that needed to be
said about the girl going outside the boundaries, but the mother did not
scold her. And very carefully she showed her daughter how to harvest the
plant.

The little girl dug up the plant and when she had it out of the soil
she found to her surprise that the root looked very much like a tiny
person. There were arms and legs and a tiny head. And there were eyes
even though they were closed. The root was all wrinkled and brown and
seemed as ancient as the forest itself.

The mother explained that the root was the most powerful part of
the plant but that whenever a young girl found her first of these plants
she must keep that root for her very own and she must keep it with her
for the rest of her life.

"But what will I do with it?" the little girl asked her mother.

And her mother looked at her with eyes of love and said, "In time you will know, my child. For each of us who travels this path finds such a root. In your time of greatest need you will understand, as each of us have before you, its purpose."

Now it was not long after this that the mother became ill. And no matter what anybody did the mother weakened more and more with each passing month and eventually she died.

The father grieved a long time but as he still had to work he had neighbors and friends help with his daughter when he was gone—and so time passed. But eventually, as always happens, he fell in love again and one day he brought his new bride home to the little house by the forest.

We know what is going to happen now don't we? Because the step-mother is a very ancient part of fairy tales and the dreamer inside us recognizes her for what she is whenever she appears. That part of us knows what she portends; trouble is not far away. Trouble always has to come from somewhere in a fairy tale. In this one it comes from the stepmother.

At first the stepmother was kind but slowly she began to change. Soon she insisted that all the gardens around the house be torn out and that the yard be landscaped like those of the rich people in town. She began to insist that she have more expensive dresses, for she has no desire to dress in simple clothes. And of course, every day when the father is gone, the little girl is forced to work for the stepmother. She is forced to spend much of her time on her knees, scrubbing the floors of the house and washing the windows and keeping weeds out of the yard.

And every night she cries herself to sleep, thinking of her mother, holding tightly to the root she gathered so long ago.

Now one of the difficult things about these kinds of fairy tales, something that has always troubled me, is the blindness of the good father. It's clear from the story that he loves his little girl, yet he brings a cruel stepmother into the house and never seems to notice what is happening. When I was young I never could understand it. If he loves his little girl so much, why doesn't he do something to help her? And the reason why he does not, it turns out, is one of the great teachings in this kind of fairy tale.

Because we live in literal times we have forgotten the teachings of the good father who cannot see. And we have forgotten the teachings of the cruel stepmother. And we have forgotten the teachings of the root that was found in the forest.

That is why these kinds of fairy tales were created. They hold our collective memories of the important teachings of those things. Those long-ago storytellers who created fairy tales understood that all things possess a shadow side. So they shaped fairy tales to hold those understandings.

When they told a story about a wise king who had a foolish and simple-minded son, they were going someplace in particular. It often turned out that when the wise king died and the foolish and simple-minded son became king, there was an evil councilor who shaped the son's rule. And that rule became evil and great harm was done to the people of that land.

What the storytellers are telling us in a tale like that is a story about the shadow side of the masculine. Not the healthy male, not what might be called the patriarchal, but rather the shadow side of the masculine, what might be better termed patriarchalism.

That the simple-minded and foolish son's father was not, in our world, a wise king but merely an average one does not alter the story's relevance for the years of the Bush presidency. Such stories are meant to teach us about the shadow side of things, and about our responsibility toward them.

The wicked stepmother, of course, is a repeating character in fairy tales. And she is about the shadow side of the feminine, just as the evil councilor is about the shadow side of the masculine. In such tales the good mother who died is code for the positive side of the feminine, what you might call its healthy expression, something that could best be termed the matriarchal. It is this part of the feminine that most of us knew in our mother's womb, perhaps the part of our mother that truly was happy to see us the day we were born. The stepmother is code for the shadow side of the feminine, something that more accurately better be called matriarchalism.

In reality what happened is that the mother did not die nor did the father remarry. Slowly over a long period of time the mother changed. The shadow side of the feminine became predominant. And that is one of the great teachings of this kind of tale.

All of us have seen this. All of us have had friends we knew when we were young, when we were teenagers perhaps. Friends who were truly joyful who then, as life progressed, became bitter because of wounds they received. Or who, for some reason, simply forgot who they are and why they are here. Tales such as these are meant to teach us about exactly that change. They hold our memories of the shadow side, a shadow side that any of us can choose at any time to follow.

And the good father who cannot see? He makes more sense now, doesn't he? The change is slow and the father doesn't want to see what is happening. Or perhaps the change is so slow he just doesn't notice. He truly is a good man, but one of the oldest teachings of all is that good men can do evil things simply because they refuse to see what is happening right in front of them. By their blindness and their silence they acquiesce to evil.

Cinderella is a perfect example of this kind of story. The two step-sisters, of course, are not stepsisters but Cinderella's real sisters who have been corrupted by the shadow side of the feminine. In our story the good mother and her child share love and closeness while spending time with plants. The stepmother however is concerned with appearances. How her yard looks and her clothes. She begins to value surface literalisms more than invisibles. We can always tell the movement of the shadow side when literalisms become more important than invisibles.

Another important code in these kinds of tales is that the girl is forced to clean the house over and over again. And she may be beaten or censored for doing a poor job of it or for tearing her dress. This kind of cleaning is always about getting rid of the ancient powers of the world. It is about removing Earth from the human realm. It is an attempt to get rid of the uncertainty that is present in all natural systems, an attempt to control the nonlinearity of Nature, to place upon it a static system of behavior in order to provide a kind of predictable security or safety. And of course Cinderella, like our little girl, spends much of her time cleaning and scrubbing as well.

The struggle that Cinderella goes through is the same one the girl in our story is struggling with. The wholeness of her nature, what you might call the 360-degree personalty that all children have when young, is under assault by the shadow side of the feminine. The tales don't really tell us why such an assault occurs. But perhaps it is because the mother has lost touch with the healthy child in herself, perhaps after too long a time of not taking care of her own needs. And now that she has lost it in herself she can no longer bear to see it in her child.

These stories are always about the shadow side and its assault on the healthy child. And they are about how the still uncorrupted child deals with that assault.

We know when we hear fairy tales such as this one that wrong things are occurring. We know immediately that what the stepmother is doing is wrong. We know that there is something in the father's blindness that is not right. We know that the child is in danger and we want to help her so that she does not forget who she is. But when we experience these things in *this* world, they are much more difficult to see. It is much harder for us to trust our feeling sense and even harder for us to say "stop" to those who are doing these things.

That is why such tales are necessary. They hold the memories of our ancestors of just these kinds of teachings. They also offer solutions, if we will listen.

Now in this story I have been telling you, every night the young girl goes to bed and weeps. She cries for the mother who died and for the pain of her daily life and she holds to her breast the root she dug so long ago. She sends to it all her pain and prayers and as often happens in tales such as these, one day something happens, one day the universe responds.

On that day, the forest man that the root really is opens his eyes and looks right at the little girl and says, "I have heard you these long nights. And as your mother told you long ago, in your deepest need you would understand my purpose in your life. I am here to help you." And at this the little girl cries and cries and says, "Tell me what to do! I am so unhappy. I want things to be the way they were."

And the forest man looks deeply into her eyes and says, "You must go into the ancient forest and there you will find what you seek."

Now, of course, we knew something like this was going to happen from the beginning of the story. A journey into the depths of the forest must always take place. The dreamer inside us knew it from the forest's first mention. In the story of Cinderella the fairy godmother is an expression of the ancient powers of the world. In our story it is the forest man who was first found in unactivated form as the root of the rare plant. And as is always true, it is our need that calls on such powers to come alive, to speak to us, and to help us, to help us not become the enemy of our souls or our memories.

The little girl, of course, is astonished by the root coming alive and speaking to her. And she is also afraid. Her mother is gone, the forest is old and deep and ancient powers live there that are better left undisturbed. How then can she go into that world by herself? She is too young, too weak, too scared to do so.

Yet the situation in which she finds herself is a terrible one. Like all of us do at the crucial turning points in our lives, she finds herself between two very difficult choices, one brutally painful that will kill her spirit in the end, the other terrifying, one that has an outcome not possible to know.

In that moment a divergence of paths emerges, and it is free will that determines which path is taken. But one thing is true, each demands a price. It just depends on what price you are willing to pay . . . and what you wish to receive in return.

CODA

A Different Kind of Thinking

ॐ

In the Western world visionaries and mystics are a good deal less common than they used to be. . . . In the currently fashionable picture of the universe there is no place for valid transcendental experiences. Consequently those who have had what they regard as valid transcendental experiences are looked upon with suspicion, as being either lunatics or swindlers. To be a mystic or visionary is no longer creditable.

ALDOUS HUXLEY

That I might know the innermost weave
of the world, witness
its dynamics and creation
and stop rummaging about in words.

GOETHE

Between the conscious and the unconscious,
the mind has put up a swing:

all Earth creatures, even the supernovas,
sway between these two trees,
and it never winds down.

Angels, animals, humans, insects by the million,
also the wheeling sun and moon;
ages go by, and it goes on.

Everything is swinging: heaven, Earth, water, fire,
and the secret one slowly growing a body.
Kabir saw that for fifteen seconds,
and it made him a servant for life.

KABIR

Epilogue

TO SEE THE SHIMMER
OF INFINITY IN THE
FACE OF THE OTHER

There was once a woman who was so trapped inside Cartesian dualism that she could find no way out. Her life felt so meaningless and she was so unhappy that she became one of Carl Jung's patients. Despite her seeking help, she knew, beyond doubt, that there was no reality other than the reductive one in which she was trapped. She continually responded to Jung's discussions of the unconscious with disbelief. But one day she came to her session and related a dream she had had the night before . . .

She had dreamed that she had been given a golden scarab beetle, a powerful symbol of death and rebirth in ancient Egypt. For some reason she could not let go of the feelings of significance she had about the beetle and she asked Jung to tell her about its meaning. Just as Jung was about to respond, he heard a gentle, insistent tapping at the window behind him. He says then that . . . "I turned round and saw a fairly large flying insect that was knocking against the window-pane from outside in an obvious attempt to get into the dark room. That seemed to me very strange. I opened the window immediately and caught the insect in the air as it flew in. It was a scarabaeid beetle, or common rose-chafer (Cetonia aurata), whose gold-green colour most nearly resembles that of a golden scarab. I handed the beetle to my patient with the words, 'Here is your scarab.'"

C. G. Jung

There are experiences most of us are hesitant to speak about, because they do not conform to every day reality and defy rational explanation. These are not particular external occurrences, but rather events of our inner lives, which are generally dismissed as figments of the imagination and barred from our memory. Suddenly, the familiar view of our surroundings is transformed in a strange, delightful, or alarming way: it appears to us in a new light, takes on special meaning. Such an experience can be as light and fleeting as a breath of air, or it can imprint itself deeply upon our minds.

Albert Hofmann

In the magical universe there are no coincidences and there are no accidents.

William Burroughs

There was an excitement in the air that could almost be tasted. Five thousand of us jammed together in Winterland for the music, for a journey that would last all night, a journey that began with Quicksilver Messenger Service, was soaring now with Jefferson Airplane, and would end with the Grateful Dead. A journey that would last a lifetime.

I was barely eighteen and the man I saw moving through the crowd seemed so very old to me. He was dressed as we all were then . . . in bright colors and flowing clothes. His trousers were green and loose and comfortable over hand-cobbled leather shoes. His shirt was hidden beneath a coat of rainbow colors. And that coat . . . a textured felt, the body of it dark blue, the big pockets on the side red, the lapels an emerald green. There was bright embroidery, twinings of yellow, red, purple, green running along the front edges of the jacket, encircling the buttons and button holes. And underneath the twining embroidery, very hard to see, was hidden a small plastic tube.

Every so often, his hand, leathered and brown, would go to the bottom edge of the coat and press it in a certain way. Then, cupped, filled with secrets, the hand would rise again, and pass something to people in the crowd.

I watched him stop and stand a few feet in front of me, begin to speak with two young women in the crowd. I can still remember how hot it was, the August air of San Francisco even more humid from the dancing and sweating and breathing of so many people in one enclosed space. The women had long chestnut hair, bound up in back—wooden sticks protruding, holding it in place—to keep it off their necks. A few wisps of that dark chestnut straggled, flowed unbound, curled along their cheeks, draped the tops of their shoulders and along the shadows cast by their clavicles. And those shoulders were tanned, golden brown, gleaming softly from the light sheen of the sweat that covered them.

One of the young women wore a white camisole, the other a more natural linen color. And those camisoles were tight, sweat-glued against their young breasts, the nipples showing dark beneath the almost transparent cloth. I could almost smell the sweet scent of them, that astonishing mix of young woman and sweat and an elusive, faint hint of perfume.

They nodded to something the man said, then his hand moved down, came up again. The cupped palm placed something tiny, hidden, in their palms. And for some reason I will never know I spoke to him as the young women walked away.

"Could I have some, too?" I said and he turned toward me.

His eyes, gray and serious, came up to meet mine, and he stopped close in front of me. He stood still then, as still as ancient memories locked into the stone of mountains. And he looked at me, he really looked.

I stood transfixed, caught by his gaze, and even in my unawareness I could sense his gaze going deep inside, touching places within me that I did not know I had. Time stopped and I was held in the embrace of moment, caught by his seeing. Our looking was so deep I can still remember the striations in his iris, the slight purple surrounding the pupil, and the wrinkles that lined out from the corners of his eyes. But mostly I remember the feeling of being seen, of someone really looking at me, into me.

I remember, too, Jefferson Airplane in the background, singing "White Rabbit" . . .

One pill makes you larger
and one pill makes you small . . .

And I remember the dancing people, the noise of the crowd, the humidity of the air, surging around us like an ocean around an island in its midst. And us, caught in the still center, held motionless in a moment outside time.

Then, as it always must . . .

the stillness began to break.

His hand, as if it were moving through a substance more viscous than air, moved down—his eyes never leaving mine—and his fingers pressed against the threads of his jacket. Slowly, oh so slowly, they came up again. He held his hand out to me then, palm up, our eyes still locked together, and on it there lay a tiny, orange cylinder. I reached and took it, my eyes still captured, and slowly brought it to my mouth. Then he nodded, sharply, as if some question had been answered, and broke the spell completely, turned, and moved off into the crowd.

The movement of the crowd caught me up, took me in its currents, swept me away into that huge space, among all those dancing people. And the band . . . they played on.

In 1970, in San Francisco, LSD was everywhere and everyone I knew, myself included, had taken it many times. It brought us laughter, and close companionship, and a slower and deeper sense of the world around us. It brought us the belief in life after birth. But that day, something different happened, as it always does for those who continue to knock on the doors of perception. The doors opened.

And the thing about doors is,
there's always something on the other side.

I fell headlong then into a world I had never known existed. I tripped and fell into the metaphysical background of the world.

There have been many stories told about that deeper world but the truth is that each of us finds the particular part of the metaphysical landscape that we are meant to find. It is not a place but rather just another part of the scenario. We trip and fall into it—irrespective of the mechanism that facilitates it—at a certain moment in our lives and it shapes all of our life thereafter.

I remember how the light changed, how it became more luminous and alive. And I remember the sudden shift that took me out of this world, into the embrace of a deeper world than I knew existed. I remember being touched, touched by the living intelligence that is underneath and behind all things. I remember its voice speaking, telling me to look, to really look. And I remember what I saw that day, just as if it were happening now. I remember seeing . . . seeing the living complexity that underlies all form. And I remember my vision traveling so far outside that place, traveling into the world, seeing the Earth, the plants, trees, rivers, each in the midst of its own life. Each filled with intelligence and soul and each and every one communicating, always communicating to everything around them. In thousands upon thousands of voices, they greeted me, welcoming me into their world. And I remember the golden threads of connection that wove them all together into a continuous seamless fabric.

I caught glimpses then of the work that lay before me and the path that I would travel. And I remember all the years I have followed it and the joys that it has brought me . . . and the grief. And still more do I remember, more than I can possibly say. As I write these words, I hear the voice of Black Elk, as if it were my voice, speaking, saying something that is and always will be true for those of us who trip and fall into the metaphysical background of the world . . .

> *I am sure now that I was then too young to understand it all, and that I only felt it. It was the pictures I remembered and the words that went with them; for nothing I have ever seen with my eyes was so clear and bright as what my vision showed me; and no words that I have ever heard with my ears were like the words that I heard. I did not have to remember these things; they have remembered themselves all these years. It was as I grew older that the meanings came clearer and clearer out of the pictures and the words; and even now I know that more was shown to me than I can tell.*[1]

And I remember, in the midst of it all, the music. The music coming from Earth and stone and plant and animal. The music that is inside everything that is, the music without which this world would not exist.

The music that passes through us, that we think is *our* music but that is in reality the Earth's music.

I remember the music and the piece of it that the Dead had captured, that they had brought into human form and sensibility, the living expression of the Earth's touch upon them.

Much later, in the early morning, when the concert was done, I remember the doors opening and us in our thousands and our colors spreading outward like butterflies into the night.

I remember how fresh and clean everything seemed, how bright the colors were. It seemed as if a filter had been taken off my eyes, as if for the first time I could really see. And I remember how keenly I felt the touch of the world upon me, a touch I still feel even as I write these words at my grandfather's desk.

And I remember what was asked of me that night, to speak for the Earth, for the plants, for all living things. That people might know they live and love, too. Know that they have intelligence and purpose. Know that they have a life of their own, filled with hopes and dreams, just as we do. Know that they are our kin.

For it was said in that timeless moment that still echoes within me there are those among us who remember deep in some part of themselves—a part that will not let them rest—the forest and the livingness of green things. It was said that it's time for them to come home. Time for them to journey deep into the forest that birthed them. Time for them to take up their work—the work that resides in the deepest parts of themselves. Time for them to speak for the green things, to teach their children the way of Earth. Time for humans to think in new ways.

There is a difference I learned, long ago, between schooling and education. Do you feel it now, in the room with you?

I was never able to find it in the analysis of chemicals or in degree programs or in any of my schools. But sometimes I find it in the soft flutter of butterflies, in the wildness of plants growing undomesticated in a forest clearing, in the laughter and running of young children, their hair flowing in the wind, and sometimes, sometimes I find it in the words of teachers who come among us from time to time—out there, far outside these walls, in the wildness of the world.

Diminuendo Al Niente

THE MOVEMENT OF GREAT THINGS

There is memory of ocean,
the swelling of waves,
the movement of great things,
just beneath the surface.
My conscious mind staggers,
a part sleeping begins to waken.
What is this great thing
That has caught us up?

Beloved . . .
Shall we find out together?
Shall we travel to a land
where two-dimensionality does not rule?
Where all that we encounter gazes back at us?
Where directions for the journey
are written in the shape and textures of the land?
Where we see, as far as the eye can touch,
the soul of us opening outward?

Shall we take that step together?
Leave the comfort of the porch,
and strike cross country,
to find the place where the Teacher lives,
the place where the big and the little become one,
the place from which we came long ago,
the place we have heard calling since before we were born?

Shall we go out Beloved
and take the path before us?
Shall we let the perfume of our love
fill our three bodies?
Come, take my hand,
it has awaited the deep you to fill it,
a length of time too long for remembering.

Come Beloved, let us take this journey together.
My feet are hungry for the first step.[1]

Appendix One

SENSORY
OVERLOAD AND
SELF-CARETAKING

By luck, a man I had met offered me a cabin in the mountains. I spent several weeks building the shelves I needed for my books. With the help of a friend, I moved in. I had a basic kitchen, water from a spring, and I set up a corner of the room as a meditation alcove.

Friends gave me all manner of research materials. A chemist offered occasional use of a laboratory. A psychiatrist promised to stand by if I went too utterly over the edge.

I was a little cocky, though, and even put a sign over the door that said DEMONS WELCOME HERE. As it turned out, the demons already knew the address.

DALE PENDELL

My surroundings had now transformed themselves in more terrifying ways. Everything in the room spun around and the familiar objects and pieces of furniture assumed grotesque, threatening forms. They were in continuous motion, animated as if driven by an inner restlessness. The lady next door, whom I scarcely recognized,

465

brought me milk . . . She was no longer [my neighbor] but rather a malevolent, hideous witch with a colored mask.

ALBERT HOFMANN

Then he goes into the wood. He didn't know that he'd been gifted with such sensitivity: he quickly absorbs all the scents; the most muffled sound won't escape him; his veins are like the veins of a leaf. Soon he's vibrating so much that he feels uneasy, he's perceiving so many things that he's in a ferment of fear, he must get out of the wood.

JULES RENARD

Security is mostly superstition. It does not exist in nature, nor do children of men as a whole experience it. Avoiding it is no safer in the long run than outright exposure. Life is either a daring adventure, or nothing.

HELEN KELLER

Every one of us who decides to follow this path makes the journey into the metaphysical background of the world by ourselves. For those of us called to this craft, we can find help in the words and teachings of those who have gone before us, but we ourselves make that journey alone. And we find, deep in the depths of the world's dreaming, the things that we are meant to find, what is our destiny to find, for we come into this world with a purpose, a function. We are meant to find certain things and then to bring them back, give them forth for those who need what we have found.

However, by its nature, we travel into that world with the deepest and most vulnerable parts of ourselves open to the touch of those metaphysical depths upon us. And what we encounter there, we *truly* encounter. For in this journey we can have no part of ourselves sequestered or protected.

There is no such thing as safety

To the extent that we have parts of ourselves hidden or sequestered, that exact degree of the metaphysical background of the world will remain invisible to us. For in such circumstance, we *can't* allow certain aspects of that world to touch us; we fear what it holds.

The work I have described in this book has called for more courage than I ever thought it possible to have, more interior work than I ever thought it possible to do. What I did not know when I began it was just how hard it would be, how difficult to feel all the things that would touch me, how hard to remain balanced in the face of them, and how much grieving would be necessary. For there are wounds there, and lost people, and damaged landscapes, and the foolishness of leaders who remained governed by the worst of themselves. There are many difficult days, times when it seems as if the darkness will never lift. The greatest challenge is finding the way through such days, coming to terms with the darkness that has been encountered, integrating its reality into my life in such a way that it does not destroy who I am,

the velvety fingers of depression

so that I do not fall into the trap of thinking the darkness removable from the world . . . and becoming a fanatic in response to such a belief, to what has hurt or frightened me so deeply.

For many, anti-drug legislation is just such a response
Nevertheless, as Annie Le Brun has so eloquently said,
people get lost exploring the Amazon
but that is not sufficient reason to prohibit exploring
the Amazon.

It is very difficult sometimes to find a path through such moments of internal darkness.

But I have long known that if we who travel this path can find in ourselves the solution to the difficulties we encounter, we then carry within ourselves the medicine necessary for our people. It is carried in our behavior, in the carriage of our bodies, in the patterns of our speech and the tone of our words. Our lives, themselves, as we live them, *are* the presence of our understanding made manifest in the world.

Buckminster Fuller, Robert Bly, Jacques Cousteau, Robert Heinlein, Joan Halifax, Stephanie Simonton, Elisabeth Kübler-Ross, William Stafford, Jane Goodall, Gregory Bateson, Eric Fromm, Frank Herbert, Ashley Montagu, Margaret Mead.

I was full of wonder at the beginning of this journey; I had no idea what I was asking of myself and my faculties when I began. It has worked my poor ego, as Goethe once put it, more than I hardly thought possible. Nevertheless, it's just part of the journey. As Mirabai once put it . . .

I take the path that ecstatic human beings have taken for centuries

and on that path, certain things await. Here is a look at some of the difficulties that can occur.

Sensory Overload

Allowing sensory gating channels to open very widely, as a way of life, as habit, can result in the constant intake of thousands upon thousands of *feeling* experiences, all imbued with complex meanings. It can become overwhelming at times; sensory overload truly is a common problem. As Franz Vollenweider put it, you may

become overloaded with excessive exteroceptive and interoceptive stimuli, which in turn could lead to a breakdown in cognitive integrity and difficulty in distinguishing self from nonself.

In other words, you can get lost in a sea of incoming, meaning-filled sensory inputs, lost in the sea of meaning in which you are now immersed.

It is crucially important to learn how to reduce sensory gating at will—and then open it again, whenever you wish—as well as learn how to take care of your self in response to the incoming meaning-filled sensory inputs you are receiving.

Reducing Sensory Gating Channels

Reduction of sensory gating at will is fairly straightforward but it does take practice. Once you habituate to more open gating, there isn't much desire to close it down again—it generally feels so good to be so alive that turning it off feels like an amputation. There literally is a disconnection that occurs and you find yourself cut off from the touch of the world upon you, alone in your own house. Nevertheless, sometimes the nervous system and the perceiving self just need a rest. To reduce gating you simply stop using the feeling sense as a perceptual tool. You just put it away for a while.

easier said than described

When using the feeling sense as a perceptual tool, there is a moving out of the self and, as well, there is an opening allowing the out there to come in here. You, as habit, are feeling the world outside yourself, continually. Often, simultaneously, working to understand the meanings of what you are feeling. In essence, you are reading the book of the world continually. It is easy to come to depend on that way of being for a sense of personal orientation.

The parts of the self that desire safety may begin using the skill to constantly monitor the exterior world to analyze intent in other people as a constant process. It can become pathological.

Once habituated, sense of self and personal orientation in space and time come to depend on the experience, so shutting it down is generally unwelcome. Exacerbating the occasional overload: the constant feeling/ sensing of the world uses a great deal of psychic energy; it can exhaust psychic reserves. These two things can then occur simultaneously: exhaustion and overload. They often go together.

The sensory reduction process is a process and simply works to reverse the steps involved in the development of enhanced sensing. You stop feeling *out there*. (Accomplishing this often becomes more difficult as the exhaustion progresses, by the way.) There are a number of ways to reduce the exterior sensing. A simple one is to focus on feeling your own heartbeat.

> Sit some place comfortable, take some deep breaths
> let all the tension in your body begin to flow out with your breath
> let the tension go out of your feet . . . your calves . . . your legs
> let the tension in your hands . . . your forearms . . . flow out with
>   your breath
> breathe the tension out of every part of your body
> s l o w l y . . . focusing all the while on your breath
> now . . . feel your heart beating inside you
> send caring to that part of you, as you would a puppy or kitten
> caress it with your caring, begin breathing into your heart
> just keep sending caring and nurturing into this part of you
> breathe it deeply into the tissues of your heart
> now . . . let that caring you have hold your entire body in its hands
> and just keep breathing that caring and nurturing
> deeper into every cell of your body

Practice this until you can maintain the state for 30 minutes at a time. This shifts the focus considerably—even in the first few minutes (though the longer you can do it, the more focus shifts). You begin to become centered in the self. The exterior inputs cease. The neural system takes the focus on the heart and breathing to be a task set and it overrides the more open gating of exterior inputs. In addition, this stops the psychic drain. The energy is no longer flowing *out there* but is now directed *in here*. Generally, when overload occurs there is an accompanying lack of self-attentiveness, the deep self is starved for caring and attention from you. This reverses that; psychic reserves build quickly. A sense of well-being immediately begins to develop.

This process does have to be practiced over a long period of time in order to habituate it so that soon after you begin feeling overloaded with sensory inputs you can immediately shift into a different state. It takes focus of mind to force the shift, since moments of overload are often accompanied by anxiety. This, by nature, tends to open gating more widely so that the deep self can scan for safety. It takes will, and practice, to just shut the thing down and focus entirely on the body.

The focus does not have to be the breath and heartbeat but it does have to be something deep in the self. I sometimes, instead, feel my four-year-old self standing beside me, feel him leaning against my right side, feel the warm bond between the two of us, and that is *all* I pay attention to.

After years, I can now hold the state for very long periods. However, within just a few moments, the sensory gating channels close and psychic energy begins to replenish. Only a day or two is necessary to restore completely even during periods of intense burnout.

Some Comments about the Concept of Safety

I need to make clear here that it is impossible to "protect" yourself in the sense that most people mean it. It's not actually a productive orientation to have when approaching the metaphysical background of the world. Conflict then tends to become a self-fulfilling prophecy. The important thing is, there really is no such thing as "protection." Safety does not exist in the real world. Let me repeat that:

Safety does not exist in the real world.

It is an illusion.

You can't "protect" yourself. That is not how the world works (even though all of us would like it to do so from time to time). The more functional approach is to: 1) Prepare yourself for the journey as best you can, developing the skill base you need to minimize adverse events; and 2) Learn how to take care of yourself so that when you do get hurt, you can competently tend to the hurt.

this is what being a professional in this realm— or any realm—means

Going into the world with the feeling sense extended is similar to when you were four years old and running around a rocky yard in shorts. Or when the training wheels came off the bike. You *are* going to fall. You are going to get skinned knees. You are going to get hurt.

And no, putting the white light around the blue light around the green light around your body is not going to eliminate adverse events. Though, on another level, that actually is a kind of self-nurturing behavior, which does help; this just isn't the most effective form of it.

How safe you feel in any circumstance is going to depend on your skill base. If you are a Navy Seal, highly trained in hand-to-hand combat, and you find yourself in a bar where someone pulls out a knife, you are still going to feel moderately safe. If you are not so trained you are going to feel very unsafe indeed.

That is why I stay out of bars where there is the likelihood of knife fights

All you can do is increase your skill base and minimize the likelihood of adverse events. Nevertheless, adverse events are *still* going to occur. You can't get rid of them.

You will need to, over time, learn to the accept the truth that there is no safety. Both Disneyland and Heaven are aberrant concepts.

The American belief that safety is a fundamental right, or even an attainable state, is unfounded. It's pathological. It expresses itself in every subculture in the United States, from the New Age to the Defense Department. And a great many unnecessary laws and regulations are passed each year in an attempt to generate it. (As an aside: it is unfortunately common that the safety measures that are enacted often result in *more* physical harm to children. Airbags—which commonly kill children—were mandated in cars by activists . . . to protect children; the rubber matting legally required on school playgrounds in England, mandated by child activists, result in *more* broken bones. [It's a physics thing.] The law of unintended consequences really is real. And . . . no plastic butter knives in the lunch box to spread the cheese; no pastries eaten into the shape of guns [that's a suspendin'] in first grade? Things are getting out of hand.)

Again, what you can do, *all you can do,* is to minimize adverse events and learn to take care of yourself if you get hurt. And you *will* get hurt from time to time. You can buy the strongest climbing rope there is, the best pitons, the best climbing shoes, study up on the terrain, develop the best skills possible, check the weather—this is what minimizing adverse events entails. But still . . . an unexpected avalanche, a sudden freak storm that no one predicted, a light plane losing altitude and crashing into the mountain—such things occur. You can't stop them. There is no such thing as safety. Remember: none of us is getting out of here alive. The most important thing is *how* we live, not the length of it.

So, let's look at a couple of real-life examples that come up when exploring the metaphysical background of the world: paranoid events and "'taking on' someone else's stuff."

Paranoid Events

It is the rare person who never experiences, while on hallucinogens or while exploring the metaphysical background of the world, a paranoid blow out. That is what Albert Hofmann was describing when he said that

> *Everything in the room spun around and the familiar objects and pieces of furniture assumed grotesque, threatening forms. They were in continuous motion, animated as if driven by an inner restlessness. The lady next door, whom I scarcely recognized, brought me milk . . . She was no longer [my neighbor] but rather a malevolent, hideous witch with a colored mask.*

At times like this the degree of fear is so strong that it is very difficult to think clearly, nevertheless . . . it's recommended. Here is how the musician Travis Holland described the experience and what he did about it.

He notes that there is a

filter effect. Where everything that's coming in through your senses goes through this filter which distorts it, and twists everything just a little bit, so that a person will say something which, when it registers on you, is a threat. Because it has been slightly filtered and amplified here, and this has been left out, and it has been rotated a few degrees, and a little color added here, it's a threat.

And that's not what came from this other person at all, it's just the way you receive it. And fortunately, while I was paranoid, I was frequently able to get out of it enough to view it objectively and see what was happening, which made it fairly easy to deal with. But it didn't stop it from happening.

But I had enough awareness of it to deal with it. And then there were dialogues that would go on in your head, with these other voices, when there was no one else around . . . or when there were other people around. Someone would say something to you, and this voice would, if what they said didn't offend you sufficiently, the voice would say, "You Know What That Really Means, Don't You?"

Well, if I couldn't stop the voice, at least I could refuse to act on what it said. So, that's what I would do, I would refuse to respond on the basis of this paranoid activity that was mine, until it went away . . .

And [the thing is], it feeds itself, the fact that you can see people edging away from you, it creates it's own substantiation.[1]

The only solution I have found that works is exactly what Holland found: you have to firmly realize that nothing is what it seems at the moment and you simply refuse, no matter how afraid you become, to act on anything you are perceiving. And you just keep on refusing until the situation passes, or you come down off the drugs, or you pass out from exhaustion. The worst thing you can do

which we all do anyway at least once or twice

is to act on what you are perceiving. Ever. It never works out well. Remember: it will pass . . . eventually. Just fasten your seatbelt and don't say or do anything in response to what you are experiencing, even if you have to redecide that every second for the next eight hours. Basically, the situation sucks, but it does pass.

The reason for the paranoia is that the self-protective part of the self gets activated and the sensory intake gets contaminated by psychological fears and confusions

that we all have inside us

and every fear we have begins playing itself out in real time, in three-dimensional space instead of inside our heads, which is where it usually plays itself out.

a classical example of projection,
the world becomes your movie screen
and you find yourself inside just about the worst
movie imaginable

The long-term solution, if you are given to periodic bouts of this dynamic (oddly enough, some people aren't), is to habituate yourself to your fear so that it no longer frightens you, so you can remain in its presence and not lose yourself. It takes the repetitious habituation of a certain response of mind, a refusal to act on the terror that is coursing through you irrespective of its strength, despite the urgings of the voice inside you telling you that you should. Over time this develops an interior default setting that clicks into place when paranoia surfaces.

Essentially: the voice that is urging you to panic is one of your consciousness modules that has become highly activated. It's come to the fore, assumed a command position, and is trying to steer the ship

onto those rocky shoals

while convincing you that the rocky shoals represent safety. Basically, that consciousness module has panicked. So, the second thing that helps is the use of various aspects of the inner council processes, which I will get into in a minute. It is imperative to make relationship with that part of you so that it does not just surge up out of the unconscious and take over, leaving you to come to your senses later amid the wreckage.

Taking On Someone Else's Stuff

This is a very common question: "If I am that open to everything, other people's stuff gets inside me. What do I do to protect myself?" Well, again, you can't "protect" yourself. The solution is something else entirely.

When you approach the world with your feeling sense engaged, you begin to actually experience *with your conscious mind* the meanings you are immersed in daily. Those meanings are already getting inside you, you just didn't notice them before . . . but your unconscious did . . . and dealt with them as best it could.

> *That it did not deal with them completely you can perceive from the fact that sometimes you just felt funny but didn't know why. And that funny feeling? It affected your state of mind and your day and your behavior and your relationships even if you didn't know what the hell was going on.*

Part of how your unconscious dealt with it was to gate the data so that your conscious mind did not get overwhelmed. So, what you are experiencing when you are more consciously open is simply a form of cognitive overload as Vollenweider and others have described it. As well, you are just not used to the process yet, much like someone who begins working construction without the muscle development to easily do so. The solution is composed of two parts: 1) experience over time; 2) developing a skill base you can use to take care of your various selves.

As you begin using your enhanced perceiving, three dynamics are coming into play: 1) More intake making it to conscious awareness; 2) The encountering of deeper, less human, or sometimes more frighteningly human, meaning fields due to a sustained focus on a single golden thread; this actually is bringing more unusual inputs inside you; 3) As these occur, when you begin to feel overwhelmed, there is an internal dynamic playing out in the inner council . . . one of your consciousness modules is becoming afraid. Several dynamics may generate that fear but, importantly, the most common is that incoming experiences may be activating old psychological confusions that you have not resolved in yourself.

> *You go into a house that is filled with rage. Your open gating channels let it in, strongly, and it floods your conscious mind. Then the memories of your rage-filled birth family and home are stimulated, they emerge once more into awareness. All the unresolved feelings and fears are activated once more. "Stuff" comes up.*

The second most common is that you have encountered a meaning that conflicts with your foundational pictures of the world.

> *You do a reading on a person at the mall and realize that they are a sociopath; they have no moral structure at all. But you don't just think it, you feel it from inside the experience itself. You see the world, for a moment, from that point of view. And that experience conflicts with your belief that all people are good (some actually aren't). This has the inevitable effect of undermining the beliefs that you use to orient yourself in society. That, in and of itself, is frightening.*

So, besides more experience, the solution demands flexibility of perspective, that is, being able to orient your consciousness from multiple perspectives while still retaining a sense of yourself. Again, this just takes practice and experience.

> *It also demands acute awareness of what "stuff" is yours and what "stuff" is not. You have to know yourself pretty well—and this necessity never ceases. You have to know what psychological confusions are yours so that when they are activated you know it is not the place or person but what the place or person has stimulated in you.*

You can also, intentionally, shut off gating, as described earlier. This gives your internal world, and your conscious mind, a break. It shuts off the input. It allows you to recover from the workout you just went through and to process the data you encountered. It reduces cognitive overload.

The most important thing, however, is direct work with your inner council and the parts that have been affected by your depth immersion. But first . . . a word about . . .

Depression

Depression is a major problem in the United States. The underlying reason for it, in my experience, comes from immersion in a world perspective that is deeply inaccurate. In other words, most people here are submerged inside an experience that denies the living reality of the external world, denies that soul, intelligence, and communicative awareness is possible with the world around us. That keeps us isolated in our own houses and the existential aloneness it generates is tremendously debilitating to the soul, to the entire self. That creates, as one of its expressions, depression. And despite the cultural emphasis on it being an abnormal state, depression is a normal, important, and irremovable element of a full life. For it is a communication about a specific circumstance, of which our Western paradigm is only the most pervasive example.

Depression is the state that occurs when the environment in which you are immersed (interior or exterior) begins sending you a communication that directly conflicts with your software, that is, one of your fundamental beliefs about the nature of things. It can be a communication about yourself, telling you, for example, that there is an inaccuracy in your perception of yourself. This could be something like . . .

You think you are a nice person but there is a rather mean part of you that you let out from time to time that is hurting people. In actuality, sometimes you are an asshole.

Because you are firmly ignoring this communication, repressing it as hard as you can, the interior you that needs you to hear it creates depression.

Depression is the way the darkness makes itself visible to us

It can also emerge because there is a part of you that really needs you to pay attention to it, because it has fundamental needs that you are not addressing.

Such as the need for more touch or play or joy in life,
or the truth that the job you are in is killing your spirit,
or the truth that being so mental all the time
is destroying your capacity to love and be loved

And because you refuse to pay attention, because you truly believe that there is no room in an adult life for touch or play or joy, that part can only get your attention by causing depression, a depression so debilitating that you are forced to deal with it. So, one way or another, it forces you to turn toward it and respond.

And, except for short term crises, pharmaceuticals are the absolute worst choice of treatment. There are reasons for this—one of the most important is that SRIs are causing major disruptions in the environment. There is an important teaching in this. We are not the center of the universe. Whether pharmaceuticals save lives or not is irrelevant; we are paying a price for using them indiscriminately. And that price? It is only going to get more costly as time goes on.

The depression that we in the United States experience as a general condition is just the same in its underlying dynamics. There is a communication that the environment is giving us. We refuse to hear it; depression emerges.

The solution is to ask yourself, whenever you experience depression, "What is the communication? What is it that I am not hearing?"—then, once understood, figuring out what to do to deal with the underlying problem.

It can take time to figure it out, even longer to figure out what to do in response. But it is the only solution I have found that actually works. Though that doesn't mean that we don't try everything else we can first. Ignoring it (first choice), television (second choice), overwork (third choice), drugs (fourth choice), sex, food, vacations, parties, sex, drugs, food, parties, vacation, suicide (constant thought), sex. It really is relentless.

> *The solution is to turn and face the darkness*
> *and find out what it is trying to tell you*
> *then to make the changes necessary to address the underlying*
> *need*

But depression, too, can and usually does pass. There are others who have been in this place before us, people *exactly* like us, who found the way through. This means that we, you, can, too. As William Stafford once put it, "Dawn comes and it comes for all but not on demand."

When the communication is truly received and acted upon, the darkness dissipates. You are not the same person that you were once you have found the way through, however; you are different. And the darkness? It will never have such a hold on you again . . . even though it will return every so often, every time there is something important coming up from the depths of yourself or the world that you do not want to hear.

Consciousness Modules

There is no way to engage in this kind of perception as a way of life, especially if you go deep with it, if you do not do specific work with the various consciousness modules that make up the self.

It is crucial to understand that the unconscious parts of the self are a great deal more powerful than the conscious mind. They respond to caring, to respect, and to negotiation. They never respond well to force. After all, they are the ones doing the heavy lifting; they are the ones that maintain the system while you are off watching television.

You can try to use shortcuts

> *everybody does in the beginning*

you can try pharmaceuticals, you can try force, you can try ignoring them, you can try locking them into boxes, you can pretty much try everything you want. The only way that I (and everyone I have read and met who has been successful at this) have found is to approach them with respect, caring, and a request to help, that is, treating them as a trusted equal and coworker and companion.

Inner Council Work

I have been working with varieties of inner council work for over forty years now. I have made a great many mistakes in the process, usually from errors in judgment (most commonly, arrogance toward the other parts of myself). Those errors have helped produce greater sophistication, and better outcomes, in the work. However, I want to bring up something specific to start with, which is a comment that I sometimes hear about inner child work.

Inner child work is crucial. *Unfortunately,* it became so popularized by John Bradshaw (and regrettably his less-accomplished clones) that I hear comments every so often to the effect of "Oh, that old thing. Give us something useful."

Well, I am.

I suggest these exercises because they actually work; they really do accomplish exactly what I am describing they can. And I have seen that they do over decades of observing hundreds of people use them. The regrettably blunt truth is: if they are not working then you are not *genuinely* doing them but only mimicking a surface expression of them, something that, *very* regrettably, some of the Bradshaw clones have encouraged. (And more irritatingly, I learned about it decades ago from some of Eric Berne's students . . . John Bradshaw didn't actually invent the process.) However . . .

A Moment in Which the Author Makes a Crucial Point or Two

I do want to make a point here: the metaphor that you use to describe the interior consciousness modules you have is irrelevant. *You don't, absolutely do not, have to call it inner child work.* The only thing important is whether or not the metaphor you use feels accurate to the modules themselves.

In my interior world, the members of my inner council don't actu-
ally like the phrase "consciousness modules," too impersonal. They
just agreed to it for this book since it is a neutral phrase most people
can hear.

Whatever descriptive you come up with, it has to feel comfortable to
your internal modules. If the metaphor is inaccurate to the way they
see themselves, it is just going to cause major problems. Because . . .
these consciousness modules? They are *intelligent,* they are *aware,* they
have their own functional areas of importance. They are independent
realities. They are self-organized systems that together make up the
you that you are. They have the same capacities as all self-organized
biological systems do. If you disrespect them, you will pay and pay and
pay. (Just an FYI on that one.) Within their area of expertise, *they*
control behavior. And nothing you can do will ever change that. (You
aren't competent to oversee your white blood cell activity, only that
system is, and it knows it. But . . . it will let you have some input, such
as using imagery to enhance its functioning. And if you establish deep
relationship with that system, you can do even more . . . but only if it
agrees to let you.)

You can make relationship with your many consciousness modules.
That is what inner council work is.

These parts of you, these modules? They are your inner council.
They are there to help the larger system, the self-organized you,
remain organized throughout your lifetime. The various psycholog-
ical modules are sources of wisdom, knowledge, perceptual capaci-
ties, strengths, insights, and behaviors that can help you through
pretty much anything you will ever face. You can consciously allow
any of them to take over as the dominant lens through which you
are approaching the world any time their particular skill base is
needed. That is why they were evolutionarily generated. They are
the intelligent expression of certain kinds of emergent behaviors.

And if all these parts are unified into one synchronized whole?
The power that emerges is immense. It is what Eric Berne referred

to as a state of individuation, being weller than well, where you have the immediate capacity for intimacy, spontaneity, awareness, and unified action always accessible.

If you do make relationship with these parts of you, they will even cede you some degree of control over their area of competence . . . but only if they truly and deeply trust your good intent—which you will have to prove through your behavior over a long period of time. It is like any relationship. Trust comes with time and trustworthy behavior. Again: if you treat them like dirt, like servants, like an impediment, as if they are stupid and you are not, they are going to make a point of getting even. And man, can they get even.

So, use whatever metaphor you want; these are just the ones that I have found to be the most potently useful. But, again, ask *them* if they like what you are calling them. And also, try to make sure that the system you are using has some underlying rationale and consistency to it.

I like the system I use, not only because after forty years I know it works, but because it is ecologically relevant . . . in both the external and internal sense of the term. You can actually see the human developmental stages out there in the world, in every self-organized biological system. The four-year-old, the child, has an ecological reality. Our internal, formerly-real-in-the-world, child is only one expression of a general condition. These parts? They have an actual reality in every part of the Gaian system.

The metaphor you use really does need some grounding in the real world. And no, most psychological theorists (and their theories) are not very useful. Most think the highly theoretical map they have created *is* the territory and the maps are almost always completely human centered; they have no ecological basis in reality. They are unrelated to the other life-forms on the planet. That never works out well in the long run.

Which brings me to an important point . . .

The "Ego"

Ego as a concept is useless. It is common, in reductive New Age texts and conversations, and in most religious traditions, to encounter the term "the ego." It is exceptionally rare to find "ego" defined, though there are several "definitions" that exist and do serve in some sort of vague way as definitional markers.

The word itself comes from the Greek and simply means "I," that is, it refers to the you that you mean when you say, "I live here," "I did this," and so on.

When schizophrenic or hallucinogenic researchers talk about ego-disintegration or ego-dissolution, loss of self control over thought process and intentionality, lack of differentiation between ego and non-ego spheres, this is what they are talking about. You don't know who "I" is for a while. (BTW, everybody has experiences like this one time or another; it is just part of the self-knowledge process. It is not pathological.)

Then there is Freud's use of the word. In his system there are, over simplistically on his part, three conscious modules of the self: id, ego, and superego. The id, in Freud's poorly developed map, is the unorganized part of the personality that contains the basic human, instinctual drives. It's motivated primarily by the desire for immediate gratification of whatever it wants. It has no morality. The ego, on the other hand, is an adaption of the self that acts to bring the id's desires to fruition in more constructive ways, essentially by delaying gratification. It acts as a mediator between the id and the external world. The superego is in essence a form of an expansive parental module, which includes the conscience, that can have a larger, more spiritual aspect to it.

Personally, I have found Freud's map to be inaccurate to the real world and the source of much confusion—though Jung (much better) and Berne (much better) both began in his system.

In Hindu/Buddhist paradigms the ego is "the spontaneous identity of an individual to represent itself." It is denoted by the Sanskrit term Ahamkara and means pretty much the same as the Greek root of the word. Ahamkara is one of several modules, in the Hindu tradition, that make up the self. However, in those systems, the Ahamkara is considered to be an illusory self that feels it must fight for itself in the world, keep its own identity intact. It is believed, because of this, to thus inter-fere with the ability to perceive the true nature of the world, which is foundationally not material, but spiritual. The focus in these traditions is often on dissolving the ego so that the "real" self can come into being.

What the adherents of that system mean in their frame of ref-erence is that the self-organized identity, the "I," that emerges out of the Ocean of Being has no ultimate reality in and of itself; it comes from the Ocean of Being and it merges back into it at death. The life it thinks it has in the meantime is an illusion. The only real-ity is the Ocean of Being. So, the insistence is on dissolving the ego and merging once more into the OB. In that system, as well, nearly all other life-forms are considered to be lesser forms of life, possessing little intel-ligence or awareness or soul. The material world is considered an illusion that blinds the self to reality, the Earth itself is denigrated, the concept of Gaia is irrelevant. Unsurprisingly, I am not a fan of this frame. Look-ing at its historical consequences over the past three millennia I find it ecologically unsound and culturally and individually damaging. (The monotheistic frames of the West are, historically, much worse.)

Hatred of the self, or of the world of form,
of the body, never works out well

A reductive form of the Hindu definition, combined with the com-mon sense of the Western "I," that is, the I that I know as I, often leads to a great deal of self-harm as well as the use of that combined vagueness for social control by power freaks in group settings. It is often used to denigrate any forceful behavior among the members of "peace" groups of whatever sort—and I am not talking about violence here, simply forceful articulation or disagreement. It is sometimes used, too, to denigrate any form of self-caretaking as being too selfish, too ego-oriented.

Individual people sometimes use it to denigrate the existence of any sort of life-affirming nurturing or caretaking within the individual. It can sometimes be used to denigrate the very existence of the self-identity that the person knows of as his or her unique self. It is often used to pro-mote a certain kind of violence toward others or the self, often for the accumulation of power over others. It's not useful.

Nevertheless . . . this part of the self does have a real existence. It is an important part of the self; it is not possible to "get rid" of the ego.

It is not possible to "get rid" of the ego.
It's an evolutionary innovation; it exists for a reason.
(No, the devil did not put it there.)
You have a right to be alive . . . and yourself
Don't ever let anybody convince you otherwise.
This recognition of the Gaian source of all internal modules
and their evolutionary necessity and our inherent
capacity to love them
is the difference between an Earth-centered spirituality
and all the others

You can make relationship with this part of the self, integrate it effectively into the inner council, and modulate its influence over behavior. Just as you can all of them. Once you do, it adds its considerable energy reserves to the life, and work, of the individual.

The "ego," in the simplest definition, is the part of us that monitors our survival. It monitors for safety and it initiates behaviors designed to keep us safe in response to what it is perceiving. It is, at root, a healthy and important part of us that wants to keep self-organization intact. It, however, has no morality. It has one function and it will do it whether we want it to or not. It decides behavior and initiates it without regard, often, to consequences. Its behavior can be extremely subtle or grossly expressed.

The way I sneakily take the slightly larger piece of pie
or the way I once erupted in rage at being disagreed with

Underneath its expressions is the desire to protect the self-organized entity of which it is a part. And . . . fear. Fear of death, of failure, of loss of self. This part of the self is the source of paranoia, the source of greed, desire for power over others, unhealthy competitiveness (yes, there is healthy competitiveness), unbridled lust for anything really. For if this part comes to believe that those things will ensure its survival it will try to obtain them. If it believes that intimacy (as it sometimes does) is dangerous, it will sabotage love. If it believes that it has to have millions of dollars to survive, then it will try to get millions of dollars. If it believes its survival is physically threatened, it will respond with violence. (And no, violence and anger in and of themselves are not inherently bad. As with everything, it is the meaning that is important, not the form. Gandhi was quite clear it was possible to kill and remain nonviolent. It just isn't very easy to do.) The form of its expression doesn't matter; whatever this part believes is necessary is, to it, necessary. In some people it remains relatively benign. It just always takes the largest piece of pie.

> *Which always, eventually, causes a marital problem*
> *the other person has this part, too. It notices everything,*
> *sooner or later.*

In some it can become megalomania. Same part, different expression.

This part of the self can, in many people, become troublesome, and it usually does, sooner or later, over the course of a lifetime. You learn to recognize its expression by how it feels. After several hundred emergences, you begin to notice that every time you do that (fill in the blank) behavior, it feels a certain way and that you usually don't feel too good about yourself afterward.

The first task is identification. The second is learning to integrate it into the self. In essence, over time, you have to learn how to moderate its influence in behavior.

> *You have to find a languaging it understands. It needs to know*
> *that there is sufficient reason to pass control to a more mature*
> *module. And, ultimately, you have to break it to bridle. You don't*
> *kill its spirit, but you break it to bridle, so that it works with you to*
> *get you where you are going. Until that happens, you just can't take*
> *your awareness off it, at all. Otherwise it will make messes.*

It often tends to reduce its activity with age, especially as the recognition that death is inevitable is accepted. This part of the self, when successfully integrated, adds tremendous power to any and all actions you take in life.

But it is crucial to learn how to parent it, to moderate its behavior. Dick Francis has a nice way of talking about what that process of moderation entails . . .

He looked at me for a while . . . "Don't you ever get muddled by emotion?"

"Yes, sometimes," I said. "But when it happens . . . I try to sort myself out. To see some logic."

"And once you see some logic, you act on it?"

"Try to." I paused. "Yes."

"It sounds . . . cold."

I shook my head. "Logic doesn't stop you feeling. You can behave logically, and it can hurt like hell. Or it can comfort you. Or release you. Or all at the same time."

After a while he said, stating a fact, "Most people don't behave logically."

"No," I said.

"You seem to think everyone could, if they wanted to?"

I shook my head. "No." He waited, so I went on diffidently, "There's genetic memory against it, for one thing. And to be logical you have to dig up and face your own hidden motives and emotions, and of course they're hidden principally because you don't want to face them. So . . . um . . . it's easier to let your basement feelings run the upper stories, so to speak, and the result is rage, quarrels, love, jobs, opinions, anorexia, philanthropy . . . almost anything you can think of. I just like to know what's going on down there, to pick out why I truly want to do things, that's all. Then I can do them or not. Whichever."[2]

The necessity to know ourselves is fundamental, to know the different parts of ourselves and their motivations and needs. We learn to see their movements through the fabric of our lives, often by the shadows they cast. Then we learn to meet the deeper needs, to moderate the behavior of the parts externally, and among and between them. This begins to generate a specific state of mind. There is a unique part of the self that begins to come forward over time. It can be described as a mature, nurturing parent of a home full of people, some younger, some older. Interestingly, when things are working well, that entire home of people flow as one synchronized whole into that more mature state of being and from there into the world. We become capable of engaging in the holy act of breaking bread with ourselves . . . and with others.

The Exercises: Self-Caretaking

There are a number of important outcomes that occur from doing these exercises over time; each is important:

1. You gain awareness of the different parts of yourself and their needs; you come to know yourself.
2. You are able to meet deep needs directly and no longer have to suffer the movements of these parts as unconscious processes. Further, you begin to heal old damage to these parts of the self that you still carry inside you.
3. You engage in a crucial ecological reclamation of the self. Any parts of the self that are abandoned become more damaged over time.
4. In this process, you begin to become your own best friend.
5. You reclaim the perceptual capacities of these parts of you.
6. As the young child ego states are reclaimed, the capacity for heart perception and the feeling sense increases substantially.
7. You have access to a great many more resources that are evolutionarily designed to help you through this life, to face adversity, to solve problems. (Each ego state will have a different solution to every problem.)
8. You initiate a process that, at its end, results in an integrated, whole human being. A state of individuation emerges, expressing itself as a unique state of mind and being.

In general, *every* developmental stage should, over time, be engaged through these kinds of exercises. *Every* additional part of the self, the part focused on survival (the "ego"), the daimon, the body (as a whole), and the body's individual parts. During the inner council exercise, other parts will emerge into awareness, each of them may need individual attention as well. Here are the initial exercises.

♌ The Inner Council Exercise

The inner council is composed of every self-organized identity that goes into making up the larger self-organized identity you know of as yourself. Working with consciousness modules entails working with them as a group, in the inner council, and individually . . . as I go into in a bit. If you have not done this before, you will soon find, as Ram Dass once put it . . .

> *when I first began to do inner work*
> *it was a mob scene in there*

The point of the council exercise is to begin to work as one unified whole, as a group of integrated consciousness modules who interact companionably and together. It takes a lot of work to get there but it is worth it. So . . .

> *Sit some place comfortable, take some deep breaths*
> *really fill up your lungs . . . and . . . hold it . . . hold it . . . hold it*
> *and breathe out*
> *just let all the tension in your body begin to flow out with your*
>   *breath*
> *let the tension flow out of your feet . . . now your calves . . . and*
>   *your legs*
> *let the tension in your hands . . . your forearms . . . flow out with*
>   *your breath*
> *let the tension flow out of every part of your body as you breathe*
>   *out*
> *now . . . see yourself standing in a clearing in the woods*
> *the sun is shining, birds are singing, there is a slight breeze*
> *and surrounding you is a forest*
> *just in front of you, there is a path,*
> *people have walked this way before you*
> *step onto the path and begin to follow it*

soon, you pass into the forest, the sun is dappled by the trees and
as you walk, the path begins to slowly drop down the hill in front
      of you
it's a gradual descent but you can feel the slight pull on your calves
as you walk, as you drop down deeper and deeper into the forest,
soon, the path begins to level out and you notice in front of you a
      stream
there are thick bushes on both sides of the stream, but the path
continues through them. You move the leaves aside with your
      hands
and notice there are stepping stones across the stream
so, carefully, you step on each one, crossing to the other side
the path continues on and you follow it
soon you come to a clearing. There is a small building in front of you
the door is open
you, carefully, walk up to the door and peer in
it's a bit dark, so it takes a few moments for your eyes to adjust
once they do, you see it is just one large room
and in the middle of it is a large table
as you walk into the room you see that
there are chairs around the table and along the sides of the room
and that some, though not all, of the chairs are occupied
one of the chairs is for you, so you walk up to the table
and sit down
these are the members of your inner council
your child is there, that young part of you that feels the world
your infant is there
and there is an old man and old woman, too
the part of you that says "no" to everything is there
and many more parts besides
some of them may be trees or birds or plants
these parts of you can appear as anything
there is no one form they will take
take a minute to notice who is there
let your eyes touch all of them, notice how they look
how they are dressed, their body posture

Are any of them talking? Do they have anything to tell you?
Do they need anything from you?
Some of them, you know, may be angry.
What is it that they are angry about?
What do they need from you?
Some of them may not talk, they want to know if you are serious first,
and over time others will come to fill the empty chairs
Begin to make relationship with them, listen to what they have to
*   say*
to what they need and want from you. Now . . .
Is there anything you need to tell them? To ask them?
Is there anything you need from them?
Spend as much time as you need with them and then . . .
Thank them for coming to be with you
for telling you about themselves, what they need
and then . . . when you are ready, tell them good-bye
for now
and stand up and go to the door and outside again
the path is there in front of you . . . begin to follow it once more
as you make your way, you can turn and look back at the house
some of them will be standing at the door, watching you walk
then turn back to the path again and follow it home
there is the stream . . . and the stones . . . and the bushes
on the other side you follow the path, rising up the hill in front of
*   you*
you pass through the forest and come to the meadow again
the birds are singing, the slight breeze is passing across the meadow
*   grasses*
you come to the place you began
and then, slowly, become aware of your body again
and your breathing
and the sound of my voice
and . . . when you are ready . . . open your eyes
and come back into the room again

This exercise will need to be repeated often. I suggested that my apprentices (when I was still teaching that way) do the exercise every morning or evening, for at least several years. I did the exercise myself daily for over two decades. Eventually, the many parts of my self integrated, the need for a formalized process was no longer necessary. Nevertheless, if a new part shows up, I do it again when I reach the moment where integration becomes timely. And parts do show up regularly, the deeper the work becomes, the more you travel into the background of the world, the more you find in yourself.

Many of the modules will need individual work. Here is a look at some of the more important . . .

✒ The Child

All life, and particularly all animal life, is sensitive to outside impressions, but the child is far and away the most sensitive organism on the entire planet . . . The child is like a diamond, I have said more than once; its many facets receive impressions as clear and sharp as etchings.

LUTHER BURBANK

(Sometimes it is helpful to make a tape recording of this exercise and then to play it back. Instead of the words "them" or "they" that I use in the exercise, use "him" or "her" and "she" or "he" and "his" or "hers"— whichever gender you are. If you practice you will find the perfect speed, pitch, and intonation for you to listen to.)

Sit someplace comfortable. Someplace you won't be disturbed. Someplace that is nurturing to you.

Close your eyes and take some deep breaths. Fill up your lungs as if they were balloons, fill them to bursting. Hold it, hold it, hold it. Then . . . slowly . . . release. As you let out the air in your lungs, let any tension you feel inside you release and flow out with your breath. Do this again . . . several times.

Begin with your toes, then your ankles, your knees. And with each breath let the tension in this part of your body flow out with your breath. Do this with each major part of your body, ending with your face, head, and neck.

Now. Imagine the floor or chair under you as two huge, cupped hands that are holding you. Let yourself relax into them, be held by them. There is no need to hold yourself up; let yourself be supported. Keep breathing and letting any tension in your body go.

Now. See, standing in front of you, the little child that you were. *How does it feel, seeing this part of you?*

Notice everything about your child. How are they dressed? How does their face look? Happy? Sad? Are you happy to see them? Do they seem happy to see you? Will they look you in the eye? Do you feel comfortable seeing them?

Notice everything.

Now (just inside yourself) ask your child if there is anything they wish to tell you. Listen carefully to make sure you hear what they say.

Now. Is there anything you wish to tell your child?

Talk and listen as much as necessary until everything has been said. Is there anything your child needs from you? Is there anything you need from your child?

Now (just inside yourself) ask your child if they will give you a hug. If the answer is yes, hold your arms out in front of you (actually do this), pick your child up, and bring them to you and hold them tight. Let your arms go around yourself and hold yourself tightly.

Let yourself feel this hug. Relax into it. Feel what it is like to hold this part of yourself so closely. Has it been too long since you gave yourself this kind of caring?

Now. Is there anything else you need to say to your child? Anything your child needs to say to you?

Let yourself be with this experience as long as you need or want to. Then, when you are finished, thank your child for hugging you and for coming to see you.

Then, when you are ready, for now, say good-bye.

We are often taught in the Western world, especially in the United States, to repress this part of us. It is a part of ourselves that feels very deeply and is very sensitive to the emotional nuances in the world. Reclaiming this part of ourselves from the bag in which it has been for so long is essential to this work. For there is no part of us that is more accessible to the field of the heart, no part that has a greater capacity to feel deeply.

Many people can have difficulty in reclaiming this part of themselves. If you imagine a close friend whom you failed to meet, three or four times in a row, for a lunch date, you can imagine the kinds of feelings that might exist in a part of you closeted away for fifteen or twenty years. Sometimes it takes a great deal of work to reestablish communication, even more to reestablish trust. This part does not respond well to demands or threats but will often respond to promises, especially if they are kept. (Usually you will have to do something in exchange. It is very important that you do it if you agree to.) It is worth the work it takes to make friends with this part of you again.

Opening the door to this part of you opens the door to reconnection to the world and all the subtle meanings within it. I often suggest that people do this exercise daily for at least a year. This part of yourself will tell you everything that is going on internally, everything that you deeply need. It will also tell you much about the world around you. It truly is possible to become your own best friend.

> *It is not necessary to tell a child, "This is wood sorrel. It looks like clover, but it's not." A child does not understand and has no need for botanical knowledge. Teach a child that clover is a green manure plant and that pearlwort is a medicinal herb useful for treating diabetes and the child will lose sight of the true reason for that plant's existence. All plants grow and exist for a reason. When we tie a child down with petty, microcosmic scientific knowledge he loses the freedom to acquire with his own hands macrocosmic wisdom. If children are allowed to play freely in a world that transcends science, they will develop natural methods of farming by themselves.*
>
> Masanobu Fukuoka

There is a reason why Luther Burbank, George Washington Carver, Helen Keller, and a great many indigenous plant peoples were all said to be like children.

↣ The Infant

Children respond to ten thousand subtle influences which would leave no more impression on a plant or on most grown-ups than

they would on a sphinx. [We should nurture this sensitivity but]
instead we pour them all into one mould, like steel wire fed through
a pin-making machine, and when they are standardized so that
you can hardly tell their minds apart we expect them to go out into
the world and make something of themselves. If they do it is in spite
of their education instead of because of it.

LUTHER BURBANK

(Sometimes it is helpful to make a tape recording of this exercise—just as you did the last one—and play it back. Instead of the words "them" or "they" that I use in the exercise, use "him" or "her" and "she" or "he" and "his" or "hers"—whichever gender you are. If you practice you will find the perfect speed, pitch, and intonation for you to listen to.)

Sit someplace comfortable. Someplace you won't be disturbed. Someplace you feel safe and nurtured.

Close your eyes and take some deep breaths. Fill up your lungs as if they were balloons, fill them to bursting. Hold it, hold it, hold it. Then . . . slowly . . . release. As you let out the air in your lungs, let any tension you feel inside you release and flow out with your breath. Do this again . . . several times.

Begin with your toes, then your ankles, your knees. And with each breath let the tension in this part of your body flow out with your breath. Do this with each major part of your body, ending with your face, head, and neck.

Now. Imagine the floor or chair under you as two huge, cupped hands that are holding you. Let yourself relax into them, be held by them. There is no need to hold yourself up; let yourself be supported. Keep breathing and letting any tension in your body go.

See, lying on the floor in front of you, the little baby that you were. *How does it feel, seeing this part of you?*

Notice everything about them. How are they dressed? How does their face look? Happy? Sad? Are their eyes open? Or closed?

Are you happy to see them? Do you feel comfortable seeing them? Do they seem happy to you? Is your baby moving? Is your baby breathing? What is the color of your baby's skin? Do your baby seem healthy? Or unhealthy? Are they are getting enough food to eat?

Notice everything about your infant.

keep breathing

Now, reach down (really do this) and pick your baby up. Hold them to your chest as you would hold and cuddle any baby, let them nestle in. Feel what it is like to hold this part of yourself so closely.

Now (even if you are a man) begin breast feeding your baby. Allow the food from inside you to flow out and into this most vulnerable part of you. Is there a nurturing that is happening now that has been too long absent? How long has it been since you comforted and took care of this most vulnerable part of yourself?

How do you feel doing this?

Now. As you are holding and feeding your baby, notice: Is there anything your baby needs from you? Anything that it wants you to do? And, as well, is there anything that you need from your baby?

In a minute it will be time to stop. But before you do, is there anything you need to say to this part of you? Is there anything else your baby needs from you?

Let yourself be with this experience as long as you want to. Then, when you are finished, look at your baby, allow the caring that is inside you to flow out and into them until they are filled up with it. And, when you are ready, thank your baby for coming to be with you, and, for now, say good-bye.

This tiny, vulnerable part of us is one that is often put in the bag of shadow. It is a part of us that is helpless and needs a special kind of food. This part of us is also very important, for it knows how to suckle at the breast of the world, to take that food into itself. And this part of you is very, very sensitive to the emotional fields and their communications. For this part of you is the one that developed within the EM field of your mother's heart. And it knows those fields as intimately as it knows anything.

There [in Nature] I can walk, and recover the lost child that I am without any ringing of a bell.

HENRY DAVID THOREAU

Infants have no words as you might have discovered—they perceive in feeling/gestalts—but that is all right, the child you met first knows lots of words. And, if you ask them to help, they are often willing to act as interpreters.

Expanding the Exercises to Every Developmental Stage

You can repeat this exercise, if you wish, with any developmental age you have lived through, from infancy to two, to four, to eight, to adolescence, young adulthood, middle age, and so on. Each has its own intelligence, its own special connections with the world. Developmental stages do not stop at twelve or sixteen; the child naturally grows to forty . . . and to eighty. It is possible to remain filled with feeling and wonder and openness at any age. Each age has its own teachings. Each is a unique developmental stage of a human being's growth. Each has unique perceptions and capacities that aid in the experience of the human condition.

I highly suggest that, over time, you work with every part of you that emerges or that captures your interest or attention. Over time, you can begin to reclaim the whole self, every part of you, and bring them together into an integrated whole as a fully interactive, healthy inner council. There is tremendous power then in any actions you take, for no part of you is holding out, uncomfortable with what you are choosing to do. *All of you*, together, is choosing, as a group, integrated whole, to life the life you then live.

It is also crucial, in this process, to integrate the body (see page 501). It is one of the most powerful parts of who you are, of the inner council.

Dealing with Specific Problems

When you run into problems with your depth encounters in the metaphysical background of the world, find the time to go to a place you are comfortable. Sit and then just ask the part of you that is upset to come and talk to you. See them on the screen of your inner vision, in your imaginal sensing. Ask them to tell you about what is troubling them. Take as long as you need for the two of you to talk it over. Assure this part of you that you will work to find a solution to the problem.

Perhaps even as you speak one will occur to you

Do this every day until you find a solution. Hug and hold this part of you if it needs it. And . . . take the problem to the inner council. The various parts of you will have different ideas, ones that did not occur to your conscious mind, that may solve the problem. If you do this, every problem you encounter can be solved. Some of them just take some work.

In this process you are working to heal your interior selves and caretake them on a regular, daily basis. There is no one alive that knows what you need better than you, and these parts of you, do. You are offering these parts a love they have always needed.

Don Conoscenti talked about the process of reclaiming a lost part of the self in one of his songs . . .

Anastasia, I have seen, all of the ghosts, haunting your streets
They will sing you their dark serenade, false lullabies will rock you
*   to sleep*
Anastasia, I have dreamed you, in the red desert sky
High above the Sangre de Cristos, with the goddess's smile
And if you're standing, at the gates of Eden, taking blame for the
*   fall*
I have left you, a ladder leaning, against the garden wall

All the cynics and the one way preachers, hammer you all day long
They will never be true believers or taste your salt tears
in the sweet light of dawn
But if you're standing, at the gates of Eden, taking blame for the fall
I have left you, a ladder leaning, against the garden wall

And if every star spoke your name, would you deny even this
If every sun, every moon, oh every road,
led back to this love that you've missed
Anastasia, I have dreamed you, in the red desert sky
High above the Sangre de Cristos,
bathed in the light of the goddess's smile.[3]

This kind of love and understanding is always necessary when you do this work in your interior world.

ﾟ The Body

It makes a wonderful difference if you find in the body an ally or an adversary.

GOETHE

Sit someplace comfortable. Someplace you won't be disturbed. Someplace you feel safe and nurtured.

Close your eyes and take some deep breaths. Fill up your lungs as if they were balloons, fill them to bursting. Hold it, hold it, hold it. Then . . . slowly . . . release. As you let out the air in your lungs, let any tension you feel inside you release and flow out with your breath. Do this again . . . several times.

Begin with your toes, then your ankles, your knees. And with each breath let the tension in this part of your body flow out with your breath. Do this with each major part of your body, ending with your face, head, and neck.

Now. Imagine the floor or chair under you as two huge, cupped hands that are holding you. Let yourself relax into them, be held by them. There is no need to hold yourself up; let yourself be supported. Keep breathing and letting any tension in your body go.

Now. See standing in front of you, your body.

How do you feel, seeing this part of you? Notice how it looks to you. Notice how it feels, how it holds itself. Does it seem happy, or sad. Mad? Ask it if there is anything it needs from you. Do you need anything from it?

Keep working with and talking to your body and listening to what it is telling you for as long as the both of you need.

Do this exercise until you can feel total and complete love for your body, until it trusts you are its best friend, until the two of you are deep and abiding friends and comrades.

It will make a tremendous difference in the work and in your life.

~ Working with Specific Organs: Bodytalk

Every part of the body has its own intelligence. It is possible to make relationship with every intelligence your body has, from your bones to your white blood cells to your heart to your brain and everything else that exists in that scenario. It's called bodytalk, and it is especially useful for bodyworkers and healers; it increases the power of your work considerably. On a personal level, it enhances health and allows sophisticated healing interventions into any physical problems you might have. So . . .

Sit someplace comfortable. Someplace you won't be disturbed. Someplace you feel safe and nurtured.

Close your eyes and take some deep breaths. Fill up your lungs as if they were balloons, fill them to bursting. Hold it, hold it, hold it. Then . . . slowly . . . release. As you let out the air in your lungs, let any tension you feel inside you release and flow out with your breath. Do this again . . . several times.

Begin with your toes, then your ankles, your knees. And with each breath let the tension in this part of your body flow out with your breath. Do this with each major part of your body, ending with your face, head, and neck.

Now. Imagine the floor or chair under you as two huge, cupped hands that are holding you. Let yourself relax into them, be held by them. There is no need to hold yourself up; let yourself be supported. Keep breathing and letting any tension in your body go.

Now, notice your lungs. Notice their shape, their color. How healthy do they seem to you? Do they seem happy? Or sad? Mad? Or scared?

Let your gaze focus on them until they come truly alive in front of you. What feelings do you have about your lungs? Let these feelings grow in intensity until they are all that you feel.

What part of your lungs stands out most clearly to your gaze? What is it about this part that is demanding your attention? What does it need from you?

Is there anything that your lungs need from you? Anything that you need from your lungs?

Do this until you can look at your lungs without any discomfort.

Now. Repeat this with your heart, your GI tract, and your skin. Or with any organ that seems to you to need attention.

Do this until you can look clearly at any organ within you and see it from multiple points of view. Do this until you have established a communication with all your organ systems, until you have a comfortability with each of them.

In this process you will discover that the nature of the organs changes. They will begin to become more aware, less unconscious, to greet you as a friend, to look forward to your visits. They will begin to interact with you. As they do, there will be an increased vitality and vibrancy to them. Astonishing really.

A Few Last Words

Irrespective of the part that emerges into your inner council, you can make relationship with it. It is a never-ending process, for you will discover new parts of yourself throughout your lifetime. It is integral to the path.

This is how you become your own best friend. And remember, other people, sometimes through no fault of their own, come and go. But . . . you will always be here. It makes a tremendous difference if you never abandon yourself.

ON THE HEALING OF SCHIZOPHRENIA

I never promised you a rose garden.

JOANNE GREENBERG

The chick's got issues, man.

SOME GUY

And that's when I realized I was Jesus.

COMMON QUOTE IN NEWS REPORTS

I have been asked by a number of people over the years about the healing of schizophrenia. This is a *very* brief look at the process.

Healing the situation isn't easy, primarily for two reasons: 1) the cultural paradigm or view of the condition is itself dysfunctional, to the extent that the paradigm itself is crazy, and 2) the depth of personal work it entails, both on the therapist's part and that of the client, is extreme. In general, depending on the severity of the cognitive fragmentation, it takes from three to five years of very focused work by a therapist that truly understands the condition and a client that is very committed.

The healing process depends on seven things: 1) accurate information about the world (this especially necessitates the abandonment of the Newtonian world view and an embrace of nonlinearity and self-organized systems); 2) depth work with the multiple conscious modules that make up every human being, especially identifying and meeting the needs that belong to each one; 3) heart-field synchronization with the therapist (who must genuinely love the client) and training of the client in heart-field synchronization as a reliable skill; 4) training in accurate responses to and identification of the incoming meaning-filled sensory data; 5) training in control of sensory gating channels, the capacity to open and shut them at will; 6) all schizophrenic conditions involve the segregation of at least one consciousness module to greater or lesser extents; that part (or parts) must ultimately be freed and reintegrated into the whole self. Due to the segregation, often over long time lines, that part becomes severely damaged. Its release from segregation involves the release of a great deal of pent up energy, including a large amount of rage. Rage work is almost always integral to the process. The pain of the part has to be received (without harm to others) so that it can reform itself along more healthy structural lines. The reclamation of this part is the only real psychological surgery involved but it is crucial to the process. And finally 7) the client has to know you will see the process through to the end. They need to know you will not bail on them part way through. This entails a depth of commitment that few Americans, and few therapists, are capable of. They will, for a time, depend on your heart field as their mechanism for identifying reality. They will be going into a darkness that they fear. They have to know you can walk there unafraid and that you will not abandon them in the dark. Don't agree to do it if you can't go the distance.

Actively working to heal schizophrenia in the American culture is fraught with peril—for the same reasons that hallucinogenic drug use is; the culture has no interest in thousands or millions of people loose in the culture with expanded sensory gating channels, actively working with the metaphysical background of the world. It undermines the dominant paradigm too significantly. Some great strides were made in the 1970s on effectively healing the condition but aggressive responses by a number of institutions resulted in such approaches being abandoned and treatment primarily confined to pharmaceuticals that are taken for decades if not a lifetime. Nevertheless, here is some depth on the process.

One: Accurate Information
about the World

As you can see from this book, the picture that our culture paints of the world in which we find ourselves is highly inaccurate. Plants are not insentient organisms, bacteria are not mindless enemies, the environment is not a static background across which humans move, intelligence and purpose are inherent in all living organisms, humans are not the only important life-form, the West is not the only rational, intelligent society. People with widely open sensory gating channels experience such truths every minute of their lives. However, in nearly all therapeutic settings they are told that such perceptions are false. Because of their sensitivity, an accurate map of the world has to be constructed for schizophrenics to replace the map absorbed from culture, family, and schooling. Quite often the shifts in the personal map are foundational. They place the person far outside the norm of the culture. The therapist has to be knowledgeable about the real nature of the world in order to help create the map. If not knowledgeable they need to actively alter their ignorance quotient in order to help their client.

This healing . . . it is not a one-way process. It never is.

In the process of new mapmaking, the therapist has to be willing to honestly answer whatever question the client asks. In essence, the process is much like a four-year-old asking why the grass is green.

*And more uncomfortable ones, such as
what were you and mommy doing last night*

All the questions have to be answered honestly and as accurately as possible.

The sensitivity of people with widely open gating channels is such that they perceive a great deal of information about the interior of other people's lives. At the most basic, they tend to be highly aware of hidden feelings. Irrespective of how good a poker player you are, they will know how you really feel.

They will see the things you hide from yourself

It is crucial that they begin to ask directly how people feel—this begins with the therapist—and get a truthful answer so they can correlate their interior awareness with the actual world. It is, in part, people lying about how they feel and what is true about the world that creates the condition.

Or by the creation of double binds as Gregory Bateson recognized,
for example
the parent telling the child "I love you"
when what they really mean is "I hate you."

This process of mapmaking lasts years. Nearly everything that has been taken for granted about the nature of reality has to be reworked, from the smallest to the largest detail.

Two: Depth Work with Multiple Conscious Modules

Multiple personality disorder is simply an extreme example of a normal condition. *All* people are multiple personalities. All people are made up of many conscious modules that, together, make up the larger self-organized whole that is their unique self. These consciousness modules are composed, primarily, of 1) every developmental age that human beings experience; 2) the body itself and every organ within it (every organ is intelligent, as is the body as a whole); and 3) a few other, less well-known parts such as the daimon.

This concept is difficult for Americans and most people in the West, the cultural illusion of a single consciousness is pervasive. Roughly, there is in each person a brand new baby, a nine-month-old, a two-year-old, a four-year-old, and so on. Each of these developmental stages possesses a unique identity . . . and specific behaviors that go along with that identity. That they can be seen existing across species shows that they are ecological innovations of long standing that serve specific functions. Each perceives a different aspect of the layered reality of the scenario we are in. A fully integrated personality would have all developmental stages in friendly association with each other, none repressed, each accessible at any time, depending on the needs of the moment.

Because the culture insists on the repression of many of these ego states (or consciousness modules), they become unconscious. Their functions and needs are unknown to most people—despite the fact that they affect behavior for everyone. All of us feel the impacts of their movements inside us daily. However, in people labeled schizophrenic these parts tend to intrude more strongly into awareness, the repression tends to be more complete, the beliefs about these parts more pathological. And the conscious mind tends to notice their existence more often as a separate entity that is influencing behavior. The belief may arise that there is another entity inside, controlling behavior or inserting crazy thoughts. The cultural map that insists there is only one single consciousness leads to tremendous confusion, and the continual feeling of being crazy. This is something that few therapists are able to dispel since *their* map is single-consciousness oriented as well.

The developmental stages, since their existence is not recognized, rarely get their needs met directly. In consequence there is a great deal of internal struggle between the different modules as each attempts to gain enough control over behavior in order to meet fundamental needs.

The need for touch in such populations of people is essential. This is a foundational need for human beings, it bypasses the linear mind, communicates the recognition of the existence of the person, and fulfills the most basic form of love. *Touch has to occur and it has to come from a genuine caring.*

Each part has to be worked with individually; often there is a lot of rage from their repression. All the emerging feelings have to be dealt with until complete. Crucially, the therapist has to be trustworthy to the individual modules. They will examine the degree of integrity of the therapist as carefully as a coyote smelling an extended hand. Any bullshit and you are through. Only through trust can this process successfully complete.

Although significant alterations in the internal conflict can be seen within short order, it generally takes several years before peaceful coexistence between the majority of parts occurs.

Three: Heart Field Synchronization

The American awareness of heart field dynamics is incredibly stunted. To a large degree that is a consequence of the abandonment of feeling as a primary cognitive approach to the world. The substitution of a mind-only reasoning process based on linear reductionism—inculcated so strongly in the school system—results in a strong repression of both the use of the heart field and caring in general.

The human heart generates an electromagnetic field that can be measured up to 10 feet from the body's surface, though it extends much further than that. The field is 5,000 times stronger than that generated by the brain. You can, in fact, feel the heart field of another person if you simply walk slowly up to them. At about 18 inches from the body you will have the experience of moving into the person's "space." Unless the person is really repressed, there will be a marked physical response at that moment.

The crucial thing is to establish a synchronization between the heart field of the person and the therapist. The client will then begin using the heart field of the therapist as a model for integrative behavior. (I deal in depth with this in *Secret Teachings of Plants,* Inner Traditions, 2004.) This is crucial. It is through this that the person is able to access a healthy interior structure. It creates a living model they can use in place of the one they received from their parents, which is, in every instance I have seen, problematical.

> *They will, for a time, use your heart field as their primary way of accessing the world around them, for it is healthier than their own. They will then begin constructing a new form for themselves, but it takes time. They will use, in the process, yours as a template for a healthy field. This is essential.*

During this the therapist must be engaged in deeply self-reflective behavior. The therapist must continually observe their own interior modules for unconscious behavior; self-awareness is crucial.

> *This kind of work demands the greatest possible self-awareness any part of you that you don't want to see will be*

activated by the client
that is part of their function in your life
to serve them, you have to become self-aware

Eric Berne spoke to this in his book *Principles of Group Treatment* (Oxford, 1966). Berne identified, primarily, five consciousness modules based on three dominants: Parent, Adult, Child (nurturing parent, critical parent, adult, natural child, adaptive child). Here are his comments . . . and necessities . . .

The Parent and Child aspects of his motivations may influence the therapist much more systematically and pervasively than he may realize. . . . The more productive question is not "Am I playing a game?" but rather "What game am I playing?" When it is discovered through supervision, for example, that a group therapist is engaged in a particular set of subversive maneuvers, this should not be a matter for surprise nor should it be taken to mean that he is unusual; rather it should be taken as a challenge and a matter for concern if a given therapist's game cannot be unmasked quickly so that self-corrective measures can be applied.

The therapist's attitude in this regard should be that of the professional rather than the amateur. He should not assume that until proven otherwise his behavior will be irreproachable, but should find out ahead of time in what respects it is likely to depart from a psychologically clear orientation. His position is analogous to that of a navigator: it is only the amateur who expects his compass to point due north; the professional assumes that there will be a deviation and wants to know what correction he should apply every time he takes a reading. In this sense the therapist, before undertaking group therapy, should "calibrate" himself so that at all times he knows in which direction he should make corrections.[1]

The synchronization of heart field between the person and the therapist is a form of re-parenting. It is crucial. It shows at a level below that of language that the person matters, that they are cared about, and that they are companioned in the darkness by someone who will go the distance with them.

And believe me, they need to know you will go the distance

Only then will they be willing to face the darkness.

Four: Training in Accurate Responses to and Identification of Incoming Data

This is continual. People labeled schizophrenic perceive things that others don't. The therapist needs some facility in this area as well. They also need to be able to support the person's perceptual frame and what they are perceiving. The client's interpretations are often skewed, so it takes time to sort it all out. It is crucial that the client learn to not act on what is perceived until the interpretations become accurate. There can be no cursory dismissal of perception by the therapist. The real question is, "What are they perceiving, and what is the correct interpretation?"

This demands the greatest possible flexibility, depth of analysis, acuity, and continual questioning about the nature of perception and meaning on the part of the therapist. It never ends. The client has to be encouraged to trust their perceptions but to be suspicious of their interpretation. Accurate interpretation occurs over time. And the therapist has to engage in a continual search for the accurate interpretation. You are helping them construct a map and compass to navigate the world. Do it well.

Five: Training in Control of Sensory Gating Channels

I have talked about this already. It will take time for them to learn how to do this. They will not usually be amenable until they become comfortable with their perceptual frame being supported. They will be afraid they will lose the capacity to open up and sense the world around them with this degree of acuity, that your goal is to shut them down. Permanently. (Most therapists do in fact intend just that.) After they begin to gain control over perception and interpretation, they will be more responsive to control over intake in general.

Six: Freeing Segregated Parts

This is one of the more difficult aspects of the work. To be frank: the segregated parts are often frightening. They are almost always possessed of homicidal rage. In the midst of heart field work, the impact of these parts on the therapist is extreme. You have to be unafraid of them. Truly unafraid. That means you have to face your own fears.

You can get one of the better description of segregated parts in *The Cathexis Reader* by Jacqui Schiff (Harper and Row, 1975). And there are a few later texts by other authors along that line that are useful as well. It's a decent beginning to the knowledge base.

These parts will only emerge if you are completely trustworthy. And when they emerge, you have to actually be able to perceive them with your feeling self, see them on the screen of your inner vision. They will show you, one time only, the wound that caused them to segregate. You will have to reach in then with your feeling self, as carefully as someone building a ship in a bottle, and touch the wound *and reshape it*. There is a part of you that has to go into that place and restructure the wound. The person cannot do it on their own. Much of the restructuring comes simply from the touch of love in just that exact place. The feeling self inserts an invisible field, made of love and directed intention, into that place. It changes things.

In this moment the client is showing the wound to someone else, without defensiveness, humbly, openly. It is something they have never done before. In that moment, you can't waver, can't fail to notice, or let your own stuff get in the way. In total service to the client you have to reach in with your directed feeling cognition and touch the wound, all of it, hold it in your heart field and then . . .

Send into it the exact meaning-filled field that is necessary to restructure the wound. That is, you receive the communication of the wound as a gestalt, you know it from inside itself. In that moment you will know everything that happened and why it is there and there will be a request for a specific response. You then craft that response, immediately, as a meaning-filled gestalt, like dolphin song, that you send back, inside the wound, deep into the part that has just revealed itself to you. And everything changes in that moment. It never goes back to the way it was.

This part? It has never trusted anyone. You will get only one chance. Don't miss it. Don't waver. Don't screw up.

It takes several years before this moment arrives, three or four sometimes. It is the actual moment of healing. On the other side, if successfully done, there is another year or so of finalizing the processes outlined above. But that is just integration, necessary before they go out into the world on their own.

Seven: Seeing Them through to the End

Crucial. Make the agreement, and keep it. And remember: always tell the truth, no matter how hard it is for you, just do it caringly. But never lie. They will always know. If you get caught in one it will often be the end of trust. And without trust, true healing cannot occur.

> *There is no reason*
> *That so many of our holy people*
> *Must remain lost.*
> *Without them, as a people,*
> *We remain lost as well.*

NOTES

Not everything that counts can be counted, and not everything that can be counted counts.

ALBERT EINSTEIN

Chapter 1. Reclaiming the Invisible

1. William Stafford, *You Must Revise Your Life,* 9–10.
2. Quoted in F. Bruce Lamb, *Wizard of the Upper Amazon,* 91.
3. Thoreau, from *Walden,* quoted in Robert Bly, *The Winged Life,* 120.
4. Albert Hofmann, *LSD: My Problem Child,* ix–x.
5. Quoted in Ibid., 199.
6. Ibid., 200.
7. Bly, *Winged Life,* 108–10.
8. Quoted in Sophy Burnham, *For Writers Only,* 12.
9. Terry Castle, "You better not tell me you forgot," 6.

Chapter 2. "The Doors of Perception"

1. Frank Ryan, *Virus X: Tracking the New Killer Plagues,* 52.
2. William Blake, *The Marriage of Heaven and Hell,* 1906.
3. Arash Javanbakht, "Sensory gating deficits, pattern completion, and disturbed fronto-limbic balance, a model for description of hallucinations and delusions in schizophrenia," 1173.
4. Franz Vollenweider, "Brain mechanisms of hallucinogens and entactogens," 268.
5. Javanbakht, "Sensory gating deficits, pattern completion, and disturbed fronto-limbic balance, a model for description of hallucinations and delusions," 1173.
6. William Stafford, *Writing the Australian Crawl,* 25–26.

Chapter 3. "And the Doorkeeper Obeys When Spoken To"

1. Davies, Chang, and Gavin, "Maturation of sensory gating performance in children with and without sensory processing disorders," 192.
2. Paula Jarrard, "Sensory Issues in Gifted Children: Synthesis of the Literature," 3.
3. M. Kisley et al., "Early postnatal development of sensory gating," 693.
4. Ibid., 696.
5. Berne, *Games People Play,* 178.
6. Kisley et al., "Early postnatal development of sensory gating," 696.
7. Markus Kiefer et al., "Neuro-cognitive mechanisms of conscious and unconscious visual perception: Form a plethora of phenomena to general principles," 58.
8. Tsuno and Mori, "Behavioral state-dependent changes in the information processing mode in the olfactory system," 362.
9. Martin Eimer, "Spatial cueing, sensory gating and selective response preparation: An ERP study on visuo-spatial orienting," 408.
10. Kiefer, Adams, and Zovko, "Attentional sensitization of unconscious visual processing," 51.
11. Ibid., 52–53.
12. Kiefer et al., "Neuro-cognitive mechanisms of conscious and unconscious visual perception," 59.
13. Ibid.
14. Hofmann, *LSD: My Problem Child,* 199.
15. Kiefer, Adams, and Zovko, "Attentional sensitization of unconscious visual processing," 54.
16. Gregory Bateson, *Mind and Nature,* 107.
17. Keifer et al., "Neuro-cognitive mechanisms of conscious and unconscious visual perception," 59–60.
18. Vaclav Havel, *The Art of the Impossible,* 166–67.

Chapter 4. "Everything Is Intelligent"

1. Michael Crichton, *The Lost World,* 2.
2. Steven Strogatz, *Sync,* 1–2.
3. Scott Camazine et al., *Self-organization in Biological Systems,* 19.
4. Ibid., 11.
5. P. C. W. Davies, "The physics of complex organisation," in Goodwin and Saunders, eds., *Theoretical Biology: Epigenetic and Evolutionary Order from Complex Systems,* 102.
6. Camazine, *Self-organization in Biological Systems,* 8, 31.
7. Yaneer Bar-Yam, *Dynamics of Complex Systems,* 10, 11.

8. Crichton, *The Lost World*, 2–3.
9. James Lovelock, "The living earth," 770.
10. Richard Lewontin, *The Triple Helix*, 89.
11. Ibid., 93.
12. Margulis and Sagan, *Dazzle Gradually*, 40.
13. Mary Midgley, *Science as Salvation*, 145.
14. Midgley, *Evolution as Religion*, 116.
15. William Day, quoted in Midgley, *Science as Salvation*, 148.
16. Midgley, *The Myths We Live By*, 119.
17. Rupert Sheldrake, *The Science Delusion*, 23.
18. Midgley, *The Myths We Live By*, 91.
19. Susan Sontag, *As Consciousness Is Harnessed to Flesh*.
20. Giorgio Samorini, *Animals and Psychedelics*, 82–83.
21. Davies, "The physics of complex organisation," in Goodwin and Saunders, eds., 109.
22. Lewontin, *The Triple Helix*, 62–63.
23. Jeremy Narby, *Intelligence in Nature*, 96.
24. Nakagaki, "Smart behavior of true slime mold in a labyrinth," 767.

Chapter 5. We Want Braaaaains

1. Quoted in Jason Godesky, "Plants are people, too."
2. Valerie Brown, "Bacteria 'R' Us."
3. Midgley, *The Myths We Live By*, 114.
4. Stuart Levy, *The Antibiotic Paradox*, 75.
5. Francisco Varela, et al., "Adaptive strategies gleaned from immune networks: viability theory and comparison with classifier systems," in Goodwin and Saunders, eds., *Theoretical Biology: Epigenetic and Evolutionary Order from Complex Systems*, 112.
6. Steven Projan, "Antibacterial drug discovery in the 21st century," in Richard Wax et al., eds., *Bacterial Resistance to Antimicrobials*, 413.
7. Williams and Lenton, *Microbial Gaia*, 5.
8. Abigail Salyers, et al., "Ecology of antibiotic resistant genes," in Richard Wax, et al., *Bacterial Resistance to Antimicrobials*, 11.
9. Levy, *The Antibiotic Paradox*, 101.
10. Quoted in Philip Frappaolo, "Risks to Human Health from the Use of Antibiotics in Animal Feeds," in William Moats, ed., *Agricultural Uses of Antibiotics*, 102.
11. Ibid.
12. Margulis and Sagan, *Dazzle Gradually*, 37.

13. Margulis and Sagan, *What Is Sex?* 55.
14. Brown, "Bacteria 'R' Us."
15. Eshel Ben-Jacob et al., "Bacterial linguistic communication and social intelligence," 366.
16. Ben-Jacob et al., "Cooperative organization of bacterial colonies: from genotype to morphotype," 779.
17. Ben-Jacob, "Bacterial self-organization: Co-enhancement of complexification and adaptability in a dynamic environment," 1283.
18. Ben-Jacob and Herbert Levine, "Self-engineering capabilites of bacteria," 197.
19. James Shapiro, "Bacteria are small but not stupid: Cognition, natural genetic engineering, and sociobacteriology," Exeter Meeting, 2006.
20. Ibid.
21. Ibid.
22. S. Bodman, T. Willey, and S. Diggle, "Cell-cell communication in bacteria," 4377–78.
23. Anthony Trewavas, "The Green Plant as Intelligent Organism," in Baluska, Mancuso, Volkmann, eds., *Communication in Plants: Neuronal Aspects of Plant Life,* 6.
24. Peggy La Cerra, "The first law of psychology is the second law of thermodynamics," 442.
25. Chakrabarti and Dutta, "An electrical network model of plant intelligence," August 29, 2002.
26. Trewavas, "The Green Plant as Intelligent Organism," in Baluska, Mancuso, Volkmann, eds., *Communication in Plants: Neuronal Aspects of Plant Life,* 8.
27. Ryan, *Virus X,* 294–95.
28. Luis Villarreal et al., "Acute and persistent viral life strategies and their relationship to emerging diseases," 1.
29. Ryan, *Virus X,* 12–13.
30. Ibid., 274, 278.
31. Ibid., 313–34.
32. Yoshida et al., "Cryptic population dynamics: Rapid evolution masks trophic interactions," 1868.
33. Hilker and Schmitz, "Disease-induced stabilization of predator-prey oscillations," 299.
34. Brenner et al., "Plant neurobiology: An integrated view of plant signaling," 414.
35. Baluska et al., "Plant synapses: Actin-based domains for cell-to-cell communcation," 106.
36. Trewavas, "Aspects of Plant Intelligence," 1.
37. Charles Darwin, *The Power of Movement in Plants,* 573.

38. Kevin Warwick, *QI*, 9.

39. Baluska et al., "Neurobiological view of plants and their body plan," in Baluska, Mancuso, Volkmann, eds., *Communication in Plants*, 31.

40. Trewavas, "The Green Plant as Intelligent Organism," in Baluska, Mancuso, Volkmann, eds., *Communication in Plants*, 3.

41. Ibid.

42. McCormack et al., "Touch-Responsive Behaviors and Gene Expression in Plants," in Baluska, Mancuso, Volkmann, eds., *Communication in Plants*, 256–67.

43. Trewavas, "The Green Plant as Intelligent Organism," in Baluska, Mancuso, Volkmann, eds., *Communication in Plants*, 4.

44. Quoted in Midgley, *Science as Salvation*, 34.

45. Baluska et al., "Neurobiological view of plants and their body plan," in Baluska, Mancuso, Volkmann, eds., *Communication in Plants*, 23.

46. Trewavas, "The Green Plant as Intelligent Organism," in Baluska, Mancuso, Volkmann, eds., *Communication in Plants*, 4–5.

47. Baluska et al., "Root apices as plant command centres," 1.

48. Trewavas, "Aspects of Plant Intelligence," 2.

49. Baluska et al., "Neurobiological view of plants and their body plan," in Baluska, Mancuso, Volkmann, eds., *Communication in Plants*, 28–29.

50. Barlow, "Darwin and the 'Root Brain'" in Baluska, Mancuso, Volkmann, eds., *Communication in Plants*, 39.

51. Ibid., 48.

52. Baluska, et al., "Neurobiological view of plants and their body plan," in Baluska, Mancuso, Volkmann, eds., *Communication in Plants*, 21.

53. Ibid., 27.

54. Ibid., 21.

55. Ibid., 28.

56. Ibid., 24.

57. Lewontin, *The Triple Helix*, 94.

58. Baluska et al., "Neurobiological view of plants and their body plan," in Baluska, Mancuso, Volkmann, eds., *Communication in Plants*, 24.

59. Crichton, *The Lost World*, 361–62.

60. Crichton, *Prey*, 251.

61. Lenton and Williams, "Gaia and evolution," 77–78.

Chapter 6. Gaia and "The Pattern that Connects"

1. Margulis and Sagan, *Dazzle Gradually*, 181.

2. Lovelock, "Reflections on Gaia," 1.

3. Lovelock, "Gaia and emergence," 1–2.

4. Crichton, *The Lost World,* 82–83.

5. Frank Herbert, *Dune,* 31, supposedly derived from either a statement by Søren Kierkegaard or slightly modified from one by Aart Van Der Leeuw, taxonomists aren't sure.

6. Quoted in Hird, "Indifferent globality," 63.

7. Ibid., 59.

8. Crichton, *The Lost World,* 337.

9. Masanobu Fukuoka, *The Natural Way of Farming,* 88.

10. Williams and Lenton, "Microbial Gaia," 6.

11. Ibid., 5.

12. Bateson, *Mind and Nature,* 21.

13. Herbert, *Dune,* 370.

14. Hird, "Indifferent globality," 63.

15. Quoted in Hird, "Indifferent globality," 59.

16. Lewontin, *It Ain't Necessarily So,* 70–72.

17. Quoted in Lane Tracy, "Is Gaia a living system?"

18. Hird, "Indifferent globality," 60.

19. Quoted in Hird, "Indifferent globality," 61.

20. Ibid., 62.

21. Fukuoka, *The Road Back to Nature,* 179.

22. Lenton, "Testing Gaia," 409.

23. Hird, "Indifferent globality," 62–63.

24. Ibid., 63.

25. Hamilton and Lenton, "Spora and Gaia: How microbes fly with their clouds," 3.

26. Ibid., 6.

27. Crichton, *Jurassic Park,* 93.

28. Midgley, ed., *Earthy Realism,* 8.

29. Trewavas, "The Green Plant as Intelligent Organism," in Baluska, Mancuso, Volkmann, eds., *Communication in Plants,* 3.

30. Tyler Volk, *Metapatterns,* viii.

31. Crichton, *Jurassic Park,* 172.

32. Volk, *Metapatterns,* viii–ix.

33. Ibid., ix.

34. Ibid., 14.

35. Ibid., 17.

36. Margulis and Sagan, *What Is Sex?* 50.

37. Ibid, 78–79.

38. Ibid., 82.
39. Ibid., 103.
40. Ibid., 123–26.
41. Buhner, *The Taste of Wild Water,* 48–49.
42. Bateson, *Mind and Nature,* 8.
43. Einstein quotes, Brainyquote.com.
44. Lovelock, "The living earth," 769.
45. Edward de Bono, Brainyquote.com.
46. Pendell, *Living with Barbarians,* 12.

Chapter 7. "Molecular Veriditas"

1. Ming and Song, "Adult neurogenesis in the mammalian central nervous system," 223.
2. Geraldine Wright, "The role of dopamine and serotonin in conditioned food aversion learning in the honeybee," 318.
3. Michael Antsey et al., "Serotonin mediates behavorial gregarization underlying swarm formation in desert locusts," 627.
4. Ibid., 629.
5. Ibid., 627.
6. Pendell, *Pharmako/poeia,* 204–5.
7. Efrain Azmitia, "Serotonin and Brain," 32.
8. Ibid., 33.
9. Ibid., 35.
10. Ibid.
11. Ibid.
12. Wu and Cooper, "Serotonin and synaptic transmission at invertebrate neuro-muscular junctions," 101.
13. Azmitia, "Serontonin and Brain," 32–33.
14. Ibid., 37.
15. Ibid., 38.
16. Ibid., 43.
17. Ibid., 43–44.
18. Ramon Pelagio-Flores et al., "Serotonin, a tryptophan-derived signal conserved in plants and animals, regulates root system architecture probably acting as a natural auxin inhibitor in *Arabidopsis thaliana,*" 490.
19. Ibid.
20. Ibid., 491.
21. Ibid., 493.

22. Akula Ramakrishna, et al., "Phytoserotonin: A review," 806.

23. Pelagio-Flores et al., "Serotonin," 498–99.

24. S. Kang et al., "Characterization of tryptamine 5-hydroxylase and serotonin synthesis in rice plants," 214.

25. Kelli Whitlock, "Casting Prozac upon the waters," 1.

26. P. Andrews et al., *Primum non nocere:* An evolutionary analysis of whether antidepressants do more harm than good," no page numbers available.

Chapter 8. The Function of Psychotropics in the Ecosystem

1. C. D. Nichols et al., "Hallucinogens and Drosophila: Linking serotonin receptor activation to behavior," 979.

2. Quoted in Pendell, *Pharmako/gnosis,* 232.

3. Hofmann, *LSD: My Problem Child,* 19.

4. Aldous Huxley, *The Doors of Perception,* 5–6, 7, 11, 15.

5. Quoted in Hofmann, *LSD: My Problem Child,* 117–18.

6. Halberstadt and Geyer, "Do psychedelics expand the mind by reducing brain activity," May 15, 2012.

7. Hofmann, *LSD: My Problem Child,* 125.

8. O'Gorman and Emmerson, "Perturbations to trophic interactions and the stability of complex food webs," 13393.

9. Ibid.

10. Ibid., 13395.

11. Ibid., 13395–96.

12. Ibid., 13396.

13. Ibid., 13393.

14. Fukuoka, *The Natural Way of Farming,* 17.

15. Duke Ellington, Brainyquote.com

16. Aldo Leopold, *A Sand County Almanac,* 149.

17. Hans Olff et al., "Parallel ecological networks in ecosystems," 1757.

18. Bateson, *Mind and Nature,* 17.

19. *Reader's Digest Great Encyclopedic Dictionary,* 1220.

20. Fukuoka, *The Natural Way of Farming,* 124–25.

21. Dawson, "The ecological niche of psychedelic plants."

22. Rick Strassman, *DMT: The Spirit Molecule,* 42.

23. Quoted in Strassman, *DMT,* 42.

24. Volk, *Metapatterns,* ix.

25. Ibid.

26. Benny Shannon, *The Antipodes of the Mind,* quoted in Pendell, *Pharmako/gnosis,* 151.

27. Crutchfield, quoted in Davies, "The physics of complex organisation," 103, in Goodwin and Saunders, eds., *Theoretical Biology*.

28. Vollenweider and Geyer, "A systems model of altered consciousness: Integrating natural and drug-induced psychoses," 495.

29. Hofmann, *LSD: My Problem Child*, 25.

30. Shannon, *The Antipodes of the Mind*, 257.

31. Jason Godesky, "Plants are people, too," 3.

32. Ibid., 7.

33. Fitz Hugh Ludlow, *The Hasheesh Eater*, 24.

34. Huxley, *The Doors of Perception*, 13.

35. Havelock Ellis, "Mescal: A new artificial paradise."

36. Hofmann, *LSD: My Problem Child*, 19.

37. Giorgio Samorini, *Animals and Psychedelics*, 78.

38. Siegel, *Intoxication*, 100, 211.

39. Pendell, *Pharmako/gnosis*, 80.

40. Edward de Bono, Brainyquote.com.

41. Quoted in Samorini, *Animals and Psychedelics*, 85.

42. Samorini, *Animals and Psychedelics*, 86.

43. Ibid.

44. Ibid., 79.

45. Hofmann, *LSD: My Problem Child*, 196–97.

46. Quoted in Pendell, *Pharmako/gnosis*, 61.

47. Ibid., 70.

48. Hofmann, *LSD: My Problem Child*, 197.

49. Samorini, *Animals and Psychedelics*, 83–84.

50. Hofmann, *LSD: My Problem Child*, 24.

51. Ibid., 199.

52. Quoted in Brandy Doyle, Book Review, "LSD, Spirituality, and the Creative Process" by Marlene Dobkin De Rios and Oscar Janiger.

Chapter 9. Inexplicable Intertangling

1. Crichton, *Prey*, ix.

2. Buckminster Fuller, *Synergetics*, 280–81.

3. Lewontin, *The Triple Helix*, 125–26.

4. Quoted in Brig Klyce, "Gaia."

5. Lewontin, *The Triple Helix*, 44.

6. Fuller, *Synergetics*, 281.

7. Midgley, *Science as Salvation*, 175.

8. Paul Krugman, The Conscience of a Liberal (blog), November 26, 2010.

9. Lewontin, *The Triple Helix,* 125.

10. Lovelock, "Climate change on a living earth."

11. Fukuoka, *The Natural Way of Farming,* 255.

12. David Seamon, *Goethe's Way of Science,* 99.

13. King, *Night Shift,* xxii.

Chapter 10. "A Certain Adjustment of Consciousness"

1. John Gardner, *The Art of Fiction,* 30–31.

2. John Dunning, *The Bookman's Wake,* 58.

3. Dick Francis, *Reflex,* 9.

4. Ibid., 154.

5. Gardner, *The Art of Fiction,* 36.

6. Gardner, *On Becoming a Novelist,* 119–21.

7. Ibid.

8. Ibid.

9. Bly, "Introduction," in *The Best American Poetry 1999,* 4–5.

10. Harry Pickens, personal commmunication, 2013.

11. Quoted in Force and Morrow, eds., *Chromatic: The Crossroads of Color and Music,* 5.

12. Pickens, personal commmunication, 2013.

13. Joe Seneca, from the movie *Crossroads.*

14. Brenda Ueland, *If You Want to Write,* 9.

15. Don Conoscenti, personal commmunication, 2013.

16. I am indebted to Willie Hunton, a mandolin player in Taos, N. Mex., for first telling me about this.

17. Kevin Compton, personal communication, 2011.

18. Eric Clapton, Q and A in *Rolling Stone,* March 14, 2013, 24.

19. Michael Ventura, from the liner notes for *Stevie Ray Vaughan and Double Trouble Texas Flood, SRV Speaks,* Sony Music, 1999.

20. From the album *Stevie Ray Vaughan and Double Trouble Texas Flood, SRV Speaks,* Sony Music, 1999.

21. Erika May Randolph, personal communication, 2013.

22. Buhner, *Sacred Plant Medicine,* 164.

23. Ueland, *If You Want to Write,* 148–49.

24. Charlie Parker, Brainyquote.com.

25. Eric Clapton, interview, 1998, quoted at www.12bar.de/intro.pho.

26. Bradford Keeney, *The Bushman Way of Tracking God,* 104.

Chapter 11. The Sea of Meaning

1. Mark Twain, *The Portable Mark Twain*, 87.
2. Rainer Maria Rilke, *The Notebooks of Malte Laurids Brigg*, 15–16.
3. Nick Cave, "Love Song Lecture," quoted at wikipedia under duende.
4. Jimmy Webb, *Tunesmith*, 17.
5. Keeney, *The Bushman Way of Tracking God*, 40.
6. Goethe, from a letter written July 23, 1820, quoted in Buhner, *The Secret Teachings of Plants*.
7. Buckminster Fuller, *Critical Path*, 133.
8. Quoted in Maureen Seaber, "The shamanic synaesthesia of the Kalahari bushmen," *Psychology Today*, Feb 15, 2012.
9. Ibid.
10. Godesky, "Plants are people, too," 4.

Chapter 12. Following Golden Threads

1. Quoted in Bly, ed., *The Darkness Around Us Is Deep*, vii.
2. Basho, quotation, yenra.com/quotations/basho.html.
3. Stafford, *Writing the Australian Crawl*, 39.
4. Bly, ed., *The Darkness Around Us Is Deep*, viii.
5. Stafford, *Writing the Australian Crawl*, 39.
6. Composer quotes on internet.
7. Stafford, *Writing the Australian Crawl*, 18.
8. William Gass, *Habitations of the Word*, 249.
9. In Bly, ed., *The Darkness Around Us Is Deep*, viii.
10. Ibid., ix.
11. Quoted in Bly, *News of the Universe*, 126.
12. Bly, *The Winged Life*, 109.
13. Bateson, *Mind and Nature*, 20.
14. Keeney, *The Bushman Way of Tracking God*, 199.
15. Quoted in Buhner, *Sacred Plant Medicine*, 40.
16. Keeney, *The Bushman Way of Tracking God*, 60.
17. Ibid.
18. Quoted in Buhner, *Ensouling Language*, 28–29.
19. Ibid., 226.
20. Quoted in Matt Cardin, "Liminality, synchronicity, and the walls of everyday reality."
21. Quoted in Buhner, *Ensouling Language*, 101–2.
22. Webb, *Tunesmith*, 13.

23. Ibid.
24. Rosanne Cash, "Don't Fact-Check the Soul," *New York Times,* April 29, 2008.
25. Berendt, *The World Is Sound,* 114.
26. Daily Mail Reporter, "Talk is cheep! Study finds human speech evolved from birdsong," *Daily Mail,* February 22, 2013.
27. Cash, "Don't Fact-Check the Soul."
28. Benjamin Bailey-Buhner, *Damaged Goods.*
29. Huxley, *The Doors of Perception,* 36.
30. Stephan Harding, "From Gaia theory to deep ecology."
31. Keller, *A Feeling for the Organism,* 201.
32. Ibid., 207.

Chapter 13. The Naturalist's Approach

1. Keller, *A Feeling for the Organism,* 140.
2. Ibid., 141.
3. Ibid., 142.
4. Ibid., 70.
5. Ibid., 198.
6. Lewontin, *Triple Helix,* 54.
7. Keller, *A Feeling for the Organism,* 198.
8. Quoted in Sylvie Shaw, "The Way of Story," www.ecopsychology.org/journal/ezine/story.html.
9. Keller, *A Feeling for the Organism,* 200.
10. Ibid., 148.
11. Ibid., 69.
12. Ibid., 117.
13. Ibid., 201.
14. Ibid., 117.
15. Harding, "From Gaia theory to deep ecology."
16. Quoted in Buhner, *The Secret Teachings of Plants,* 198.
17. Keller, *A Feeling for the Organism,* 80.
18. Ibid., 125.
19. Bly, *News of the Universe,* 212–13.
20. Keller, *A Feeling for the Organism,* 200.
21. Henri Bortoft, *The Wholeness of Nature,* 51.
22. Ibid., 53–54.
23. Keller, *A Feeling for the Organism,* 122.
24. Quoted in ibid., 150–51.

25. Bortoft, *The Wholeness of Nature.*
26. Bly, *American Poetry*, 274–75.
27. Ibid., 262.
28. Henri Corbin, "Mundus Imaginalis."
29. Godesky, "Plants are people, too," 5.
30. Quoted in Buhner, *Ensouling Language*, 179.
31. Keller, *A Feeling for the Organism*, 126.
32. Gardner, *The Art of Fiction*, 36.
33. Seamon, *Goethe's Way of Science*, 46.
34. Keller, *A Feeling for the Organism*, 122.
35. Ibid., 144.
36. McFadden, *Quantum Evolution*, 268.
37. Ibid.
38. Ibid., 269.
39. Ibid., 186.
40. Ibid., 270.
41. Keller, *A Feeling for the Organism*, 199.
42. Ibid., 199–200.
43. Ibid., 204.
44. Samuel Delaney, *The Fall of the Towers*, 156.
45. Lovelock, "Gaia and emergence."

Chapter 14. The Imaginal World

1. Thoreau, *Journal*, October 4, 1859.
2. I read this story of the dolphin child long ago and have told it many times (in my own various words and interpretations) in workshops and lectures. The original can be read here: Lyall Watson, "The Biology of Being: A Natural History of Consciousness" in David Lorimer et al., *The Spirit of Science* (N.Y.: Continuum International Publishing Group, 1999).
3. Le Brun, *Reality Overload*, 200.
4. Bly and Woodman, *The Maiden King*, 5.
5. Ibid.
6. Corbin, "Mundus Imaginalis."
7. McFadden, *Quantum Evolution*, 184.

Chapter 15. The Dreaming of Earth

1. Bly and Woodman, *The Maiden King*, 5.
2. Lao-tzu, *Tao-Te Ching*, 65.

3. Fukuoka, *The Natural Way of Farming*, 181.
4. Quoted in Bortoft, *The Wholeness of Nature*, 265.
5. Bortoft, *The Wholeness of Nature*, 84.
6. Ibid.
7. Corbin, "Mundus Imaginalis."
8. Seaberg, "The shamanic synaesthesia of the Kalahari bushmen."
9. Quoted in Pendell, *Pharmako/gnosis*, 36.
10. Pendell, *Living with Barbarians*, 1.
11. Crichton, *Prey*, 261.
12. Leibert, trans., *Rumi: Fragments, Ecstacies*, 15.
13. Buhner, *The Taste of Wild Water*, 13.

Chapter 16. Reemergence into Classical Newtonian Space

1. Quoted in Hervier, *The Details of Time*, 56.
2. Harrison, *Seeds of Change Catalogue*, 1994, 67.
3. S. Ahabala, "Oscillations in Plants," in Baluska, Mancuso, Volkmann, eds., *Communication in Plants*, 261.
4. Volkov, "Electrophysiology and Phototropism," in Baluska, Mancuso, Volkmann, eds., *Communication in Plants*, 351.
5. Berendt, *The World Is Sound*, 116.
6. Quoted in ibid., 118.
7. Seaberg, "The shamanic synaesthesia of the Kalahari bushmen."
8. Ibid.
9. Berendt, *The World Is Sound*, 89–90.
10. Kruse and Julicher, "Oscillations in cell biology," 20–26.
11. Quoted in Campbell and Doman, *Healing at the Speed of Sound*, 102.
12. Quoted in Daniel Miller, "The amazing images that let us 'see' music (and could even help us communicate with dolphins)."
13. Berendt, *The World Is Sound*, 77.
14. [https]://aguasonics.com.
15. Berendt, *The World Is Sound*, 80.

Chapter 17. The Ecological Function of the Human Species

1. Nigel Clark, "Ex-orbitant globality," 166.
2. Guillette, "Impacts of endocrine disruptors on wildlife," 5.
3. Quoted in Clark, "Ex-orbitant globality," 172.
4. Quoted in ibid., 165.
5. Clark, "Ex-orbitant globality," 173.

6. Ibid., 174.

7. Ibid., 175.

8. Ibid., 184.

9. Crichton, *Jurassic Park,* 367.

10. Lewontin, *The Triple Helix,* 102–3.

11. Quoted in Sagan, *Notes from the Holocene,* 12.

12. Staff Writer NASA, "Earth microbes on the moon," September 1, 1998.

13. Ibid.

14. Ibid.

15. Rilke, "All Will Come Again," available in numerous places on the Internet, e.g., www.reclaimingthewildsoul.com, accessed December 13, 2013.

16. Quoted in Keller, *A Feeling for the Organism,* 205–6.

Chapter 18. "The Road Not Taken"

1. Midgley, *Science as Salvation,* 170.

2. Quoted in Adam Phillips, "Am I a Spaceman?" 27.

3. Krugman, The Conscience of a Liberal (blog), 10/07/11.

4. Jenny Diski, "Short cuts," 36.

5. Adam Phillips, "A Seamstress in Tel Aviv," 6.

6. Deresiewicz, "The disadvantages of an elite education," 1.

7. Ibid., 2.

8. Ibid., 8.

9. Lovelock, *Homage to Gaia,* 5.

10. Clark, "Ex-orbitant globality," 171.

11. Le Brun, *Reality Overload,* xii.

12. John Ioannidis, "Why most published research findings are false," 686.

13. Freedman, "Lies, damned lies, and medical science," 2010.

14. Ibid.

15. Ibid.

16. Baez, "Ban Elsevier."

17. Krugman, "In praise of econowonkery," blog, May 11, 2013.

18. Shapin, *Never Pure,* 54.

19. Krugman, "Fine Austrian Whines," blog, February 20, 2013.

20. Crichton, *Jurassic Park,* x–xi.

21. Marcia Angell, "Drug companies and doctors: A story of corruption," *The New York Review of Books,* January 15, 2009.

22. Quoted in Cavoukian, "The environment is dead: Long live mother nature," 2012.

23. Heinrich, Heine, and Norenzagan, "The weirdest people in the world?" 2010.

24. Fuller, *Critical Path,* xi.

25. Alan Boyle, "Gamers solve molecular puzzle that baffled scientists," NBCNews .com, January 8, 2013.

26. Daily Mail Reporter, "Schoolboy cracks age-old math problem," *Daily Mail,* May 23, 2012.

27. Clark, "Ex-orbitant globality," 169.

28. Ibid., 175.

29. Quoted in ibid., 175.

Chapter 19. Becoming Barbarian

1. Saul, *Voltaire's Bastards,* 30, 36.

2. Walker, *Living by the Word,* 35.

3. Quoted in Fuller, *Critical Path,* xii.

4. Stafford, *A Scripture of Leaves,* 7.

5. Harding, "Earth system science and Gaian science."

Epilogue. To See the Shimmer of Infinity in the Face of Another

1. John Neihardt, *Black Elk Speaks,* 49.

Diminuendo Al Niente. The Movement of Great Things

1. Buhner, *The Taste of Wild Water,* 60–61. For Julie.

Appendix One. Sensory Overload and Self-Caretaking

1. Travis Holland, *Texas Genesis,* 87.

2. Francis, *The Danger,* 103–4.

3. Don Conoscenti, lyrics to "Anastasia," *Mysterious Light* Cogtone, 2000.

Appendix Two. On the Healing of Schizophrenia

1. Berne, *Principles of Group Treatment,* 22.

BIBLIOGRAPHY

The only thing that interferes with my learning is my education.

ALBERT EINSTEIN

The problem with digital books is that you can always find what you are looking for but you need to go to a bookstore to find what you weren't looking for.

PAUL KRUGMAN

I read from 200 to 300 books per year and, when writing, perhaps 10,000 journal, newspaper, and blog articles over the same period. In the course of that I read a great many wonderful things (and a lot of terrible ones). However, over the past forty years there are a few books that stand out because they shifted my perceptual frame so significantly that they altered the course of my life. They are, in the order in which I found them: *Dune, The Limits to Growth, Black Elk Speaks, Games People Play, The Kabir Book, Gaia: A New Look at Life on Earth, The Art of the Impossible, The Winged Life, Voltaire's Bastards,* and *Sex at the Margins.* Be warned, some of these books are hand grenades disguised as nonfiction; they stir things up, considerably. Nevertheless, I highly recommend them. The work of Mary Midgley, Evelyn Fox Keller, Myra Hird, and Lynn Margulis are also important reading; they examine the assumptions and logical problems in the current Western world view and do so with extreme intelligence while at the same time offering a much more accurate paradigm. Annie Le Brun's *Reality Overload* is an important companion to Saul's *Voltaire's Bastards* and is especially revealing regarding the assaults on imaginal thinking and perception. The work of Corbin, Hillman, Bortoft, and Seamons is important reading if you are interested in depth perception of the world and a deeper understanding of our place in that process. Of my books, *Lost Language of Plants* is important if you wish to understand the chemical communication of plants in more depth, *Secret Teachings of Plants* if you wish to explore in depth the possibilities of heart perception, and *Ensouling Language* if you wish more depth on golden threads, aisthesis, and inducing intentional dreaming and imaginal sensing.

The following are the books, journal papers, and news articles I used as resources for this book. Those with an asterisk are highly recommended if you wish to go deeper into the material.

Books

Aaronson, Bernard, and Humphry Osmond. *Psychedelics*. Garden City, N.Y.: Doubleday, 1970.

Abram, David. *Becoming Animal*. N.Y.: Pantheon, 2010.

* Agustin, Laura Maria. *Sex at the Margins: Migration, Labour Markets, and the Rescue Industry*. London: Zed Books, 2007.

Alexandersson, Olof. *Living Waters: Viktor Shauberger and the Secrets of Natural Energy*. Dublin, Ireland: Gateway, 1990.

Allman, John Morgan. *Evolving Brains*. N.Y.: Scientific American Library, 1999.

Bailey-Buhner, Benjamin. *Damaged Goods*. A novel in progress, copyright 2013, all rights reserved, Benjamin Bailey-Buhner.

* Baluska, Frantisek. *Plant-Environment Interactions: From Sensory Plant Biology to Active Plant Behavior*. Berlin: Springer, 2009.

* Baluska, F., S. Mancuso, D. Volkmann, eds. *Communication in Plants: Neuronal Aspects of Plant Life*. Berlin: Springer, 2006.

Bar-Yam, Yaneer. *Dynamics of Complex Systems*. Reading, Mass.: Addison-Wesley, 1997.

Barabasi, Albert-Laszlo. *Linked*. N.Y.: Plume, 2003.

Bartholomew, Alick. *Hidden Nature: The Startling Insights of Viktor Schauberger*. Kempton, Ill.: Adventures Unlimited Press, 2005.

Bateson, Gregory. *Mind and Nature*. N.Y.: E. P. Dutton, 1979.

Basho, Matsuo. *The Narrow Road to the Deep North*. N.Y.: Penguin, 1966.

Benyus, Janine. *Biomimicry*. N.Y.: Harper, 1997.

Berendt, Joachim-Ernst. *The World Is Sound*. Rochester, Vt.: Destiny Books, 1991.

Berne, Eric. *Games People Play*. N.Y.: Grove, 1964.

———. *Principles of Group Treatment*. London: Oxford University Press, 1966.

Blake, William. *The Marriage of Heaven and Hell.* Boston, Mass.: John Luce, 1906.

Bly, Robert. *American Poetry: Wilderness and Domesticity.* N.Y.: Harper and Row, 1990.

———, ed. *The Best American Poetry 1999,* series ed. David Lehman. N.Y.: Scribner, 1999.

———, ed. *The Darkness Around Us Is Deep: Selected Poems of William Stafford.* N.Y.: HarperPerennial, 1993.

* ———. *The Kabir Book.* Boston, Mass.: Beacon Hill, 1977.

———. *News of the Universe.* San Francisco, Calif.: Sierra Club Books, 1980.

* ———. *The Winged Life: The Poetic Voice of Henry David Thoreau.* San Francisco, Calif.: Sierra Club Books, 1986.

Bly, Robert, and Marion Woodman. *The Maiden King.* N.Y.: Henry Holt, 1998.

* Bortoft, Henri. *The Wholeness of Nature: Goethe's Way of Science.* N.Y.: Lindisfarne Press, 1996.

Bose, Jagadis. *Growth and Tropic Movement of Plants.* London: Longmans, Green, 1929.

———. *Irritability of Plants.* New Delhi, India: Discovery House, 1999.

———. *The Nervous Mechanism of Plants.* London: Longmans, Green, 1926.

———. *Physiology of the Ascent of Sap.* London: Longmans, Green, 1924.

———. *Plant Autographs and Their Revelations.* N.Y.: Macmillan, 1927.

———. *Plant Response.* N.Y.: Longmans, Green, 1906.

Bowles, Samuel, and Herbert Gintis. *A Cooperative Species: Human Reciprocity and Its Evolution.* Princeton, N.J.: Princeton University Press, 2011.

* Buhner, Stephen Harrod. *Ensouling Language.* Rochester, Vt.: Inner Traditions, 2010.

———. *Herbal Antibiotics: Natural Alternatives for Treating Drug-resistant Bacteria,* 2nd ed. North Adams, Mass.: Storey Publishing, 2012.

———. *Herbal Antivirals: Natural Alternatives for Treating Drug-resistant Viruses.* North Adams, Mass.: Storey Publishing, 2013.

* ———. *The Lost Language of Plants.* White River Junction, Vt.: Chelsea Green, 2002.

———. *Sacred Plant Medicine.* Rochester, Vt.: Bear and Company, (1996) 2006.

* ———. *The Secret Teachings of Plants.* Rochester, Vt.: Bear and Company, 2004.

———. *The Taste of Wild Water.* Silver City, N.M.: Raven Press, 2009.

Burkhardt, Richard. *The Spirit of System: Lamarck and Evolutionary Biology.* Cambridge, Mass.: Harvard University Press, 1995.

Burnham, Sophy. *For Writers Only.* N.Y.: Ballantine, 1994.

Camazine, Scott, et al. *Self-organization in Biological Systems.* Princeton, N.J.: Princeton University Press, 2001.

Campbell, Don, and Alex Doman. *Healing at the Speed of Sound.* N.Y.: Hudson Street Press, 2011.

Capra, Fritjof. *The Hidden Connections*. N.Y.: HarperCollins, 2002.

Changeux, Jean-Pierre. *Neuronal Man*. N.Y.: Pantheon, 1985.

Coats, Callum. *Living Energies*. Dublin, Ireland: Gateway, 2001.

Corning, Peter. *Nature's Magic: Synergy in Evolution and the Fate of Humankind*. Cambridge, U.K.: Cambridge University Press, 2003.

Crichton, Michael. *Congo, Sphere,* and *Eaters of the Dead*. N.Y.: Wings Books, 1994.

———. *Jurassic Park*. N.Y.: Knopf, 1990.

———. *The Lost World*. London: Arrow Books, 1997.

———. *Next*. N.Y.: Harper, 2006.

———. *Prey*. N.Y.: HarperCollins, 2002.

Darwin, Charles. *The Power of Movement in Plants*. London: John Murray, 1880.

Davidson, Richard, and Sharon Begley. *The Emotional Life of Your Brain*. N.Y.: Hudson Street Press, 2012.

Delaney, Samuel. *The Fall of the Towers*. N.Y.: Bantam, 1982.

Dixon, Royal. *The Human Side of Plants*. N.Y.: Frederick A. Stokes, 1914.

Doyle, Richard. *Darwin's Pharmacy: Sex, Plants, and the Evolution of the Noosphere*. Seattle: University of Washington Press, 2011.

Dunning, John. *The Bookman's Wake*. N.Y.: Scribner, 1995.

Eisley, Loren. *The Night Country*. Lincoln: University of Nebraska Press, 1997.

Everett, Daniel. *Don't Sleep, There Are Snakes: Life and Language in the Amazonian Jungle*. N.Y.: Pantheon, 2008.

Force, Chris, and Scott Morrow, eds. *Chromatic: The Crossroads of Color and Music*. Chicago: Alarm Press, 2011.

Francis, Dick. *The Danger*. N.Y.: Fawcett, 1984.

———. *Three to Show: Dead Cert, Nerve, Odds Against*. N.Y.: Harper and Row, 1969.

———. *Reflex*. N.Y.: Putnam, 1981.

Freedman, David. *Wrong: Why Experts Keep Failing Us—and How to Know When Not to Trust Them*. N.Y.: Little, Brown, 2010.

* Fukuoka, Masanobu. *The Natural Way of Farming*. Tokyo: Japan Publications, 1985.

* ———. *The Road Back to Nature*. Tokyo: Japan Publications, 1987.

Fuller, R. Buckminster. *Critical Path*. N.Y.: St. Martins, 1981.

———. *Synergetics: Explorations in the Geometry of Thinking*. N.Y.: Macmillan, 1975.

Gardner, John. *The Art of Fiction*. N.Y.: Vintage, 1991.

———. *On Becoming a Novelist*. N.Y.: Norton, 1999.

Garrels, Scott, ed. *Mimesis and Science*. East Lansing: University of Michigan Press, 2011.

Gass, William. *Habitations of the Word*. Ithaca, N.Y.: Cornell University Press, 1997.

Gluck, Mark, and Catherine Myers. *Gateway to Memory: An Introduction to Network Modeling of the Hippocampus and Learning*. Cambridge, Mass.: MIT Press, 2001.

Goodwin, B., and P. Saunders, eds. *Theoretical Biology: Epigenetic and Evolutionary Order from Complex Systems*. Edinburgh, Scotland; Edinburgh University Press, 1989.

* Havel, Vaclav. *The Art of the Impossible*. N.Y.: Knopf, 1997.

Harding, Stephan. *Animate Earth*. White River Junction, Vt.: Chelsea Green, 2006.

Harrison, Kathleen. *Seeds of Change Catalogue, 1994.*

* Herbert, Frank. *Dune*. Philadelphia, Pa.: Chilton, 1965.

* Hervier, Julien. *The Details of Time: Conversations with Junger*. N.Y.: Marsilio, 1995.

Hill, Peggy. *Vibrational Communications in Animals*. Cambridge, Mass.: Harvard University Press, 2008.

* Hillman, James. *The Soul's Code*. N.Y.: Random House, 1996.

* ———. *The Thought of the Heart and the Soul of the World*. N.Y.: Spring Publications, 1998.

Hinton, David, trans. *Mountain Home: The Wilderness Poetry of Ancient China*. N.Y.: New Directions, 2005.

*Hofmann, Albert. *LSD: My Problem Child*. N.Y.: McGraw-Hill, 1980.

Holland, Julie, ed. *Ecstasy: The Complete Guide*. Rochester, Vt.: Park Street Press, 2001.

Holland, Travis (as told to Mike Williams). *Texas Genesis: A wild ride through Texas Progressive Country Music 1963–1978, with digressions as seen through the warped mind of Travis Holland*. Austin, Tex.: B. F. Deal Publishing, 1978, Special Collectors Edition, one of 100 copies.

Howarth, William. *The Book of Concord: Thoreau's Life as a Writer*. N.Y.: Viking, 1982.

* Huxley, Aldous. *The Doors of Perception*. N.Y.: Thinking, Ink, 2011.

James, William. *On Some of Life's Ideals*. N.Y.: Henry Holt and Company, 1900.

Jantsch, Erich. *The Self-organizing Universe*. N.Y.: Pegamon Press, 1980.

Keeney, Bradford. *The Bushman Way of Tracking God*. N.Y.: Atria, 2010.

* Keller, Evelyn Fox. *A Feeling for the Organism: The Life and Work of Barbara McClintock*. N.Y.: W. H. Freeman, 1983.

———. *Making Sense of Life*. Cambridge, Mass.: Cambridge University Press, 2002.

———. *The Mirage of a Space Between Nature and Nurture*. Durham, N.C.: Duke University Press, 2010.

———. *Refiguring Life*. N.Y.: Columbia University Press, 1995.

———. *Reflections on Gender and Science*. New Haven, Conn.: Yale University Press, 1985.

———. *Secrets of Life, Secrets of Death*. N.Y.: Routlege, 2002.

Kempermann, Gerd. *Adult Neurogenesis*. Oxford, U.K.: Oxford University Press, 2006.

King, Stephen. *Night Shift*. Garden City, N.J.: Doubleday, 1978.

Ksenzhek, Octavian, and Alexander Volkov. *Plant Energetics*. San Diego, Calif.: Academic Press, 1998.

La Cerra, Peggy, and Roger Bingham. *The Origin of Minds*. N.Y.: Harmony Books, 2002.

Lamb, F. Bruce. *Rio Tigre and Beyond*. Berkeley, Calif.: North Atlantic Books, 1985.

* ———. *Wizard of the Upper Amazon*. Boston, Mass.: Houghton Mifflin, 1974.

Lanner, Ronald. *Made for Each Other*. N.Y.: Oxford University Press, 1996.

Lanza, Robert, and Bob Berman. *Biocentrism*. Dallas, Tex.: Benbella Books, 2009.

Lao-Tzu. *Tao Te-Ching*. N.Y.: Modern Library, 1989.

LeBrun, Annie. *The Reality Overload*. Rochester, Vt.: Inner Traditions, 2008.

Leopold, Aldo. *For the Health of the Land*. Washington, D.C.: Island Press, 1999.

* ———. *A Sand County Almanac*. Oxford, U.K.: Oxford University Press, 1987.

Levy, Stuart. *The Antibiotic Paradox*. N.Y.: Plenum Press, 1992.

* Lewontin, Richard. *It Ain't Necessarily So: The Dream of the Human Genome and Other Illusions*. N.Y.: New York Review Books, 2000.

———. *The Triple Helix: Gene, Organism, and Environment*. Cambridge, Mass.: Harvard University Press, 2000.

* Lewontin, Richard, and Richard Levins., *Biology Under the Influence*. N.Y.: Monthly Review Press, 2007.

Liebert, Daniel, trans. *Rumi: Fragments and Ecstacies*. Sante Fe, N. Mex.: Sunstone Press, 1981.

Lovelock, James. *The Ages of Gaia*. N.Y.: Bantam, 1990.

———. *Gaia: A New Look at Life on Earth*. N.Y.: Oxford University Press, 1979.

———. *Healing Gaia*. N.Y.: Harmony Books, 1991.

———. *Homage to Gaia*. Oxford, U.K.: Oxford University Press, 2000.

———. *The Revenge of Gaia*. London: Allen Lane, 2006.

———. *The Vanishing Face of Gaia*. N.Y.: Basic, 2009.

Ludlow, Fitz Hugh. *The Hasheesh Eater: Being Passages from the Life of a Pythagorean*. New Brunswick, N.J.: Rutgers University Press, 2006.

Margulis, Lynn. *Symbiotic Planet*. N.Y.: Basic, 1998.

Margulis, Lynn, and René Fester. *Symbiosis as a Source of Evolutionary Innovation*. Cambridge, Mass.: MIT Press, 1991.

Margulis, Lynn, and Lorraine Olendzenski, eds. *Environmental Evolution*. Cambridge, Mass.: MIT Press, 1992.

Margulis, Lynn, and Dorion Sagan, *Acquiring Genomes: A Theory of the Origins of Species*. N.Y.: Basic, 2003.

———. *Dazzle Gradually: Reflections on the Nature of Nature*. White River Junction, Vt.: Chelsea Green, 2007.

———. *Microcosmos: Four Billion Years of Microbial Evolution*. N.Y.: Touchstone, 1986.

———. *What Is Sex?* N.Y.: Simon and Schuster, 1997.

Masson, Jeffrey, and Susan McCarthy. *When Elephants Weep: The Emotional Lives of Animals*. N.Y.: Delacorte, 1995.

McFadden, Johnjoe. *Quantum Evolution*. N.Y.: Norton, 2000.

McKenzie, D. F. *Making Meaning*. Amherst: University of Massachusetts Press, 2002.

Midgley, Mary. *Animals and Why They Matter*. Athens: University of Georgia Press, 1983.

———. *Beast and Man*. London: Routledge, 1979.

*———, ed. *Earthy Realism: The Meaning of Gaia*. Exeter, U.K.: Societas, 2007.

———. *Evolution as Religion*. London: Routledge, 1985.

———. *The Myths We Live By*. London: Routledge, 2004.

———. *Science and Poetry*. London: Routledge, 2001.

———. *Science as Salvation*. London: Routledge, 1992.

———. *Wisdom, Information, and Wonder*. London: Routledge, 1989.

* Miller, Douglas, ed. *Goethe, The Collected Works*, vol. 12: Scientific Studies. Princeton, N.J.: Princeton University Press, 1988.

Moats, William, ed. *Agricultural Uses of Antibiotics*. Washington, D.C.: American Chemical Society, 1986.

Montagu, Ashley. *On Being Human*. N.Y.: Henry Schuman, 1951.

Narby, Jeffrey. *Intelligence in Nature*. N.Y.: Tarcher, 2005.

Neihardt, John. *Black Elk Speaks*. N.Y.: William Morrow and Co., 1932.

Nutt, David. *Drugs Without the Hot Air*. Cambridge, U.K.: UIT, 2012.

O'Connell, Caitlin. *The Elephant's Secret Sense*. N.Y.: Free Press, 2007.

* Pendell, Dale. *Pharmako/gnosis*. Berkeley, Calif.: North Atlantic Books, 2009.

* ———. *Pharmako/poeia*. Berkeley, Calif.: North Atlantic Books, 2009.

———. *Living with Barbarians*. Sebastopol, Calif.: Wild Ginger Press, 1999.

Pikovsky, Arkady, M. Rosemblum, and J. Kurths. *Synchronization: A Universal Concept in Nonlinear Sciences*. Cambridge, U.K.: Cambridge University Press, 2001.

Powell, Simon. *Darwin's Unfinished Business: The Self-organizing Intelligence of Nature*. Rochester, Vt.: Park Street Press, 2012.

Renard, Jules. *Nature Stories*. N.Y.: New York Review Book, 2011.

Restak, Richard. *Brainscapes*. N.Y.: Hyperion, 1995.

Rilke, Ranier Marie. *The Notebooks of Malte Laurids Brigg*. N.Y.: Norton, 1949.

Rollins, James. *Black Order*. N.Y.: Harper, 2006.

Roshchina, Victoria. *Neurotransmitters in Plant Life*. Enfield, N.H.: Science Publishers, 2001.

Ryan, Frank. *Virus X: Tracking the New Killer Plagues*. N.Y.: Little, Brown, 1997.

Sabini, Meredith, ed. *The Earth Has Soul: C. G. Jung on Nature, Technology, and Modern Life*. Berkeley, Calif.: North Atlantic Books, 2008.

Sagan, Dorion. *Notes from the Holocene*. White River Junction, Vt.: Chelsea Green, 2007.

Samorini, Giorgio. *Animals and Psychedelics: The Natural World and the Instinct to Alter Consciousness*. Rochester, Vt.: Park Street Press, 2002.

✻ Saul, John Ralston. *Voltaire's Bastards: The Dictatorship of Reason in the West.* N.Y.: Vintage, 1992.

Schultes, Richard Evans, Albert Hofmann, and Christian Rätsch. *Plants of the Gods: Their Sacred, Healing, and Hallucinogenic Powers,* revised and expanded. Rochester, Vt.: Healing Arts Press, 1998.

✻ Seamon, David. *Goethe's Way of Science.* Albany: State University of New York, 1998.

Shannon, Benny. *The Antipodes of the Mind: Charting the Phenomenology of the Ayahuasca Experience.* Oxford, U.K.: Oxford University Press, 2010.

Shapin, Steven. *Never Pure: Historical Studies of Science as if It Was Produced by People with Bodies, Situated in Time, Space, Culture, Society, and Struggling for Credibility and Authority.* Baltimore, Md.: Johns Hopkins University Press, 2010.

✻ Sheldrake, Rupert. *The Science Delusion.* London: Coronet, 2012.

Shepard, Florence, ed. *Encounters with Nature: Essays by Paul Shepard.* Washington, D.C.: Island Press, 1991.

✻ Shepard, Odell, ed. *The Heart of Thoreau's Journals.* Mineola, N.Y.: Dover, 1961.

Shepard, Paul. *Nature and Madness.* Athens: University of Georgia Press, 1982.

Shulgin, Alexander, and Ann Shulgin. *TiHKAL: The Continuation.* An online book comprising part 2 of TiHKAL, www.erowid.org/library/books_online/thikal/thikal16.shtml.

Siegel, Ronald. *Intoxication: The Universal Drive for Mind-altering Substances.* Rochester, Vt.: Park Street Press, 2005.

Sontag, Susan. *As Consciousness Is Harnessed to Flesh.* London: Hamish Hamilton, 2012.

Stafford, William. *A Scripture of Leaves.* Elgin, Ill.: Brethren Press, 1989.

✻ ———. *Writing the Australian Crawl.* Ann Arbor: University of Michigan Press, 1978.

———. *You Must Revise Your Life.* Ann Arbor: University of Michigan Press, 1986.

Steele, Edward, R. Lindley, and R. Blanden. *Larmarck's Signature: How Retrogenes are Changing Darwin's Natural Selection Paradigm.* Reading, Mass.: Helix Books, 1998.

Strassman, Rick. *DMT: The Spirit Molecule.* Rochester, Vt.: Park Street Press, 2001.

Stringer, Chris. *Lone Survivors.* N.Y.: Times Books, 2012.

Strogatz, Steven. *Sync: The Emerging Science of Spontaneous Order.* N.Y.: Hyperion, 2003.

Thoreau, Henry David. *The Journal of Thoreau,* vols. 1 and 2. Mineola, N.Y.: Dover Publications, 1962.

✻ Twain, Mark. *Life on the Mississippi.* Boston, Mass.: James Osgood, 1883, chapters 4–13.

———. *The Portable Mark Twain.* N.Y.: Viking Press, 1968.

Tyson, Scott. *The Unobservable Universe.* Albuquerque, N.M.: Galaxia Way, 2011.

Ueland, Brenda. *If You Want to Write.* St. Paul, Minn.: Graywolf Press, 1987.

Ventura, Michael. *Letters at 3 AM: Reports on Endarkenment.* Dallas, Texas: Spring Publications, 1998.

Verstosick, Frank. *The Genius Within: Discovering the Intelligence of Every Living Thing*. N.Y.: Harcourt, 2002.

Volk, Tyler. *CO_2 Rising*. Cambridge, Mass.: MIT Press, 2008.

———. *Gaia's Body: Towards a Physiology of Earth*. Cambridge, Mass.: MIT Press, 2003.

———. *Metapatterns*. N.Y.: Columbia University Press, 1995.

———. *What Is Death?* N.Y.: Wiley, 2002.

Wainwright, Stephen. *Axis and Circumfrence*. Cambridge, Mass.: Harvard University Press, 1988.

Walker, Alice. *Living by the Word*. N.Y.: Harcourt, 1988.

Warwick, Kevin. *QI: The Quest for Intelligence*. London: Piatkus, 2000.

Wax, Richard, et al., eds. *Bacterial Resistance to Antimicrobials,* 2nd ed. Boca Raton, Fla.: CRC Press, 2008.

Webb, Jimmy. *Tunesmith*. N.Y.: Hyperion, 1998.

Whitfield, John. *In the Beat of a Heart: Life, Energy, and the Unity of Nature*. Washington, D.C.: Joseph Henry Press, 2006.

Wink, Michael, and Ben-Erik Van Wyk. *Mind-altering and Poisonous Plants of the World*. Portland, Oreg.: Timber Press, 2008.

Witzany, Gunther. *Biocommunication and Natural Genome Editing*. Berlin: Springer, 2010.

Journal Papers, Articles, and Various Websites

Ackland, G., and I. Gallagher. "Stabilization of large generalized Lotka-Volterra foodwebs by evolutionary feedback." *Physical Review Letters* 93, no. 15 (2004): 158701.

Adams, J. "Chemical interactions with pyramidal neurons in layer 5 of the cerebral cortex: Control of pain and anxiety." *Current Medical Chemistry* 16, no. 27 (2009): 3476–9.

Adler, Lawrence, and Merilyne Waldo. "Counterpoint: A sensory gating-hippocampal model of schizophrenia." *Schizophrenia Bulletin* 17, no. 1 (1991): 19–24.

Adler, L., G. Rose, R. Freedman. "Neurophysiological studies of sensory gating in rats: Effects of amphetamine, phencyclidine, and haloperidol." *Biological Psychiatry* 21, no. 8–9 (1986): 787–98.

AFP, "Online gamers crack AIDS enzyme puzzle." September 19, 2011, games.yahoo .com/blogs/plugged-in/online-gamers-crack-aids-enzyme-puzzle-161920724.html.

al-Amin, H., and S. Schwarzkopf. "Effects of the PCP analog dizocilpine on sensory gating: Potential relevance to clinical subtypes of schizophrenia." *Biological Psychiatry* 40, no. 8 (1996): 744–54.

Albrecht, M., et al. "Interaction diversity within quantified insect food webs in restored and adjacent intensively managed meadows." *Journal of Animal Ecology* 76, no. 5 (2007): 1015–25.

Alonso, M., et al. "Turning astrocytes from the rostral migratory stream into neurons:

A role for the olfactory sensory organ." *Journal of Neuroscience* 28, no. 43 (2008): 11089–102.

Alverez-Buylla, A., et al. "The heterogeneity of adult neural stem cells and the emerging complexity of their niche." *Cold Spring Harbor Symposium on Quantitive Biology* 73 (2008): 357–65.

Alworth, L., and S. Buerkle. "The effects of music on animal physiology, behavior, and welfare." *Laboratory Animals* (N.Y.) 42, no. 2 (2013): 54–61.

Andrews, P., et al. "*Primum non nocere*: An evolutionary analysis of whether antidepressants do more harm than good." *Frontiers in Psychology* 3, article 117 (2012): no page numbers available.

Angell, Marcia. "Drug companies and doctors: A story of corruption." *The New York Review of Books,* January 15, 2009.

Antsey, M., et al. "Serotonin mediates behavioral gregarization underlying swarm formation in desert locusts." *Science* 323 (2009): 627–30.

Arnao, Marino, and Josefa Hernandez-Ruiz. "The physiological function of melatonin in plants." *Plant Signaling and Behavior* 1, no. 3 (2006): 89–95.

Asner, Gregory, and Roberta Martin. "Airborne spectranomics: Mapping canopy chemical and taxonomic diversity in tropical forests." *Frontiers in Ecology and the Environment* 7, no. 5 (2009): 269–76.

Azmitia, Efrain. "Modern views on an ancient chemical: Serotonin effects on cell proliferation, maturation, and apoptosis." *Brain Research Bulletin* 56, no. 5 (2001): 413–24.

———. "Serotonin and brain: Evolution, neuroplasticity, and homeostasis." *International Review of Neurobiology* 77 (2007): 31–56.

Baez, John Carlos. "Ban Elsevier," www.johncarlosbaez.wordpress.com/2012/01/26/banelsevier.

Baluska, F., S. Mancuso, D. Volkmann, and P. W. Barlow. "The 'root-brain' hypothesis of Charles and Francis Darwin: Revival after more than 125 years." *Plant Signaling and Behavior* 4, no. 12 (2009): 1121–27.

———. "Root apices as plant command centres: The unique 'brain-like' status of the root apex transition zone." *Biologia Bratislava* 59, supplement 13 (2004): 1–13.

Baluska, F., D. Volkmann, and D. Menzel. "Plant synapses: Actin-based domains for cell-to-cell communication." *Trends in Plant Science* 10, no. 3 (2005): 106–11.

Bassler, B. "How bacteria talk to each other." *Current Opinions in Microbiology* 2, no. 6 (199): 582–87.

Ben-Jacob, E. "Bacterial self-organization: Co-enhancement of complexification and adaptability in a dynamic environment." *Philosophical Transactions of the Royal Society of London,* series A, 361 (2003): 1283–1312.

Ben-Jacob, E., I. Becker, Y. Shapira, and H. Levine. "Bacterial linguistic communication and social intelligence." *Trends in Microbiology* 12, no. 8 (2004): 366–72.

Ben-Jacob, E., I. Cohen, and D. L. Gutnick. "Cooperative organization of bacterial colonies: From genotype to morphotype." *Annual Reviews of Microbiology* 52 (1998): 779–806.

Ben-Jacob, E., and H. Levine. "Self-engineering capacities of bacteria." *Journal of the Royal Society, Interface* 3 (2006): 197–214.

Benes, Francine, and Sabina Berretta. "GABAergic interneurons: Implications for understanding schizophrenia and bipolar disorder." *Neuropsychopharmacology* 25, no. 1 (2001): 1–27.

Bentivoglio, M. "Musical skills and neural functions: The legacy of the brains of musicians." *Annals of the New York Academy of Sciences* 999 (2003): 234–43.

Bermudez, I., D. Beadle, and J. Benson. "Multiple serotonin-activated currents in isolated, neuronal somata from locust thoracic ganglia." *Journal of Experimental Biology* 165 (1992): 43–60.

Bermudez, P., et al. "Neuroanatomical correlates of musicianship as revealed by cortical thickness and voxel-based morphometry." *Cerebral Cortex* 19, no. 7 (2009): 1583–96.

Blenau, W., and M. Thamm. "Distribution of serotonin (5-HT) and its receptors in the insect brain with focus on the mushroom bodies: Lessons from *Drosophila melanogaster* and *Apis mellifera*." *Arthropod Structure and Development* 40, no. 5 (2011): 381–94.

Bodman, S., J. Willey, and S. Diggle. "Cell-cell communication in bacteria: United we stand." *Journal of Bacteriology* 190, no. 13 (2008): 4377–91.

Bond, Anthony. "The buzz and the bees: Flowers use electrical fields to communicate with insects." *Daily Mail*, February 21, 2013.

Boyle, Alan. "Gamers solve molecular puzzle that baffled scientists." NBCNews.com, January 8, 2013.

Braff, David, and Mark Geyer. "Sensorimotor gating and schizophrenia." *Archives of General Psychiatry* 47 (1990): 181–88.

Brenner, E., et al. "Plant neurobiology: An integrated view of plant signaling." *Trends in Plant Science* 11, no. 8 (2006): 413–19.

Brown, B., and C. Swan. "Dendritic network structure constrains metacommunity properties in riverine ecosystems." *Journal of Animal Ecology* 79, no. 3 (2010): 571–80.

Brown, Valerie. "Bacteria 'R' Us." www.psmag.com/science-r-us-23628.

Cadenhead, K., et al. "Sensory gating deficits assessed by the P50 event-related potential in subjects with schizotypal personality disorder." *American Journal of Psychiatry* 157, no. 1 (2000): 55–59.

Cadotte, M. "Metacommunity influences on community richness at multiple spatial scales: a microcosm experiment." *Ecology* 87, no. 4 (2006): 1008–16.

* Cardin, Matt. "Liminality, synchronicity, and the walls of everyday reality." www
.teemingbrain.com/2012/07/23/liminality-synchronicity-and-the-walls-of-everyday-
reality.

Cash, Roseanne. "Don't Fact-Check the Soul." *New York Times,* April 29, 2008.

Castle, Terry. "You better not tell me you forgot." *London Review of Books* 34, no. 18
(2012): 3–11.

Cavoukian, Raffi. "The environment is dead: Long live mother nature." *Common
Dreams,* May 23, 2012.

Chaio, J., and B. Cheon. "The weirdest brains in the world." *The Behavorial and Brain
Sciences* 33, no. 2–3 (2010): 88–90.

Chakrabarti, Bikas, and Omjyoti Dutta. "An electrical network model of plant intelligence." Talk given at the Condensed Matter Days, August 29–31, 2002.

Clapham, David. "TRP channels as cellular sensors." *Nature* 426 (2003): 517–24.

Clapton, Eric. Q and A in *Rolling Stone.* March 14, 2013, 24.

Claridge, A. W., S. C. Barry, S. J. Cork, and J. M. Trappe. "Diversity and habitat relationships of hypogeous fungi. I. Study design, sampling techniques and general
survey results." *Biodiversity and Conservation* (2000) 9: 151–73.

———. "Diversity and habitat relationships of hypogeous fungi. II. Factors influencing the
occurence and number of taxa." *Biodiversity and Conservation* (2000) 9: 175–99.

* Clark, Nigel. "Ex-orbitant globality." *Theory, Culture, and Society* 22, no. 5 (2005):
165–85.

Clementz, B., et al. "Poor P50 suppression among schizophrenia patients and their
first-degree biological relatives." *American Journal of Psychiatry* 155, no. 12
(1998): 1691–94.

Conner, J., et al. "NGF is essential for hippocampal plasticity and learning." *The Journal of Neuroscience* 29, no. 35 (2009): 10883–89.

* Corbin, Henri. "Mundus Imaginalis, or the Imaginary and the Imaginal." hermetic
.com/moorish/mundus-imaginalis.html.

Cozzi, N., et al. "Dimethyltryptamine and other hallucinogenic tryptamines exhibit
substrate behavior at the serotonin uptake transporter and the vesicle monamine
transporter." *Journal of Neural Transmission* 116, no. 12 (2009): 1591–99.

Csaba, G., and Pal Katalin. "Effects of insulin, triodothyronine, and serotonin on plant
seed development." *Protoplasma* 110 (1982): 20–22.

Cvrckova F., H. Lipavska, and V. Zarsky. "Plant Intelligence." *Plant Signaling and
Behavior* 4, no. 5 (2009): 394–99.

Dacks, A., T. Christensen, and J. Hildebrand. "Modulation of olfactory information
processing in the antenna lobe of Manduca sexta by serotonin." *Journal of Neurophysiology* 99, no. 5 (2008): 2077–85.

Daily Mail Reporter. "High-speed evolution: Study shows salmon can change their genes in a single generation." *Daily Mail,* December 19, 2011.

———. "Memory of chimpanzees is far better than human, study reveals." *Daily Mail,* February 15, 2013.

———. "Schoolboy cracks age-old maths problem." *Daily Mail,* May 23, 2012.

———. "Talk is cheep! Study finds human speech evolved from birdsong." February 22, 2013.

Daszak, P., et al. "Emerging infectious diseases of wildlife—threats to biodiversity and wildlife." *Science* 287 (2000): 443–49.

Davies, Patricia, and William Gavin. "Validating the diagnosis of sensory processing disorders using EEG technology." *American Journal of Occupational Therapy* 61, no. 2 (2007): 176–87.

Davies, Patricia, Wen-Pin Chang, and William Gavin. "Maturation of sensory gating performance in children with and without sensory processing disorders." *International Journal of Psychophysiology* 72, no. 2 (2009): 187–97.

Dawson, Kim. "The ecologic niche of psychedelic plants." *Maps Bulletin* 19, no. 1 (no year noted): 57–8.

de Bono, Edward. www.brainyquote.com/quotes/authors/e/edward_de_bono.html.

de Castro, A., et al. "Diversity of soil fungal communities of Cerrado and its closely surrounding agriculture fields." *Archives of Microbiology* 190 (2008): 129–39.

del Angel-Meza, A., et al. "A tryptophan-deficient corn-based diet induces plastic responses in cerebellar cortex cells of rat offspring." *International Journal of Developmental Neuroscience* 19, no 4 (2001): 446–53.

Deresiewicz, William. "The disadvantages of an elite education." *The American Scholar,* Summer 2008, www.theamericanscholar.com.

Diski, Jenny. "Short cuts." *London Review of Books* 34, no. 24 (2012): 36.

Doyle, Brandy. Book Review. "LSD, Spirituality, and the Creative Process by Marlene Dobkin De Rios and Oscar Janiger." *MAPS* xiv, no. 1, Summer 2004.

Editorial Comment. "Toward a future for Gaia theory." *Climatic Change* 52 (2002): 423–30.

Edwards, C., et al. "Sensory gating impairments in heavy cannabis users are associated with altered neural oscillations." *Behavioral Neuroscience* 123, no. 4 (2009): 894–904.

Eimer, Martin. "Spatial cueing, sensory gating and selective response preparation: An ERP study on visuo-spatial orienting." *Electroencephalography and Clinical Neurophysiology* 88 (1993): 408–20.

Einstein, Albert. www.brainyquote.com/quotes/authors/a/albert_einstein.html.

Eisen, A., et al. "Melatonin agonists modulate 5-HT2A receptor-mediated neurotransmission: Behavioral and biochemical studies in the rat." *Journal of Pharmacology and Experimental Therapeutics* 273, no. 1 (1995): 304–8.

Ellington, Duke. www.brainyquote.com/quoes.authors/d/duke_ellington.html.

Ellis, Havelock. "Mescal: A new artificial paradise." www.mescaline.com/artificialparadise/index.html.

Ellstrand, Norman, and Kristina Schierenbeck. "Hybridization as a stimulus for the evolution of invasiveness in plants?" *PNAS* 97, no. 13 (2000): 7043–50.

Emmerson, Mark, and Jon Yearsley. "Weak interactions, omnivory and emergent food-web properties." *Proceedings of the Royal Society of London* 271 (2004): 397–405.

Eyjolfsdottir, Gudridur. "Investigation of the funga of Surtsey 2008." *Surtsey Research* 12 (2009): 105–11.

Free, Andrew, and Nicholas Barton. "Do evolution and ecology need the Gaia hypothesis?" *Trends in Ecology and Evolution* 22, no. 11 (2007): 611–19.

* Freedman, David. "Lies, damned lies, and medical science." *The Atlantic,* November 2010.

Fride, E. "Endocannabinoids in the central nervous system: An overview." *Prostaglandins, Leukotrines, and Essential Fatty Acids* 66, no. 2–3 (2002): 221–33.

Garcia-Domingo J., and J. Saldana. "Food-web complexity emerging from ecological dynamics on adaptive networks." *Journal of Theoretical Biology* 247, no. 4 (2007): 819–26.

Gartz, J. "Biotransformation of tryptamine derivatives in the mycelial cultures Psilocybe." *Journal of Basic Microbiology* 29, no. 6 (1989): 347–52.

Gartz, J., G. Adam, and H. Verbrodt. "Growth-promoting effect of a brassinosteroid in mycelial cultures of the fungus *Psilocybe cubensis.*" *Naturwissenschaften* 77, no. 8 (1990): 388–89.

Gayle, Damien. "How a beetle can use the stars to navigate its way across the vast deserts of Africa." *Daily Mail,* January 24, 2013.

Geyer, M. "Why study hallucinogenic drugs in animals?" *The Heffter Review of Psychedelic Research* 1 (1998): 33–38.

Geyer, M., and D. Braff. "Startle habituation and sensorimotor gating in schizophrenia and related animal models." *Schizophrenia Bulletin* 13, no. 4 (1987): 643–48.

Geyer, M., and R. Light. "LSD-induced alterations of investigatory responding in rats." *Psychopharmacology* 65, no. 1 (1979): 41–47.

Geyer, M., L. R. Peterson, G. J. Rose, et al. "The effects of lysergic acid diethylamide and mescaline-derived hallucinogens on sensory-integrative function: Tactile startle." *Journal of Pharmacology and Experimental Therapeutics* 207, no. 3 (1978): 837–47.

Geyer, M., and F. Vollenweider. "Serotonin research: Contributions to understanding psychoses." *Trends in Pharmacological Sciences* 29, no. 9 (2008): 445–53.

Ghisolfi, E., et al. "Impaired P50 sensory gating in post-traumatic stress disorder secondary to urban violence." *International Journal of Psychophysiology* 51, no. 3 (2004): 209–14.

Gianchino, C., and V. Taylor. "Lineage analysis of quiescent regenerative stem cells in the adult brain by genetic labeling reveals spatially restricted neurogenic niches in the olfactory bulb." *European Journal of Neuroscience* 30, no. 1 (2009): 9–24.

Glasper, E., and E. Gould. "Sexual experience restores age-related decline in adult neurogenesis and hippocampal function." *Hippocampus,* March 5, 2013, epub ahead of print.

✱ Godesky, Jason. "Plants are people, too." http://rewild.info/anthropik/2007/08/plants-are-people-too/index.html.

Goldman, Rakic. "The 'psychic' neuron of the cerebral cortex." *Annals of the New York Academy of Sciences* 868 (1999): 13–26.

Goodman, S., and S. Greenland. "Why most published research findings are false: Problems in the analysis." *PloS Medicine* 4, no. 4 (2007): e168.

Goodwin, Brian. "Reclaiming a Life of Quality." *Journal of Consciousness Studies* 6, no. 11–12 (1999): 229–35.

Goudard, A., and M. Loreau. "Nontrophic interactions, biodiversity, and ecosystem functioning: An interaction web model." *The American Naturalist* 171, no. 1 (2008): 91–106.

Gravel, D., et al. "Persistence increases with diversity and connectance in trophic metacommunities." *PLoS* 6, no. 5 (2011): e19374.

Greenwood, Veronique. "How fungi create the Amazon's clouds." Time.com, September 5, 2012.

Gross, T., et al. "Generalized models reveal stabilizing factors in food webs." *Science* 325 (2007): 747–50.

Grunwald, T., et al. "Neuronal substrates of sensory gating within the human brain." *Biological Psychiatry* 53, no. 6 (2003): 511–19.

Guichard, Frederic. "Interaction strength and extinction risk in a metacommunity." *Proceedings of the Royal Society,* series B 272 (2005): 1571–76.

Guillette, Louis. "Impacts of endocrine disruptors on wildlife." *Endocrine Disruptors and Pharmaceutically Active Compounds in Drinking Water Workshop,* Center for Health Effects of Environmental Contamination, April 19–21, 2000, www.cheec.uiowa.edy/conferences/edc_2000/guillette.html.

Guzman, Gaston. "Supplement to the monograph of the genus Psilocybe." *Bibliotheca Mycologica* 159 (1995): 91–141.

Guzman, G., J. Allen, and J. Gartz. "A worldwide geographical distribution of the neurotropic fungi, an analysis and discussion." *Ann. Mus. Civ Rovereto* 14 (1998): 189–280.

Halberstadt, A. L., M. R. Buell, V. L. Maston, et al. "Modification of the effects of 5-methoxy-N,N-dimethyltryptamine on exploratory behavior in rats by monamine oxidase inhibitors." *Psychopharmacology* 201, no. 1 (2008): 55–66.

Halberstadt, A. L., and M. Geyer. "Do psychedelics expand the mind by reducing brain activity?" *Scientific American* (May 15, 2012).

———. "LSD but not lisuride disrupts prepulse inhibition in rats by activating the 5-HT2A receptor." *Psychopharmacology* 208 (2010): 179–89.

———. "Multiple receptors contribute to the behavioral effects of indoleamine hallucinogens." *Neuropharmacology* 61, no. 3 (2011): 364–81.

Hamilton, W., and T. Lenton. "Spora and Gaia: How microbes fly with their clouds." *Ethology, Ecology and Evolution* 10 (1998): 1–16.

Harding, Stephan. "Earth system science and Gaian science." www.schumachercollege .org.uk/learning-resources/earth-system-science-and-gaian-science.

———. "From Gaia theory to deep ecology." www.gn.apc.org/schumachercollege/ articles/stephan.htm.

Harvey, John. "Role of the serotonin 5-HT2A receptor in learning." *Learning and Memory* 10, no. 5 (2003): 355–62.

Harvey, J., et al. "Selective remodeling of rabbit frontal cortex: Relationship between 5-HT2A receptor density and associative learning." *Psychopharmacology* 172, no. 4 (2004): 435–42.

Heinrich, J., S. Heine, and A. Norenzayan. "The weirdest people in the world?" *The Behavioral and Brain Sciences* 33, no. 2–3 (2010): 61–83.

Herholz, S., and R. Zatorre. "Musical training as a framework for brain plasticity: Behavior, function, and structure." *Neuron* 76, no. 3 (2012): 486–502.

Hilker, F., and K. Schmitz. "Disease-induced stabilization of predator-prey oscillations." *Journal of Theoretical Biology* 255, no. 3 (2008): 299–306.

Hird, Myra. "Coevolution, symbiosis, and sociology." *Ecological Economics* 69 (2010): 737–42.

* ———. "Indifferent globality: Gaia, symbiosis, and 'other worldliness.'" *Theory, Culture, and Society* 27, no. 2–3 (2010): 54–72.

Holland, M., and A. Hastings. "Strong effect of dispersal network structure on ecological dynamics." *Nature* 456, no. 7223 (2008): 792–94.

Hong, X., et al. "Neuroleptic effects on P50 sensory gating in patients with first-episode never medicated schizophrenia." *Schizophrenia Research* 108, no. 1–3 (2009): 151–57.

Hopfield, J. "Neural networks and physical systems with emergent collective computational abilities." *Proceedings of the National Academy of Sciences USA*, 79 (1982): 2554–58.

Howeth, J., and M. Leibold. "Species dispersal rates alter diversity and ecosystem stability in pond metacommunities." *Ecology* 91, no. 9 (2010): 2727–41.

Hugget, R. "Ecosphere, biosphere, or Gaia? What to call the global ecosystem." *Global Ecology and Biogeography* 8 (1999): 425–31.

Hunt, J., and M. Bonsall. "The effects of colonization, extinction and competition on coexistence in metacommunities." *Journal of Animal Ecology* 78, no. 4 (2009): 866–79.

Hyman, S., and E. Nestler. "Initiation and adaptation: A paradigm for understanding psychotropic drug action." *American Journal of Psychiatry* 153, no. 2 (1996): 151–62.

Ingram, T., L. Harmon, and J. Shurin. "Niche evolution, trophic structure, and species turnover in model food webs." *The American Naturalist* 174, no. 1 (2009): 56–67.

Inoue, Jun-ichi, and Bikas Chakrabarti. "Competition between ferro-retrieval and anti-ferro orders in a Hopfield-like network model for plant intelligence." http://arxiv .org/pdf/cond-mat/0408209.pdf.

Ioannidis, John. "Why most published research findings are false." *PloS Medicine* 2, no. 8 (2005): e124.

———. "Why most published research findings are false: Author's reply to Goodman and Greenland." *PloS Medicine* 4, no. 6 (2005): e215.

Ishihara, A., et al. "The tryptophan pathway is involved in the defense of rise against pathogenic infection via serotonin production." *The Plant Journal* 54, no. 3 (2008): 481–95.

Istok, E., et al. "Expressive timing facilitates the neural processing of phrase boundaries in music: Evidence from event-related potentials." *PLoS One* 8, no. 1 (2013): e55150.

Jabot, Franck, and Jordi Bascompte. "Bitrophic interactions shape biodiversity in space." *PNAS* 109, no. 12 (2012): 4521–26.

James, C., et al. "Musical training intensity yields opposite effects on grey matter density in cognitive versus sensorimotor networks." *Brain Structural Function,* February 14, 2013, epub ahead of print.

Jancke, L., et al. "Pre-attentive modulation of brain responses to tones in coloured-hearing synasthetes." *BMC Neuroscience* 13 (2012): 151.

Janiger, O., and M. Dobkin de Rios. "LSD and creativity." *Journal of Psychoactive Drugs* 21, no. 1 (1989): 129–34.

Jarrard, Paula. "Sensory Issues in Gifted Children: Synthesis of the Literature, 2008." www.spdfoundation.net/pdf/sensoryissuesingiftedchildren.pdf.

Javanbakht, Arash. "Sensory gating deficits, pattern completion, and disturbed fronto-limbic balance, a model for description of hallucinations and delusions in schizophrenia." *Medical Hypothesis* 67 (2006): 1173–84.

Jeltsch, F., et al. "Pattern formation triggered by rare events: Lessons from the spread of rabies." *Proceedings of the Royal Society of London* 264 (1997): 495–503.

Jha, S., et al. "5-HT2A/2C receptor blockade regulates progenitor cell proliferation in the adult rat hippocampus." *Neuroscience Letters* 441, no. 2 (2008): 210–14.

Jiang, W., et al. "Cannabinoids promote embryonic and adult neurogenesis and produce anziolyltic- and antidepressant-like effects." *The Journal of Clinical Investigation* 115, no. 11 (2005): 3104–16.

Johnson, D., et al. "Toxicity and hazard of selective serotonin reuptake inhibitor antidepressants fluozetine, fluvoxamine, and sertraline to algae." *Ecotoxicology and Environmental Safety* 67, no. 1 (2007): 128–39.

Johnson, O., J. Becnel, and C. Nichols. "Serotonin 5-HT2 and 5-HT1A-like receptors differentially modulate aggressive behaviors in *Drosophila melanogaster*." *Neuroscience* 158, no. 4 (2009): 1292–1300.

———. "Serotonin receptor activity is necessary for olfactory learning and memory in *Drosophila melanogaster*." *Neuroscience* 192 (2011): 372–81.

Jones, M., et al. "The mode of action of thidiazuron: auxins, indoleamines, and ion channels in the regeneration of *Echinaces purpurea*." *Plant Cell Reports* 26, no. 9 (2007): 1481–90.

Jonsson, Patrik. "New research opens a window on the minds of plants." *Christian Science Monitor,* March 3, 2005.

Joober, R., et al. "Publication bias: What are the challenges and can they be overcome?" *Journal of Psychiatry and Neuroscience* 37, no. 3 (2012): 149–52.

Kaji, Ryuji. "Basal ganglia as a sensory gating device for motor control." *The Journal of Medical Investigation* 48 (2001): 142–46.

Kaji, R., et al. "Abnormal sensory gating in basal ganglia disorders." *Journal of Neurology* 252, supplement 4 (2005): 13–16.

Kalia, C., et al. "LSD induced genetic damage in barley." *Chromosoma* 32 (1970): 142–51.

Kanan, C. "Recognizing sights, smells, and sounds with gnostic fields." *PLoS One* 8, no. 1 (2013): e54088.

Kang, K., S. Kang, K. Lee, et al. "Enzymatic features of serotonin biosynthetic enzymes and serotonin biosynthesis in plants." *Plant Signaling and Behavior* 3, no. 6 (2008): 389–90.

Kang, K., Y. S. Kim, S. Park, and K. Beck. "Senescence-induced serotonin biosynthesis and its role in delaying senescence in rice leaves." *Plant Physiology* 150 (2009): 1380–93.

Kang, K., K. Lee, S. Park, et al. "Enhanced production of melatonin by ectopic overexpression of human serotonin N-acetyltransferase plays a role in cold resistance in transgenic rice seedlings." *Journal of Pineal Research* 49, no. 2 (2010): 176–82.

Kang, S., et al. "Characterization of tryptamine 5-hydroxylase and serotonin synthesis in rice plants." *Physiology and Biochemistry* 26 (2007): 2009–15.

Karnani, Mahesh, and Arto Annila. "Gaia again." *Biosystems* 95 (2009): 82–87.

Kazansky, A. B. "Gaia as an autopoietic system: New vistas, in Human Being, Nature, Society: Actual Problems." *Proceedings of the 13th International Conference of Young Scientists,* St. Petersburg State University Publishing, 2002, 3–8.

Keay, Susan, and Averil Brown. "Colonization by *Psilocybe semilanceata* of roots of grassland flora." *Mycological Research* 94, no. 1 (1990): 49–56.

———. "Interactions between *Psilocybe semilanceata* and fungi of its habitat." *Mycological Research* 93, no. 4 (1989): 554–56.

Khozhai, L. "Formation of the astroglia in the mouse cortex after temporary prenatal blockade of serotonin synthesis." *Neuroscience and Behavioral Physiology* 36, no. 3 (2006): 275–78.

Kiefer, Markus. "Executive control over unconscious cognition: Attentional sensitization of unconscious information processing." *Frontiers in Human Neuroscience* 6, no. 61 (2012): no page numbers noted.

Kiefer, Markus, Sarah Adams, and Monika Zovko. "Attentional sensitization of unconscious visual processing: Top-down influences on masked priming." *Advances in Cognitive Science* 8, no. 1 (2012): 50–61.

Kiefer, M., et al. "Neuro-cognitive mechanisms of conscious and unconscious visual perception: From a plethora of phenomena to general principles." *Advances in Cognitive Psychology* 7, special issue (2011): 55–67.

Kieniewicz, Paul. "Gaia and plate tectonics." http://paulkieniewicz.co.uk/?page_id=257.

Kisley, M., and Z. Cornwell. "Gamma and beta neural activity evoked during a sensory gating paradigm: Effects of auditory, somatosensory and cross-modal stimulation." *Clinical Neurophysiology* 117, no. 11 (2006): 2549–63.

Kisley, M. A., T. L. Noecker, and P. M. Guinther. "Comparison of sensory gating to mismatch negativity and self-reported perceptual phenomena in healthy adults." *Psychophysiology* 41 (2004): 604–12.

Kisley, M. A., S. D. Polk, R. G. Ross, et al. "Early postnatal development of sensory gating." *Neurophysiology, Basic and Clinical* 14, no. 5 (2003): 693–97.

Kleidon, Axel. "Beyond Gaia: Thermodynamics of life and earth system functioning." *Climatic Change* 66 (2004): 271–319.

———. "Non-equilibrium thermodynamics, maximum entropy production and Earth-system evolution." *Philosophical Transactions of the Royal Society,* series A, 368 (2010): 181–96.

———. "Testing the effect of life on Earth's functioning: How Gaian is the Earth system?" *Climatic Change* 52 (2002): 383–89.

Kleidon, A, Y. Malhi, P. Cox. "Maximum entropy production in environmental and ecological systems." *Philosophical Transactions of the Royal Society,* series B, 365 (2010): 1297–1302.

Klyce, Brig. "Gaia." www.panspermia.org/gaia.htm.

Kolbert, Elizabeth. "Spoiled Rotten: Why do kids rule the roost." *The New Yorker,* July 2, 2012.

Krause, M., et al. "Auditory sensory gating in hippocampus and reticular thalamic neurons in anesthetized rats." *Biological Psychiatry* 53 (2003): 244–53.

Krugman, Paul. "Fine Austrian whines." The Conscience of a Liberal (blog). *New York Times,* krugman.blogs.nytimes.com, February 20, 2013.

———. "In praise of econowonkery." The Conscience of a Liberal (blog). *New York Times,* krugman.blogs.nytimes.com, May 11, 2013.

———. "Open science and the econoblogosphere." The Conscience of a Liberal (blog). *New York Times,* krugman.blogs.nytimes.com, January 17, 2012.

———. "The power of conventional wisdom." The Conscience of a Liberal (blog). *New York Times,* krugman.blogs.nytimes.com, September 27, 2010.

Kruse, Karsten, and Frank Julicher. "Oscillations in cell biology." *Current Opinions in Cell Biology* 17 (2005): 20–26.

Kurthen, M., et al. "Towards a functional topography of sensory gating areas: Invasive P50 recording and electrical stimulation mapping in epilepsy surgery candidates." *Psychiatry Research* 155, no. 2 (2007): 121–33.

La Cerra, Peggy. "The first law of psychology is the second law of thermodynamics: The energetic evolutionary model of the mind and the generation of human psychological phenomena." *Human Nature Review* 3 (2003): 440–47.

La Cerra, Peggy, and Roger Bingham. "The adaptive nature of the human neurocognitive architecture: An alternative model." *Proceedings of the National Academy of Sciences USA* 95 (1998): 11290–94.

Lackovic, Z. "Psychoactive drugs and neuroplasticity." *Psychiatria Danubina* 19, no. 3 (2007): 202–5.

Lee, Pei-Tseng, et al. "Serotonin-mushroom body circuit modulating the formation of anesthesia-resistant memory in Drosophila." *PloS* 108, no. 33 (2011): 13794–99.

Lenton, Timothy. "Clarifying Gaia: Regulation with or without natural selection," in *Scientists Debate Gaia: The Next Century,* S. Schneider et al., eds., 15–25. Cambridge, Mass.: MIT Press, 2004.

———. "Gaia and natural selection." *Nature* 394 (1998): 439–47.

———. "Introduction to the Gaia theory," in *Earth System Science,* Guerzoni et al., eds., 9–29. Siena, Italy: University of Siena Press.

———. "Testing Gaia: The effect of life on Earth's habitability and regulation." *Climatic Change* 52 (2002): 409–22.

Lenton, Timothy, and James Lovelock. "Daisyworld is Darwinian." *Journal of Theoretical Biology* 206 (2000): 109–16.

Lenton, Timothy, and Marcel van Oijen. "Gaia as a complex adaptive system." *Philosophical Transactions of the Royal Society of London,* series B 357 (2002): 683–95.

Lenton, Timothy, and David Wilkinson. "Developing the Gaia theory: A response to the criticisms of Kirchner and Volk." *Climatic Change* 58 (2003): 1–12.

Lenton, Timothy, and Hywel Williams. "Gaia and evolution," in *Gaia in Turmoil: Cli-*

mate Change, Biodepletion, and Earth Ethics in an Age of Crisis, Crist and Rinker, eds., 61–84. Cambridge, Mass.: MIT Press, 2009.

———. "Microbial Gaia: A new model for the evolution of environmental regulation." *Gaia circular,* Geological Society of London, 2007.

Lijffijt, M., et al. "P50, N100, P200 sensory gating: Relationships with behavioral inhibition, attention, and working memory." *Psychophysiology* 46, no. 5 (2009): 1059.

Liu, Z., et al. "Synchrony of spatial populations induced by colored environmental noise and dispersal." *Biosystems* 98, no. 2 (2009): 115–21.

Loeuille, N., and M. Leibold. "Ecological consequences of evolution in plant defenses in a metacommunity." *Theoretical Population Biology* 74, no. 1 (2008): 34–45.

Loreau M., and R. Holt. "Spatial flows and the regulation of ecosystems." *American Naturalist* 163, no. 4 (2004): 606–15.

Lovelock, James. "Climate change on a living earth," draft copy of lecture delivered to a public meeting of the Royal Society, October 29, 2007.

———. "Gaia and emergence: A response to Kirchner and Volk." *Climatic Change* 57 (2003): 1–3.

———. "The living earth." *Nature* 426 (2003): 769–70.

———. "Reflections on Gaia." American Geophysical Union Chapman Conference, Valencia. *Scientists Debate Gaia.* MIT press, 2004. http://mitpress2.mit.edu/books.chapters/0262194988chapm1.pdf.

Ludewig, K., et al. "Deficits in prepulse inhibition and habituation in never-medicated first-episode schizophrenia." *Biological Psychiatry* 54, no. 12 (2003): 121–28.

Ma, D., et al. "Glial influences on neural stem cell development: Cellular niches for adult neurogenesis." *Current Opinions in Neurobiology* 15, no. 5 (2005): 514–20.

Marek, G., and G. Aghajanian. "LSD and the phenethylamine hallucinogen DOI are potent partial agonists at the 5-HT2A receptors on interneurons in rat piriform cortex." *Journal of Pharmacology and Experimental Therapeutics* 278, no. 3 (1996): 1373–82.

Margulis, Lynn. "Gaia by any other name." http://mitpress2.mit.edu/books/chapters/0262693690chapm2.pdf.

Masler, E. "Responses Heterodera glycines and Meloidogyne incognita to exogenously applied neuromodulators." *Journal of Helminthology* 81, no. 4 (2007): 421–27.

Matheson, T., S. Rogers, and H. Krapp. "Plasticity in the visual system is correlated with a change in lifestyle of solitarious and gregarious locusts." *Journal of Neurophysiology* 91, no. 4 (2004): 1–12.

Matsushima, Y., et al. "Historical overview of psychoactive mushrooms." *Inflammation and Regeneration* 29, no. 1 (2009): 47–58.

McCormick, David, and Thierry Bal. "Sensory gating mechanisms of the thalamus." *Current Opinion in Neurobiology* 4 (1994): 550–56.

McDowell, Adam. "Westerners vs. the world: We are the WEIRD ones." *National Post,* August 21, 2010.

McGehee, D. "Nicotine and synaptic plasticity in prefrontal cortex." *Science's STKE* 399 (2007): pe44.

Miller, Daniel. "The amazing images that let us 'see' music (and could even help us communicate with dolphins)." *Daily Mail,* January 30, 2013.

Ming, G., and H. Song. "Adult neurogenesis in the mammalian central nervous system." *Annual Reviews of Neuroscience* 28 (2005): 223–50.

Mittman, S., and M. Geyer. "Dissociation of multiple effects of acute LSD on exploratory behavior in rats by ritanserin and propranolol." *Psychopharmacology* 105, no. 1 (1991): 69–76.

Morris, C., D. Georgakopoulos, and D. Sands. "Ice nucleation active bacteria and their potential role in precipitation." *Journal De Physique* IV 121 (2004): 87–103.

Murakami, M., et al. "State-dependent sensory gating in olfactory cortex." *Neuron* 46, no. 2 (2005): 285–96.

Musical quotations. http://musiced.about.com/od.beginnersguide/a/bg.htm.

Nadkarni, Nalini. "Diversity of species and interactions in the upper tree canopy of forest ecosystems." *American Zoology* 34 (1994): 70–78.

———. "Tropical rainforest ecology from a canopy perspective." *Academic Press* (1988), http://academic.evergreen.edu/n/nadkarnn/cv/pdf.

Naish, Darren. "Tool use in crocodylians: Crocodiles and alligators use sticks to attract waterbirds." *Scientific American,* November 30, 2013.

Nakagaki, T. "Smart behavior of true slime mold in a labyrinth." *Research in Microbiology* 152, no. 9 (2001): 767–90.

Neal, J., R. Benedict, and L. Brady. "Interrelationship of phosphate nutrition, nitrogen metabolism, and accumulation of key secondary metabolites in saprophytic cultures of *Psilocybe cubensis, Psilocybe cyanescens,* and *Panaeolus campamulatus.*" *Journal of Pharmaceutical Sciences* 57, no. 10 (2010): 1661–67.

Nesse, R., and K. Berridge. "Psychoactive drug use in evolutionary perspective." *Science* 278, no. 5335 (1997): 63–66.

Neutel, A., J. Heesterbeek, and P. de Ruiter. "Stability in real food webs: Weak links in long loops." *Science* 296 (2002): 1120–23.

Nichols, C., E. Garcia, and E. Sanders-Bush. "Dynamic changes in prefrontal cortex gene expression following lysergic acid diethylamide administration." *Molecular Brain Research* 111, no. 1–2 (2003): 182–88.

Nichols, C., et al. "Hallucinogens and Drosophila: Linking serotonin receptor activation to behavior." *Neuroscience* 115, no. 3 (2002): 979–84.

Nielen, Lisbeth, and Alfred Kaszniak. "Awareness of subtle emotional feelings: A comparison of long-term meditators and nonmeditators." *Emotion* 6, no. 3 (2006): 392–405.

Nielsen, L., et al. "Electric currents couple spatially separated biogeochemical processes in marine sediment." *Nature* 463, no. 7284 (2010): 1071–74.

O'Brien, Gerard, and Jon Opie. "The disunity of consciousness." *Australian Journal of Philosophy* 76 (1998): 378–95.

O'Gorman, Eoin, and Mark Emmerson. "Perturbations to trophic interactions and the stability of complex food webs." *PNAS* 106, no. 32 (2009): 13393–98.

Ogjakova, Mariela, and Christina Hadjiivanova. "Animal neurotransmitter substances in plants." *Bulgarian Journal of Plant Physiology* 23, no. 1–2 (1997): 94–102.

Olff, H., et al. "Parallel ecological networks in ecosystems." *Philosophical Transactions of the Royal Society,* series B 364 (2009): 1755–79.

Orozco-Suarez, S., et al. "Corn feeding during development induces changes in the number of serotonergic neurons in the raphe nuclei." *International Journal of Developmental Neuroscience* 21, no. 1 (2003): 13–22.

Ouagazzal, A., et al. "Effect of LSD on prepulse inhibition and spontaneous behavior in the rat: A pharmacological analysis and comparison between two rat strains." *Neuropharmacology* 25, no. 4 (2001): 565–75.

Palenicek, T., M. Balikova, V. Bubenikova-Valesova, and J. Horacek. "Mescaline effects on rat behavior and its time profile in serum and brain tissue after a single subcutaneous dose." *Psychopharmacology* 196, no. 1 (2008): 51–62.

Palenicek, T., Z. Hilnak, V. Bubenikova-Valesova, et al. "Sex differences in the effects of N,N-diethyllysergamide (LSD) on behavioural activity and prepulse inhibition." *Progress in Neuropharmacology and Biological Psychiatry* 34, no. 4 (2010): 588–96.

Palmer, Jason. "Amoebas show primitive farming behaviour as they travel." *BBC News,* January 19, 2011.

Park, S., and K. Back. "Melatonin promotes seminal root elongation and root growth in transgenic rice after germination." *Journal of Pineal Research* 53, no. 4 (2012): 385–89.

Peat, David. "The Saving of planet Gaia." *New Scientist,* March 18, 2006.

Pelagio-Flores, R., et al. "Serotonin, a tryptophan-derived signal conserved in plants and animals, regulates root system architecture probably acting as a natural auxin inhibitor in *Arabidopsis thaliana.*" *Plant and Cell Physiology* 52, no. 3 (2011): 490–508.

Phillips, Adam. "Am I a Spaceman?" *London Review of Books* 33, no. 20 (2011): 27–29.

———. "A Seamstress in Tel Aviv." *London Review of Books* 11, no. 17 (1989): 6–7.

Postle, Bradley. "Delay-period activity in prefrontal cortex: One function is sensory gating." *Journal of Cognitive Neuroscience* 17, no. 11 (2005): 1679–90.

Pow, Helen. "Meet the toughest animal on the planet." *Daily Mail,* February 17, 2013.

Quednow, B., et al. "Psilocybin-induced deficits in autonomic and controlled inhibition are attenuated by ketanserin in healthy human volunteers." *Neuropsychopharmacology* 37, no. 3 (2012): 630–40.

Ramakrishna, A., P. Giridhar, and G. Ravishankar. "Indoleamines and calcium channels influence morphogenesis in in vitro cultures of *Mimosa pudica*." *Plant Signaling and Behavior* 4, no. 12 (2009): 1136–41.

Ramakrishna, A., et al. "Phytoserotonin: A review." *Plant Signaling and Behavior* 6, no. 6 (2011): 800–809.

Rappaport, John. "Inventing Medical Reality (parts one and two)." http://jonrappaport.wordpress.com/2012/02/22.

Ray, S. M., S. S. Park, and A. Ray. "Pollen tube guidance by the female gametophyte." *Development* (1997) 124: 2489–98.

Reading, N., and V. Sperandio. "Quorum sensing: The many languages of bacteria." *FEMS Microbiology Letters* 254, no. 1 (2006): 1–11.

Riba, J., A. Rodriguez-Fornells, and M. Barbanoj. "Effects of ayahuasca on sensory and sensorimotor gating in humans as measured by P50 suppression and prepulse inhibition of the startle reflex, respectively." *Psychopharmacology* 165 (2002): 18–28.

Roschchina, V. "Chemical signaling in plant microspore cells." *Izv Akad Nauk Ser Biology* 4 (2006): 414–20.

Roy, S., and J. Chattopadhyay. "The stability of ecosystems: A brief overview of the paradox of enrichment." *Journal of Bioscience* 32, no. 2 (2007): 421–28.

Rozin, R. "The weirdest people in the world are a harbinger of the future of the world." *The Behavioral and Brain Sciences* 33, no. 2–3 (2010): 108–9.

Saah, Tammy. "The evolutionary origins and significance of drug addiction." *Harm Reduction Journal* 2, no. 8 (2005): no page numbers listed.

Sadasivaiah, R., G. Collins, and D. Davis. "Effect of LSD on mitotic and meiotic plant chromosomes." *Chromosoma* 44 (1973): 309–18.

Saigusa, T., et al. "Amoebae anticipate periodic events." *Physical Review Letters* 100, no. 1 (2008): 018101.

Sänger, J., V. Müller, and U. Lindenberger. "Intra- and interbrain synchronization and network properties when playing guitar in duets." *PLoS One,* September 10, 2013.

Sanoitis, A. "Evolutionary and anthropological approaches towards understanding human need for psychotropic and mood altering substances." *Journal of Psychoactive Drugs* 42, no. 4 (2010): 477–84.

Sanyal, T., et al. "Effects of prenatal loud music and noise on total number of neurons and glia, neuronal nuclear area and colume of chick brainstem auditory nuclei, field L and hippocampus: A steriological investigation." *International Journal of Developing Neuroscience,* March 1, 2013, epub ahead of print.

Savonenko, A., et al. "Impaired cognition, sensorimotor gating, and hippocampal long term depression in mice lacking the prostaglandin E2 EP2 receptor." *Experimental Neurology* 217, no. 1 (2009): 63–73.

Schekman, Randy. "How journals like *Nature, Cell,* and *Science* are damaging science: The incentives offered by top journals distort science, just as big bonuses distort banking." *The Guardian,* December 9, 2013.

Schellnhuber, H. "Earth system analysis and the second Copernican revolution." *Nature* 402, supplement, (1999): C19–23.

Schindler, E., et al. "Serotonergic and dopaminergic distinctions in the behavioral pharmacology of (+-)-1-(2,5-dimethoxy-4-idophenyl)-2-aminopropane (DOI) and lysergic acid diethylaminde (LSD)." *Pharmacology, Biochemistry, and Behavior* 101, no. 1 (2012): 69–76.

Scialdone, A., S. T. Mugford, D. Feike, et al. "Arabidopsis plants perform arithmetic division to prevent starvation at night." *eLife,* elife.elifesciences.orb/content/2/e00669.

Science News. "Genetic circuit allows both individual freedom, collective good [in bacteria]." April 22, 2013.

Seaberg, Maureen. "The shamanic synaesthesia of the Kalahari bushmen." *Psychology Today,* February 15, 2012.

Sel, A., and B. Calvo-Merino. "Neuroarchitecture of musical emotions." *Reviews in Neurology* 56, no. 5 (2013): 289–97.

Sessa, Ben. "From sacred plants to psychotherapy." www.rcpsych.ac.uk/pdf/ben%20sessa20%20sacred%20to%20psychotherapy.pdf.

Sessini, Phillipa. "Modeling the Gaia Hypothesis: Daisyworld." http://dspace.ucalgary.ca/bitstream/1880/46480/2/2007-857-09.pdf.

* Shapiro, James. "Bacteria are small but not stupid: Cognition, natural genetic engineering, and sociobacteriology." *Studies in History and Philosophy of Biological and Biomedical Science* 38, no. 4 (2007): 807–19.

Shaw, Sylvie. "The way of story," www.ecopsychology.org/journal/ezine/story.html.

Sherman, A., et al. "Auditory rhythms are systemically associated with spatial-frequency and density information in visual scenes." *Psychonomic Bulletin and Review,* February 20, 2013, epub ahead of print.

Staff writer. "Earth microbes on the moon." *Space Science News* (1998), science.nasa.gov/science-news/science-at-nasa/1998/ast01sep98_1/.

Stella, N. "Cannaboid signaling in glial cells." *Glia* 48, no. 4 (2004): 267–77.

Stone, J., M. Sherwood, and G. Carroll. "Canopy microfungi: Function and diversity." *Northwest Science* 70, special issue (1996): 37–45.

Strick, C., et al. "Modulation of NMDA receptor function by inhibition of D-amino acid oxidase in rodent brain." *Neuropharmacology* 61, no. 5–6 (2011): 1001–15.

Stuntz, S., et al. "Diversity and structure of the arthropod fauna within three canopy epiphyte species in central Panama." *Journal of Tropical Ecology* 18 (2002): 161–76.

Sudgen, Andrew. "Hairy, spiny or naked." *London Review of Books* 35, no. 3 (2013): 33.

Sullivan, R., and E. Hagan. "Psychotropic substance-seeking: Evolutionary pathology or adaptation?" *Addiction* 97 (2002): 389–400.

Suzuki, K., and T. Yoshida. "Non-random spatial coupling induces desynchronization, chaos, and multistability in a predator-prey-resource system." *Journal of Theoretical Biology* 300 (2012): 81–90.

Taupin, P. "Adult neurogenesis and neuroplasticity." *Restorative Neurology and Neuroscience* 24, no. 1 (2006): 9–15.

———. "Adult neurogenesis in mammals." *Current Opinions in Molecular Therapy* 8, no. 4 (2006): 345–51.

———. "Neurogenesis in the adult central nervous system." *Comptes Rendes Biologies* 329, no. 7 (2006): 465–75.

Taylor, Bron. "Earth and nature-based spirituality (Part 1): From deep ecology to radical environmentalism." *Religion* 31 (2001): 175–93.

Thebault, Elisa, and Colin Fontaine. "Stability of ecological communities and the architecture of mutualistic and trophic networks." *Science* 329 (2010): 853–56.

Thiese, Neil. "Implications of postmodern biology for biology: The cell doctrine." *Laboratory Investigation* (2006): 1–10.

Thoma, R., et al. "Schizophrenia diagnosis and anterior hippocampal volume make separate contributions to sensory gating." *Psychophysiology* 45, no. 6 (2008): 926–35.

Thome, J., and A. Eisch. "Neurogenesis: Relevance for pathophysiology and pharmacotherapy of psychiatric diseases." *Nervenarzt* 76, no. 1 (2005): 11–19.

Tracy, Lane. "Is Gaia a living system." www.systemsoflife.org/sites/systemsoflife.org/files/99040_0.pdf.

Tregellas, J., D. B. Davalos, D. C. Rojas, et al. "Increased hemodynamic response in the hippocampus, thalamus and prefrontal cortex during abnormal sensory gating in schizophrenia." *Shizophrenia Research* 92, no. 1–3 (2007): 262–72.

Tregellas, J., J. Ellis, S. Shatti, et al. "Increased hippocampal, thalamic, prefrontal hemodynamic response to an urban noise stimulus in schizophrenia." *American Journal of Psychiatry* 16, no. 3 (2009): 354–60.

Trewavas, Anthony. "Aspects of Plant Intelligence." *Annals of Botany* 92 (2003): 1–20.

———. "Aspects of plant intelligence: An answer to Firn." *Annals of Botany* 93 (2004): 353–57.

———. "Green plants as intelligent organisms." *Trends in Plant Science* 10, no. 9 (2005): 413–19.

Trewavas, A., and F. Baluska. "The ubiquity of consciousness, cognition and intelligence in life." *EMBO Reports* 12 (2011): 1221–25.

Trapp, S., H. Schroll, and F. Hamker. "Open and closed loops: A computational approach to attention and consciousness." *Advances in Cognitive Psychology* 8, no. 1 (2012): 1–8.

Tsuno, Yusuke, and Kensaku Mori. "Behavioral state-dependent changes in the information processing mode in the olfactory system." *Communicative and Integrative Biology* 2, no. 4 (2009): 362–64.

Tupper, Kenneth. "Enteogens and existential intelligence: The use of plant teachers as cognitive tools." *Canadian Journal of Education* 27, no. 4 (2002): 499–516.

Uchida, S., and B. Drossel. "Relation between complexity and stability in food webs with adaptive behavior." *Journal of Theoretical Biology* 247, no. 4 (2007): 713–22.

Ujihara, H. "Mechanisms of psychotropics action in relation to CNS neurogenesis." *Nihon Yakurigaku Zasshi* 123, no. 5 (2004): 319–28.

Urban, M., and D. Skelly. "Evolving metacommunities: Toward an evolutionary perspective on metacommunities." *Ecology* 87, no. 7 (2006): 1616–26.

Vasseur, D., and J. Fox. "Environmental fluctuations can stabilize food web dynamics by increasing synchrony." *Ecological Letters* 10, no. 11 (2007): 1066–74.

Viegas, Jennifer. "Dolphins appear to do nonlinear mathematics." *NBC News,* July 17, 2012.

Villarreal, L., et al. "Acute and persistent viral life strategies and their relationship to emerging diseases." *Virology* 272 (2000): 1–6.

Volkov, A., et al. "Plant electrical memory." *Plant Signaling and Behavior* 3, no. 7 (2008): 490–92.

Vollenweider, Franz. "Brain mechanisms of hallucinogens and entactogens." *Dialogues in Clinical Neuroscience* 3, no. 4 (2001): 265–79.

Vollenweider, Franz, and Mark Geyer. "A systems model of altered consciousness: Integrating natural and drug-induced psychoses." *Brain Research Bulletin* 56, no. 5 (2001): 495–507.

Wadhwa, S., et al. "Quantitative study of plasticity in the auditory nuclei of chick under conditions of prenatal sound attenuation and overstimulation with species specific and music sound stimuli." *International Journal of Developing Neuroscience* 17, no. 3 (1999): 239–53.

Walter, Lisa, and Nephi Stella. "Cannabinoids and neuroinflammation." *British Journal of Pharmacology* 141, no. 5 (2004): 775–85.

Wardle, D. "The influence of biotic interactions on soil biodiversity." *Ecology Letters* 9, no. 7 (2006): 870–86.

Whitlock, Kelli. "Casting Prozac upon the waters." *University of Georgia Research Magazine,* Summer 2005.

Williams, Hywel, and Timothy Lenton. "Environmental regulation in a network of simulated microbial ecosystems." *Proceedings of the National Academy of Sciences USA* 105, no. 30 (2008): 10432–37.

Williams, T., et al. "Distinct neural generators in sensory gating in schizophrenia." *Psychophysiology* 48, no. 4 (2011): 470–78.

Winkleman, Michael. "Psychointegrator plants: Their roles in human culture, consciousness and health," in *Yearbook of Cross-cultural Medicine and Psychotherapy,* 9–53. VWG: Berlin, 1996.

Woollaston, Victoria. "Fennel is no fun but chili chats to basil: Researchers find 'talking' plants grow best when next to friendly neighbors." *Daily Mail* online, May 6, 2013.

Wright, Geraldine. "The role of dopamine and serotonin in conditioned food aversion learning in the honeybee." *Communicative and Integrative Biology* 4, no. 3 (2011): 318–20.

Wu, Wen-Hui, and Robin Cooper. "Serotonin and synaptic transmission at invertebrate neuromuscular junctions." *Experimental Neurobiology* 21, no. 3 (2012): 101–12.

Yoshida, T., et al. "Cryptic population dynamics: Rapid evolution masks trophic interactions." *PLoS Biology* 5, no. 9 (2007): e235.

Young, Neal, J. Ioannidis, and O. Al-Ubaydli. "Why current publication practices may distort science." *PLoS Medicine* 5, no. 10 (2008): e2o1.

Zachariou, M., et al. "Sensory gating and its modulation by cannabinoids: Electrophysiological, computational and mathematical analysis." *Cognitive Neurodynamics* 2, no. 2 (2008): 159–70.

Zhou, D., et al. "Influence of physical parameters of sound on the sensory gating effects of N40 in rats." *Neuroscience Letters* 432 (2008): 100–104.

INDEX

PLANT INTELLIGENCE
AND THE
IMAGINAL REALM

"The twentieth century was the great age of physics, and the twenty-first is the age of biology. According to Stephen Harrod Buhner, we must interact empathically with the biosphere by opening our perceptual gates to perceive through all body sensations. He deliciously explores music, writing, art, and plants as tools for reclaiming our feeling sense of nature. *Plant Intelligence and the Imaginal Realm* is a work of heartfelt wisdom written so exquisitely that it took my breath away, a must read for anyone who wants to achieve *keystone intelligence*—empathic immersion within Earth's dreaming."

BARBARA HAND CLOW, AUTHOR OF *AWAKENING THE PLANETARY MIND: BEYOND THE TRAUMA OF THE PAST TO A NEW ERA OF CREATIVITY*

"Stephen Harrod Buhner's *The Lost Language of Plants* and *The Secret Teaching of Plants* taught a generation of herbalists to trust our sense that the world was alive and speaking to us. *Plant Intelligence and the Imaginal Realm* takes us further down that path of remembering and re-enchantment, awakening our capacity to tap directly in to the Gaian mind. Be warned: if you read this book, you will never be the same again."

SEAN DONAHUE, TRADITIONAL HERBALIST AND INSTRUCTOR, SCHOOL OF WESTERN HERBAL MEDICINE AT PACIFIC RIM COLLEGE